Making Disability Modern

Making Disability Modern

Design Histories

Edited by
Elizabeth Guffey and Bess Williamson

BLOOMSBURY VISUAL ARTS
LONDON • NEW YORK • OXFORD • NEW DELHI • SYDNEY

BLOOMSBURY VISUAL ARTS
Bloomsbury Publishing Plc
50 Bedford Square, London, WC1B 3DP, UK
1385 Broadway, New York, NY 10018, USA
29 Earlsfort Terrace, Dublin 2, Ireland

BLOOMSBURY, BLOOMSBURY VISUAL ARTS and the Diana logo
are trademarks of Bloomsbury Publishing Plc

First published in Great Britain 2020
Reprinted 2022

© Editorial content and introductions, Elizabeth Guffey and Bess Williamson, 2020

© Individual chapters, their authors, 2020

Elizabeth Guffey and Bess Williamson have asserted their right under the Copyright, Designs and Patents Act, 1988, to be identified as Editors of this work.

For legal purposes the Acknowledgments on p.ix constitute an extension of this copyright page.

Cover design: Olivia D'Cruz

Cover image: Izzy Wheels ©, 2018. Wheel design by James Earley. Photo by Sarah Doyle

All rights reserved. No part of this publication may be reproduced or transmitted in any form or by any means, electronic or mechanical, including photocopying, recording, or any information storage or retrieval system, without prior permission in writing from the publishers.

Bloomsbury Publishing Plc does not have any control over, or responsibility for, any third-party websites referred to or in this book. All internet addresses given in this book were correct at the time of going to press. The author and publisher regret any inconvenience caused if addresses have changed or sites have ceased to exist, but can accept no responsibility for any such changes.

A catalogue record for this book is available from the British Library.

A catalog record for this book is available from the Library of Congress.

ISBN:	HB:	978-1-3500-7043-1
	PB:	978-1-3500-7042-4
	ePDF:	978-1-3500-7045-5
	ePub:	978-1-3500-7044-8

Typeset by Integra Software Services Pvt. Ltd.

To find out more about our authors and books visit www.bloomsbury.com and sign up for our newsletters.

Contents

List of Images vii
Acknowledgments ix

Introduction: Rethinking Design History through Disability, Rethinking Disability through Design *Elizabeth Guffey and Bess Williamson*   1

Part 1 Designers and Users from Craft to Industry

1 The Material Culture of Gout in Early America *Nicole Belolan* 19

2 Walking Cane Style and Medicalized Mobility *Cara Kiernan Fallon* 43

3 Artificial Limbs on the Panama Canal *Caroline Lieffers* 61

4 Technologies for the Deaf in British India, 1850–1950 *Aparna Nair* 77

Part 2 Disability and World-Making in the Twentieth Century

5 The Ideologies of Designing for Disability *Elizabeth Guffey* 101

6 Architecture, Science, and Disabled Citizenship *Wanda Katja Liebermann* 113

7 Disability and Modern Chemical Sensitivities *Debra Riley Parr* 131

8 Design for Deaf Education: Early History of the NTID *Kristoffer Whitney* 143

9 Designing the Japanese Walking Bag *Elizabeth Guffey* 159

Part 3 Making Disability Digital

10 The Politics and Logistics of Ergonomic Design   *Jennifer Kaufmann-Buhler*   177

11 Designing Emergency Access: Lifeline & LifeCall   *Elizabeth Ellcessor*   193

12 3D-Printed Prosthetics and the Uses of Design   *Bess Williamson*   209

13 Materializing User Identities & Digital Humanities   *Jaipreet Virdi*   225

Index   242

List of Images

1.1	Unidentified artist. "An attack of the Gout," 1818–1825. Doc. 699. Courtesy, The Winterthur Library: Joseph Downs Collection of Manuscripts and Printed Ephemera	24
1.2	Gout crane, wood and linen, United States, 1800–1840, 82" H., 1.231.2. Courtesy of Old Sturbridge Village	26
2.1	Gorham Cane Heads, Illustrated Price List of Otto Young & Co., Gorham Company Archives, John Hay Library, Brown University, Providence, RI. Image sourced from Brown University Library	45
2.2	Men's Fashions, 1918. Images from Sears, Roebuck, and Co. Catalog, Spring 1918, catalog 136L. Image sourced from Ancestry.com	48
3.1	From *American Medicine* 19, no. 5 (May 1913): 5	65
4.1	Advertisement for the Stolz Electrophone in an Indian newspaper. Credit: From NewsBank, inc. and the Center for Research Libraries. All Rights Reserved	84
5.1	Harry Kerr. Goldsmith believed most wheelchair users required assistance leaving home (1956). Getty Images/Harry Kerr/Stringer	107
6.1	Typical original residential unit plan, with wheelchair stamp, Het Dorp, Arnhem, the Netherlands, Van den Broek and Bakema, 1963–1965	119
6.2	A resident applying lipstick, looking in an angled mirror, Van den Broek and Bakema, 1963–1965	123
8.1	Close-up of the cluster classrooms from the floor plans. Courtesy of RIT/NTID Deaf Studies Archive, Rochester Institute of Technology	148
8.2	Cluster-classroom logo on the dedication program. Courtesy of RIT/NTID Deaf Studies Archive, Rochester Institute of Technology	149
9.1	SWANY promotional website 2001. Permission Etsuo Miyoshi	165
11.1	Illustration of the full system, from "Closed-Loop Emergency Alarm and Response System," U.S. patent, 1977	195
11.2	An "ornamental design" for the alarm transmitter, from a 1985 Lifeline US patent; current designs are quite similar in shape and simplicity	197
12.1	"Deborah" wearing Bespoke Fairings, bespokeinnovations.com (archived). Courtesy of Scott Summit	212

12.2	"Raptor Reloaded by e-NABLE," 3D printed hand prosthesis with elastic components, 2014. Thingiverse.com	216
13.1a	Amelia Woods's conversation tube pouch. Courtesy of Ken Seiling Waterloo Region Museum (1970.006.001)	231
13.1b	Amelia Woods's conversation tube. Courtesy of Ken Seiling Waterloo Region Museum (1970.007.001)	231
13.2	Andrew Gawley's prothesis. Grey Roots Museum and Archives collection, object ID 1973.100.001	233

Acknowledgments

This collection began as a conference at the Hagley Museum and Library, hosted by the Center for the History of Business, Technology, and Society. Our thanks go to the original presenters at the conference and to Roger Horowitz, Carol Lockman, Erik Rau, and the late Lynn Catanese for their support of an accessible and rigorous discussion of design, technology, and disability at Hagley. At the conference, we benefitted from comments from Katherine Ott, Jeffrey Brune, and Beth Linker. As we proposed the collection of chapters to Bloomsbury Press, three anonymous reviewers also provided useful perspective.

Our contributors here have been generous with their research and writing, finding time for edits and image permissions. Several have moved from graduate school to post-PhD life since the start of writing, and we are excited to bring their important work to publication. As we have developed this project, we have received helpful input from our colleagues Aimi Hamraie, Ashley Shew, and Josh Halstead. Our longtime colleague and editor Maggie Taft provided sharp editing and insight at key points in the manuscript's development. We are also thankful to graduate students Carrie Wright, Sophie Jenkins, and Nick Duque-Robayo at SAIC, and Noriko Okada at Purchase College, who assisted with editing and formatting.

Introduction: Rethinking Design History through Disability, Rethinking Disability through Design

ELIZABETH GUFFEY AND BESS WILLIAMSON

This introduction has two aims. The first is to preview and set the context for the chapters on design and disability in this volume. The second is to propose a persistent link that binds them together: a "design model of disability" that encapsulates the way that design has been deployed as a "fix" for the physiological and social experiences of disability in modern history. The chapters in the volume examine the alternately harmonious and tense, but always compelling relationship between designers, architects, medical professionals, and those people whose bodies and minds do not fit the norms that have shaped the modern world. Taken together, these studies offer a new, historically rooted perspective on design's role in constructing the meaning of disability over two centuries. Among the clutter of prosthetic legs and ear horns is a rich if almost completely overlooked history that goes beyond ideas of medical "progress" or technological curiosity. These chapters show ways in which design—broadly conceived as the processes of planning and making the material world—played an active role in shaping the meaning of disability in the modern world. In many cases, the structures and products of modern design created barriers by preventing disabled bodies from moving through space and society. In others, they could alleviate disability or provide useful tools for political agendas or the expression of disability identity. The chapters in this volume aim to identify this wide range of interventions as a narrative whole of disability reshaped in modernity.

Devices that responded to the needs of people with disabilities can be found throughout human history, but beginning in the late eighteenth-century, the category of "assistive" or "adaptive" devices began to emerge to reconcile the misfits of disabled bodies with the rhythms and forms of modern life.[1] The contributors to this volume show how this shift was inextricably linked to larger processes of modernity that reshaped medicine, social life, culture, and global economies. Through their analyses, three approximate eras of design development emerge, each offering distinct approaches. First, in the eighteenth and nineteenth centuries, custom making allowed for a certain adaptive flexibility to serve the varying needs of disabled and chronically ill people. As new industries and inventions often replaced these smaller and more flexible approaches, the demands of standardization and mass-production also reduced design possibilities for non-typical bodies. Meanwhile, additional forces, such as cultural imperialism and class status, cast some choices as preferable to others. The chapters in the second part, "World-Making," show how disability was a part of broader design shifts of the twentieth century toward large-scale planning and increasingly global and diverse consumer cultures. In the civil rights-focused era of the later twentieth century, design was additionally proposed as a means to make a new world—one which included disabled people as equal and protected citizens. The demands for accessibility as a civil right produced not only new laws, but also new theories of design's social responsibilities. Finally, the third part includes perspectives on the digital era as a distinct period of design possibility. New technologies and devices reorient the relationships between designers, manufacturers, and users in ways that will, once again, reshape the worlds of disabled people.

The chapters in this collection trace a modern design history of disability, a process of "making disability modern" that redefined relationships between body and technology within the hegemonies of mass production and the modern state. The distinct ways that designers approached disability, we find, merit examination along with other major social forces that have shaped the meanings of ability and disability in modern life. Proposals to improve and refine the built environment—the driving ethos of modern design—drew on and reinforced industrial and medical definitions of "normal" bodily size, shape, and ability. At the same time, disabled people's roles as agents in design, whether as makers, users, or activists, represent a history not often captured in trajectories of taste or style.

Defining Modernity

It is tempting to see the intersection of design and disability as a relatively recent development, and even a response to growing legislation. The Americans with Disabilities Act (1990) in the United States and the Disability Discrimination Act (1995) in the United Kingdom each mandated that architects and designers consider and accommodate those with cognitive, sensory, and mobility impairments, and set the stage for international declarations such as the United Nations Convention on the Rights of Persons with Disabilities (2006).[2] Without losing sight of these developments, however, these design histories tell a larger story of how modern design defined disability over a longer period and in varied arenas of life.

While "modernity" is a historical term with widely varying applications, within design, "Modernism" refers to an aesthetic style as well as mindset of production and planning. Modernism is associated with avant-garde architecture and design of the late nineteenth through the mid-twentieth century that took on spare, geometric forms and materials like steel, glass, and chrome. But it was also an ideology that involved a near idolization of new technologies inspired by the orderly world of factories, and a fascination with innovative methods of making. Modernist designers reshaped many areas of everyday life following the vaunting sense that progress could be found in the new. As Judy Attfield has written, even beyond the rarefied realm of trained designers and architects, practices of modernity in design have been defined by a "vision of change as beneficial."³ This Modernist attachment to change paralleled modern medical approaches to cure and intervention. Indeed, many architects viewed structures and cities themselves as near-medical instruments, clearing away germs and making way for an idealized modern body.⁴

From the time that Louis Sullivan coined the phrase "form follows function," ideas of practical functionality shaped definitions of the style that we call Modernism. In its exaltation of rationality, Modernism had little room for bodies and abilities that existed outside of statistical averages, standardized forms, and other narrowly defined ideals. The theorist and historian Lennard Davis suggests that as a result, disability might be cast as a kind of "dismodernism," creating a "difficulty" for the idea of improvement and progress in modernity.⁵ Within design history, scholars likewise point out that Modernism implicitly enshrined bodily and racial ideals. Streamlined Modernist design of the interwar years, for example, mirrored eugenic agendas to eliminate the atypical, abnormal, or perceived "inferior."⁶ Prominent Modernist designers including Le Corbusier in France and Henry Dreyfuss in the United States laid out statistically driven, anthropomorphic charts of human bodies as guides for the design of buildings and products.⁷ Le Corbusier's *The Modulor* (1945) and Dreyfuss's *Measure of Man* (1955) translated available statistics into a single image of a male (or in Dreyfuss's case, one male and one female) figure, formalizing the image of a normative body as the most suited to Modern design environments.⁸ Beyond the plans of individual architects and designers, standardized work routines, mass-produced products, and rationalized architecture defined physical normalcy in the modern era in terms of who was and was not able to use them. In this sense, many aspects of twentieth-century design actually created the inaccessibility that later activists worked to undo.

The Modernist push to standardize and rationalize is only one facet of design's engagement with disability. At the same time as leading architects engaged a predilection for so-called standard bodies, designers and laypersons proposed technological fixes to the isolation and marginalization of disabled people. Many designers developed technological adaptations to address specific disabled populations. For example, Lillian Gilbreth and her husband Frank, known for their "time-motion" efficiency studies in factories in the 1920s, developed a prototype of a typewriter that required only one arm to operate for amputee veterans of the First World War.⁹ Henry Dreyfuss, too, took up the charge of designing for disabled veterans, inviting amputees of the Second World War into his office. After observing "how they co-ordinated their muscles to operate the steel substitutes for what they call their 'meat hands,'" Dreyfuss produced a modest, streamlined arm aiming to "ma[ke] easier for the wearer further to develop this remarkable ability."¹⁰ These forays into designing for disabled users preceded a fuller design exploration of "access" starting in the 1950s and 1960s.

While mainstream, professional designers occasionally worked on specialized applications for disabled users, disabled people themselves also used design to adapt or invent their own devices and, in some case, transform industries. One of the great design successes of the twentieth-century history of wheelchairs was the portable, foldable metal chair developed by Herbert Everest, himself an engineer paralyzed in a mining accident, and his neighbor and fellow engineer Harry Jennings. Their manufacturing company, Everest & Jennings, maintained primacy in the wheelchair market until the late twentieth century.[11] Two generations after they introduced their pioneering design Marilyn Hamilton, an athlete paralyzed in hang-gliding accident, brought sporty design and bright colors to wheelchairs with Quickie, a company whose wheelchairs became bestsellers and challengers to the older chrome-style Everest & Jennings chairs.[12] To these breakout stories we might add generations of anonymous disabled people and their families who devised adaptations to their houses, cars, and work equipment to improve the function of their daily lives.[13]

As a catch-all term referring to nearly any human practice of planning and making, design gained particular cultural relevance in the industrial era. The work of constructing a world that included disabled people was performed by professional makers, their clients, and the often-unnamed technologists, craftspeople, and tinkerers whose work populated the abundant modern material world. And as the histories included in this book show, when it came to applications related to disability, design can just as often solidify barriers as challenge them.

The Design Model of Disability

Scholars of disability studies often speak of "models" of disability. Doing this means tracing attitudes across time and culture and ultimately suggesting that the meanings of disease, impairment, and disability have been highly variable. Medieval beliefs about physical difference might be associated with a moralistic mindset; through much of Western history disability was considered a form of divine judgment, karma, or some type of retribution. These perceptions were deeply linked to social inequality and led to the founding of charitable organizations as well as sequestration in separate towns or buildings.[14] Meanwhile, some forms of disability, for example dwarfism or blindness, were treated with reverence of a kind; people with dwarfism were "collected" and employed as "wonders" in European courts.[15] These attitudes were only overshadowed with the rise of science as we know it today. With the Enlightenment in the seventeenth century came a more individualized approach toward conditions of illness and physical difference, less likely to evoke fear or wonder and more commonly framing disability as a mishap or error to be treated or cured.[16]

Efforts to redefine disability as an individual bodily pathology to be fixed, cured, or eliminated are associated with the rise of the "medical model" of disability in the nineteenth century. Modern medical practice redefined physical "problems," as well as their roots, care, and treatment, and produced disability as a pathological condition inherent to an individual body (and thus curable or treatable in sterile isolation). The "medical model" thus identifies not only an approach to disability, but also the sites and devices that have been brought to bear on the disabled body from the nineteenth century to the present day. Just as medical professionalism bourgeoned, so too did the places where people with disabilities could be sent. Nineteenth-century hospitals and asylums thrived and were promoted as places of both treatment and refuge, sharing the characteristic of removing disability from mainstream society.

Only in the late 1960s did advocacy-minded scholars and community leaders begin to cohesively reframe these models and identify what they called a "social model" of disablement. Issued as a direct challenge to the "medical model," this newer model posited disability as a condition defined and perpetuated by society itself.[17] This model gave a conceptual tool to emerging rights movements to identify aspects of the disability experience not encapsulated in diagnosis. As activist Irving Zola argued, a medical definition of disability implicitly "evokes the image of many ascribed traits, such as weakness, helplessness, dependency, regressiveness, abnormality of appearance and depreciation of every mode of physical and medical functioning."[18] By contrast, the social model emphasized the role of external factors in shaping disabled lives, including education, living conditions, and legal guardianship. Tom Shakespeare summarizes the insights of the social model as pointing out "that many of the problems which disabled people face are generated by social arrangements, rather than by their own physical limitations."[19] As a unified Disability Rights movement emerged in the United States and Europe in the 1960s, the social model helped to bring a focus on changeable policies and institutions, as well as the shared experience of people across different categories of disability.

More recently, scholars have challenged the limiting binary of the "social" versus "medical" models, particularly by asserting the ways in which embodied experience of disability is part of a social understanding of identity and as a political/relational reflection of power structures.[20] Complementing these analyses, we argue that this intellectual scaffolding has room for a *design model of disability* to identify a distinct approach to disability in the modern industrial era and continuing to this day. This design model identifies disability as a phenomenon that can be treated or ameliorated through digital or material things. In practices of planning and production, we argue, design defines the categories of ability and disability in ways that are distinct from medical and social categories alone. And while social and medical models categorize disabilities according to their respective frameworks, designed technologies and interfaces are profoundly shaping questions of "function" and "normalcy" to this day.

If modern medicine defined disability as physiological pathology, static, and contained within an individual body, design has defined disability through function in the material—and increasingly digital–environments. Like medicine, design's professional penchant for invention seeks to resolve or at least improve the condition of disability through technological change. Unlike medicine, design shifts the focus from an individual's body and condition or diagnosis to the external environment: for example, a ramp can be useful for people with a variety of mobility impairments who use wheeled devices; enlarged screen type, voice commands, and closed captioning are used on digital devices by people with a range of disabilities, often overlapping. In this sense, the design model of disability differs from the medical model because it does not envision bodily cure or rehabilitation as the only response to disability. Instead, it delivers agency to material—and increasingly digital—artifacts by imagining that objects and spaces can do the work of inclusion. Thus, while physical and digital barriers have sometimes been used to illustrate the social model, efforts to change them often rely on design. From curb cuts and ramps to web accessibility standards, design has been suggested as a cure-all for eliminating prejudice, social awkwardness, and exclusion.[21]

A design model of disability is not offered here as an ideal, but as a common approach in design and related professions. Although not identified as a discrete "model" as here, this approach has accumulated both advocates and critics over time. As scholar Ashley Shew has observed, in our technology-focused society, disabled people are often pressured to adopt new and challenging devices. Calling this phenomenon "techno-ableism," Shew questions an ideology suggesting that "using technologies to restore physical abilities is the key to addressing disability—and that disabled bodies are inferior when they are not properly equipped with these technologies."[22] The design model can go wrong, sometimes over-prescribing futuristic technology while neglecting mundane design concerns in everyday spaces.[23] By contrast, Aimi Hamraie and Kelly Fritsch suggest the term "crip technoscience" to refer to the many ways disabled people engage with the technological world. While crip technoscience may include acts of professional design, this field stretches to include "practices of critique, alternation, and reinvention of our material-discursive world." Hamraie and Fritsch's "Crip Technoscience Manifesto" (2019) revises Modernist notions of design. Instead of emphasizing "standard" or "universal" design, they point to the "messy, non-innocent, contradictory, and nevertheless crucial work" of disabled people.[24] While techno-ableism can be discussed without reference to crip technoscience, by juxtaposing them within a design model of disability we can identify points for both critique and promise.

As the chapters in this volume indicate, the design model of disability helps us not only address the historical problem of disabled people's access to the world, but also trace these questions of design and agency in the modern era. These stories reveal that design's connection to disability cannot solely be summarized in terms of medical treatment or social compliance. By offering a series of artifact-focused histories, this book provides a picture of how design has shaped experiences and meanings of disability through professional and amateur practices, official and unofficial treatments, and creative endeavors that intersect with medical, social, and other powers seeking to define what it means to be disabled.

Designing Disability: Terminology

Design that considers disability has taken a variety of names, some of which indicate the precarious place that disabled people have occupied in designers' minds. Much like the many definitions of modernity, words such as "access," "assistive," and "accommodation" can be considered narrowly or in their most capacious sense, while others, now outdated—"self-help," "handicapped," or "crippled"—are telling about shifting notions of disability within society. Noting changes in terms is important not for political correctness but rather to identify the very real and very deep power structures that still inform the status of people with disabilities in society. The development of more neutral terms, for example "universal" or "inclusive" design, marked a deliberate move away from terms of diminishment. They also do hidden work in design, implicitly asserting that disability is relevant to all design practice and is not solely a "special" or separate concern.

Before the nineteenth century, there were no unifying terms or ideology for design related to disability. As the early chapters in this volume show, the things of disabled people's everyday lives were often made by artisanal makers, or as variations among general manufacturing categories, such as carriages, furniture, or metal and wood works. Only with the advent of specialized rehabilitation fields such as physiatry, orthopedics, and occupational therapy did a recognizable vocabulary begin to emerge for this form of design.[25] In the early twentieth century, as these fields first developed, they offered a new category of tools described as "self-help aids" and "rehabilitation devices," or by specialized names such as prosthetics (replacing a body part) and orthotics (supporting a body part).[26] By the 1960s, these tools were more likely to be referred to as *adaptive* or *assistive* equipment. These terms identified devices specifically made for disabled bodies and most often available through specialized stores or by medical prescription.

By definition, terms such as "adaptive" and "assistive" suggest a separate category of technologies for disabled people, in contrast to unlabeled, general categories of technology and design.[27] But in practice, devices often move more freely between categories, depending on their context or even the lived moment when they are put to use.[28] A recent example is Apple's iPad, which was designed to function as a digital tablet with applications selected by the user. If used to send email, read books, watch videos, and other planned uses, it is categorized as a standard consumer device. But when an iPad is used as a speaking device, for example becoming a platform for AAC (Augmentative and Alternative Communication), it immediately slips into the category of assistive technology.[29] These digital devices highlight the reality that many technologies not readily identified as "assistive" are actively used and useful for disabled people.[30]

As architects and planners of the twentieth century addressed the built environment as a whole to reflect disabled people's participation, their terms indicated bias as well as aspiration. In the 1950s and 1960s, advocates described efforts at "barrier-free" design, defining the approach more by what would be absent than what would be present. The term "accessible," by contrast, gave a positive characteristic to these approaches and linked them to broader rights-related developments in the society at large. But as these terms became more widely used, they also came to connote a certain legalistic approach. Today, "access" is encoded in a variety of legal policies, including the Americans with Disabilities Act, the UK's Disabilities Discrimination Act, and the United Nations Convention on the Rights of Persons with Disabilities. As a result, "accessible" tends to refer rights of citizenship that are often defined as resting with the individual. Within these rights systems, Kelly Fritsch writes, "access" is conceived as "an individual state of affairs in which the problem to be resolved arises from the particular body incapable of gaining access."[31]

In the last several decades designers and disability advocates have suggested terms to further clarify a series of newer goals deemed possible through design. "Universal design" and "inclusive design" emerged in the late twentieth to early twenty-first century; each has different adherents and subtly distinct claims, but both center on the notion that designing for disabled people should not be an isolated design endeavor. In 1985, the US architect Ronald Mace coined the term "universal design" to describe the goal of design that would address both disabled and non-disabled users, rather than requiring "special concessions" for disabled people.[32] In a time when "accessible" was often associated with a legal standard providing the minimum levels of accommodation, Mace and his collaborators imagined universal design to represent an entire philosophy of design rather than government regulation. Widely published in the 1990s, their "Seven Principles of Universal Design" named core concepts such as "equitable use," "flexibility," and "tolerance for error." Their efforts also reflect how fully the design model of disability had developed since the barrier-free movement toward defining affirmative design principles.

Likewise, the notion of "inclusive design" surfaced in European design circles in the 1990s, but has gradually become global in use. There is no clearly defined edge that separates this term from "universal design," and both seek solutions that benefit a range of users: the goal is to design "products and/or services that are accessible to, and usable by, as many people as reasonably possible … without the need for special adaptation or specialised design."[33] But "inclusive design" can also stress a more profoundly social dimension and encompass many categories of overlooked users. In abandoning idealized bodies and types, in recent years inclusive design has expanded beyond disabled persons. Here, the flexible and adaptive characteristics of universal design can shift to designers' practical awareness of different languages, cultures, genders, and ages, as well as abilities.[34] At the same time, inclusive design has scaled back the expectations of universal design; instead of expecting to develop perfect design solutions usable by everyone, it aims to identify specific answers to carefully identified problems.

In recent years, a new wave of design voices has expanded the scope in other directions, challenging the notion of a "mainstream" design entirely and proposing ways of designing that center disability in new ways. And again the terms surrounding such design shift. At Gallaudet University, the United States' longest-operating university for deaf and hard of hearing students, architects proposed DeafSpace, an architectural strategy that prioritizes the experience of deaf people, while also acknowledging some of the benefits to other marginalized users.[35] In other contexts such as the product design world, where digital tools of rapid prototyping and custom manufacturing have gained foothold, the notion of "mass production" itself is under critique. Technical approaches that allow for smaller-batches or customized designs, particularly through digital production, offer the promise of eliminating the compromises in "universal" or "inclusive" strategies. With these tools at hand, some designers have suggested ideas such as "resonant" design or "design for one," methods that embrace the individual distinctiveness of users rather than seeking generalized "universal" solutions.[36]

The evidence presented in these chapters suggests that design cannot and does not cure everything, and that a multiplicity of possible approaches exists at any given time in history. Moreover, as the "design model of disability" suggests, the choices designers, users, and others make are deeply contextual. The chapters in this book describe how factors such as availability of materials and information, social acceptability of various kinds of design, and overall societal enthusiasm for technological improvement all play a part in how disability is defined vis-a-vis design. And while this historical work often maps the exclusion and oppression of disabled people in modern Western society, we hope that it also suggests pathways out of this exclusion. In addressing the possibilities for engagement with disability rather than sidelining disability into legalistic or marginal categories, we argue that disability was, indeed, central to the development of modern design and its ambitions. Moreover, we envision models for including disabled people and their design knowledge in mainstream design history as has not previously been done. If disability has been a part of the modern design world, the future of design may only benefit from greater inclusion and recognition of disability as a form of human diversity and an origin-point for design knowledge and creativity.

Notes

1. Elizabeth Guffey, *Designing Disability: Symbols, Space, and Society* (London: Bloomsbury Publishing, 2017), 3–6.
2. Christina Cogdell, "Design," in *Keywords for Disability Studies*, ed. Rachel Adams, Benjamin Reiss, and David Serlin (New York: New York University Press, 2014), 59–60.
3. Judy Attfield, *Wild Things: The Material Culture of Everyday Life* (Oxford: Berg, 2000), 32.
4. Margaret Campbell, "What Tuberculosis Did for Modernism: The Influence of a Curative Environment on Modernist Design and Architecture," *Medical History* 49, no. 4 (December 2005): 463–88.
5. Lennard J. Davis, *Bending over Backwards: Disability, Dismodernism, and Other Difficult Positions* (NYU Press, 2002).
6. Christina Cogdell, *Eugenic Design: Streamlining America in the 1930s* (Philadelphia: University of Pennsylvania Press, 2004); Fabiola López-Durán, *Eugenics in the Garden: Transatlantic Architecture and the Crafting of Modernity* (Austin: University of Texas Press, 2018).
7. Aimi Hamraie, *Building Access: Universal Design and the Politics of Disability* (Minneapolis: University Of Minnesota Press, 2017); Lance Hosey, "Hidden Lines: Gender, Race, and the Body in Graphic Standards," *Journal of Architectural Education* 55, no. 2 (November 2001): 101–12.

8. Hosey, "Hidden Lines: Gender, Race, and the Body in Graphic Standards"; Hamraie, *Building Access*, 29–38.
9. Elspeth Brown, "The Prosthetics of Management: Time Motion Study, Photography, and the Industrialized Body in World War I America," in *Artificial Parts, Practical Lives: Modern Histories of Prosthetics*, ed. Katherine Ott, David Serlin, and Stephen Mihm (New York: New York University Press, 2002), 249–81.
10. Henry Dreyfuss, *Designing for People* (New York: Grossman Publishers, 1974), 27; David Harley Serlin, *Replaceable You: Engineering the Body in Postwar America* (Chicago: University of Chicago Press, 2004), 21–56.
11. Guffey, *Designing Disability*, 37–40.
12. Joseph P Shapiro, *No Pity: People with Disabilities Forging a New Civil Rights Movement* (New York: Times Books, 1993), 211–213.
13. Bess Williamson, "Electric Moms and Quad Drivers: People with Disabilities Buying, Making, and Using Technology in Postwar America," *American Studies* 52, no. 1 (2012): 5–30.
14. Henri-Jacques Stiker, *A History of Disability* (Ann Arbor: University of Michigan Press, 1999), 65–91; Michel Foucault, *Madness and Civilization: A History of Insanity in the Age of Reason*, trans. Richard Howard (New York: Knopf Doubleday Publishing Group, 2013), 3–38.
15. Irina Metzler, *A Social History of Disability in the Middle Ages: Cultural Considerations of Physical Impairment* (Routledge, 2013), 90.
16. Roger Cooter, "The Disabled Body," in *Medicine in the Twentieth Century*, ed. Roger Cooter and John V Pickstone (Amsterdam: Harwood Academic Publishers, 2000).
17. Tom Shakespeare, *Disability Rights and Wrongs* (London: Routledge, 2006), 9–10.
18. Irving Kenneth Zola, "Self, Identity, and the Naming Question: Reflection on the Language of Disability," in *The Social Medicine Reader*, ed. Gail Henderson, Nancy M.P. King, Ronald P. Strauss, and Sue E. Estroff (Durham, NC: Duke University Press, 1997), 79.
19. Shakespeare, *Disability Rights and Wrongs*, 10.
20. Shakespeare, *Disability Rights and Wrongs*; Alison Kafer, *Feminist, Queer, Crip* (Bloomington, Indiana: Indiana University Press, 2013).
21. Early regulations for access emphasized that people should not need to ask for help to access spaces such as library stacks. Richard K Scotch, *From Good Will to Civil Rights: Transforming Federal Disability Policy*, 2nd ed (Philadelphia: Temple University Press, 2001), 73–74.
22. Ashley Shew, "Different Ways of Moving through the World," *Logic Magazine*, no. 5 (Fall 2018): 207.
23. Ashley Shew, "Stop Depicting Technology as Redeeming Disabled People," *Nursing Clio*, April 23, 2019, https://nursingclio.org/2019/04/23/stop-depicting-technology-as-redeeming-disabled-people/.
24. Aimi Hamraie and Kelly Fritsch, "Crip Technoscience Manifesto," *Catalyst: Feminism, Theory, Technoscience* 5, no. 1 (2019): 1.

25 Roger Cooter, *Surgery and Society in Peace and War: Orthopaedics and the Organization of Modern Medicine, 1880–1948* (Basingstoke: Macmillan in association with the Centre for the History of Science Technology and Medicine, University of Manchester, 1993).
26 Some period sources that catalog these different categories include Edward W. Lowman and Howard A. Rusk, *Self-Help Devices, Part 1* (New York: Institute of Physical Medicine and Rehabilitation, New York University Medical Center, 1962); Sidney Licht, *Orthotics Etcetera* (Baltimore, Md: Waverly Press, 1966).
27 Sara Hendren, "All Technology Is Assistive," *Wired*, October 16, 2014, https://www.wired.com/2014/10/all-technology-is-assistive/.
28 Sara Hendren, "All Technology Is Assistive," *Wired*, October 16, 2014, https://www.wired.com/2014/10/all-technology-is-assistive/; Meryl Alper, for example, describes the varying attitudes of families who use iPads as communication devices and see them as consumer, medical, or educational devices. Meryl Alper, *Giving Voice: Mobile Communication, Disability, and Inequality* (Cambridge, MA: The MIT Press, 2017).
29 Alper, *Giving Voice*.
30 Hendren, "All Technology Is Assistive."
31 Kelly Fritsch, "Accessible," in *Keywords for Radicals: The Contested Vocabulary of Late-Capitalist Struggle*, ed. Clare O'Connor, A. K. Thompson, and Kelly Fritsch (Chico, Calif.: AK Press, 2016), 24.
32 Ronald Mace, "Universal Design: Barrier Free Environments for Everyone," *Designers West*, November 1985; Aimi Hamraie, "Universal Design Research as a New Materialist Practice," *Disability Studies Quarterly* 32, no. 4 (September 25, 2012), http://dsq-sds.org/article/view/3246.
33 "What Is Inclusive Design?," *Inclusive Design Toolkit*, accessed February 28, 2019, http://www.inclusivedesigntoolkit.com/whatis/whatis.html.
34 "What Is Inclusive Design?," *Inclusive Design Research Centre*, accessed February 28, 2019, https://idrc.ocadu.ca/about-the-idrc/49-resources/online-resources/articles-and-papers/443-whatisinclusivedesign.
35 "DeafSpace," *Gallaudet University*, accessed February 28, 2019, https://www.gallaudet.edu/campus-design-and-planning/deafspace.
36 Graham Pullin, *Design Meets Disability* (Cambridge, Mass: MIT Press, 2009), 93.

Bibliography

Alper, Meryl. *Giving Voice: Mobile Communication, Disability, and Inequality*. Cambridge, MA: The MIT Press, 2017.
Attfield, Judy. *Wild Things: The Material Culture of Everyday Life*. Oxford: Berg, 2000.
Brown, Elspeth. "The Prosthetics of Management: Time Motion Study, Photography, and the Industrialized Body in World War I America." In *Artificial Parts, Practical Lives: Modern Histories of Prosthetics*, ed. Katherine Ott, David Serlin, and Stephen Mihm, 249–281. New York: New York University Press, 2002.

Campbell, Margaret. "What Tuberculosis Did for Modernism: The Influence of a Curative Environment on Modernist Design and Architecture." *Medical History* 49, no. 4 (December 2005): 463–488.

Cogdell, Christina. *Eugenic Design: Streamlining America in the 1930s*. Philadelphia: University of Pennsylvania Press, 2004.

Cogdell, Christina. "Design." In *Keywords for Disability Studies*, ed. Rachel Adams, Benjamin Reiss, and David Serlin. New York: New York University Press, 2014.

Cooter, Roger. *Surgery and Society in Peace and War: Orthopaedics and the Organization of Modern Medicine, 1880–1948*. Basingstoke: Macmillan in association with the Centre for the History of Science Technology and Medicine, University of Manchester, 1993.

Cooter, Roger. "The Disabled Body." In *Medicine in the Twentieth Century*, ed. Roger Cooter and John V Pickstone. Amsterdam: Harwood Academic Publishers, 2000.

Davis, Lennard J. *Bending Over Backwards: Disability, Dismodernism, and Other Difficult Positions*. New York: New York University Press, 2002.

"DeafSpace." *Gallaudet University*. Accessed February 28, 2019. https://www.gallaudet.edu/campus-design-and-planning/deafspace

Dreyfuss, Henry. *Designing for People*. New York: Grossman Publishers, 1974.

Foucault, Michel. *Madness and Civilization: A History of Insanity in the Age of Reason*. Translated by Richard Howard. New York: Knopf Doubleday Publishing Group, 2013.

Fritsch, Kelly. "Accessible." In *Keywords for Radicals: The Contested Vocabulary of Late-Capitalist Struggle*, ed. Clare O'Connor, A. K. Thompson, and Kelly Fritsch. Chico, CA: AK Press, 2016, 23–26.

Guffey, Elizabeth. *Designing Disability: Symbols, Space, and Society*. London: Bloomsbury Publishing, 2017.

Hamraie, Aimi. "Universal Design Research as a New Materialist Practice." *Disability Studies Quarterly* 32, no. 4. (September 25, 2012). http://dsq-sds.org/article/view/3246.

Hamraie, Aimi. *Building Access: Universal Design and the Politics of Disability*. Minneapolis: University of Minnesota Press, 2017.

Hamraie, Aimi, and Kelly Fritsch. "Crip Technoscience Manifesto." *Catalyst: Feminism, Theory, Technoscience* 5, no. 1 (2019): 1–34.

Hendren, Sara. "All Technology Is Assistive." *Wired*, October 16, 2014. https://www.wired.com/2014/10/all-technology-is-assistive/

Hosey, Lance. "Hidden Lines: Gender, Race, and the Body in Graphic Standards." *Journal of Architectural Education* 55, no. 2 (November 2001): 101–112.

Kafer, Alison. *Feminist, Queer, Crip*. Bloomington: Indiana University Press, 2013.

Licht, Sidney. *Orthotics Etcetera*. Baltimore, MD: Waverly Press, 1966.

López-Durán, Fabiola. *Eugenics in the Garden: Transatlantic Architecture and the Crafting of Modernity*. Austin: University of Texas Press, 2018.

Lowman, Edward W., and Howard A. Rusk. *Self-Help Devices, Part 1*. New York: Institute of Physical Medicine and Rehabilitation, New York University Medical Center, 1962.

Mace, Ronald. "Universal Design: Barrier Free Environments for Everyone." *Designers West* 33, no. 1 (November 1985).

Metzler, Irina. *A Social History of Disability in the Middle Ages: Cultural Considerations of Physical Impairment*. New York: Routledge, 2013.

Pullin, Graham. *Design Meets Disability*. Cambridge, MA: MIT Press, 2009.

Scotch, Richard K. *From Good Will to Civil Rights: Transforming Federal Disability Policy*. 2nd ed. Philadelphia, PA: Temple University Press, 2001.

Serlin, David Harley. *Replaceable You: Engineering the Body in Postwar America*. Chicago, IL: University of Chicago Press, 2004.

Shakespeare, Tom. *Disability Rights and Wrongs*. London: Routledge, 2006.

Shapiro, Joseph P. *No Pity: People with Disabilities Forging a New Civil Rights Movement*. New York: Times Books, 1993.

Shew, Ashley. "Different Ways of Moving through the World." *Logic Magazine* 1, no. 5 (Fall 2018): 207–213.

Shew, Ashley. "Stop Depicting Technology as Redeeming Disabled People." *Nursing Clio*, April 23, 2019. https://nursingclio.org/2019/04/23/stop-depicting-technology-as-redeeming-disabled-people/

Stiker, Henri-Jacques. *A History of Disability*. Ann Arbor: University of Michigan Press, 1999.

Anonymous. "What Is Inclusive Design?" *Inclusive Design Research Centre*. Accessed February 28, 2019. https://idrc.ocadu.ca/about-the-idrc/49-resources/online-resources/articles-and-papers/443-whatisinclusivedesign

"What Is Inclusive Design?" *Inclusive Design Toolkit*. Accessed February 28, 2019. http://www.inclusivedesigntoolkit.com/whatis/whatis.html

Williamson, Bess. "Electric Moms and Quad Drivers: People with Disabilities Buying, Making, and Using Technology in Postwar America." *American Studies* 52, no. 1 (2012): 5–30.

Part 1 Designers and Users from Craft to Industry

In the opening chapter of this part, Nicole Belolan highlights the creative work of adaptation to disability in the eighteenth century. In her account, Philadelphia gentleman John Lukens commissioned, invented, borrowed, and refashioned an array of things to deal with the debilitating condition of gout. A man of ample means, some of Lukens's assistive devices—like the phaeton carriage that he commissioned to get around—were grandiose. But other early Americans, she argues, relied on a variety of devices in order to live with disability in the preindustrial age. The preindustrial normalcy of disability is evident in a rich material culture that includes Lukens's well-appointed carriage along with other ad hoc, improvised, or adapted aids for support. Over the next two centuries, material objects and designed environments would increasingly be celebrated for their ability to cure—or treat—disability. But in the preindustrial era disabled people, family members, craftspeople, servants, and enslaved workers routinely made things accommodate and mitigate disability in everyday life.[1]

Functional and stylish equipment documented or preserved through history tell us not only about the biographies of historical figures, but also about rarely studied forms and techniques of craft, including customization for both function and style. At a time when most disabled people lived at home, they, their friends, and their families designed their own devices and environments. As physical impairments were a common part of pre and early industrial life, this approach was widespread. By the late nineteenth century, designed interventions like Braille, hearing aids, and wheelchairs were being mass produced and available for purchase by or prescription to disabled users. Their histories also interlink with strains of national ambition, industry, war, and conquest.

Disabling the Industrial Revolution

The design histories in this volume mark out the early modern period as the onset of industrialization. In the context of mass production and communication, definitions of disability were closely intertwined with shifting notions of utility and fashion in everyday material life. Cara Fallon's study of nineteenth-century canes available to consumers reveals the variety and sheer faddishness of designs on sale once mechanization and the American system of production took over. As her study notes, in an earlier age canes may have functioned as mobility aids, but by the nineteenth century they were fashionable enough that middle-class users typically owned several and could choose from a huge variety of handcrafted models. When canes fell out of fashion—partly because they once again became medicalized in the twentieth century—this variety and stylishness all but disappeared.

Much of the documented history of design and disability has been from a Western perspective, but Aparna Nair documents how these dynamics played out in India with distinctive colonial implications. In British India, patented, designed, and mass-produced technologies like ear trumpets were presented to deaf colonial subjects as part of the purported benefits of colonial rule. Better-off Indians could buy for themselves audiphones and electrophones, but tended to disdain the indigenous form of communication known as the "language of the fingers." Capitalizing on this stigma, colonial authorities emphasized oralism and instilled an increasing reliance on mass-produced devices imported from the West. But these impulses were hardly limited to India. In the early twentieth century, modernity was more and more associated with design.

In a broader sense, the Industrial Revolution itself was a source of disability. Factory labor was dangerous, especially because the rise of unskilled labor led industry to view people (not machines) as disposable. Work injuries were common and resulted in little recompense, whether in industrial-era coal mines or in automobile factories.[2] This was also the case in great feats of engineering, like the construction of the Panama Canal, a project that transformed modern life by facilitating easier maritime trade between the Pacific and the Atlantic Oceans and reshaped the lives of many laborers due to the large numbers of injuries and amputations. Caroline Lieffers investigates how prosthesis design became a synecdoche of the United States' growing global design presence, especially in Panama. As Lieffers argues, the distribution of more modern, designed limbs reproduced inequities based on race, class, and nation in the US Empire.

Throughout the premodern world, a rich variety of improvised, adapted, or specially made aids suggests that disability was accommodated as a normal feature of everyday life. As society industrialized in the nineteenth century, more and more patented, and mass-produced designs replaced the ad hoc systems and devices used before the Industrial Revolution. The emergence of professional design in the late nineteenth century did not abolish non-professional innovation. But designed answers to disablement became more and more common. By the beginning of the twentieth century, to be disabled and living in the modern era often meant using some kind of designed device.

Notes

1 Abrams, *Revolutionary Medicine*; Dea H. Boster, *African American Slavery and Disability: Bodies, Property, and Power in the Antebellum South, 1800–1860* (New York: Routledge, 2013).
2 Rose, *No Right to Be Idle*; Blackie, "Disability, Dependency, and the Family in the Early United States."

Bibliography

Abrams, Jeanne E. *Revolutionary Medicine: The Founding Fathers and Mothers in Sickness and in Health*. New York: New York University Press, 2013.

Altschuler, Sari. *The Medical Imagination: Literature and Health in the Early United States*. Early American Studies. Philadelphia: University of Pennsylvania Press, 2018.

Blackie, Daniel. "Disability, Dependency, and the Family in the Early United States." In *Disability Histories*, ed. Susan Burch and Michael Rembis. Chicago: University of Illinois Press, 2014.

Boster, Dea H. *African American Slavery and Disability: Bodies, Property, and Power in the Antebellum South, 1800–1860*. New York: Routledge, 2013.

Rose, Sarah F. *No Right to Be Idle: The Invention of Disability, 1840s-1930s*. Chapel Hill: University of North Carolina Press, 2017.

1 The Material Culture of Gout in Early America

NICOLE BELOLAN

Applying the last coat of varnish onto the phaeton Pennsylvania Surveyor General John Lukens (1720–89) ordered in 1789, a worker at George Hunter's internationally acclaimed coach-making shop in Philadelphia likely took pride in knowing his light blue paint job would soon be seen throughout the city's streets.[1] Once the varnish dried, we can envision another worker hopping into the open, four-wheel carriage, taking the reins of a horse, and delivering Lukens's recreational coach—which set him back the princely sum of $200 plus an annual luxury tax—to his home at Market Street between 6th and 7th streets, just a short walk from the Pennsylvania State House (now Independence Hall).[2]

Likely enlivened at the prospect of tooling around in his new pleasure carriage, we can imagine Lukens approaching the lower-than-ordinary entrance, slowly taking one step at a time into the capacious seating area, and settling down on the seat. After all, a man with gout, a crippling form of arthritis, who would eventually require a coffin measuring an unusually broad two feet, three inches across the shoulders, needed the "very low" and "roomy" phaeton design, as Hunter recorded in his daybook.[3] Despite the disabling pain gout caused, Lukens used his new carriage to navigate his world, perhaps en route to the American Philosophical Society where he was a member. Lukens was sixty-nine and a widower, but he still probably enjoyed showing off his wealth and station to everyone who noticed the spectacle of the carriage passing through the city's corridors.

We can imagine that after taking a spin around Philadelphia, Lukens returned his new prized possession to his home. There, he slowly climbed the stairs to his bedchamber where he enjoyed the physical comfort provided by a bed chair, two night chairs (indoor toilets), and an invalid chair (wheelchair).[4] Or, he may have enveloped himself in the welcoming wings and soft upholstery provided by an easy chair. Perhaps Dinah, his servant of African descent, or his nurse Sarah Coombs, hustled around him, propping up his swollen, gouty limbs and fluffing the pillow on his invalid chair should he tire of the easy chair.[5] The furniture, which his wife had likely put to good use before her death after a "long and painful illness" the previous year, may have groaned with his weight, and Lukens probably groaned with disabling pain.[6] When it was time to turn in, Lukens slept in his bedstead, though he owned six in a time and place where one bedstead would have been considered a luxury.

To live with and manage physical disabilities such as gout in early America, people like Lukens, rich and poor alike, improvised material solutions within their physical and social environments.[7] They did this in collaboration with friends, family, craftspeople, servants, and enslaved people using whatever resources they had at hand. They commissioned, invented, borrowed, and refashioned an array of objects ranging from specially designed phaetons to shoes to sooth and conceal the painful, disabling disease of gout. They wanted to stay mobile and active and pursue everyday life and activities.[8] Individuals' reputations depended, in part, on whether they looked well-groomed and healthy as well as whether they contributed to their families and communities. They used objects and people to get the job done.[9]

Today, to access places, people, and activities, Americans with disabilities tend to use and alter mass-marketed objects in conjunction with more specially made items. We typically classify objects people with disabilities use to engage with the world "assistive technology" or "assistive devices." Historian Katherine Ott defines these objects as things that "enhance such capacities as mobility and agility, sensory apprehension, communication, and cognitive action."[10] Examples Ott lists include prosthetic limbs and hearing aids, among many other objects. People often acquire such tools through medical professionals or purveyors of medical devices. People sometimes alter such objects using materials they find around the house to customize them to their bodies.[11]

When John Lukens had gout, there was no formalized assistive technology industry from which he could purchase what we would call an "accessible" carriage. Instead, Lukens worked closely with his Philadelphia carriage-maker to design and construct a phaeton that was at the height of fashion but that was also fit for someone who had trouble getting around.[12] Lukens's carriage would have been lower to the ground and roomier inside (and therefore more accessible, to use the modern term) than the typical four-wheeled phaeton or recreational carriage of his time.[13] Lukens's carriage-makers probably had limited experience making conveyances for disabled people. Therefore, the objects they designed were vernacular, or objects made using few or no guides for construction.[14] Most often, making those goods was part of a much more robust business for something else. For example, many furniture-makers or turners made wooden artificial limbs for individuals when they were not making chairs or sofas.

The reputations of people with gout depended, in part, on their ability to stay mobile and active as participants to their families and communities. Moving beyond discussion of the late-eighteenth-century international appetite for gouty satire, this chapter addresses the lived experience of this disabling impairment and its social implications in early America. In this chapter, I first explore gout as a medical condition as it was conceived in the eighteenth century. Then, I examine the objects people with gout and their caregivers used to contend with the disabling disease. Early Americans with a variety of disabilities used many of these objects—such as bedsteads, easy chairs, and bed chairs—to live with and manage their impairments in everyday life. Lukens's experience with gout serves as a case study through which to highlight objects' importance in facilitating mobility but also shaping the meaning of disability in early America.

A Long-Standing Condition

Gout is not a new disease. Archaeologists uncovered human remains marked by gout that date back to ancient Egypt.[15] Doctors have identified three major gout "epidemics": one that took place during the Roman Empire, another that took place in the eighteenth and nineteenth centuries, and a contemporary epidemic.[16] Two of the most high-profile men in Revolutionary-era Atlantic world, Benjamin Franklin and William Pitt, had gout. Franklin remains the best known, and contemporary essayists (and people this author has talked to about their research) often invoke Franklin's plight.[17] But farmers, poor people, and women in early America got gout too, highlighting the fact that gout was not just a "disease of kings" but a common ailment most people would have been familiar with.

In the eighteenth century as now, gout was a chronic, non-lethal, and non-contagious condition best managed with a combination of lifestyle changes and medications. Today, the Center for Disease Control and Prevention defines gout as a rheumatic disease that results in "pain," "swelling," "redness," and "heat" in the joints.[18] We know that gout is caused by a combination of genetic and environmental factors. Genetic factors may contribute to whether someone gets gout. In addition, consuming foods high in purines, such as organ meat, and alcohol (particularly beer), also determine whether someone might develop the disease. When someone eats purine-rich foods, the body produces uric acid to process the purines. If there is too much uric acid in someone's body, it can accumulate in joints in the form of crystals that form lumps and bumps (sometimes called tophi).[19] If untreated, gouty hands, for instance, can grow to the size of a boxing glove.[20] Because the skin stretches rapidly on a part of the body where that type of expansion does not ordinarily happen quickly, the joint becomes tender and unable to withstand much pressure.[21]

Gout affected the rich and the poor alike in early America. When it came to gout, some early Americans believed that people developed gout because gout itself was a mechanism that would rid the body of other illnesses. They believed gout balanced the humours and prevented other diseases.[22] Lukens and his contemporaries rightly suspected some of the environmental causes. John Wesley's *A Collection of Receipts. For the Use of the Poor* (1745), republished at least thirty-seven times throughout Europe and the United States well into the nineteenth century, advised gouty readers to avoid "flesh" (or meat) and "strong drink."[23] Some people like Wesley believed that diets heavy in alcohol and meat—whether those of elites or the poor—threatened to bring on gout. John Lukens's gout may have been affected by his alcohol intake. The Philadelphia Quaker Meeting disowned him in 1784, citing misdeeds such as "Intemperance of Drinking."[24]

Everyone in early America knew the bodily and material signs of gout since they were common and difficult to hide. The physical embodiment of the condition was so distinctive that sometimes Anglo-Americans even used the term "gouty" to refer to other swollen or distorted things such as animal limbs.[25] But this term was rooted in the changes it wrought on the human body. Nineteenth-century medical specimen hands now preserved in the Mütter Museum's collections show how the crystals can form disfiguring, tender lumps and knobs called tophi.[26] Tophi can limit the ability to walk, write, or move more generally. The swelling was familiar enough that Anglo-Americans used the term "gouty" to refer generally to misshapen legs or lameness. In 1767, one "servant lad named Cassius Belliger" with "remarkable *gouty* feet, and subject to a weakness in his limbs." Despite Cassius's impairment, he somehow managed to run away from his master, Israel Pemberton in Philadelphia.[27] Whether Cassius suffered from true gout is unclear, but the term clearly telegraphed a kind of distinctive disfigurement that readers of *The Pennsylvania Gazette* were expected to immediately recognize and understand.

Gout was and is painful.[28] Gout shaped Lukens's life at least by the 1770s when he was in his fifties. Writing in a shaky hand in the margins of his 1778 *Almanack*, he noted a November attack of gout that affected one of his wrists and both of his feet.[29] Other sufferers were more direct in chronicling their discomfort. Moody Follansbee (b. 1729?), a Massachusetts farmer, wrote in the 1760s about his gouty fits in a series of journal entries, also in an almanac, that included the word "pain" nine times.[30] Some observers were even more explicit. In a letter to the *Pennsylvania Packet*, one person with gout described the disease as "the greatest bodily Infirmities."[31]

Treatments for the condition varied. Indeed, Lukens and his contemporaries turned to a variety of resources to manage and live with this painful, potentially debilitating and disabling disease. Early Americans relied on doctors (if they could afford them or if they had access to them at reduced or cost-free rates at institutions such as the Pennsylvania Hospital, established in 1751 in Philadelphia). They also called on lay medicine dispensed via family or familiar receipts or recipes, written or communicated orally. And finally, people with gout looked to printed medical advice aimed at ordinary readers and advertisements placed by businesses in newspapers.[32] We know a little bit about which of these resources Lukens exploited.[33]

Late in his life, Lukens called on one of the best-educated physicians in British North America. Around the time of Lukens's death in 1789, Dr. Adam Kuhn (1741–1817), who had studied botany and medicine in Europe, cared for Lukens.[34] Kuhn held several prominent roles as a medical leader in early Philadelphia. When Lukens died in 1789, Kuhn held the post as one of the physicians at the Pennsylvania Hospital, served at the Philadelphia Dispensary, and was a member of the College of Physicians.[35] Lukens may have known Kuhn as a fellow member of the American Philosophical Society.

Like many of his elite contemporaries, Lukens also relied on lay medical knowledge dispensed and labor performed by at least one compensated woman, Sarah Coombs, and probably his servant of African descent Dinah.[36] Coombs lived with the family since at least 1762 as a "Child under their Care," according to Quaker Meeting records.[37] If Coombs was not Lukens's niece by blood, she was in practice, as he left her £100 in addition to the £49, 14 shillings, and 6 pence he owed her for

"4 years Service in his Family as House Keeper & Nurse."[38] Coombs likely knew the family's medical needs inside and out, as we can assume she also cared for John's wife Sarah Lukens before she died in 1788.[39]

John Lukens also benefitted from care performed by individuals of African descent. Dinah, described as "a Negro Wench," and whose precise type of servitude or enslavement remains unclear, worked in his household. When Lukens died in 1789, an estate appraiser valued Dinah's remaining service at £25.[40] Given the extent of Lukens's household and the interminable nature of gout and Sarah Lukens's final illness, we can surmise that Dinah played an equally critical role in providing direct medical care or facilitating that care by collaborating with Kuhn, Coombs, the Lukens family, and others. When they were not administering medicine, changing linens, or otherwise maintaining furniture used by Lukens and his wife, they may have assisted with moving or carrying them.[41] South Carolina planter-merchant elite Ann Ashby Manigault (1705–82), who also had gout, wrote about being "carried down stairs" and otherwise moved around at home people due to her gout and related infirmities, work that was probably done by enslaved people.[42]

Despite gout's characterization as a natural cleansing disease, there was no shortage of prescriptions in popular medical books, advertisements for medicines in newspapers, and prescriptions in family home recipe books for managing it. For example, Lukens likely used "1 bottle [of] Gout Cordial," listed among his property and valued at 40 shillings and 3 pence upon his death, on at least one occasion.[43] Probably an alcohol-based curative, he may have acquired the medicine after seeing a newspaper advertisement for such a cordial listed among other medicines.[44]

If Lukens had paged through the most popular lay medical manuals printed and circulated in early America during the second half of the eighteenth century, he would have come across a number of approaches for treating gout. A sample: Don't overeat or drink.[45] Exercise outside. Or, exercise outside using a piece of furniture with springs called a chamber or exercise horse, which one merchant marketed as capable of providing relief for "Rheumatic and Gouty patients."[46] Drink "bitter tincture of rhubarb" or "a pint of strong infusion of elder-buds [probably referring to a shrub], dry or green, morning and evening."[47] Drink milk and water and eat vegetables and grains.[48] Place "raw, lean beef-stake" on your affected limb, or "Rub [it] with warm treacle, and then bind on a flannel smeared therewith."[49] All of these suggestions would have taken time to prepare, work that, in an elite household like Lukens's, would have been done by enslaved people, servants, or family members.

Manuscript home receipt books offered a similar array of steps to relieve the pain and swelling. Philadelphian Elizabeth Byles's (b. 1733) recipe book included two recipes for managing gout. One instructed readers that "as soon as it begins the Atackt take a spoonful of brimstone Morn[ing] and Night, and Wash it don With a glass of Mountain Win[e] this Cured a person who had it bad."[50] This particular recipe suggests gout could be more or less painful and disabling depending on the individual.

Whether or not those cures worked on "the greatest bodily Infirmities" is another question.[51] Writers of popular medical manuals referred to gout as something that made a person into a "Cripple" and that felt like "torture."⁵² People with gout reported on cycles of probably unpredictable setbacks and improvements. Moody Follansbee noted in January of 1767 that his gout "confined [him] to [his] bed for a week," and he "was unable for some days to turn in [his] bed [without] help."⁵³ By April, he could "go about [his] Room," and by October, he could go "as far as [his] gate," sometimes with crutches.⁵⁴ Prescriptive literature prescribed eating and drinking better, but for chronic cases like Follansbee's and Lukens's, authors of those tomes also suggested turning to laudanum, made from opium.⁵⁵ The image in Figure 1.1, depicting what the artist called "An attack of the Gout," though dating from the early nineteenth century, represents a rare, non-satirical, American depiction of a man suffering from gout in his home setting, surrounded by curatives and a mess he had no time or ability to clean.

Many of the objects in this material culture of gout functioned not only to mitigate pain but also to help people with the disease remain functional in society and work against stereotypes. Even as gout caused very real pain and disabling discomfort and limited people's contributions to society in the eighteenth century, gout also carried profound social stigma. In fact, critics in Britain and America took relentless aim at gout as a disease caused by excess. Satirical images, like Thomas Rowlandson's 1785 *Comfort in the Gout*, often painted gouty sufferers as elite, overweight, helpless,

Figure 1.1 Unidentified artist. "An attack of the Gout," 1818–1825. Doc. 699. Courtesy of The Winterthur Library: Joseph Downs Collection of Manuscripts and Printed Ephemera.

conspicuous figures.[56] In America, criticisms, such as those made by Philadelphia physician Benjamin Rush, carried an additional, political tone. In 1772, Rush referred to gout as a "dreadful scourge of intemperance" and insisted that for men like Lukens to participate in their "Public business," they must refrain from drinking wine and developing gout so that they might stay active in "these exalted spheres," such as politics and war, "which [they] are called to fill."[57] Since Lukens held the public position of Surveyor General, Rush's comments were certainly aimed at people like him.[58]

More Than Physical Comfort: Symbolic and Social Objects

And so for someone like John Lukens to remain functional in society while disabled, people used objects such as a specially designed phaeton. At home, they improvised with other objects and people to enjoy physical and social comfort and maintain a veneer of gentility.[59] For example, people like Lukens could sit upright in upholstered, soft easy chairs before they were ready to venture into public. Some early Americans of lesser means (or limited access to urban centers) made their own comfortable easy-style chairs.[60] They altered wooden side chairs and armchairs by adding wooden panels to the sides like "wings" of an easy chair, stuffing, and upholstery from whatever fabric they may have had at hand.[61]

Some early Americans borrowed objects to remain upright and involved in their household's social and familial activities. Lukens owned two "bed chairs," which resembled the upper portions of easy chairs; like easy chairs, bed chairs also allowed disabled people to sit upright in warmth and comfort while they spent extended periods of time in bed. Those with lesser means improvised by borrowing or renting bed chairs from people like Lukens. For example Elizabeth Drinker of Philadelphia lent her family's bed chair to her network of family, friends, and neighbors on numerous occasions throughout the late eighteenth century.[62] If an individual needed a bed chair but did not know someone like the Drinkers, cabinet-maker Thomas Burling in New York City rented bed chairs to customers.[63]

Some early Americans improvised by designing vernacular objects meant specifically to address gout. Dr. Joseph Trumbull (1756–1824) in Worcester, Massachusetts, for example, designed an adjustable gout crane, seen in Figure 1.2, on which gouty people could rest their aching limbs and elevate them at home. The crane itself would have been attached or affixed to a window or wall, and the user could have raised the sling up and down using a pulley mechanism. In addition to the crane he made for himself, Trumbull also donated one to the Massachusetts General Hospital.[64] Furniture-makers designed specialty items exclusively for gout, but few have survived to the present day. In London, for instance, cabinet-maker George Hepplewhite pictured the adjustable "gouty stool" designed to "comfort the afflicted" alongside furniture associated with impairment such as easy chairs in his 1794 design book. These high-end accouterments were probably difficult to acquire outside urban settings, which may explain Trumbull's inventiveness.

Figure 1.2 Gout crane, wood and linen, United States, 1800–1840, 82" H., 1.231.2. Courtesy of Old Sturbridge Village.

People used these objects to remain actively upright while maintaining a form of gentility and sociability at home. At home and in public, people disabled by gout had to worry about how their legs and feet looked to others since that's where gout often showed up visibly. In early America, this was a particular concern for public figures like Lukens. Fit and functional legs were favored as important components of Anglo-American male beauty.[65] Gout or not, such men expected to have their legs admired and they were often put on display. Elite men, or at least those working in genteel trades, like Connecticut merchant Elijah Boardman pictured in an often-illustrated 1789 portrait by Ralph Earl, wore breeches to the knee and hose, which conformed tightly to their calves.[66] Working men like sailors wore more loose-fitting trousers, usually down to their shoes, but even this style of pants drew the viewer's eye to the ankles along the outlines of the lower and upper leg.[67] On the other hand, the flannels and shoes people with gout wore on their legs tended to highlight their tender, lumpy, and distended limbs. Wealthy gout sufferers might hide their gout—at least momentarily—by traveling by special conveyances much like Lukens's improvised phaeton and with a soft blanket made and marketed specifically for people with gout, but the working poor had fewer means to hide it.[68] A 1777 Philadelphia runaway advertisement, for instance, described John Groase, "a noted villain and a great cheat," as "very lame in his hands and feet with the gout."[69] Furthermore, the bulky wrappings and flannels associated with gout were so commonplace that at least one British escaped convict used them to hide in plain sight. Described in the 1736 records of London's central circuit court, the Old Bailey, the escapee pretended to have gout to avoid detection while still wearing his heavy—and revealing—prison irons. Working man Daniel Malden testified as to how he "wrapp'd [his] Irons close to [his] Legs, as if [he] had been gouty or lame" using "Rags and pieces of [his] Jacket" so as to avoid drawing notice upon escaping from prison.[70] This getup hid Malden's prison irons on the part of his body that would most likely have been visibly enflamed if he had had gout.[71]

Malden used fabric around his legs to simulate a common way to care for and hide gouty limbs: wrapping them in several layers of flannel fabric, as we can see in Rowlandson's *Comfort in the Gout*. These physically necessary wrappings made gout all the more visually apparent, making it nearly impossible to hide the disease. Gout sufferers and other people who were sick used soft fabrics like flannel close to the body for several reasons. For early Americans, flannel or the "soft nappy stuff of wool" was commonly worn as everyday clothing but also for health.[72] People used flannel to manage a variety of bodily concerns such as keeping warm and preventing disease. The fabric, often wrapped around the leg like a bandage, concealed the disfiguring and debilitating lumps gout produced. Flannel also induced perspiration, which early Americans believed rid the body of disease and relieved pain.[73] The fabric could also absorb fluid excretion since it was possible (in extreme cases) for gouty joints to leak.

When it came to their footwear, early Americans with gout continued to improvise. Many satirical depictions of people with gout featured large, distinctive feet and footwear.[74] Those with gout lamented that walking around on gouty feet felt like walking on rocks, so, as a consequence, they modified shoes or had special shoes made to manage pain and hide unsightly swelling.[75] These shoes varied in design; there was no one pattern to make a "gout shoe" since everyone's body was different. Some people commissioned oversized shoes.[76] Others cut their shoes so that they had more room for their swollen extremity.[77] In some cases, gouty people wore shoes made of fabric like the archaeological example uncovered in London.[78] These shoes were cut with parts similar to those seen on traditional late-eighteenth-century shoes, and the user tied them to their legs. Like gouty legwear, gouty footwear, too, would have concealed gouty lumps and bumps. But because these shoes, like flannel wrappings, were so visible, they had the undesired result of drawing attention to the disease.

Whether or not Lukens went out and about with lumps and bumps protruding beneath flannels or when he was experiencing less acute and visible symptoms of gout, he knew he had to get going so he could maintain his presence in Rush's "exalted spheres." Rolling through the streets of Philadelphia, John Lukens's phaeton allowed him to remain active among his peers despite his ailments. The phaeton's elegance may have distracted onlookers momentarily, but if they looked for more than a few seconds, they would have noticed how low to the ground the phaeton was and how roomy it was inside compared to others. The estate auctioneer obscured the meaning of Lukens's material world when he simply referred to the phaeton as an "invalid carriage."[79] Lukens used objects for more than simply curing, fixing, or medically caring for his body. He also used the phaeton for more than just getting around. With these objects, Lukens performed socioeconomic and political status. Lukens was a wealthy man who held a public office in colonial and early national Philadelphia. He needed to maintain that status while suffering from the disabling disease of gout, which he did in part by commissioning a fine conveyance he may have hoped would distract from stigma associated with his disabling disease.[80] In doing so, Lukens deployed improvisation of design to live with and manage disability, showing an early example of the many ways people with disabilities used and continue to use things in their everyday lives.

Acknowledgments: The author thanks the many individuals and groups who have read and offered suggestions for improving this work, including by not limited to Kasey Grier, Christine Heyrman, Arwen Mohun, Beth Linker, Tyler Putman, Katherine Ott, colleagues from the 2018 NEH Summer Institute Global Histories of Disability, and the editors of this volume.

Notes

1 George and William Hunter daybooks, May 27, 1789, and August 4, 1789, Vol. 1, 1788–1791, MS. Amb. 45661, Historical Society of Pennsylvania (HSP). The entry noting that the Lombart chaise was blue (May 27) is now missing from the manuscript,

but former Colonial Williamsburg Foundation wheelwright Andy De Lisle emailed the author notes from old transcriptions of the account books. The August 4 entry noting that the carriage Lukens wanted to emulate was "light blue" remains intact. Andrew De Lisle to author, August 18, 2017.

2   Ibid., June 2 and August 8, 1789, and [Death Notice], *The Independent Gazetteer*, Philadelphia, PA, October 16, 1789, 3, America's Historical Newspapers, Readex. All historic newspaper sources from America's Historical Newspapers, Readex, unless otherwise noted. For more about the Hunter shop, see Richard E. Powell, Jr., "Coachmaking in Philadelphia: George and William Hunter's Factory of the early Federal Period," *Winterthur Portfolio* 28, no. 4 (1993): 247–277.

3   David Evans daybooks, October 15, 1789, Am. 9115, HSP.

4   John Lukens, Will and Inventory, 1789, No. 157, Book U, p. 380, Philadelphia, PA, Microfilm Roll 1, 1789, Winterthur Library: Downs Collection of Manuscripts and Printed Ephemera and John Lukens, and Vendue Lists, 1790, Folder 44, Papers of the Estate of John Lukens, 1789–1900 & undated, Manuscript Group 489: Lukens-Lenox Papers, 1702–1900, Pennsylvania State Archives, Microfilm, University of Delaware Library Special Collections.

5   John Lukens Inventory and Vendue Lists.

6   [Death Notice], *Pennsylvania Packet*, Philadelphia, PA, March 7, 1788, 3. In his *Sermons to gentlemen upon temperance and exercise*, Philadelphia physician Benjamin Rush wrote about going into the bedchamber of a man with gout and told readers that should "not [be] alarmed at his groans." Benjamin Rush, *Sermons to gentlemen upon temperance and exercise* (Philadelphia, PA: Printed by John Dunlap, in Market-Street, 1772), 25, Early American Imprints, Series I: Evans, 1639–1800, Readex.

7   By "live with" and "manage," I mean making choices about (rather than "coping with" or "overcoming") how to live with physical disability. Using the phrases "managing" and "living with" restores agency to people with disabilities. Using phrases like "overcoming disability" is unpopular with people with disabilities because when we use a phrase like that, we suggest disabilities must be conquered or "cured" in order to live good or successful lives. See Paul K. Longmore and Lauri Umansky, "Introduction: Disability History: The Margins to the Mainstream," in *The New Disability History: American Perspectives*, eds. Paul K. Longmore and Lauri Umansky (New York: New York University Press, 2001), 16–17.

8   Examples of activities not typically part of everyday like include war, large-scale organized religious worship, natural disasters, etc. Historian Jack Larkin informs my definition of everyday life. Jack Larkin, *The Reshaping of Everyday Life, 1790–1840* (New York: Harper & Row, 1988), xiii. For more on everyday life and aesthetics, see David Morgan, *Visual Piety: A History and Theory of Popular Religious Images* 1998 (Berkeley: University of California Press, 1999), 12–17.

9   Objects like Lukens's phaeton are central to understanding lived experience of disability in early America. As disability historian and material culture scholar Katherine Ott noted, "One of the most difficult modalities of peoples' lives to retrieve from the past is

how bodies move," but that "[o]bjects can help restore that lost knowledge." Katherine Ott, "Disability Things: Material Culture and American Disability History, 1700–2010," in *Disability Histories*, eds. Susan Burch and Michael Rembis (Chicago: University of Illinois Press, 2014), 120.

10   Katherine Ott, "Prosthetics," in *Keywords for Disability Studies*, eds. Rachael Adams, Benjamin Reiss, and David Serlin (New York: New York University Press, 2015), 140.

11   Ott, "Prosthetics," 140–141. See, for example, Sara Hendren and Caitrin Lynch at Olin College of Engineering, "Engineering at Home," accessed August 12, 2019, http://engineeringathome.org

12   Lukens's carriage was not unique. At least one of his European counterparts "the Lord Bishop of Rochester," Francis Atterbury, according to a 1722 newspaper account, "was seiz'd at his House" for plotting "High Treason" and "carry'd thither [to the Tower of London] in his own Coach, which was adapted to his Illness of the Gout, of which he is extremely lame." "London, August 21," *The New-England Courant*, Boston, MA, October 29, 1722, 2. In addition, James Logan (1674–1751), who broke his hip is 1728, noted to a friend that on at least one occasion, he borrowed what he described as an "easie chaise" (or carriage). James Logan to Peter Collinson, October 2, 1736, Alvertthorpe Letterbook A, Collection 2011, James Logan papers 1670–1749, HSP. For more on Logan and his material experience with disability, see Nicole Belolan, "'Confined to Crutches': James Logan and the Material Culture of Disability in Early America," *Pennsylvania Legacies* 17, no. 2 (2017): 6–11.

13   To get a sense of what a typical phaeton of the period looked like, see Phaeton, 1775–1785, United States or France, Gift of the Johnstown Historical Society, 1955, Long Island Museum, 258, accessed August 15, 2019, http://longislandmuseum.pastperfectonline.com/

14   This definition is inspired by James Deetz's distinction between *vernacular* and *academic* architecture. James Deetz, *In Small Things Forgotten: An Archaeology of Early American Life* 1977 (New York: Anchor Books 1996), 125–127. For more on defining vernacular "practices," see Arwen P. Mohun, *Risk: Negotiating Safety in American Society* (Baltimore, MD: Johns Hopkins University Press, 2013), 261, fn. 3.

15   Juliet Rogers and Tony Waldron, *A Field Guide to Join Disease in Archaeology* (West Sussex, England: John Wiley & Sons Ltd, 1995), 79. Thank you to Elizabeth Craig-Atkins and Karen Harvey for bringing this source to my attention.

16   MD Gerald F. Falasca, "Metabolic Diseases: Gout," *Clinics in Dermatology* 24, no. 6 (November–December 2006): 498. Thank you to Elizabeth Craig-Atkins and Karen Harvey for bringing this source to my attention. For more on gout identified in bones from the Roman London, see Alex Werner, *London Bodies: The Changing Shape of Londoners from Prehistoric Times to the Present Day* (London: Museum of London, 1998), 37.

17   For a recent example, see Josh Max, "When a Vegan Gets Gout," *New York Times*, July 5, 2018, https://www.nytimes.com/2018/07/05/well/family/when-a-vegan-gets-gout.html.

18 "Gout," Center for Disease Control and Prevention, last reviewed January 28, 2019, http://www.cdc.gov/arthritis/basics/gout.htm. For contemporary medical perspectives on gout, see David S. Newcombe and Dwight R. Robinson, *Gout: Basic Science and Clinical Practice* (New York: Springer, 2013) and The Gout Education Society, 2019, http://gouteducation.org/
19 "Gout," Center for Disease Control and Prevention.
20 Jonathan S. Dunham, MD, Personal interview, March 11, 2014.
21 For more on the distinction between gout and other types of arthritis, see Roy Porter and G.S. Rousseau, *Gout: The Patrician Malady* (New Haven, CT: Yale University Press, 1998), 7–10.
22 Ibid., 71–85.
23 John Wesley, *A Collection of Receipts. For the Use of the Poor* (Chester: Printed by Peter Joynson, 1745?), 13, ECCO, Gale. Wesley expanded this pamphlet and published it as *Primitive Physic*, versions of which circulated in England and America into the nineteenth century. Deborah Madden, "Wesley as Adviser on Health and Healing," in *Cambridge Companion to John Wesley*, ed. Randy L. Maddox and Jaso E. Vickers (New York: Cambridge University Press, 2010): 176; 179–180. Some scholars have suggested that one reason for the seemingly high instance of gout among middling and elites of the eighteenth and nineteenth centuries may be due to lead leaching into wine store in barrels soldered using lead. See Alfred J. Bollet, *Plagues & Poxes: The Impact of Human History on Epidemic Disease* (New York: Demos Medical Publishing, 2004), 198–199. For more on heavy drinking among all classes in early America, see W.J. Rorabaugh, *The Alcoholic Republic: An American Tradition* (New York: Oxford University Press, 1979) and Peter Thompson, *Rum Punch & Revolution: Taverngoing & Public Life in Eighteenth-Century Philadelphia* (Philadelphia: University of Pennsylvania Press, 1999).
24 Whitfield J. Bell, Jr., "John Lukens (1720–1789)," in *Patriot Improvers: Biographical Sketches of Members of the American Philosophical Society*, Vol. 1, 1743–1768 (Philadelphia, PA: American Philosophical Society, 1997), 314–320.
25 Oxford English Dictionary Online, s.v., gouty, accessed August 12, 2019.
26 "Hands with Gout," Nineteenth century, The College of Physicians of Philadelphia Digital Library, 2202.1, Human Hands in Preserving Fluid, accessed August 12, 2019, http://www.cppdigitallibrary.org/items/show/2608
27 [Runaway advertisement], *The Pennsylvania Gazette*, Philadelphia, PA, October 22, 1767, 4.
28 For more on the role pain played in early Americans' lives, see Elaine Forman Crane, "'I Have Suffer'd Much Today': The Defining Force of Pain in Early America," in *Through a Glass Darkly: Reflections on Personal Identity in Early America*, ed. Ronald Hoffman, Mechal Sobel, and Fredrika J. Teute (Chapel Hill: University of North Carolina Press, 1997): 370–403.
29 John Lukens Diary, November 18, 1778, inside *Poor Will's Almanack for the Year of Our Lord, 1778; Being the Second after Leap Year* (Philadelphia, PA: Printed and Sold by Joseph Crukshank, in Market-Street, between Second and Third Streets, opposite

Elbow-Land), No. 17, Eastwick Collection, 1746–1929, Mss.974.811.Ea7, American Philosophical Society.

30 Moody Follansbee diaries, 1765–1766, *Pre-Revolutionary Diaries at the Massachusetts Historical Society*, microfilm edition, 13 reels (Boston: Massachusetts Historical Society, 1988), reel 4.1–2. Hereafter referred to as Follansbee diaries.

31 PHILANTHROPOS, [Letter and Epitaph], *Pennsylvania Packet*, Philadelphia, PA, September 5, 1782, 1.

32 Jeanne E. Abrams, *Revolutionary Medicine: The Founding Fathers and Mothers in Sickness and in Health* (New York: New York University Press, 2013), 20.

33 For one historian's take on the value of integrating medical history into disability history, see Beth Linker, "On the Borderland of Medical and Disability History: A Survey of the Field," *Bulletin of the History of Medicine* 87, 4 (2013): esp. 502–503, 505, and 520. For more on the relationship between medical history and disability history, see Catherine Kudlick, "Social History of Medicine and Disability History," in *The Oxford Handbook of Disability History*, ed. Michael Rembis, Catherine Kudlick, and Kim E. Nielsen, (New York: Oxford University Press, 2018), 105–124.

34 Receipt for payment to Adam Kuhn, July 31, 1789, Folder 489m.18, Papers of the Estate of John Lukens. Samuel Powel Griffitts, *Biographical Notice of Doctor Adam Kuhn* (Philadelphia PA: Printed by William Fry, 1818), 4, Early American Imprints, Series II: Shaw-Shoemaker, 1801–1819, Readex.

35 Ibid., 5.

36 See, for example, the case studies of several "founding" families in Jeanne E. Abrams, *Revolutionary Medicine: The Founding Fathers and Mothers in Sickness and in Health* (New York: New York University Press, 2013).

37 Certificate of Removal, October 25, 1762, Quaker Meeting Records, Certificates of Removal, 1762–1764, MR Ph:397, Swarthmore College, accessed online August 12, 2019, via Ancestry.com. U.S., Quaker Meeting Records, 1681–1935.

38 Receipt for payment of Sarah Coombs, November 16, 1789, Folder 489m.18, Papers of the Estate of John Lukens, 1789–1900 & undated, Manuscript Group 489: Lukens-Lenox Papers, 1702–1900, Pennsylvania State Archives, Microfilm, University of Delaware Library Special Collections, and Lukens Inventory.

39 [Death Notice], *Pennsylvania Packet*, March 7, 1788.

40 Lukens Inventory and Vendue Lists.

41 Servants, slaves, family, friends, and furniture manufacturers performed work that extends and builds on historian Kathleen's Brown's concept of "body work," or the "cleaning, healing, caring" labors performed to help people meet their needs. Kathleen M. Brown, *Foul Bodies: Cleanliness in Early America* (New Haven, CT: Yale University Press, 2009), 5.

42 Ann Ashby Manigault, March 1776, "Diary of Ann Ashby Manigault," in *Extracts from the Journal of Mrs. Ann Manigault 1754–1781*, ed. Mabel J. Webber (Charleston: South Carolina Historical Society, 1920,) 112–113, accessed via Alexander Street Press. Upon Ann's husband Gabriel's death in 1781, he owned several hundred enslaved individuals. Clay Scott Graubard, "Documenting the University of Pennsylvania's Connection

to Slavery," The University of Pennsylvania, Class of 2019, April 19, 2018, 25, https://archives.upenn.edu/wp-content/uploads/2018/12/CSGraubard_Documenting-the-University-of-Pennsylvanias-Connection-to-Slavery.pdf. To learn about how Manigault descendants' slaves mutilated Ann and Gabriel's portraits, see Jennifer Van Horn "The Dark Iconoclast": African Americans' Artistic Resistance in the Civil War South, The Art Bulletin, 99, 4 (2017): 141–143.
43 Lukens Vendue Lists.
44 [Advertisement for E. Poinsett], *City Gazette and Daily Advertiser*, Charleston, SC, April 5, 1788, 4.
45 For two examples, see John Tennent, *Every man his own doctor: or, The Poor Planter's Physician* (Williamsburg, VA: 1751, 41), Early American Imprints, Series I: Evans, 1639–1800, Readex, and William Buchan, MD, *Domestic Medicine: or, a Treatise on the Prevention and Cure of Diseases by Regimen and Simple Medicines* (Philadelphia, 1784), 296, Evans, 1639–1800, Readex.
46 "A Chamber Horse," *Independent Journal*, New York, August 2, 1788, 4. For more on chamber horse history and modes of construction, see Nancy Britton and Heather Porter, "Upholstery Springs: Their Introduction and Early Development in Britain and America," in *The Forgotten History-Upholstery Conservation*, ed. Karin Lohm (Linköping, Sweden: Linköping University, 2011), 128–129.
47 William Buchan, *Domestic Medicine* (Philadelphia, 1784), 299, and John Wesley, MA, *Primitive Physic: or, An easy and natural method of curing most diseases* (Philadelphia, PA: Printed by Prichard & Hall, in Market-Street, and sold by John Dickins, in Fourth Street, near Race Street, 1789), 99, Early American Imprints, Series I: Evans, 1639–1800, Readex.
48 Eliza Smith, *The compleat housewife: or, Accomplish'd gentlewoman's companion* (Williamsburg, VA: Printed and sold by William Parks, 1742), 193, Early American Imprints, Series I: Evans, 1639–1800, Readex.
49 John Wesley, MA, *Primitive Physic*, 99.
50 Elizabeth Byles, Recipe Book, No. 167, William Ball Collection, Winterthur Library: Downs Collection of Manuscripts and Printed Ephemera, Col. 613, 00x179.2.
51 PHILANTHROPOS, Ibid.
52 John Tennent, *Every man his own doctor*, 42, and William Buchan, *Domestic Medicine*, 297.
53 Follansbee diaries, January 1767.
54 Ibid., April–November 1767.
55 Eliza Smith, *The compleat housewife*, 194, and Buchan, *Domestic Medicine*, 301.
56 Porter and Rousseau, *Gout*, 248. For more on the visual culture of gout, see Julie Anderson, Emm Barnes, and Emma Shackleton, *The Art of Medicine: Over 2,000 Years of Images and Imagination* (Chicago, IL: University of Chicago Press, 2011), 138–139. For additional fictional depictions of gouty invalid in print, see Robert Montgomery Bird, *Sheppard Lee: Witten by Himself*, 1836 (New York: New York Review of Books, 2008) and "The Invalid Fisherman," *The Gem* (Philadelphia, PA: Published by Henry F. Anners,

1839): 206–211. Thank you to Sari Altschuler and Cristobal Silva for suggesting I take a look at *Sheppard Lee*.

57 Rush, *Sermons to gentlemen upon temperance and exercise*, 24.

58 Many colonial Americans revered William Pitt, who had gout, because he championed the repeal of the Stamp Act. Newspapers regularly reported on Pitt's public political appearances. See, for example, "On Mr. PITT's bring indisposed with the GOUT," *Boston Evening-Post*, May 16, 1757, 3, and "LONDON, February 25," *Newport Mercury*, Newport, Rhode Island, April 28, 1766, 2. Many of those reports included sympathetic references to his gout and the objects he used to get around because of it. Pitt's gout was such an important part of his identity that a poem written from the perspective of a 1770 statue erected in response to the erection of a George the III statue in New York included a reference to Pitt's gout. "THE SPEECH OF THE STATUE, OF THE Right Hon. William Pitt, EARL OF CHATHAM., To the Virtuous and Patriotic Citizens of New-York," (New York: Printed by Hugh Gaine, 1770), Early American Imprints, Series I: Evans, 1639–1800, Readex.

59 In *The Invention of Comfort*, John E. Crowley suggests that the concept of "physical comfort" developed around 1800. I add that comfort also encompassed a social component. John E. Crowley, *The Invention of Comfort: Sensibilities and Design in Early Modern Britain and Early America* (Baltimore, MD: The Johns Hopkins University Press, 2001), 142 and 292. As David Yosifon and Peter N. Stearns explain, around 1750, Americans began to emphasize the importance maintaining good posture, which was considered a sign of self-control. David Yosifon and Peter N. Stearns, "The Rise and Fall of American Posture," *The American Historical Review* 103, no. 4 (1998): 1059. Richard L. Bushman, *The Refinement of America: Persons, Houses, Cities* (New York: Alfred A. Knopf, 1992), 99 and 446, and John F. Kasson, *Rudeness and Civility: Manners in Nineteenth-Century Urban America* (New York: Hill and Wang, 1990), 34.

60 Robert F. Trent noted that, in conjunction with other forms such as bed chairs, chamber pots, close stools, and gout stools, easy chairs played critical roles in "a complex of nursing" in early American bedchambers. I build on his analysis and add that disabled people and their families, servants, slaves, and acquaintances also used these objects as part of living and managing with disability and impairment (not just nursing). Robert F. Trent, "Mid-Atlantic Easy Chairs, 1770–1820: Old Questions and New Evidence," in *American Furniture*, ed. Luke Beckerdite (Hanover, NH: Chipstone Foundation, distributed by University Press of new England, 1993), 209.

61 Examples of such chairs can be found at the following museums: The National Museum of American History (which the author studied in person), Old Sturbridge Village, the Sherman Historical Society in Connecticut, and the John Greenleaf Whittier Birthplace in Haverhill, MA. For a fictional depiction of the same type of furniture, see Maria Catharine Sedgwick, *The city clerk and his sister; and other stories* (Philadelphia, PA: Willis P. Hazard, 1851).

62 See *The Diary of Elizabeth Drinker*, ed. Elaine Forman Crane (Boston, MA: Northeastern University Press, 1991). Drinker's diary is searchable online through North American Women's Letter's and Diaries database, published by ProQuest's Alexander Street.
63 Thomas Burling, "cabinet and chair-maker," *Daily Advertiser*, New York, January 3, 1788, 4.
64 Maria Louisa Trumbull Cogswell, "The Trumbull Mansion and Its Occupants," *Proceedings of the Worcester Society of Antiquity* 17 (1900), 241–243, Google Books. For another unique, vernacular object Benjamin Franklin made to live with gout, see David Waldstreicher's "The Long Arm of Benjamin Franklin," in *Artificial Parts, Practical Lives: Modern Histories of Prosthetics* (New York: New York University Press, 2002), 200–236.
65 For more on the beauty of men's legs in eighteenth and early-nineteenth-century Anglo-American culture, see Karen Harvey, "Men of Parts: Masculine Embodiment and the Male Leg in Eighteenth Century England," *Journal of British Studies* 54, 4 (2015): 797–821.
66 Ralph Earl, Elijah Boardman, 1789, Oil on canvas, 83" X 51", The Metropolitan Museum of Art, Bequest of Susan W. Tyler, 1979, 1979.395, https://www.metmuseum.org/art/collection/search/10830
67 This British image by Francis Wheatley depicts clothing of the type sailors would have worn throughout the Atlantic world, including America. *The Sailor's Return*, 1786, Oil on canvas, 470mm X 381mm, BHC1076, National Maritime Museum, Greenwich, London, Caird Collection, http://collections.rmg.co.uk/collections/objects/12568.html#oxEHlF1gcK6djljV.99
68 For an example of a "Silk Quilt" for "gouty and rheumatic invalids" sold during Lukens's life, see "To Be Sold." *The Pennsylvania Gazette*, February 1, 1775, 4. For an account of soft fabric marketed to people with gout, see "ELIZABETH-TOWN, October 10," *New-Jersey Journal* (Elizabethtown), October 10, 1792, 3. For more on similar objects in the British context, see David M. Turner and Alun Withey, "Technologies of the Body: Polite Consumption and the Correction of Deformity in Eighteenth-Century England," *History* 99, no. 338 (2014): 294.
69 [Runaway advertisement], *Pennsylvania Evening Post*, Philadelphia, PA, June 28, 1777, 344.
70 Old Bailey Proceedings Online (www.oldbaileyonline.org, version 8.0, 12 August 2019), *Ordinary of Newgate's Account*, November 1736 (OA17361102).
71 Still, people almost exclusively associated gout with wealth. This criticism continued through the twenty-first century. Contemporary reporters continue to cite eighteenth- and early-nineteenth-century satirical depictions of gout whether or not the average American with gout uses those images as a reference point. See Jane E. Brody, "'Disease of Kings' Trickles Down to the Rest," *New York Times*, May 9, 2011, https://www.nytimes.com/2011/05/10/health/10brody.html, and Eric Nagourney, "Why Do I Have Gout?" *New York Times*, April 26, 2013, https://www.nytimes.com/2013/04/27/booming/why-do-i-have-gout.html

72 Samuel Johnson, *A Dictionary of the English Language*, s.v. flannel, https://archive.org/details/dictionaryofengl01johnuoft, Internet Archive. For more on the healthful benefits of flannel, see: Benjamin Rush, M.D., *Directions for preserving the health of soldiers: recommended to the consideration of the officers of the Army of the United States* (Lancaster, PA: Printed by John Dunlap, in Queen-Street, 1778), 4, ECCO, Gale, M. D. Benjamin Rush, *Medical inquiries and observations* (Philadelphia, printed. London, reprinted for C. Dilly, in the Poultry, 1789), 162, ECCO, Gale, and William Buchan, M.D., *Domestic Medicine; Or, A Treatise on the Prevention and Cure of Diseases*, 16th ed., (London: Printed for A. Strahan, and T. Cadell Jun. and W. Davies, [Successors to mr. Cadell,] in the Strand; and J. Balfour, and W. Creech, Edinburgh, 1798), 383, ECCO, Gale, and M.D. William Buchan, *A Letter to the Patentee, Concerning the Medical Properties of the Fleecy Hosiery* (London—PRINTED: New-York-Re-printed by G. Forman, No. 156 Front-Street, For F. Wetherhill, 1794), Early American Imprints, Series I: Evans, 1639–1800, Readex.

73 Buchan, *Domestic Medicine*, 383. Flannel was also used for similar purposes with liver disorders. Steven J. Peitzman, *Dropsy, Dialysis, Transplant: A Short History of Failing Kidneys* (Baltimore, MD: Johns Hopkins University Press): 45–57.

74 For contemporary findings on how shoes affect gout sufferers' "foot paint, impairment, and disability," see Keith Rome et. al, "Footwear Characteristics and Factors Influencing Footwear Choice in Patients with Gout," *Arthritis Care & Research* 63, 11 (2011): 1599–1604.

75 "On annual white-washings," *The American Museum: Or, Repository of Ancient and Modern Fugitive Pieces & Prose and Poetical*, Philadelphia, PA, January 1787, 48, American Periodicals, ProQuest.

76 [No Title], *The Nightingale; or A Melange de Literature; a Periodical Publication*, Boston, MA, 1, Iss. 7, May 24, 1796, 83, American Periodicals, ProQuest.

77 See visual satires of the period, such as "Hob in the Well," (Publish'd as the act directs, September 4, 1793, by T. Prattent, 46 Cloth Fair, West Smithfield, London), The Lewis Walpole Library, http://hdl.handle.net/10079/digcoll/552196 and Thomas Rowlandson, "Comfort in the Gout," (Published July1, 1802, by S.W. Fores, 50 Piccadilly, London, Originally published 1785), The Lewis Walpole Library, http://hdl.handle.net/10079/digcoll/976404

78 According to the archaeology report, the bones of Abraham Favenc, which included gout boots, did not show signs of gout. That said, the report notes that "bony characteristics associated with gout are only rarely observed in skeletal examples." Margaret Cox, Life and Death in Spitalfields 1700 to 1850, CBA Occasional Papers No. 21 (1996), 76, https://archaeologydataservice.ac.uk/archiveDS/archiveDownload?t=arch-284-1/dissemination/pdf/cba_op_021.pdf. See page 73, figure 68 for gout boots, currently in the collection of the Museum of London. Regardless, as Winterthur curator Linda Eaton suggested, the relatively large size of the shoes suggests they were used by someone who had a foot impairment.

79 [Lukens estate auction], *Federal Gazette*, Philadelphia, PA, November 6, 1789, 3.

80 In the mid–late eighteenth century, the term "invalid" had a primarily medical association. The term *invalid* did not become common shorthand for furniture or devices designed and marketed to disabled people until the mid- to late nineteenth century. Samuel Johnson defined an invalid (n) as "one disabled by sickness or hurts." *A Dictionary of the English Language*, 6th ed. (London: J. F. And C. Rivington, 1785) s.v. "invalide," The Internet Archive, https://archive.org/details/dictionaryofengl01johnuoft/page/n6. Corinne Kirchner and Liat Ben-Moshe, *Encyclopedia of American Disability History*, ed. Susan Burch (New York: Facts on File, 2009), s.v. Invalid and Invalidism.

Bibliography

Abrams, Jeanne E. *Revolutionary Medicine: The Founding Fathers and Mothers in Sickness and in Health*. New York: New York University Press, 2013.

Anderson, Julie, Emm Barnes, and Emma Shackleton. *The Art of Medicine: Over 2,000 Years of Images and Imagination*. Chicago, IL: University of Chicago Press, 2011.

Bell, Whitefield, J., Jr. "John Lukens, 1720–1789." In *Patriot Improvers: Biographical Sketches of Members of the American Philosophical Society*. Vol. 1, 1743–1768. Philadelphia, PA: American Philosophical Society, 1997, 314–320.

[Advertisement for E. Poinsett]. 12/19/2019 *City Gazette and Daily Advertiser*, Charleston, SC, April 5, 1788, 4. America's Historical Newspapers. Readex.

Belolan, Nicole. "'Confined to Crutches': James Logan and the Material Culture of Disability in Early America." *Pennsylvania Legacies* 17, no. 2 (2017): 6–11.

Bird, Robert Montgomery. *Sheppard Lee: Written by Himself*. 1836. New York: New York Review of Books, 2008.

Bollet, Alfred J. *Plagues & Poxes: The Impact of Human History on Epidemic Disease*. New York: Demos Medical Publishing, 2004.

Nancy, Britton, and Heather Porter. "Upholstery Springs: Their Introduction and Early Development in Britain and America." In *The Forgotten History-Upholstery Conservation*, ed. Karin Lohm (Linköping, Sweden: Linköping University, 2011), 118–147.

Brody, Jane E. "'Disease of Kings' Trickles Down to the Rest." .*New York Times*, May 9, 2011, https://www.nytimes.com/2011/05/10/health/10brody.html

Brown, Kathleen M. *Foul Bodies: Cleanliness in Early America*. New Haven, CT: Yale University Press, 2009.

Buchan, William, MD. *Domestic Medicine: or, a Treatise on the Prevention and Cure of Diseases by Regimen and Simple Medicines*. Philadelphia, PA, 1784. Evans, 1639–1800. Readex.

Buchan, William, M.D. *Domestic Medicine;.Or, A Treatise on the Prevention and Cure of Diseases*. 16th ed. London: Printed for A. Strahan, and T. Cadell Jun. and W. Davies, [Successors to mr. Cadell,] in the Strand; and J. Balfour, and W. Creech, Edinburgh, 1798. ECCO. Gale.

Buchan, William, M.D. *A Letter to the Patentee, Concerning the Medical Properties of the Fleecy Hosiery*. London—PRINTED: New-York-Re-printed by G. Forman, No. 156 Front-Street, For F. Wetherhill, 1794. Early American Imprints, Series I: Evans, 1639–1800. Readex.

Bushman, Richard L. *The Refinement of America: Persons, Houses, Cities*. New York: Alfred A. Knopf, 1992.

Certificate of Removal, October 25, 1762. Quaker Meeting Records, Certificates of Removal, 1762–1764, MR Ph:397, Swarthmore College. Accessed online August 12, 2019, via Ancestry.com. U.S., Quaker Meeting Records, 1681–1935.

Elizabeth Byles Recipe Book. 1759. Winterthur Library: Downs Collection of Manuscripts and Printed Ephemera.

"A Chamber Horse." *Independent Journal*, New York, August 2, 1788, 4. America's Historical Newspapers. Readex.

Crane, Elaine Forman. "'I Have Suffer'd Much Today': The Defining Force of Pain in Early America." In *Through a Glass Darkly: Reflections on Personal Identity in Early America*, ed. Ronald Hoffman, Mechal Sobel, and Fredrika J. Teute, 370–403. Chapel Hill: University of North Carolina Press, 1997.

Cogswell, Maria Louisa Trumbull. "The Trumbull Mansion and Its Occupants," *Proceedings of the Worcester Society of Antiquity* 17 (1900): 241–255. Google Books.

Cox, Margaret. "Life and Death in Spitalfields 1700 to 1850." CBA Occasional Papers No. 21 (1996), https://archaeologydataservice.ac.uk/archiveDS/archiveDownload?t=arch-284-1/dissemination/pdf/cba_op_021.pdf

Crowley, John E. *The Invention of Comfort: Sensibilities and Design in Early Modern Britain and Early America*. Baltimore, MD: Johns Hopkins University Press, 2001.

[Death Notice]. *The Independent Gazetteer*, Philadelphia, PA, October 16, 1789, 3. America's Historical Newspapers. Readex.

[Death Notice]. *Pennsylvania Packet*, Philadelphia, PA, March 7, 1788, 3. America's Historical Newspapers. Readex.

Deetz, James. *In Small Things Forgotten: An Archaeology of Early American Life*. 1977. New York: Anchor Books, 1996.

Drinker, Elizabeth. *The Diary of Elizabeth Drinker*, ed. Elaine Forman Crane. Boston, MA: Northeastern University Press, 1991.

Dunham, Jonathan S. MD. Personal interview. March 11, 2014.

"ELIZABETH-TOWN, October 10." *New-Jersey Journal* (Elizabethtown). October 10, 1792, 3. America's Historical Newspapers. Readex.

Earl, Ralph. *Elijah Boardman*, 1789, Oil on canvas, The Metropolitan Museum of Art, Bequest of Susan W. Tyler, 1979, 1979.395. Accessed August 15, 2019. https://www.metmuseum.org/art/collection/search/10830

Evans, David. Daybooks. Am.9115. Historical Society of Pennsylvania.

Falasca, Gerald F., MD. "Metabolic Diseases: Gout." *Clinics in Dermatology* 24, no. 6 (November–December 2006): 498–508.

Hunter, George and William. Daybooks. Amb. 45661. Historical Society of Pennsylvania.

"Gout." *Center for Disease Control and Prevention*. Last reviewed January 28, 2019. http://www.cdc.gov/arthritis/basics/gout.htm

The Gout Education Society. 2019. http://gouteducation.org/

Graubard, Clay Scott. "Documenting the University of Pennsylvania's Connection to Slavery." The University of Pennsylvania, Class of 2019, April 19, 2018. Available at https://archives.upenn.edu/wp-content/uploads/2018/12/CSGraubard_Documenting-the-University-of-Pennsylvanias-Connection-to-Slavery.pdf

Griffitts, Samuel Powel. *Biographical Notice of Doctor Adam Kuhn*. Philadelphia, PA: Printed by William Fry, 1818. Evans. Early American Imprints, Series II: Shaw-Shoemaker, 1801–1819. Readex.

"Hands with Gout." Nineteenth century, Human Hands in Preserving Fluid, The College of Physicians of Philadelphia Digital Library, 2202.1. Accessed August 12, 2019. http://www.cppdigitallibrary.org/items/show/2608

Harvey, Karen. "Men of Parts: Masculine Embodiment and the Male Leg in Eighteenth Century England." *Journal of British Studies* 54, no. 4 (2015): 797–821.

Hendren, Sara, and Caitrin Lynch. "Engineering at Home." Olin College of Engineering. Accessed August 15, 2019. http://engineeringathome.org

"Hob in the Well." Publish'd as the act directs, September 4, 1793, by T. Prattent, 46 Cloth Fair, West Smithfield, London. The Lewis Walpole Library. Accessed August 15, 2019. http://hdl.handle.net/10079/digcoll/552196

"The Invalid Fisherman." In *The Gem*. Philadelphia, PA: Published by Henry F. Anners, 1839. 206–211.

Johnson, Samuel. *A Dictionary of the English Language*. London: J. F. And C. Rivington et. al., 1785. Accessed August 15, 2019. https://archive.org/details/dictionaryofengl01johnuoft

Kasson, John F. *Rudeness and Civility: Manners in Nineteenth-Century Urban America*. New York: Hill and Wang, 1990.

Kirchner, Corinne, and Liat Ben-Moshe. *Encyclopedia of American Disability History*, ed. Susan Burch. New York: Facts on File, 2009.

Kudlick, Catherine. "Social History of Medicine and Disability History." In *The Oxford Handbook of Disability History*, ed. Michael Rembis, Catherine Kudlick, and Kim E. Nielsen, 105–124. New York: Oxford University Press, 2018.

Larkin, Jack. *The Reshaping of Everyday Life, 1790–1840*. New York: Harper & Row, 1988.

Linker, Beth. "On the Borderland of Medical and Disability History: A Survey of the Field." *Bulletin of the History of Medicine* 87, no. 4 (Winter 2013): 499–535.

Logan, James. Papers 1670–1749. Collection 2011. Historical Society of Pennsylvania.

"LONDON, February 25." *Newport Mercury*, Newport, Rhode Island, April 28, 1766, 2. America's Historical Newspapers. Readex.

"London, August 21." *The New-England Courant*, Boston, MA, October 29, 1722, 2. America's Historical Newspapers, Readex.

Longmore, Paul K., and Lauri Umansky. "Introduction: Disability History: The Margins to the Mainstream." In *The New Disability History: American Perspectives*, ed. Paul K. Longmore and Lauri Umansky, 1–29. New York: New York University Press, 2001.

Lukens, John. Diary. Inside *Poor Will's Almanack for the Year of Our Lord, 1778; Being the Second after Leap Year* (Philadelphia, PA: Printed and Sold by Joseph Cruikshank, in Market-Street, between Second and Third Streets, opposite Elbow-Land), No. 17. Eastwick Collection, 1746–1929, Mss.974.811.Ea7. American Philosophical Society.

[Lukens estate auction]. *Federal Gazette*, Philadelphia, PA, November 6, 1789, 3. America's Historical Newspapers. Readex.

John Lukens Will and Inventory. 1789. No. 157, Book U, p. 380, Philadelphia, PA, Microfilm Roll 1. Winterthur Library: Downs Collection of Manuscripts and Printed Ephemera.

John Lukens Vendue lists. 1790. Folder 44, Papers of the Estate of John Lukens, 1789–1900 & undated, Manuscript Group 489: Lukens-Lenox Papers, 1702–1900, Pennsylvania State Archives. Microfilm, University of Delaware Library Special Collections.

Manigault, Ann Ashby. In *Extracts from the Journal of Mrs. Ann Manigault 1754–1781*, ed. Mabel J. Webber. Charleston, SC: South Carolina Historical Society, 1920. Accessed via Alexander Street Press. Proquest.

Phaeton. United States or France, 1775–1785, Gift of the Johnstown Historical Society, 1955, Long Island Museum, 258. Accessed August 15, 2019. http://longislandmuseum.pastperfectonline.com/

Madden, Deborah. "Wesley as Advisor on Health and Healing." In *Cambridge Companion to John Wesley*, ed. Randy L. Maddox and Jaso E. Vickers. Vol. 1, 76–189. New York: Cambridge University Press, 2010.

Max, Josh. "When a Vegan Gets Gout." *New York Times*, July 5, 2018, https://www.nytimes.com/2018/07/05/well/family/when-a-vegan-gets-gout.html

Mohun, Arwen P. *Risk: Negotiating Safety in American Society*. Baltimore, MD: Johns Hopkins University Press, 2013.

Moody Follansbee diaries. 1765–1766. *Pre-Revolutionary Diaries at the Massachusetts Historical Society*, microfilm edition, 13 reels (Boston: Massachusetts Historical Society, 1988), reel 4.1–2.

Morgan, David. *Visual Piety: A History and Theory of Popular Religious Images*. 1998. Berkeley: University of California Press, 1999.

Nagourney, Eric. "Why Do I Have Gout?" *New York Times*. April 26, 2013, https://www.nytimes.com/2013/04/27/booming/why-do-i-have-gout.html

Newcombe, David S., and Dwight R. Robinson. *Gout: Basic Science and Clinical Practice* (New York: Springer, 2013).

[No Title]. *The Nightingale; or A Melange de Literature; a Periodical Publication*, Boston, MA, 1, Iss. 7, May 24, 1796: 83. American Periodicals. ProQuest.

Oxford English Dictionary Online. "On Mr. PITT's bring indisposed with the GOUT." *Boston Evening-Post*, May 16, 1757, 3. America's Historical Newspapers. Readex.

Ott, Katherine. "Disability Things: Material Culture and American Disability History, 1700–2010." In *Disability Histories*, ed. Susan Burch and Michael Rembis, 119–135. Chicago: University of Illinois Press, 2014.

Ott, Katherine. "Prosthetics." In *Keywords for Disability Studies*, ed. Rachael Adams, Benjamin Reiss, and David Serlin. New York: New York University Press, 2015.

Peitzman, Steven J. *Dropsy, Dialysis, Transplant: A Short History of Failing Kidneys*. Baltimore, MD: Johns Hopkins University Press.

Powell, Jr., E. Richard. "Coachmaking in Philadelphia: George and William Hunter's Factory of the Early Federal Period." *Winterthur Portfolio* 28, no. 4 (1993): 247–277.

Old Bailey Proceedings Online (www.oldbaileyonline.org, version 8.0, August 12, 2019). *Ordinary of Newgate's Account*, November 1736 (OA17361102).

"On annual white-washings." *The American Museum: Or, Repository of Ancient and Modern Fugitive Pieces & Prose and Poetical*, Philadelphia, PA, January 1787: 48–53. American Periodicals. ProQuest.

PHILANTHROPOS. [Letter and Epitaph]. *Pennsylvania Packet*, Philadelphia, PA, September 5, 1782, 1. America's Historical Newspapers. Readex.

Porter, Roy, and G.S. Rousseau. *Gout: The Patrician Malady*. New Haven, CT: Yale University Press, 1998.

Receipt for payment of Sarah Coombs. November 16, 1789. Folder 489m.18, Papers of the Estate of John Lukens, 1789–1900 & undated, Manuscript Group 489: Lukens-

Lenox Papers, 1702–1900, Pennsylvania State Archives, Microfilm, University of Delaware Library Special Collections.

Rogers, Juliet, and Tony Waldron. *A Field Guide to Joint Disease in Archaeology*. West Sussex, England: John Wiley & Sons Ltd, 1995.

Rome, Keith, et. al. "Footwear Characteristics and Factors Influencing Footwear Choice in Patients with Gout," *Arthritis Care & Research* 63, no. 11 (2011): 1599–1604.

Rorabaugh, W. J. *The Alcoholic Republic: An American Tradition*. New York: Oxford University Press, 1979.

Rowlandson, Thomas. "Comfort in the Gout." Pubd. July1, 1802, by S.W. Fores, 50 Piccadilly, London, Originally published 1785. The Lewis Walpole Library. Accessed August 15, 2019, http://hdl.handle.net/10079/digcoll/976404

[Runaway advertisement]. *The Pennsylvania Gazette*, Philadelphia, PA, October 22, 1767, 4. America's Historical Newspapers. Readex.

[Runaway advertisement]. *Pennsylvania Evening Post*, Philadelphia, PA, June 28, 1777, 344. America's Historical Newspapers. Readex.

Rush, Benjamin, M.D. *Directions for preserving the health of soldiers: recommended to the consideration of the officers of the Army of the United States*. Lancaster, PA: Printed by John Dunlap, in Queen-Street, 1778. Gale. ECCO.

Rush, Benjamin. M. D. *Medical inquiries and observations*. Philadelphia, printed. London, reprinted for C. Dilly, in the Poultry, 1789. Gale. ECCO.

Rush, Benjamin. *Sermons to gentlemen upon temperance and exercise*. Philadelphia, PA: Printed by John Dunlap, in Market-Street, 1772. Early American Imprints, Series I: Evans, 1639–1800, Readex.

Sedgwick, Maria Catharine. *The city clerk and his sister; and other stories*. Philadelphia, PA: Willis P. Hazard, 1851.

Smith, Eliza. *The compleat housewife: or, Accomplish'd gentlewoman's companion*. Williamsburg, VA: Printed and sold by William Parks, 1742. Early American Imprints, Series I: Evans, 1639–1800. Readex.

"THE SPEECH OF THE STATUE, OF THE Right Hon. William Pitt, EARL OF CHATHAM., To the Virtuous and Patriotic Citizens of New-York." New York: Printed by Hugh Gaine, 1770. Early American Imprints, Series I: Evans, 1639–1800. Readex.

Tennent, John. *Every man his own doctor: or, The Poor Planter's Physician*. Williamsburg, VA: 1751. Early American Imprints, Series I: Evans, 1639–1800. Readex.

"Thomas Burling, cabinet and chair-maker." *Daily Advertiser*, New York. January 3, 1788, 4. America's Historical Newspapers. Readex.

Thompson, Peter. *Rum Punch & Revolution: Taverngoing & Public Life in Eighteenth-Century Philadelphia*. Philadelphia: University of Pennsylvania Press, 1999.

"To Be Sold." *The Pennsylvania Gazette*, February 1, 1775, 4. America's Historical Newspapers. Readex.

Trent, Robert F. "Mid-Atlantic Easy Chairs, 1770–1820: Old Questions and New Evidence." In *American Furniture*, ed. Luke Beckerdite. 201–211. Hanover, NH: Chipstone Foundation, distributed by University Press of New England, 1993.

Turner, David M., and Alun Withey. "Technologies of the Body: Polite Consumption and the Correction of Deformity in Eighteenth-Century England." *History* 99, no. 338 (2014): 775–796.

Van Horn, Jennifer. "'The Dark Iconoclast': African Americans' Artistic Resistance in the Civil War South." *The Art Bulletin* 99, no. 4 (2017): 133–167.

Waldstreicher, David. "The Long Arm of Benjamin Franklin." In *Artificial Parts, Practical Lives: Modern Histories of Prosthetics*, 200–236. New York: New York University Press, 2002.

Wheatley, Francis. *The Sailor's Return*, 1786, Oil on canvas, National Maritime Museum, Greenwich, London, Caird Collection, BHC1076. Accessed August 15, 2019, http://collections.rmg.co.uk/collections/objects/12568.html#oxEHIF1gcK6djljV.99

Werner, Alex. *London Bodies: The Changing Shape of Londoners from Prehistoric Times to the Present Day*. London: Museum of London, 1998.

Wesley, John. *A Collection of Receipts. For the Use of the Poor*. Chester: Printed by Peter Joynson, 1745?. ECCO. Gale.

Wesley, John, MA. *Primitive Physic: Or An easy and natural method of curing most diseases*. Philadelphia, PA: Printed by Prichard & Hall, in Market-Street, and sold by John Dickins, in Fourth Street, near Race Street, 1789. Early American Imprints, Series I: Evans, 1639–1800. Readex.

Yosifon, David, and Peter N. Stearns. "The Rise and Fall of American Posture." *The American Historical Review* 103, no. 4 (1998): 1057–1095.

2 Walking Cane Style and Medicalized Mobility
CARA KIERNAN FALLON

"Every well-dressed man without exception, carries a cane," wrote the *Chicago Daily Tribune* in 1890.[1] Engraved, enameled, lacquered, and jewel-encrusted canes filled the shops and cluttered the streets of turn-of-the-century fashionable society. There were "at least 2000 different styles and handles" of canes according to the *Boston Daily Globe*, while fashion houses of Tiffany & Co., the Gorham Company, and the House of Fabergé marketed sterling silver and diamond-encrusted "limited edition" canes to their well-heeled patrons.[2] Although traditionally the province of monarchs and men—dignitaries ranging from Louis XIV to George Washington carried canes; Voltaire, Rousseau, and Dickens had several—canes also rose to the height of fashion for women in the late nineteenth century. Newspapers claimed that Queen Victoria, who used a walking stick "habitually" due to her rheumatism, inspired the "cane fad" in women from Paris to New York.[3] Even the "new woman has made her debut on State street," added the *Tribune*. "She carries a cane. So bring forth your walking sticks."[4] Associated with the powerful, the intelligent, and the fashion-forward, canes were even used to assert or elevate one's status, being able to "give dignity where dignity is most needed."[5] From the early modern courts of absolutist monarchs to the high society of the early twentieth century, a marvelous variety of canes accompanied the powerful, the fashionable, the wealthy, the old, the young, the lame, and the dignified.[6] Yet, by the end of the twentieth century, canes had been transformed into medical devices resisted by the elderly and stigmatized by the broader public. Ebony, hickory, snakewood, and other sticks topped with silver and gemstone handles were replaced by instruments with aluminum shafts, rubber tips, and ergonomic handles tested for gait optimization. Cane sales moved from fashion houses to medical supply shops, while physical therapists and physicians grouped canes into the category of "mobility aids," alongside crutches, walkers, and wheelchairs. Late-twentieth-century surveys reported older adults resisted using canes, while gerontologic nurses and physicians designed interventions to encourage their use.[7]

This chapter analyzes the cane's fall from fashion, its standardization as a medical tool, and its implications for the meanings and experiences of walking impairments, particularly in older adults. It demonstrates how the diversity of late-nineteenth-century canes became streamlined into a medical aid prescribed, fitted, and quantified by health professionals and how changes in fashion and medical research foregrounded impairment as they erased markers of social status and community belonging. It demonstrates how the loss of the fashionable cane was more than the loss of an accessory—it altered the experience of physical decline in old age, removing a multifaceted object that provided dignity and balance while introducing new moments of conflict and negotiation of impairment in later life. The old and impaired have received comparatively little scholarly attention; their experiences reflect a significant and overlooked category not only in disability histories, but also in studies of design.[8] This chapter thereby provides insight into the nearly ubiquitous experience of impairment in old age and the role of the cane in mediating the relationships between aging, disability, and stigma in the history of design.

By drawing together the history of the cane and the evolving experience of impairment in old age, this chapter illuminates how aspects of American design history—the materials of daily living, their cost and construction, fashions, social customs, and symbolic meaning of nearly ubiquitous items—have shaped the experiences of aging and disability over the course of the twentieth century. Tracing the ways canes have changed—how their users, uses, and meanings have evolved over time—elucidates the effect of materials on the experiences of disability, the role of fashion in accentuating or obscuring impairment, and the impact of medicine and material culture in shaping social access and exclusion, status, and stigma. Moreover, it helps delineate how cane design itself was significant in helping individuals negotiate the boundaries of ablement and disablement.

"A Cane for Every Hand"

In 1906, renowned American silver manufacturer, the Gorham Company, displayed life-size images of silver-engraved cane heads in its annual catalog to "meet the ever-growing demand" for canes.[9] The pages featured sterling silver, ivory, buckhorn, whalebone, 18-karat gold, and jewel-encrusted cane handles, displayed alongside sterling silver desk sets, cigar boxes, bronze matchbox stands, and ladies' combs, hairbrushes, and hand mirrors. A sterling silver cane head on an ebony stick cost $16.80 (approximately $500 today), while an 18-karat gold cane handle with solid gold ornamentation went for $96.00 (around $2,400 today).[10] The 1915 Gorham Catalog offered an even more extensive selection of canes: 108 pages of canes featured 790 different styles of canes, umbrellas, whips, and riding crops.[11] Ladies' umbrellas and parasols were made from a variety of fine white pearl with gold-filled bands, gold-embossed and silk taffeta heads, displayed alongside silver cigar boxes, ornate berry dishes, sterling silver snuff boxes, porcelain shaving cups, gold collar buttons, and diamond-mounted pendants for the wealthiest of patrons. Tiffany & Co. manufactured exclusive cane heads and competed with Russian House of Fabergé, whose master designer Mikhail Perkhin created opulent cane heads of sapphire, diamond, ivory, and emerald gemstones. Meanwhile, turn-of-the-century department stores including Macy's, Wanamakers, McCreary's, and Lord & Taylor sold "useful gifts" of canes and umbrella sets and retail shops along the stretch of New York City's "Ladies' Mile," displayed the occasional cane in their windows.

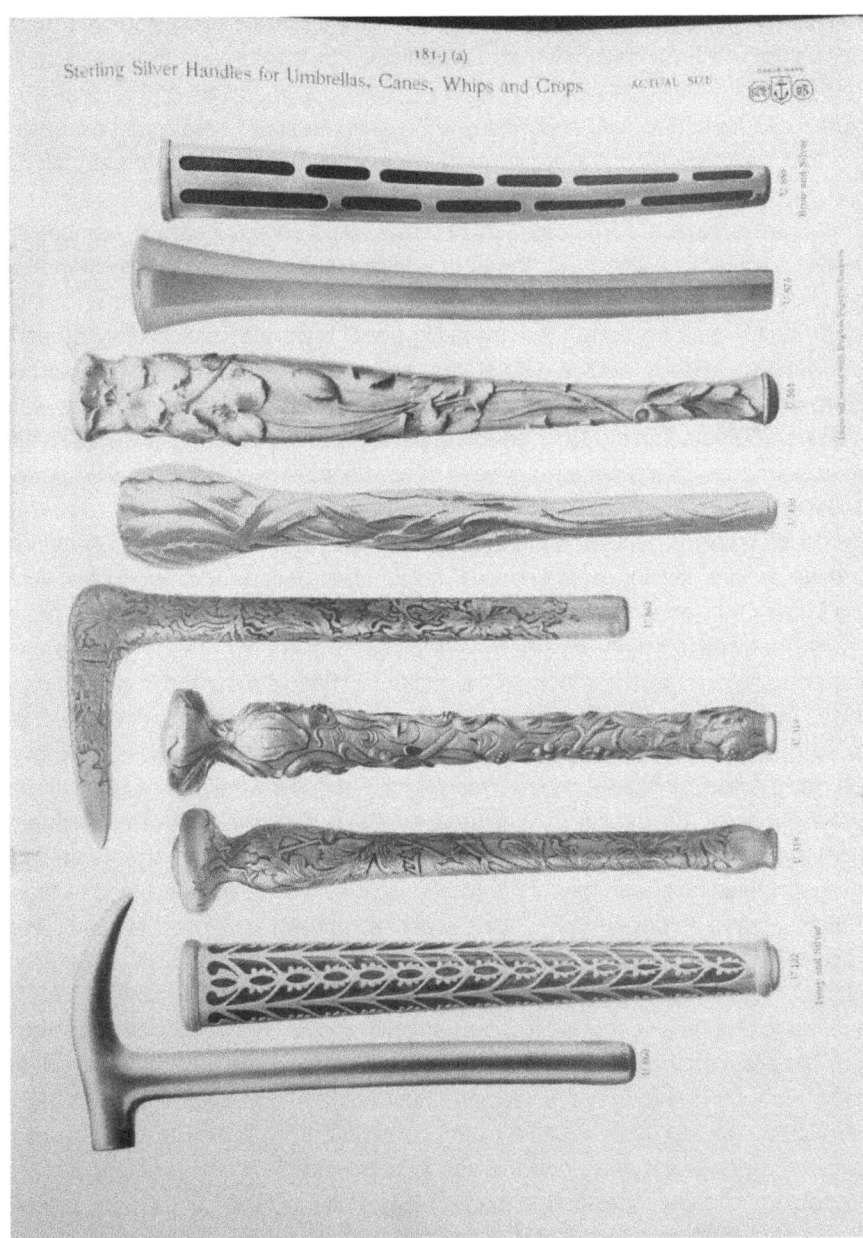

Figure 2.1 Gorham Cane Heads, Illustrated Price List of Otto Young & Co., Gorham Company Archives, John Hay Library, Brown University, Providence, RI. Image sourced from Brown University Library.

Previously items owned by the wealthy and aristocratic, acquired in Europe or special ordered, passed down through families or hand-made by skilled family members, canes expanded into middle-class fashion at the close of the nineteenth century.[12] Gorham, Fabergé, and Tiffany & Co. manufactured ornate and expensive canes and cane heads for the wealthier classes, while emerging department stores began selling canes alongside umbrellas and parasols, and advertised them in local and national newspapers. The category of canes was fluid and inclusive—umbrellas, parasols, riding whips, and other forms of walking "sticks" were marketed together with canes, sold in gift sets, and often used interchangeably. The terms "cane," "stick," "staff," "walking cane," and "walking stick" were also used fluidly by cane sellers, fashion houses, and novelty stores, and the owners of canes bequeathed them to future generations in their wills.[13] Canes, umbrellas, and riding crops were also grouped together in industry reports of supply and demand, as raw materials of cane, reed, rattan, and other lumber were shared across categories when imported for US manufacturing.[14]

Particular fashions circulated in the late nineteenth and early twentieth centuries, with their designs serving as markers of social stratification. The "world travelers" of the Lotos Club, an exclusive New York City establishment, were known to prefer "curious" materials brought back from their global excursions.[15] Union League men were said to favor a black bamboo with a buck-horn handle mounted in silver, a cane that was "a good cane to walk with," "showy, yet strong," "and a formidable weapon at close quarters."[16] Cane shafts of English ash, a light brown hue resembling olive wood, were called "unsightly" by the *Washington Post*, but were "all the rage among the young men of the Capital."[17] Whangee, an Asian bamboo, signaled wealth and discernment: "The possession of a perfect specimen of this case argues at once that a good price has been paid for it. Moreover, it cannot be imitated; and to these two facts it owes its popularity."[18] Cane styles also reflected attunement to changing prices through trade. As ebony became "much cheaper" since the "opening up of Africa," "the old-fashioned, black ebony stick has fallen into complete disuse."[19] Different age groups also tended toward particular styles: "English ash and partridge wood, pimento, or the wood of the pepper tree, is the most popular material for young men's canes now on the market," declared the *Washington Post* in 1903. "Cherry sticks are still used to some extent by old men, while the German weichsel, and French furze wood stick, and the acacia canes are now the most popular and fashionable of old age canes on the market."[20] The "fashionable canes of the present season," according to regional and national newspapers, drew from styles of both young and old.[21]

Whether used as a weapon, an indicator of formality, an expression of pedigree, or as a walking support, a cane's design and use also displayed personality. According to cane makers, the objects could reveal an owner's attributes. One cane seller claimed, "I can generally tell the nature of a man by the cane he carries." Here is an "eminent lawyer," he explained, with a "strong, sound malacca cane, with a bone or ivory handle … he grasps it firmly … just as he employs his hand when laying down the law." In contrast, he noted, "this dudish fellow coming along," who brandished a cane that was "thin, but without pith; plenty of varnish, but no backbone." "Isn't it exactly a counterpart of himself?"[22] Turn-of-the-twentieth-century men and women moved with canes in a variety of ways, and etiquette books explained proper "use" of canes. "Canes and umbrellas should not be carried under the arm horizontally, endangering the eyes and ribs of other pedestrians," explained Agnes Morton's *Etiquette* in 1911.[23] Inside the home, Emily Holt's *Encyclopaedia of Etiquette* explained, "A very punctilious man accounts it the better form to carry in his hat and cane when making a first formal call, because to leave them behind implies a familiarity with the house and hostess that he dares not claim."[24] She instructed that a man should place his cane, as well as his overcoat and overshoes, in the hall before entering the drawing room.[25] "Should a caller insist, however, on clinging to these belongings—either for mere formality's sake or even simply to insure their safety ... he must be strictly mindful that it gets in nobody's way."[26] Carrying a cane expressed formality and respect for the hostess, and a certain divergence from drawing room customs was permitted to "insure their safety." Queen Victoria "leaned heavily on" her canes due to her rheumatism, former Governor of New York and Democratic Senator David Hill "carrie[d] it free, applying it to the use intended," and still others adhered to the "dude" style of "hooking it over the arm."[27]

On the other hand, "caning"—a beating imparted with a cane—also emerged as a more violent use of the object; newspapers recounted canings with regularity. Famous canings included President Andrew Jackson's caning of Thomas Swann in 1806 and the Congressional battle between Preston Brooks and Charles Sumner over abolitionism in 1856, which resulted in Brooks beating Sumner until his cane shattered.[28] Books and magazines even explained the "art" of self-defense with a cane. Women's fashions described "Protection and Diversion" as one of the uses of a cane for women—the *Boston Daily Globe*, for example, noted that women could use a "walking stick ... to keep off an aggressor till help might arrive," or "to toss aside fallen branches," fend off an "overzealous farmer's dog," and "finally it can be used by a woman as a means of defense just as well as by a man."[29] Canes displayed etiquette, style, personality, background, and even the potential for physical violence.

Although canes were fashionable accessories and markers of social status, their "more serious purpose" remained as a walking aid.[30] "Carrying" a cane was common rhetoric in the early twentieth century, though twirling, tapping, swatting, and even "leaning heavily" on canes were mentioned with regularity. Popular accounts asserted, "There can be no doubt that the legitimate use of a walking-stick is to assist weakened limbs to bear the superincumbent weight of the body."[31] Highly ornamented handles did not preclude walking support—doctors commented on hand and back injuries from cane heads and clothing stores sold silk cane head covers to protect owners' hands from elaborate handles.[32] Cane makers described the "heavier" and "more substantial" canes preferred by old men, noting that "elderly gentlemen are very fond of theirs."[33] Old women were also discerning patrons: "Elderly ladies

Figure 2.2 Men's Fashions, 1918. Images from Sears, Roebuck, and Co. Catalog, Spring 1918, catalog 136L. Image sourced from Ancestry.com.

frequently purchase crutch-handled sticks, and they are very particular in their choice of wood or cane," explained one cane seller.[34] One of the most basic functions of the cane was widely recognized as an aid in walking, and this assistance encompassed different features over the life course. As the "pride of youth and the solace of old age," ubiquitous canes were designed so they could gradually offer support for their owners, even if not all deployed them as such.

The Cane and the Crutch

Canes and crutches shared the function of walking support, but canes were imbued with a multiplicity of meanings derived from their personalized handles and shafts, their expensive and rare materials, and their associated usage by both able-bodied and impaired individuals. In the early twentieth century, some amateur historians even created a genealogy of cane design based on class (and carefully separated the cane from the crutch). In *The Walking-Stick Papers*, Robert Cortes Holliday argued that the cane was used by ancient rulers and in early modern courts, descended from the traveling staff, the sword, and the scepter. In a more sporting fashion, it was also associated with golf clubs and riding crops. "The prehistoric ape, we are justified in assuming," wrote Holliday in his 1918 account, "struggled upright upon a cane." "The cane, so to speak, with which primitive man wooed his bride, defended his life, liberty and pursuit of happiness, and brought down his food, was (like all canes which are in good taste) admirably chosen for the occasion."[35]

In these popular accounts, canes had the ability to function as walking aids, indeed, that was their most basic function, but they were not defined by it. A crutch, however, foregrounded a user's acute needs. In medical literature and consumer publications, "crutches" functioned as walking aids for a population described and depicted as wounded soldiers, beggars, and those with severe injuries—typically the poor and severely disabled. As tools for the needy and disabled, crutches lacked whimsy; canes delighted in personal style and splendor that transformed an aid into an accessory, elevating rather than detracting from one's social status.[36] Cane design, and the materials it used, reinforced these meanings, influencing consumers and creating social customs that mediated the experience of disability.

The Old Man and His Stick: Gender and Genealogy of the Cane

Cane designs varied substantially so that they could be used across the life course, with different purposes in different life stages. The acquisition of a cane was often social rather than medical in early life, and while serving the function of support at older ages, it also conveyed many other meanings. Because of their ubiquity, canes concealed slight and gradual debilities in walking, and they allowed their owners to subtly incorporate greater walking support. Because cane design was so varied, they conveyed many different meanings, including wealth, status, and style, among others—and as such, canes were not solely signs of physical health. With their fabled connections to learned and genteel society, they were enjoyed by the young and the old as an ornament of dress as well as an instrument for balance or stability. Because their association with the elderly was portrayed as expected and natural, the use of canes by the old did not stigmatize the instrument, nor did possession of a cane stigmatize an owner. Canes could be carried by "the very youthful and the very aged, the powerful, the distinguished, the patrician, the self-important," and "those who fancy to exalt themselves."[37]

In fact, when canes were affiliated with the impairments of the elderly, this still did not preclude stylish designs, nor their use as an honor or award. In 1909, the *Boston Post* commended the "vigor and longevity of New England Manhood" by presenting a gold-headed cane to the oldest citizens of 700 New England towns.[38] Editor and publisher, Edwin A. Grozier, declared that the *Boston Post* Cane was a "handsome and substantial gift," taking over a year to make, with ebony logs shipped from the Congo and cut, dried, recut, shellacked, and then varnished and polished by hand. A gold head was made of 14-karat gold, cut, sized, and soldered, then filled with a hard composition and chased (hand-ornamented), and polished by J.F. Fradley & Co., one of the leading manufacturers of fine canes. The "Boston Post cane is not merely an ornamental cane," Grozier explained. "It is designed for everyday usuage [sic] and will last for many years."[39] The *Boston Post* also set up a repair service for the canes through F. Joseph Bianco, a jeweler in East Boston, who reportedly repaired around eighteen of these canes per year between 1909 and 1953.[40] The *Boston Post* Canes were billed as "especially interesting for what they signify, for they are intended as a tribute to honored and useful lives, to thrift, to temperance, and right living, and above all, to the superb vigor of New England manhood."[41] Sunday editions of the *Boston Post* included photographs and brief biographies of the recipients. Solomon Talbot, age 95, was the first recipient to have his photograph published in the *Boston Post* on August 21, 1909, calling the cane "one of the signal honors of my long life."[42] Women advocated for award of the canes and convinced Grozier to include them as "citizens" eligible for the cane by the 1930s. Moreover, it wasn't only the elderly who used them—Grozier gave the remaining canes from the first shipment to his staff at the *Boston Post* for Christmas presents—the same canes were ultimately shared between the oldest New England residents and the newspaper staff.

But, while men had access to the image of the "venerable old man" using a cane, important differences in the experience of aging and impairment were manifested by gender. In fact, "lighter" and "daintier" cane designs became periodically fashionable for women. Catalogs of Gorham and Tiffany & Co. marketed cane heads and parasol handles for women, and ladies' canes were described as longer and lighter than the men's canes—sometimes up to 48 inches tall—with ornate ivory handles and tassels adding a "dignified air."[43] Some papers reported that "a woman might have 10 or 12 canes, each one prettier than the other."[44] "Swagger canes," wrote the *New York Times* in 1913, appeared in London, Paris, and Rome as "the most fashionable women, old and young, are carrying them, so that they are quite as usual as a parasol would be here."[45]

Canes brokered interpersonal relationships and social customs, took part in public promenade and domestic etiquette, and served as symbols of social class, style, and personality. They were high-fashion, exquisite, and often expensive items that reflected economic choices, social stratification, and group belonging. Canes were multivalent—they had symbolic power, but also practical uses. One could quite literally lean on a cane, or gradually take on its support and balance as needed, while partaking in the customs and fashions of his or her particular social group. Canes conjured up the "Colonel of the Old South, the Bohemian, the bookworm, the artist, and the villain." And, as Holliday exclaimed, "who ever heard of a fairy godmother without a cane?"[46]

From Fashion House to Hospital to Nursing Home

And yet, canes gradually disappeared from fashionable society in the second quarter of the twentieth century. Elite and middle-class catalogs charted this decline: in 1915, the Gorham Company filled 108 pages with nearly 800 different canes and cane head designs, but by 1941, canes were completely absent from its pages. Among the middle classes, Sears, Roebuck & Company catalogs sold men's "finest genuine malacca canes" through 1929, but by the end of the following decade, offered only "convalescent" canes.[47]

To some extent, this was because of earlier connections of canes to the aristocratic and genteel, the formal and traditional, and as such, their popularity was undermined as American dress codes became increasingly casual into the mid-twentieth century.[48] Men began recounting concerns about making a "spectacle" of themselves while carrying an ornate cane, and some described the cane as clumsy when entering and alighting from automobiles, a new luxury item and class marker.[49] Still others surmised that the rise of buses, automobiles, bicycles, and concurrent decline in horse-drawn transport decreased sales of the riding crop along with the cane.[50] Products from sewing machines to vacuum cleaners were marketed in home goods catalogs as electric-powered, "modernistic," and "streamlined," while children's toy automobiles, toy telephones, and even toy cash registers highlighted aspirations embodied in sleek, mechanistic elements of mid-twentieth-century technologies.[51] With their hard-won genealogies of aristocratic tradition, canes were increasingly cast aside in the aspirational imagery of the modern middle class.

Changes in medical treatment also contributed to the decline of the fashionable cane and rise of the medical cane. On the heels of two World Wars and a series of devastating polio epidemics, rapidly expanding professions of orthopedics and physical therapy eagerly employed canes, developed new training methods for their use, and encouraged adjustments to their materials and designs. While the Red Cross held charity drives collecting unused canes to donate to wounded soldiers, orthopedic surgeons and physical therapists shuttled veterans through rehabilitation programs and produced an abundance of medical literature on the training of the wounded and impaired on canes.[52] George Deaver, medical director for the Institute for the Crippled and Disabled, and physical therapy technician Mary Eleanor Brown explained in 1946, "canes are more difficult to use than crutches," and "often it is necessary to teach subjects how to use crutches before they are put on canes."[53] They asserted that the "principal justification for a cane is to maintain balance," and the "use of canes rests on the extent of the disability."[54] Physicians and physical therapists also developed training exercises with canes to make injured veterans more "self-sufficient" and able to "carry out the activities of daily living which are basic to his vocation and avocations," underscoring the increased importance of a cane in compensating for disabilities.

In conjunction with training exercises, physical therapists and physicians discussed how to standardize canes, make professional adjustments, and ensure the design and materials reiterated the cane's medical purposes. "The common standard cane is 36 inches," Deaver and Brown explained, and "usually any size other than 36 inches must be adjusted or made especially."[55] This, they explained, was to "allow a bend at the elbow of approximately 30 degrees … this height allows the greatest power to be drawn from the participating muscle groups."[56] Donald Covalt, clinical director of the Institute of Physical Medicine and Rehabilitation at Bellevue Medical Center, and rehabilitation course director Edith Buchwald also emphasized that canes should be "carefully adjusted" by doctors and physical therapists to the correct height.[57] Subsequent publications reiterated that canes "should be fitted … by a physician or physical therapist" and that "the patient should receive instruction in their use."[58]

A range of professionals also encouraged other changes to canes that mimicked crutches and braces, including rubber tips for safety and aluminum alloys for strength and lighter weight. While rubber cushions had been manufactured and affixed to wooden crutches as early as the 1860s (and became increasingly common in the following decades), jewelers continued to employ primarily metal ferrules on the ends of canes into the late 1930s.[59] In the 1940s, however, industrial designers experimented with crutch-cane combinations for wounded soldiers and physical therapists encouraged the use of rubber cushions for shock absorption and preventing slipping. In 1940, for example, New York inventor Philip Cederstrom patented a "Cane Crutch" design combining forearm crutches with a cane handle and shaft, ending with a "resilient crutch tip" to "minimize shocks."[60] Industrial designer Thomas Lamb also developed a crutch-cane, the Lamb Lim-Rest, in the early 1940s. The design included a detachable cane with an underarm crutch, cane handle, and a rubber "cushion" tip to prevent slipping.[61] Mid-century physical therapists such as Deaver and Brown encouraged, "A cane should be strong and contain a good large soft rubber cap for its base, such as has already been described for crutches."[62] By

1947, one patent application for ice-grips summarized, "Most canes and crutches are covered at the lower end with a tip of rubber or similar material."[63]

Heavier wooden shafts were also replaced with lighter-weight aluminum bodies. Crutch-canes such as Lamb's Lim-Rest, adjustable forearm crutches, and other combinations of crutches and canes swapped wooden shafts for lightweight metals at mid-century, while physical therapists encouraged the use of aluminum canes for rehabilitation. An "aluminum cane has been devised which can be adapted to any length until the right length is found," wrote Covalt and Buchwald in 1953.[64] Aluminum shafts ending in rubber tips emphasized safety, uniformity, and support for injury and impairment above all else. These changes linked canes with a spectrum of other devices long focused on walking impairments, including crutches, braces, and wheelchairs, ultimately solidifying the object's transition from a multivalent accessory to a device based on medical need.[65]

Mainstream media reflected these shifts: whereas news articles in the 1890s interviewed cane sellers and men-about-town who described "carrying" canes and "wearing" walking sticks, by the 1950s, physicians, nurses, and physical therapists were quoted as they described canes in terms of "use," "need," and "support" for "patients" on canes as "mobility aids."

While physicians and physical therapists re-configured the cane as a medical device, medical attention to aging bodies established impairment as the result of particular disease processes in need of medical treatment, rather than an inevitable part of growing old. As the second half of the century progressed, physicians analyzed the problems of arthritis, osteoporosis, falls, and hip fractures, debating their relationships to the processes of "normal" aging.[66] Furthermore, as the medical establishment began to rethink the advance of disease and its role in old age, canes became integrated into the debate. "Old age cannot be cured," explained geriatrician William Morton in a 1953 Congressional Lecture, "but its concomitant disabilities [can be] made tolerable and the remaining years more enjoyable."[67] Like many in the period, he noted that the "simplest [mechanical aid] is a stick, but patients have to be taught how best to use it."[68] Covalt and Buchwald added that "arthritic patients" and individuals suffering from the long-term "effects of poliomyelitis" also should be "prescribed" a cane, while others, including the clinical director of the National Institute of Arthritis and Metabolic Diseases, advised that patients with arthritis should continue to exercise and that "canes and crutches may help."[69]

Public health campaigns reiterated the importance of lightweight, aluminum canes with rubber tips for safety purposes in the elderly. Metropolitan Life Insurance Company's pamphlet, "Safety for the Aging Population," distributed in the mid-1950s, encouraged older policyholders to use a rubber "vacuum cup" tip on their canes to "make it safer."[70] The National Safety Council similarly emphasized, "Use a rubber-tipped cane if you need to—and use it proudly."[71]

As the cane transitioned into a medical device signaling impairment and need, physicians also remarked on the rising stigma of the instrument. If only "the cane were restored to popular favor," orthopedic surgeon Walter Blount said in 1956, "thousands of Americans would be helped, particularly those who have bone and joint injuries."[72] He added, "Early degenerative hip disease may require no treatment other than weight reduction and a stick in the opposite hand."[73] He issued a "plea" for his medical colleagues to bring the walking stick back to favor—"If they would do so ... it would be a lot easier to get the lame and the decrepit to carry canes."[74] Physicians made public recommendations for the elderly to take up exercising with "that walking stick," and papers reported that "doctors want to bring the walking stick back—this time for 'safety.'"[75]

While the National Safety Council beseeched the elderly to use a cane "proudly," subsequent public health campaigns addressed the growing reluctance to cane use by suggesting that older individuals "pledge to use canes" to reduce their risk of balance and gait problems leading to falls.[76] Medical and public health efforts to bring back the cane emphasized safety over style, overlooking the importance of the cane's role in conveying social connections beyond physiological need, the ubiquity of its use that facilitated these meanings, and the ways that these factors together produced the multifaceted object touted as practical and desirable.

Growing attention in medicine and public health to falls, fractures, osteoporosis, and arthritis brought the cane under further medical scrutiny. Research studies in the 1970s and 1980s tracked the effect of canes on gait patterns in the elderly and described the benefits of a cane as a mobility aid for arthritis and osteoporosis.[77] Although conflicting data emerged on the efficacy of canes in preventing falls and fractures, public health campaigns continued to endorse their use, bolstered by the recommendations of physicians and physical therapists. Growing rates of hip replacement surgeries also brought more elderly into rehabilitation programs, with the cane as a tool for post-operative recovery. Rising medical attention to the issues of old age led to new cane designs—including three- and four-pronged canes, canes with fold-out seats or fold-up shafts, and canes providing biometric feedback—emphasizing that old age could be better understood and negotiated, and cane design might help achieve this.

Of course, as the cane fell from fashion and became streamlined into a medical tool, it increasingly became an object of shame, rather than of pride; it transformed from a device for any age to an aid for the old and disabled, from an emblem of power to a sign of weakness. This history underscores the importance of appearance, whimsy, individuality, and social relationships—needs that go beyond the physical—in the use and design of objects for the elderly impaired. It shows how material things affect meaning, how meaning affects experience, and how experience shapes social relationships, feelings of access and exclusion, and the boundaries of disability. Finally, the history of the cane points to a time when physical ailments were considered part of life rather than individually experienced medical events—a time in which all people were temporarily able-bodied in a life course perspective—and the role of fashions, materials, and customs of cane carrying in negotiating the boundaries of old age and disability.

Notes

1. "Spring Styles in Canes," *Chicago Daily Tribune*, May 11, 1890, 11.
2. "All About Canes," *Boston Daily Globe*, November 16, 1885, 2.
3. "Fashions in Canes," *Los Angeles Times*, March 10, 1895, 14. "New Woman Carries a Cane," *Chicago Daily Tribune*, December 27, 1896, 23.
4. "New Woman Carries a Cane," *Chicago Daily Tribune*, 23.
5. "Walking Canes," *Cincinnati Enquirer*, April 13, 1903, 4.
6. Most manufacturers, etiquette books, and primary sources used the terms "cane," "stick," "walking stick," and "walking cane" interchangeably. Riding crops and umbrellas were often used for promenading as well as for riding or weather protection. This chapter uses the terms provided by the sources, defaulting to the term "cane."
7. Eileen J. Porter, Jacquelyn J. Benson, Sandy Matsuda, "Older Homebound Women: Negotiating Reliance on a Cane or Walker," *Qualitative Health Research* 21, no. 4 (April 21, 2011): 539.
8. Much of the excellent and expansive literature on the historical specificity of disability has focused on questions of congenital disabilities, childhood and education, war-related disabilities, and problems of employment with working-age populations. Special issues in the *Bulletin of the History of Medicine* ("On the Borderland of Medical and Disability History" 87, no. 4 Winter 2013), *Perspectives: The Newsmagazine of the American Historical Association* 44, no. 8, 2006, and *Social History of Medicine* 19, no. 3, 2006, reflect these central preoccupations. Historical examinations of old age, by contrast, have focused on the social status and economic welfare of the elderly and the rise of gerontological sciences. For example, see Carole Haber, *Beyond Sixty-Five: The Dilemma of Old Age in America's Past* (Cambridge: Cambridge University Press, 1983), W. Andrew Achenbaum, *Shades of Gray: Old Age, American Values, and Federal Policies since 1920* (New York: Little, Brown and Company, 1983), William Graebner, *A History of Retirement: The Meaning and Function of an American Institution, 1885–1978* (New Haven, CT: Yale University Press, 1980), David Hackett Fisher, *Growing Old in America* (Oxford: Oxford University Press, 1978), and Carole Haber and Brian Gratton, *Old Age and the Search for Security: An American Social History* (Bloomington: Indiana University Press, 1994).
9. Catalog of Sterling Silver Small Wares, Toilet Ware, Desk Furnishings, Umbrellas, Canes, Pipes, Commercial Bronze, etc. Gorham Manufacturing Co., 1906–1907, Brown University Archives, John Hay Library, Providence, Rhode Island.
10. *Illustrated Price List of Otto Young & Co.* (Chicago, IL: Press of Donohue & Henneberry, 1900), John Hay Library, Brown University Archives, Providence, Rhode Island. The Consumer Price Index began in 1913. Combined with other inflation calculations, it provides a general parameter for the magnitude of change. Bureau of Labor Statistics, Consumer Price Index History Table, available at: http://www.bls.gov/cpi/tables.htm
11. Gold Line, Dresserware, Canes, Umbrellas, Desksets, Mesh Bags, Belt Buckles, The Gorham Company, August 1, 1915, John Hay Library, Brown University, Providence, Rhode Island.

12 On bourgeois dress and conspicuous consumption, see Thorstein Veblen, *The Theory of the Leisure Class: An Economic Study in the Evolution of Institutions* (New York, 1899).
13 For example, Benjamin Franklin bequeathed his walking stick to George Washington, Thomas Jefferson willed his gold-mounted cane to James Madison, which Madison passed to Thomas J. Randolph, and John Quincy Adams left four canes to his descendants. George Washington's Last Will and Testament, July 9, 1799, The Papers of George Washington Digital Edition (Charlottesville: University of Virginia Press, Rotunda, 2008) and James Madison, Will and Codicil April 19, 1835, *The Writings of James Madison, Comprising His Public Papers and His Private Correspondence*, Vol. 9, 1819–1836, ed. Gaillard Hunt (New York: G.P. Putnam's Sons, 1900).
14 Schedule A, Classification of Imports and Exports of Foreign Commodities, Department of Commerce (Washington, DC: US Government Printing Office, May 28, 1915).
15 "Fashions in Canes," *Los Angeles Times*, 14.
16 Ibid.
17 "Canes of the Season," *Washington Post*, November 29, 1903, B3.
18 "Fashions in Canes," *Los Angeles Times*, 14.
19 "Canes of the Season," *Washington Post*, B3.
20 Ibid.
21 Ibid.
22. Language of Canes: Character Indicated by the Walking-Stick," San Francisco Chronicle, November 11, 1884, 3.
23 Agnes H. Morton, *Etiquette: Good Manners for All People, Especially Those Who Dwell within the Broad Zone of the "Average"* (Philadelphia, PA: Penn Publishing Company, 1911), 160.
24 Emily Holt, *Encyclopaedia of Etiquette* (Garden City and New York: Doubleday, Page & Company, 1922), 38.
25 On Victorian hall customs, see Kenneth L. Ames, "Meaning in Artifacts: Hall Furnishings in Victorian America," *Journal of Interdisciplinary History* 9, no. 1 (Summer, 1978): 19–46.
26 Holt, *Encyclopaedia of Etiquette*, 38.
27 "Fashions in Canes," *Los Angeles Times*, 14.
28 Historians have analyzed the altercation's reflection of racial tensions before the Civil War. See, for example, Manisha Sinha, "The Caning of Charles Sumner: Slavery, Race, and Ideology in the Age of the Civil War," *Journal of the Early Republic* 23, no. 2 (Summer 2003): 233–262 and William James Hull Hoffer, *The Caning of Charles Sumner: Honor, Idealism, and the Origins of the Civil War* (Baltimore, MD: Johns Hopkins University Press, 2010).
29 Sarah Bernhardt, "Advocates Tall Walking Cane for Women," *Boston Daily Globe*, November 17, 1912, 55.
30 "Walking Canes," *Cincinnati Enquirer*, 4.
31 John R. Jackson, "Walking-Sticks," *Good Words* 12 (January 1871): 509–512.
32 "Fashions in Canes," *Los Angeles Times*, 14.

33 "The Walking Staff," *Detroit Free Press*, October 24, 1886, 18.

34 "Character in Canes," *Phrenological Journal and Science of Health* 80, no. 1 (January 1885): 45.

35 Robert Cortes Holliday, "On Carrying a Cane," in *The Walking-Stick Papers* (New York: George H. Doran Company, 1918), 13–14.

36 On delight in altering mass market designs, see Bess Williamson, "Electric Moms and Quad Drivers: People with Disabilities Buying, Making, and Using Technology in Postwar America," *American Studies* 52, no. 1 (2012): 5–30.

37 Holliday, "On Carrying a Cane," 15.

38 "Oldest Citizens," *Boston Post*, August 30, 1909.

39 Edwin A. Grozier to Town Selectmen, August 2, 1909, in Barbara Staples, *The Bay State's Boston Post Canes: The History of a New England Tradition* (Lynn, MA: Fleming Press, 1997), 24.

40 Staples, *Bay State's Boston Post Canes*, 25–29.

41 "Oldest Citizens," *Boston Post*.

42 Staples, *Bay State's Boston Post Canes*, 29.

43 "Language of Canes: Character Indicated by the Walking-Stick," *San Francisco Chronicle*, November 11, 1884, 3.

44 Bernhardt, "Advocates Tall Walking Cane," 55.

45 "Walking Sticks a Feminine Fad," *New York Times*, June 1, 1913, 74.

46 Holliday, "On Carrying a Cane," 20. In some versions of Cinderella, including the 1922 mini-play adapted by Lindsey Barbee, the Fairy Godmother waved her "cane."

47 As indicated in index listing of goods in Sears Roebuck & Company biannual fall and spring catalogs. "Finest genuine Malacca canes" in Sears, Roebuck & Company Catalog, Fall 1929, 232.

48 On increasingly casual American styles, see David Yosifon and Peter N. Stearns, "The Rise and Fall of American Posture," *American Historical Review* 103, no. 4 (October 1998): 1057–1095 and Peter N. Stearns, *American Cool: Constructing an Emotional Style* (New York: New York University Press, 1994).

49 E. Stanley Johnson, "Remarks on Canes and Spats," *New York Times*, March 30, 1941 and "The Cane Losing Favor Abroad," *New York Times*, July 12, 1931, SM11.

50 W.L. Julyan, "Before Carrying a Stick," *The Field*, December 26, 1957, 1194.

51 Wholesale Catalog, *Novelties, Gift Goods, Diamonds, Watches, Jewelry, Silverware, Furniture, Etc., Catalog*, N. Sure Company, 1935, Brown University Archives, Providence, Rhode Island.

52 On the development of physical therapy and orthopedic surgery, see Beth Linker, *War's Waste: Rehabilitation in World War I America* (Chicago, IL: University of Chicago Press, 2011) and Naomi Rogers, *Polio Wars: Sister Kenny and the Golden Age of American Medicine* (Oxford and New York: Oxford University Press, 2013).

53 George Deaver and Mary Eleanor Brown, "The Challenge of Crutches: Living with Crutches and Canes," *Archives of Physical Medicine and Rehabilitation* 27, no. 11 (November 1946): 683–703.

54 Ibid., 688.

55 Ibid., 688–689.
56 Ibid., 689.
57 Donald A. Covalt and Edith Buchwald, "Aids to Ambulation," *American Journal of Nursing* 53, no. 9 (September 1953): 1085–1088.
58 Robert H. Jebsen, "Use and Abuse of Ambulation Aids," *JAMA* 199, no. 1 (January 2, 1967): 63–68.
59 Natural rubber was used by indigenous American populations, but its sensitivity to temperature limited its uses. Early-nineteenth-century experimenters developed the process of vulcanization—heating natural rubbers with sulfur to make them more durable—and Thomas Hancock (Great Britain) and Charles Goodyear (United States) were each awarded patents for vulcanizing rubber in 1845. This process expanded rubber manufacturing to an array of goods in the late nineteenth century. Crutches, for example, could be found to use rubber cushions sporadically from the 1860s on—for example, Bugbee's Crutch described a rubber cushion with a retractable steel spike on the end of the crutch. "Bugbee's Crutch," *Scientific American* XIV, no. 19 (May 5, 1866): 314. On the history of the rubber industry, see John A. Tully, *The Devil's Milk: A Social History of Rubber* (New York: Monthly Review Press, 2011).
60 Philip Cederstrom, "Cane Crutch," U.S. Patent no. 2,192,766, United States Patent and Trademark Office, March 5, 1940.
61 The Lamb Lim-Rest: The Modern Cane-Crutch Combination, c. 1942–1945, Series I, Thomas Lamb Papers (Accession 2181), Hagley Museum and Library, Wilmington, Delaware.
62 Deaver and Brown, "The Challenge of Crutches," 688–689.
63 Sidney H. Richards, "Nonskid Devices for Crutches and the Like," US Patent No. 2,449,509, United States Patent and Trademark Office, September 14, 1948.
64 Covalt and Buchwald, "Aids to Ambulation," 1088.
65 For more on the expectations of self-sufficiency, see, for example, Linker, *War's Waste* and Williamson, "Electric Moms and Quad Drivers."
66 On the mid-twentieth-century transformation of osteoporosis from an inevitable condition of aging to a disease, see Gerald N. Grob, *Aging Bones: A Short History of Osteoporosis* (Baltimore, MD: Johns Hopkins University Press, 2014), 54–85. On the shifting boundaries of hypertension and pre-hypertension, see Jeremy A. Greene, *Prescribing by Numbers: Drugs and the Definition of Disease* (Baltimore, MD: Johns Hopkins University Press, 2006). On the transformation of atherosclerosis, see Robert A. Aronowitz, "The Social Construction of Coronary Heart Disease Risk Factors," in *Making Sense of Illness: Science, Society, and Disease* (Cambridge: Cambridge University Press, 1998), 111–144.
67 Morton, "The Elderly Patient," 5.
68 Ibid.
69 Covalt and Buchwald, "Aids to Ambulation," 1085 and Faye Marley, "Arthritis Strikes One out of Five Families," *Austin Statesman*, December 21, 1961, B9.
70 "Getting down to Brass Tacks," Welfare Division Pamphlets, 1953–1957, Metropolitan Life Archives, New York.

71 "Getting on—Safely," National Safety Council Pamphlet, 1958, National Safety Council Archives, Itasca, Illinios.
72 "Orthopedic Surgeon Would Bring Back the Walking Cane," *Daily Boston Globe*, February 6, 1956, 5.
73 Ibid.
74 "The Cane," *Hartford Courant*, February 15, 1956, 14.
75 Herbert Black, "Walking Lost Art? Nonsense!" *Boston Globe*, November 12, 1961, 63.
76 "Aged Warned: Take Pledge and Use Canes," *Atlanta Daily World*, April 17, 1963, 3.
77 J.F. Aloia, S.H. Cohn, J.A. Ostuni, R. Cane, K. Ellis, "Prevention of Involutional Bone Loss by Exercise," *Annals Internal Medicine* 89, no. 3 (September 1978): 356–358. Also see: L. Bennett, M.P. Murray, E.F. Murphy, T.T. Sowell, "Locomotion Assistance through Cane Impulse," *Bulletin Prosthetics Research* 10, no. 31 (Spring 1979): 38–47 and L. Ceder, L. Ekelund, S. Inerot, L. Lindberg, E. Odberg, C. Sjolin, "Rehabilitation after Hip Fracture in the Elderly," *Acta Orthopaedica Scandinavica* 50 (December 1979): 681–688.

3 Artificial Limbs on the Panama Canal
CAROLINE LIEFFERS

In the fall of 1911, New York City's most renowned artificial limb manufacturer, the A.A. Marks Company, released a lavish new piece of advertising. Going beyond its usual thick catalogues and elegant trade cards, the company issued what it called a folder, a massive celebration of its products that spread across the recto and verso of a huge paper sheet the size of a double-page newspaper spread. The text began by focusing on the Marks artificial limbs' adaptability to various points and types of amputation, as well as the promise of successful social reintegration for wearers. But the campaign did not stop there. "Over forty thousand have been made and sent to all parts of the world. Worn in all climates from the tropics to the artics [sic]," it read. A turn of the page invited readers to imagine a completely new environment for prostheses, and indeed for Americans: the construction of the Panama Canal. "This stupendous work has been planned and executed by brains, muscles, and machinery," the advertisement noted, but the project's immensity and drama had also come at great bodily cost. The United States' construction of the Panama Canal, officially running from 1904 to 1914 but extending well beyond that, recruited tens of thousands of workers, and many of them met with what the folder listed as "accidents, premature blasts, railroad cars and steam shovels [that] have blown off and crushed arms and legs." Men were blinded and deafened, fingers, hands, and arms were lost, and hundreds of legs were amputated. The US government's Isthmian Canal Commission, responsible for nearly every element of the construction as well as daily life in the strip of American-controlled land known as the Canal Zone, had selected Marks's limbs to serve as replacements for workers "maimed in the service."[1]

This chapter examines the role of artificial limbs as tools of American expansion and empire, specifically in the construction of the Panama Canal. Whether at the center of eager advertisements or in the background of triumphant accounts of the United States' engineering and managerial prowess, American-made prostheses were presented as unproblematic technologies that returned men to useful labor and remedied any hint of violence stemming from the United States' expansion into Central America. The reality, though, was much more complicated. This stunning new waterway, meant to facilitate a modern and global American power for the new twentieth century, would prove to be a man-made fault line separating seemingly deserving and productive workers from supposedly expendable and unproductive liabilities.

This chapter uses the stories of four men injured in the Canal project—Alessandro Comba, Wilfred McDonald, James Chandler, and Melford Hymison—to make sense of the imperial lives of artificial limbs. In spite of advertisers' optimistic rhetoric, prostheses were often painful, fragile, and expensive, and their material shortcomings deepened extant divisions between white and black, innocent and culpable, citizen and foreigner, laborer and dependent, binaries that defined life at this new edge of empire. Through the provision of these state-of-the-art devices, Canal administrators sought to govern the movement, labor, somatics, and appearance of the casualties of their expansionary power, taking on what scholar Jasbir Puar has, in a different context, labeled the imperialist's "right to maim," and complementing it with a medical–technological "right to fix" on terms most favorable to their metropolitan interests.[2] But artificial limbs, those apparatuses of American achievement, worked with and in and sometimes against colonized bodies and landscapes, their supposed invisibility and intimacy with the body rendering them exemplars of what Ann Laura Stoler has called "the less perceptible effects of imperial interventions and their settling into the social and material ecologies in which people live and survive."[3] Injured workers and their prostheses—some ill-fitting, some broken down—persisted as debris of humanity and machinery well after the initial enthusiasm for the project subsided. The Canal presented a vision of boundless American technology and know-how, but workers who lost limbs troubled such easy assumptions. These injured men posed persistent ethical and managerial challenges for the Canal's administrators, and in many cases they sought out their own networks of care and community. They worked through, resisted, and repaired the United States' global and local destructions and designs, and enacted their own forms of self-determination through their bodily technologies.

Artificial Limbs and American Power

The A.A. Marks Company was founded by Amasa Abraham Marks in 1853 and later operated by his sons. It rose to prominence along with other prosthesis manufacturers during the Civil War, as tens of thousands of amputation survivors returned home to their civilian occupations.[4] Like its nineteenth-century rivals, the Marks Company presented its product as smooth, light, quiet, and most importantly, useful, the pinnacle of modern techniques of manufacture that could imitate the body and restore a wearer "to the equals [sic] of his fellow-men in every employment of life."[5] Indeed, the company's promotional pamphlet "From the Stump to the Limb," dating from around 1890, took readers through the stages of an artificial limb's construction, suggesting that the prosthesis was a hybrid between quality craftsmanship—each log of willow or bass thoughtfully trimmed and shaped by hand, for example—and new technology, including power saws and lathes, a kiln-dry contrived by A.A. Marks himself, and vulcanized rubber. The company's particular feature, in fact, was the use of rubber hands and feet on its appliances, which supposedly secured "naturalness in walking, ease to the stump, and great durability."[6] The limb was apparently the culmination of human skill and sensitivity, as well as constant innovation and ingenuity.

Marks's prostheses were not only popular in the United States: one of the walls of the manufacturer's Broadway showroom hosted a dramatic display of thousands of envelopes from foreign countries visibly addressed to A.A. Marks and bearing postage stamps, cancellation marks, and en route stamps that documented their journeys around the world. "This panorama has excited much comment," read "From the Stump to the Limb," arguing that the display "stands as indisputable evidence of the foreign relations of the house."[7] Indeed, the Panama Canal was hardly the first time A.A. Marks's artificial limbs had been a synecdoche for the growing global presence of the United States and its goods. In 1860, the young Amasa Abraham had presented one of his limbs as a gift to the first Japanese delegation to the United States, and by the early twentieth century the A.A. Marks catalog featured the story of a Spanish-American War correspondent who was shot in the spine in Cuba, as well as an account of an Armenian Christian missionary whose American-made artificial limb was stolen during his people's persecution.[8] Marks's advertising materials were available in Spanish, Portuguese, Italian, French, and German, and the enterprising manufacturer made eager use of rail and mail to ship its legs to any market with the money to buy them, provisioning the United States' creative power and technological prowess to a world that seemed to be sorely in need of them.[9]

The Panama Canal offered yet another opportunity for the ambitious company. In 1904 the United States embarked on one of the greatest engineering challenges that the world had ever known, enacting what historian Julie Greene has identified as the country's confidence in its "gifts to world civilization" as well as "pride in its rising stature as a first-class imperial power."[10] Boosters depicted the Canal project as the culmination of American progress and potential. For his Fourth of July speech in 1911, Chief Engineer and Canal Commission Chairman George Washington Goethals described the United States and its workers as "cutting a highway of commerce through what was a plague spot of the world." In doing so, he continued, "they are showing the world how to rid itself of all plague spots." These "agents of the American nation" were the advance guard in an extraordinary new era of progress.[11]

The task was as immense as the nation's vision and rhetoric. The project began with an attempt to discipline the landscape—draining swamps, killing mosquitoes, and initiating a whole-scale sanitation effort, both within the ten-mile-wide Canal Zone and in the adjacent coastal cities of Colon and Panama City. The work continued with even more dramatic reshaping of the environment. The world's largest dam had to be built to stop the Chagres River, creating massive Gatun Lake, which drowned villages and forced the relocation of a nineteenth-century railway. "Never before has man dreamed of taking such liberties with nature," wrote an awed reporter.[12] Locks of a kind never before conceived, let alone built, had to be constructed at each end of the Canal. But the greatest challenge of all was the Culebra Cut, later renamed the Gaillard Cut. Known as Hell's Gorge among the workers, it was a colossal artificial valley excavated from the mountains, averaging 120 feet in depth over nine miles.[13] Tens of millions of cubic yards of dirt had to be moved, necessitating some sixty million pounds of dynamite, and a new railway system had to be constructed to bring laborers and machinery in and out and haul away hundreds of trainloads of excavated material each day.[14] Journalists marveled at the scale of the engineering, and in exchange for this monumental effort, the government and its supporters assured Americans that the Canal would make the United States a world power, able to move its goods and naval forces quickly between oceans. The route from New York to Yokohama via San Francisco, for example, would be shortened by more than 3700 miles; Japan would be over 1800 miles closer to New York than it was to Liverpool.[15] Through man's work as "titanic remodeler," as the *Washington Post* put it, the United States could ensure military mobility and access to global markets.[16]

Remodeling the landscape was not only a task for the engineers and machines that captivated American reporters, though; it was, more importantly, the work of laborers, many of whom were similarly hacked up, hauled away, or remade. The United States officially employed some 45,000 foreign workers for the project, and a little under half, around 19,900, were from Barbados, while the rest came from elsewhere in the Caribbean and Latin America, Spain, Italy, and a smattering of other countries.[17] These men were relegated to the bottom part of the pay scale, and the most dangerous work. Massive steam shovels intensified the Isthmus's heat and humidity, and hospital and funeral cars on the trains carried out the bodies of those hurt or killed in the shoveling and the dynamiting.[18] Those who survived would be shipped to one of the Canal Zone's American-run hospitals for free treatment. Starting around late 1907 or early 1908, the Isthmian Canal Commission began officially providing artificial limbs for those injured in the course of their duties, with the appliances supposedly furnished "irrespective of color, nationality, or character of work engaged in."[19] This was a notable development in a labor environment deeply stratified by distinctions between employees paid in gold and those paid in silver, a binary that mapped largely (though not completely) onto parallel divisions into "skilled" and "unskilled" labor, American citizens and precarious foreign workers, unmarked whiteness and black racialization.[20] There were, however, caveats to this administrative largesse: the laborer had to be deemed not culpable for his injury before he could qualify, and the injury had to have occurred in the line of duty.[21] These conditions technically excluded injuries incurred during breaks, for example, or when a worker was hurt on one of the labor trains that were essential to moving employees to and from their work sites.[22] Even so, by 1912, the Commission had provided over 200 artificial limbs, and one of the Canal's early historians testified that many of the recipients "were able to return to work."[23]

A.A. Marks was a key provider of these prostheses from the start. Despite expressions of interest from the Staggs Aluminum-Rawhide Artificial Limb Company and the Erickson Artificial Limb Company, for example, American administrators generally favored Marks's products because they believed that the company made a "better and less expensive limb." There were certainly dissenters, and rival manufacturers did receive occasional orders, but Marks courted the Canal's administrators aggressively.[24] A company representative made a trip to the Isthmus, and to edge out the competition Marks offered incentives like fitting kits and measuring tapes, as well as a reduced price.[25] In most cases, the manufacturer was even willing to accept orders based on measurements rather than casts. This was a serious advantage in humid and distant Panama, where plaster casts—already troublesome to make—required shellacking to preserve their integrity, and shipping, moreover, was inconvenient and expensive. The company would even fix any errors in measurement and make alterations and corrections without additional cost to the Commission.[26] Marks also offered varied color options to fit the Canal Zone's diverse population of workers, and by the 1930s the company had developed a color chart to match limbs to wearers' skin tones, with options of "black," "negro," "mulatto," and "quadroon."[27] "White" was not mentioned. "We believe that is it unnecessarily ludicrous for a negro to wear a pink leg," the manufacturer wrote, a statement that suggests an attempt to satisfy the company's and the administrators' aesthetic standards and sensibilities as much as the wearers'.[28]

The A.A. Marks Company was not just eager for the Panama Canal's business; it also quickly turned its role as chief purveyor into a larger advertising opportunity. In medical journals and newspapers the manufacturer boasted that its waterproof construction and rubber components made the Marks appliance the only suitable option for Panama's tough physical work and fearfully humid climate, and it even promised to send "an attractive little book showing the canal, with map in colors … free to any doctor who will request it."[29] Marks's advertisements often featured woodcuts of the massive steam shovels and awe-inspiring Culebra Cut (Figure 3.1), positioning the company's prostheses at the forefront of technological

Figure 3.1 From *American Medicine* 19, no. 5 (May 1913): 5.

and engineering achievement. The United States, in this depiction, fulfilled its expansionary aims by also ostensibly empowering the disabled body, using machinery to remake the man as it remade the landscape. In its rhetorical ideal, the Canal Zone was the epitome of American ingenuity and drive, a site where both the artificial limb and the ambitious nation could fulfill their potential.

Reality and Resistance

Historians have argued that the Panama Canal epitomized an exceptionalist narrative of US imperialism. Despite recurring tensions with low-paid workers, the government and citizens of Panama, and even occasional opponents at home, the Canal project cast the country's expansion in a benevolent and humane light, a show of American strength without American threat.[30] The provision of artificial limbs enacted this same power—and ostensible goodwill—at the scale of the individual body. Yet justice and dignity for people injured in the Canal project were intimately tied to their ability to help the state achieve its larger ends, and close analysis of the Canal's records reveals the complexities and limits of this American benevolence in practice. The material lives of artificial limbs entwined with the politics of imperial power over landscapes, labor, and human mobility and migration. National and racial prejudice, assumptions about guilt and responsibility, and bureaucratic entanglements reduced injured workers in many cases to seemingly little more than balance sheets of social cost and productivity.

Alessandro Comba was an Italian laborer on the Canal project, one of more than 11,000 Europeans brought to the Isthmus on contracts under the assumption that they would be more productive than the black West Indians who made up the majority of the diggers.[31] On September 21, 1907, after less than a year in the Zone, Comba was working at what was called the "Sosa Yard," probably a cluster of train tracks near Corozal at the Pacific end of the Canal. He was carrying a can of water on his head to refresh his gang of fellow workers, and as he crossed the railroad tracks, a train engine struck him, crushing his legs. He was rushed to nearby Ancon hospital, where both of his limbs were amputated.[32] A year later, his stumps considered healed, he was sent to New York City, where he was fitted with artificial legs at St. Vincent's Hospital.[33] With such an expensive outlay on his treatment, the Isthmian Canal Commission expected that he would return to work in Panama, but the prostheses, probably supplied by A.A. Marks, did not live up to their promise. "The stumps of his limbs are very tender," wrote the Commission Chairman, "and probably will never permit the use of the limbs with which he has been fitted."[34] Almost immediately, Comba was back in the hospital in Panama. Any plans to provide him with some sort of light employment on the Canal were dashed, and in June 1909 the Commission decided that he would be sent to New York once again, fitted with another set of prostheses, and then deported back to Europe.[35] He landed July 6, 1909, was taken to the charity hospital on Blackwell's Island, and by December of that year he had been moved to the hospital at Ellis Island, where he waited to be sent home.[36] The Canal Commission had little use for an employee who did not meet their expectations of successful rehabilitation with artificial limbs, and whose status as an Italian national left him with little reason to remain in the Canal Zone, let alone the United States.

With a family to support and a mere thirty days of paid meritorious sick leave to compensate him for his injury, Comba asked the Canal Commission for financial relief, and the Bureau of Immigration and Naturalization delayed his warrant for deportation several times to allow Congress time to approve a payment of $500.[37] The bill had the support of the Canal Commission's Chairman, the Italian ambassador, and even the Secretary of War. The wheels of bureaucracy, however, turned slowly. From his bed in Ellis Island Hospital in April of 1910, Comba wrote to President Taft, pleading for resolution:

> I have been here a very long time waiting for Congress to decide my case, and in the mean time my wife and three children are in Europe in the worst misery, as I know you to have a kind heart I beg of you to decide my case as soon as possible so that I may go back to my family.[38]

Though the Senate passed a measure for his relief, the House of Representatives adjourned in 1910 before taking any action.[39] The Bureau of Immigration and Naturalization would delay no longer. Comba was finally deemed a "public charge," incapable of self-support and thus ineligible to remain in the United States.[40] An association of Italian immigrants fought to keep him in the country, and the story, simmering since the previous year, quickly garnered the attention of newspapers across the nation: "Loses Legs in Gov't Service, Is Barred from Adopted Land," mourned a headline in the *Labor World*.[41] The *New York Times* called Comba "a living example of how the great Republic treats its servitors when they come upon evil days" and insisted on "better and decenter" liability and compensation laws worthy of "our National dignity."[42] The *Los Angeles Herald* had an even blunter assessment: "Comba Sent Back to Italy Because Legs Were Cut Off." He had helped "Uncle Sam dig the big ditch" and was apparently so capable that he was already in line for promotion at the time of his accident.[43] Workers' compensation was a growing concern in Progressive-Era America, and the US government, these articles implied, was shamefully cavalier with human life. By failing to recognize the sacrifices of its workers—particularly when they did not have the benefit of citizenship—on such a conspicuous project as the Panama Canal, the country was endangering its reputation at home and abroad. One reader of a similar article in the *New York Herald* even wrote to President Taft, asking "If the law does not give redress, can not sentiment, common humanity induce Congress to do something …?"[44] Moved, perhaps, by this publicity, Congress finally passed a bill to provide Comba with $500 in 1912, nearly five years after his accident, and the money was noted in budgetary disbursements.[45] But it is unlikely that Comba received it. He had already been sent back to Europe in the summer of 1910.[46]

Comba's case illuminates the expanding American empire's fault lines of citizenship and productivity: artificial limbs, with their waterproof endurance, promised to transcend precarious immigration status and undo injuries sustained in the name of national expansion. Yet, when the realities of fit and pain failed the wearer and his work, the full brunt of imperial impatience bore down. Irremediable disability could not be reconciled with the vision of modernity exemplified by the Panama Canal.

Other men were denied the chance even to try such artificial limbs. If a worker was deemed to have been at fault for his injury, official policy initially stated that he would have to purchase his own appliance. If he could not afford to buy a prosthesis to help him get back to work, the laborer risked destitution, deportation, or both. Jamaican Wilfred McDonald was one such example. He told his story in a letter to the Canal administrators on May 25, 1913, and his rare voice should be quoted at length:

> I have ben Serveing the ICC [Isthmian Canal Commission] and the PRR [Panama Railroad] in the caypasoity as Train man From the yea 1906 until my misfawchin wich is 1912 Sir without eny Fear i am Speaking Nothing But the Truth to you I have no claim comeing to me. But for mercy Sake I am Beging you To have mercy on me By Granting me a Pair of legs for i have lost both of my Natrals. I has a Mother wich is a Whido, and too motherless childrens which During The Time when i was working i was the only help to the familys.

McDonald closed his letter as "your Truley Sobadinated Clyante," testifying all too accurately to his position in the face of the Canal's imposing centralized bureaucracy and frequently unforgiving policies.[47]

Jamaica, like many sugar-dependent economies in the British Caribbean, had been experiencing decades of labor migration, low wages, and economic turmoil by the early 1900s, and many families struggled even to reach subsistence; McDonald's mother and children, if they were not already living on the Isthmus, may have relied on his remittances.[48] But McDonald's most profound "misfortune" may have been that his loss of both legs at the lower third was deemed his own fault, as it had occurred outside of his official duties. Legally, he was entitled to nothing.[49] Yet Canal administrators realized that they might accidentally create a population of public charges, especially when men evaded or refused deportation or were forced to remain in hospital for lack of other options.[50] In a policy already informally in place and made official in November 1913, the Chief Sanitary Officer was permitted to furnish injured-but-liable employees, and occasionally even non-employees, with peg legs at the Commission's expense. The appendages would be provided "in any case in which he [the Chief Sanitary Officer] considers that the interests of the I.C.C., [Isthmian Canal Commission] or Canal Zone Government will be benefited thereby."[51] The simple peg legs were meant to help men earn a livelihood. They are "more serviceable, last longer, and are cheaper to repair than the manufactured article with the steel joints and rubber feet, which will not stand the rough usage they are put to by a laboring man," John L. Phillips, the Acting Chief Sanitary Officer, wrote to Goethals.[52] Marks's idealized advertising, evidently, did not provide the full story. The company's attractive and sophisticated limbs were less durable than promised, and, in practice, these expensive devices were reserved for better-paid employees, or as a reward for those deemed non-liable. The modern bodies they made were apparently not for desperate and destitute laborers who supposedly brought on their injuries themselves. There was a further rationale for peg legs, too, one that highlighted the fundamental racism of Canal Zone governance: in 1914, Chief Health Officer Charles Mason explained that "the West Indian negro, as a rule, has not sufficient intelligence to care for and use properly an artificial limb."[53] Goethals, by this point Governor of the Canal Zone, agreed.[54]

McDonald, however, proved an exception. With a double amputation, peg legs would be almost impossible for him to wear, but Colon Hospital Superintendent Claude Pierce explained that artificial limbs would likely enable McDonald at least to walk, though perhaps with the help of crutches or some other support.[55] Phillips concurred. He wrote to Goethals:

> [McDonald is] perfectly helpless in his present condition, and will no doubt remain a charge on the Commission indefinitely. Peg-legs would be of no service to him, but I believe that he could learn to walk and earn a livelihood if he had two artificial legs, which can be secured for $75.00 apiece. At present it is costing the Commission something over $300.00 a year to maintain this man.[56]

Though McDonald's case was not to act as a precedent, the administration determined that it would be in their best interests to provide him with the limbs.[57]

Not all men benefited from such generosity—or rather, such economic calculus. In June of 1909, for example, Barbadian James Chandler lost his right foot below the knee; as in McDonald's case, the injury occurred outside of his official duties. He was released from the hospital on crutches and relied on his friends and schoolmates to help him purchase an artificial leg to facilitate his return to work. After several years, however, he needed a replacement. He pleaded his case to the Chairman in a handwritten letter: "I works as switchman and flagman in sun and rain and the leg now is broken all down I am suppose to work on crutches again which is very distressing and hurtful I am beging you Sir to do your level best in helping me with an artificial leg." Chandler took pains to describe his work "for the United States of America Government with their canal during that period of time I work pretty hard and obeyed orders so far as conscern."[58] Much like the journalists in Comba's case, Chandler understood that appealing to the Commission's sense of responsibility and the significance of the national project of Canal-building might garner sympathy. Indeed, as the First World War loomed, other workers perceived new opportunities for leverage. A group of six men injured on the Canal, for example, complained of the potential damage their poor treatment could do to the United States in the context of impending military conflict: "My Lord," their representative, Henry Gordan, wrote to President Wilson, "do you believe that when These able bodied men See the treatments of a Poor crippled they would ever devote their Energies, to Perform the duty of a noble hero, to Which their country had Given them a natural Liking?"[59]

In Chandler's case, the Commission, not wanting to set a precedent, offered only a peg leg.[60] But his story also offers a glimpse of the social life of workers on the

Canal Zone, and particularly West Indian workers, who formed deep networks of friendship and care that allowed injured men their own forms of self-fashioning and self-determination. They designed the lives they could, with the bodies and technologies they could, within the constraints of America's larger visions of the world. Melford Hymison, apparently also sometimes known as Wilfred, was another such man. A black laborer from Costa Rica, he was struck by a train while in the line of duty on March 10, 1913—the construction year that witnessed the highest number of leg amputations. He was about twenty-two years old, and his right foot was gone. Hymison received an artificial leg, but only two years later he complained that it was unserviceable, probably worn out from hard physical work. The Commission, trying to save money, offered him a peg leg as a replacement.[61]

Hymison, however, was not satisfied. He paid for a new artificial leg in 1917, and ordered another replacement in 1926 via the Canal authorities, using deductions from his wages as an office helper. But he was not pleased with the product, which had been supplied by the Staggs Aluminum-Rawhide Artificial Limb Company. The prosthesis, he declared, was "something inferior, not properly fitted, and in fact something no human should have worn."[62] This was not the first complaint about the company's products, and the leg was sent back to the United States for alterations; the government would absorb its cost, and Hymison was to be furnished with a Marks limb instead.[63] In 1931, Hymison received another replacement limb, which he again sent back for alterations.[64] The same device was repaired in 1933, and in 1934, Hymison made yet another complaint. This time the chief of Gorgas (formerly Ancon) Hospital's surgical clinic had had enough, writing, "we have spent more time and money on this complaining, letter-writing, syphilitic employee than he is worth." He continued, "Recommend (1) issuing him a pair of crutches if he will not wear his new limb, and (2) Deportation to Costa Rica."[65] Staying in the Canal Zone was a privilege granted only to the productive and the compliant. But Hymison persisted, safe in a community of proud and allied workers, workers who may well have helped him purchase some of those legs. His injured body survived long after the construction was completed, a testament to American power's lasting forces of destruction and remaking, forces that bound together men, landscapes, and technologies. In 1959, he was the Master of Ceremonies for the Canal Zone Retired Workers Association, and he finally passed away in Panama City, aged seventy-four, in 1966.[66] He had defied the administrators' prejudices and power over his body, his somatics, and his belonging.

Prostheses were rhetorically and culturally designed and negotiated by their different users, often in contentious circumstances. Imperialism undoubtedly created disabilities through its violent remaking of lands and waters. As the A.A. Marks Company itself admitted, "[a] work of this magnitude, though conducted in the most careful way, means the loss of many legs and arms."[67] An article in the Panama *Star and Herald* even dared to reckon the "Cost of the Panama Canal in Human Legs." Over 400 were lost between 1905 and 1921, peaking with 93 in 1913 alone.[68] America's imperial imposition, however, did not stop at infrastructure and injury.

The United States was confident in its capacity to remake or remove the casualties of its power, erasing any attendant damage and claiming benevolence through the provision of modern artificial limbs and functional peg legs. However awesome the empire's vision and rhetoric may have been, though, they were riddled with the fractures and fault-lines of citizenship and culpability, inescapable race and compulsory productivity. Though artificial limbs helped many men return to work, America's ambitious project, in the end, outstripped the nation's ability and, on occasion, its humanity. Laborers bore their missing legs and hard-won prostheses for the rest of their lives, left to make their own meanings out of a Canal that was never meant to be theirs, but to which they had sacrificed an irreplaceable part of themselves.

Notes

1. A.A. Marks, "Among the Rubber Footed," advertising folder, Oversize 79, Folder 7, NMAH.AC.0060.S01.01.Artificial, Warshaw Collection of Business Americana, National Museum of American History Archives, Smithsonian Institution.
2. Jasbir K. Puar, *The Right to Maim: Debility, Capacity, Disability* (Durham, NC: Duke University Press, 2017).
3. Ann Laura Stoler, "Introduction: 'The Rot Remains': From Ruins to Ruination," in *Imperial Debris: On Ruins and Ruination*, ed. Ann Laura Stoler (Durham, NC: Duke University Press, 2013), 4.
4. The history of artificial limbs in the United States, particularly in the post–Civil War era, has been well documented. See, for example, Laurann Figg and Jane Farrell-Beck, "Amputation in the Civil War: Physical and Social Dimensions," *Journal of the History of Medicine and Allied Sciences* 48, no. 4 (1993): 454–475; Lisa Herschbach, "Prosthetic Reconstructions: Making the Industry, Re-Making the Body, Modeling the Nation," *History Workshop Journal* 44 (1997): 23–57; David D. Yuan, "Disfigurement and Reconstruction in Oliver Wendell Holmes's 'The Human Wheel, Its Spokes and Felloes,'" in *The Body and Physical Difference: Discourses of Disability in the Humanities*, ed. David T. Mitchell and Sharon L. Synder (Ann Arbor: University of Michigan Press, 1997), 71–88; and Guy Hasegawa, *Mending Broken Soldiers: The Union and Confederate Programs to Supply Artificial Limbs* (Carbondale: Southern Illinois University Press, 2012), among many others.
5. A.A. Marks, "From the Stump to the Limb," 2, Box 1, Folder 11, NMAH.AC.0060.S01.01.Artificial, Warshaw Collection of Business Americana. Studies on this subject include, among others, Erin O'Connor, *Raw Material: Producing Pathology in Victorian Culture* (Durham, NC: Duke University Press, 2000), 102–147; and Stephen Mihm, "'A Limb Which Shall Be Presentable in Polite Society': Prosthetic Technologies in the Nineteenth Century," in *Artificial Parts, Practical Lives: Modern Histories of Prosthetics*, ed. Katherine Ott, David Serlin, and Stephen Mihm (New York: New York University Press, 2002), 282–299.
6. Marks, "From the Stump to the Limb," 25.
7. Ibid., 20.

8   Unidentified New York newspaper, [June 1860], quoted in [George Edwin] Marks, ed., *A Treatise on Artificial Limbs, with Rubber Hands and Feet* (New York: A.A. Marks, 1896), 20; A.A. Marks Company, *Manual of Artificial Limbs* (New York: A.A. Marks, 1914), 339–346 and 353–357.
9   Marks, "Among the Rubber Footed."
10 Julie Greene, *The Canal Builders: Making America's Empire at the Panama Canal* (New York: Penguin, 2009), 5.
11 George W. Goethals, "Address Delivered by Col. Geo. W. Goethals, U.S.A., at Cristobal, C.Z., July 4, 1911," 3, in Goethals, Gov. George W., File 2: Personal File, January 1, 1911 to September 30, 1913, Box 3, Governors' Personal Correspondence, Entry A1 34-CC, RG 185, National Archives and Records Administration, College Park, MD (hereafter abbreviated RG 185).
12 Arthur Bullard, *Panama: The Canal, the Country and the People* (New York: Macmillan, 1914), 47.
13 Vaughan Cornish, "The Panama Canal in 1908," *The Geographical Journal* 33, no. 2 (1909): 167; Ira E. Bennett, *History of the Panama Canal: Its Construction and Builders* (Washington, DC: Historical Publishing Company, 1915), 140.
14 Bennett, *History of the Panama Canal*, 141–143.
15 Cornish, "Panama Canal," 173.
16 "Remodeling the Earth: How Man Is Changing Nature's Work to Meet the Demands of Modern Conditions," *Washington Post*, March 5, 1911, MS4.
17 Velma Newton, *The Silver Men: West Indian Labour Migration to Panama, 1850–1914* (Kingston: Institute of Social and Economic Research, University of the West Indies, 1984), 41–42.
18 Recollections of Charles F. Williams, in *Roosevelt Medal-Holders' Tape-Recorder Guest Book: The Word-for-Word Reminiscences of Thirty-Five Old Timers Who Helped Dig the Panama Canal*, ed. Loron Brodie Burnham (Balboa Heights: Isthmian Historical Society, 1958), 14, in Panama Canal Museum Collection, Smathers Libraries, University of Florida.
19 Bennett, *History of the Panama Canal*, 425.
20 See, for example, Greene, *Canal Builders*; Michael L. Conniff, *Black Labor on a White Canal: Panama, 1904–1981* (Pittsburgh, PA: University of Pittsburgh Press, 1985); Lancelot S. Lewis, *The West Indian in Panama: Black Labor in Panama, 1850–1914* (Washington, DC: University Press of America, 1980); Newton, *Silver Men*; Trevor O'Reggio, *Between Alienation and Citizenship: The Evolution of Black West Indian Society in Panama, 1914–1964* (Lanham, MD: University Press of America, 2006); Olive Senior, *Dying to Better Themselves: West Indians and the Building of the Panama Canal* (Kingston: University of the West Indies Press, 2014).
21 Bennett, *History of the Panama Canal*, 425.
22 "Memorandum for the Chairman," July 23, 1913, in File 2-L-5, Part 1, Box 47, General Correspondence, 1905–14, Entry PI 153 30, RG 185 (hereafter General Correspondence, 1905–14); D.C. Howard, "Memorandum to the Governor: Request

of Charles Radcliff for Arm," August 29, 1917, in File 2-L-5, Part 2, Box 169, General Records, 1914–34, Entry A1 34-B, RG 185 (hereafter General Records, 1914–34).

23 Bennett, *History of the Panama Canal*, 425.

24 Letter from Charles Mason to Chief Sanitary Officer, January 14, 1913; letter from Lloyd Noland to "Sir," March 20, 1909; letter from Acting General Purchasing Officer to Chief Quartermaster, May 18, 1911, in File 2-L-5, Part 1, Box 47, General Correspondence, 1905–14.

25 Letter from Emory Staggs to F.C. Boggs, December 14, 1912; letter from Acting General Purchasing Officer to Chief Quartermaster, March 25, 1912; letter from William L. Marks to W.C. Gorgas, December 22, 1908; letter from A.A. Marks to F.C Boggs, March 27, 1911, in File 2-L-5, Part 1, Box 47, General Correspondence, 1905–14.

26 Letter from E.D. Anderson to E.H. Erickson Artificial Limb Company, July 21, 1931, and memorandum fragment from H.P. Makel, June 27, 1931, in File 2-L-5, Part 3, Box 169, General Records, 1914–34; letter from Charles Mason to Chief Sanitary Officer, January 14, 1913.

27 Letter from A.L. Flint to Chief Quartermaster, August 16, 1933, in File 2-L-5, Part 3, Box 169, General Records, 1914–34.

28 Letter from Marks Artificial Limb Company to Panama Canal Purchasing Department, July 27, 1933, in File 2-L-5, Part 3, Box 169, General Records, 1914–34.

29 "The Panama Canal," *Medical Herald* 35, no. 2 (February 1916): 65.

30 Greene, *Canal Builders*, 9; see also Alexander Missal, *Seaway to the Future: American Social Visions and the Construction of the Panama Canal* (Madison: University of Wisconsin Press, 2008).

31 Greene, *Canal Builders*, 161; Cornish, "Panama Canal," 169–170; *Annual Report of the Isthmian Canal Commission and the Panama Canal for the Fiscal Year Ended June 30, 1914* (Washington, DC: Government Printing Office, 1914), 294.

32 Personal Injury Reports, January 11, 1906 to October 1, 1907, pages 148–149, in Personal Injury Registry Books Box 1 (January 11, 1906 to June 18, 1908), Entry A1 170, RG 185; letter from William Rogers to William Williams, November 15, 1909, File 52730/82, Box 759, Immigration and Naturalization Service Case Files, Entry 9, RG 85, National Archives and Records Administration, Washington DC (hereafter RG 85); letter from George W. Goethals, February 2, 1909, in "Alessandro Comba," Senate Report 864, 61st Congress, 2d Session, June 16, 1910, US Congressional Serial Set 5590, Session Volume D (Washington, DC: Government Printing Office, 1910), 1.

33 Letter from Robert Watchorn to Daniel J. Keefe, January 8, 1909, in File 52730/82, Box 759, Immigration and Naturalization Service Case Files, Entry 9, RG 85.

34 Letter from George W. Goethals, February 2, 1909, in "Alessandro Comba," Senate Report 864.

35 "One Hundred and Forty-Seventh Meeting," September 21, 1908, in *Minutes of Meetings of the Isthmian Canal Commission, July–December 1908* (Washington, DC: Government Printing Office, 1910), 1685; "One Hundred and Fifty-Third Meeting,"

June 10, 1909, in *Minutes of Meetings of the Isthmian Canal Commission, January–December 1909* (Washington, DC: Government Printing Office, 1910), 1712.

36. Letter from Benj. S. Cable, April 30, 1910, in "Alessandro Comba," Senate Report 864.
37. Letter from George W. Goethals, February 2, 1909, in "Alessandro Comba," Senate Report 864.
38. Letter from Alexander [sic] Comba to W.H. Taft, April 13, 1910, in File 52730/82, Box 759, Immigration and Naturalization Service Case Files, Entry 9, RG 85.
39. Letter from Charles Earl to Commissioner of Immigration, Ellis Island, June 28, 1910, in File 52730/82, Box 759, Immigration and Naturalization Service Case Files, Entry 9, RG 85.
40. Telegram from St. Raphael Society to Department of Commerce and Labor, July 8, 1910; and Deportation Warrant No. 1679, December 4, 1909, in File 52730/82, Box 759, Immigration and Naturalization Service Case Files, Entry 9, RG 85; "Same Old Story," *The Labor Argus*, January 6, 1910, 3.
41. "Loses Legs in Gov't Service, Is Barred from Adopted Land," *The Labor World*, December 25, 1909, 1.
42. "Topics of the Times," *New York Times*, July 13, 1910, 6.
43. "Injured while Working on Canal, then Deported," *Los Angeles Herald*, July 13, 1910, 3.
44. Letter from Ilka Teitelbaum to William Howard Taft, July 12, 1910, in File 52730/82, Box 759, Immigration and Naturalization Service Case Files, Entry 9, RG 85.
45. 37 Stat. 1261, "An Act for the Relief of Alessandro Comba," July 10, 1912, in *Treaties and Acts of Congress Relating to the Panama Canal* (Washington, DC: Government Printing Office, 1917), 64; *Combined Statement of the Receipts and Disbursements, Balances, etc. of the United States during the Fiscal Year ended June 30, 1913*, House of Representatives Document 396, 63d Congress, 2d Session (Washington, DC: Government Printing Office, 1913), 149.
46. "Injured while Working on Canal," 3; letter from J. Ter Kuile to Commissioner General of Immigration, July 12, 1910, in File 52730/82, Box 759, Immigration and Naturalization Service Case Files, Entry 9, RG 85.
47. Letter from Wilfred McDonald to "Sir" [Acting Chief Sanitary Officer], May 25, 1913, in File 2-L-5, Part 1, Box 47, General Correspondence, 1905–14.
48. Bonham C. Richardson, *The Caribbean in the Wider World, 1492–1992: A Regional Geography* (Cambridge: Cambridge University Press, 1992), 137; Newton, *Silver Men*, especially Chapter 1.
49. Letter from John L. Phillips to Chairman, June 9, 1913, and letter from Claude Pierce to Acting Chief Sanitary Officer, June 7, 1913, in File 2-L-5, Part 1, Box 47, General Correspondence, 1905–14.
50. Letter from W.C. Gorgas to Chairman, August 21, 1913, in File 2-L-5, Part 1, Box 47, General Correspondence, 1905–14.
51. "Peg Legs May Be Furnished Free," *The Canal Record* 7, no. 14 (November 26, 1913): 124.
52. Letter from John L. Phillips to Chairman, October 24, 1913, in File 2-L-5, Part 1, Box 47, General Correspondence, 1905–14.

53 Letter from Charles Mason to Governor of the Panama Canal, April 18, 1914, page 1, in File 2-L-5, Part 2, Box 169, General Records, 1914–34.
54 Letter from George Goethals to Chief Health Officer, April 27, 1914, in File 2-L-5, Part 2, Box 169, General Records, 1914–34.
55 Letter from Claude Pierce to Acting Chief Sanitary Officer, June 7, 1913, in File 2-L-5, Part 1, Box 47, General Correspondence, 1905–14.
56 Letter from John L. Phillips to Chairman, June 9, 1913, in File 2-L-5, Part 1, Box 47, General Correspondence, 1905–14.
57 Letter from H.F. Hodges to Acting Chief Sanitary Officer, June 11, 1913, in File 2-L-5, Part 1, Box 47, General Correspondence, 1905–14.
58 Letter from James Chandler to "Honoured Sir" [Goethals], May 30, 1913, in File 2-L-5, Part 1, Box 47, General Correspondence, 1905–14.
59 Letter from Henry Gordan to President Wilson, November [8?], 1916, page 3, in File 72-C-1/G, Part 1, Box 1277, General Records, 1914–34.
60 Letter from H.F. Hodges to James Chandler, June 11, 1913, in File 2-L-5, Part 1, Box 47, General Correspondence, 1905–14.
61 Letter from J.C. Twomey to Superintendent, Gorgas Hospital, March 7, 1934, in File 2-L-5, Part 3, Box 169, General Records, 1914–34.
62 Letter from W. Hymison to Superintendent, Ancon Hospital, December 23, 1926, in File 2-L-5, Part 2, Box 169, General Records, 1914–34.
63 Memorandum for File 2-L-5, January 4, 1927; and letter from W.P Chamberlain to W. Hymison, January 18, 1927, in File 2-L-5, Part 2, Box 169, General Records, 1914–34.
64 Letter from J.C. Twomey to Superintendent, Gorgas Hospital, March 7, 1934.
65 Letter from T.W. Earhart to Superintendent, Gorgas Hospital, March 6, 1934, in File 2-L-5, Part 3, Box 169, General Records, 1914–34.
66 "CZ Retired Workers Install Officers; Committee Meets," *The Panama American*, February 14, 1959, 8; "Melford Hymison," August 24, 1966, Gorgas Hospital Mortuary Records, 1906–1991, RG 185, accessed via Ancestry.com.
67 "Helpful Hints for the Busy Doctor," *Texas Medical Journal* 33, no. 3 (1917): 148.
68 "Cost of the Panama Canal in Human Legs," *Panama Star and Herald*, August 30, 1921.

4 Technologies for the Deaf in British India, 1850–1950

APARNA NAIR

In the last decade of the nineteenth century, deafness in colonial India appeared to capture the imagination of the public of the British metropole.¹ Sparked in part by the 1889 publication of the report of the *Royal Commission on the Blind, Deaf and Dumb and Idiots and Imbeciles*, deaf activists and their advocates in Britain urged that the government extend its recommendations and findings toward the colonies also. Newspapers in the colony and the metropole began to examine and discuss the status and the needs of the deaf Indian subject.² In metropolitan spaces that advocated for the deaf like as the British Deaf and Dumb Association, the "plight" of the deaf in India as well as the paucity of nascent educational efforts in the colony was a part of this discussion. To cite just one instance, at the World Congress of the Deaf in 1893, Francis Maginn noted that while in "other parts of the world," 500 special schools provided for the deaf, "in the whole of the vast territory of India, there is but one, of recent foundation, containing less than thirty pupils."³ This commentary came after a long public encomium to the colonial education system and its contributions toward the "hearing masses" in India. A stronger representation was made in 1897, when 600 British "deaf-mutes" signed a petition to Queen Victoria, in her capacity as the Empress of India, claiming to communicate on behalf of all her "educated deaf-mute" subjects. The petition urged that the "blessings of civilization and religion" be extended to these "living sufferers from life-long deafness." Missionaries were also an active part of this conversation. At the Congress of the Deaf and Dumb in Liverpool in 1899, a representative of the Zenana missionary, Miss Swainson, provided an account of the 200,000 "deaf and dumb" in India—including the existence of three schools catering to only 100 deaf children.⁴ All of these accounts share certain attributes: they are all framed by a quantitative assessment of the deaf in India, which was consistently used to underscore the large numbers of deaf colonial subjects living under the rule of the British Crown. These public debates, newspaper reports, and letters also concurrently pointed out that this population tended to be more isolated from the purported benefits of colonial rule as they were being felt by their hearing counterparts, which was presented as a failure.⁵ Similarly, all these discussions also identified the deaf colonial subject as an ideal opportunity to illuminate the essential benevolence of empire. For these advocates, the deaf colonial subject constituted a unique deserving object through which to demonstrate the benefits of the metropolitan systems of education for the deaf, the superiority of oralism, and the scientific and technological advantages of colonialism.

This chapter asks if colonialism succeeded in altering the possibilities and methods of communication and interaction for the deaf in British India and to what extent the transmission of designs for disability were indeed transformative for deaf Indian lives. Further, this chapter examines the extent to which colonialism had significant impacts on the quotidian lives of the deaf colonial subject in India. In order to partially answer these questions, this chapter begins by describing the contours of deaf histories as tangible in the colonial and missionary archives. Next, the chapter examines the introduction of imported devices that claimed to "cure" deafness to explore what impacts these "Western" designs had on the everyday experiences of deafness. Finally, this chapter describes and analyzes *Kar Pallavi Bhasha*, an indigenous sign language that was observed among the deaf in west India. I argue that *Kar Pallavi Bhasha* is an important indigenous technological response of the Indian deaf to the needs of the community. Moreover, this form of communication emerged independent of and outside of the missionary schools for the deaf, which were nonetheless touted as being educational and technological pioneers for the deaf in India. While existing sources tell us little about the ways in which this language was utilized by the community, its very survival in the colonial archive suggests that it may have been more widespread than one might have expected. It also points to the existence of forms of communication very different from the devices designed and imported by British colonizers. Lastly, relative to the audiphone or electrophone, indigenous sign language is far more likely to have had more meaningful impacts on the quotidian lives of the deaf.

Technology, like biomedicine, had been an integral part of the histories of empire. Varying in scale from "everyday" technologies like the bicycle and typewriter to technologies of the body like vaccination and technologies of transport like the railways, these devices, machines, and processes embodied the putative advantages and scientific superiority of the metropole were utilized as material evidence of the colonizer's "modernity," served as a litmus test of the colonial subjects' own embrace of the "West," the "modern," and the "scientific," and eventually also came to be co-opted to narrate nationalist sentiment, perform religious or social identities.[6] Older scholarship has interpreted colonial technology as a "tool of Empire," but the transfer of technologies from the metropole to the colony had also sparked unexpected and significant indigenous engagement and "dialogues."[7] This chapter continues this focus on technology but extends it to specific designs for disability, including audiphones, ear trumpets, and sign language itself. This analytical focus allows us some ingress into the everyday adaptations and adjustments to deafness, aspects of the historical deaf experience that are not immediately evident when we consider the glimpses of deafness in the archives of the colonial state, or those of local elites or in the missionary records. Further, in these records, the deaf colonial subject is often devoid of agency and is often portrayed as a passive recipient of the philanthropic and scientific beneficence of the colonial state or missionary actors. Further, through the lens of technologies, we can not only position deafness at the intersection of the broader histories of consumption, capitalism, colonialism, and class, but also situate indigenous sign language as an innovative technological adaptation to deafness that had potentially more impacts on the everyday lives of deaf Indians compared to imported designs from the metropole.

Deafness in British India

Before describing designed responses to deafness, I would like to examine some of the ways in which colonialism may have impacted the Indian deaf community. The colonial archive offers complicated and sometimes contradictory impressions of deaf worlds and deaf experiences. The fragmentary evidence offers a picture of deaf lives that often do not support the perception of deafness as a cause for social abjection and isolation. One of the very most obvious sources that give us some sense of deafness in colonial India is the imperial census. A behemoth endeavor that involved thousands of enumerators, census administrators, local headmen, and other intermediaries, the imperial censuses of British India had enumerated four categories of "infirmity" from 1871 to 1930—blindness, deaf-muteness, insanity, and leprosy.[8] Census administrators constantly worried about the definitions and the boundaries of the four enumerated categories of infirmity. In the case of deaf-muteness they urged enumerators to include only those were congenitally deaf and "mute," and to exclude all others.[9] Further, enumerators were instructed to ensure that those who were deaf due to old age and debility were to be excluded, although it is debatable to what extent these rules were followed in the field.[10] The prevalence of deaf-muteness reported in the imperial censuses tended to fluctuate, but was reported to be slightly higher than that in Britain. Gender differences were also enumerated: in 1891, for instance, the prevalence of deaf-muteness was reported to be 9/10,000 for males and 6/10,000 for females.[11] Despite the routine measurement of all four categories of infirm through the imperial census, estimates such as these were consistently derided as unreliable and the census itself unsuitable to enumerate infirmity in general. While this may have been particularly true for leprosy and insanity, deaf-muteness was believed to be both easier and more accurate to enumerate. Unlike leprosy or insanity, deaf-muteness appeared to elicit fewer negative reactions, as is suggested by some of the rare ethnographic details on the worlds of the deaf contained in the imperial census. For instance, some reports suggest that the figure of the "deaf-mute" was received with "awe" and elicited kindly treatment from families and communities.[12] Concealment of impairment among deaf-mutes and their families was also considered unlikely in general because in rural India, the deaf were usually well known in their own communities. Many were "practically a village character and well known and recognized as such."[13]

Deafness is also tangible within the archives on colonial biomedicine. British physicians had long held that India was a space that represented a unique set of corporeal threats to the colonizer's body and mind. In a similar vein, physicians also debated the mechanisms through which residence in India may have produced or exacerbated deafness. Writing in the *Lancet*, Wright (a surgeon-aurist) commented that he had treated a "great number" of Europeans who had departed for India with perfect hearing and returned "extremely deaf, a fact of which, he noted, that the East India Company was well aware."[14] While aurists like Wright generally appeared to agree that a residence in India predisposed the British toward partial or complete deafness, they disagreed on the causes. Metropolitan medical discourses understood deafness as the effect of climate and environment on the body. Wright speculated on whether the higher prevalence of hearing impairments among East-India men was a result of the climate, "modes of living, or the general medical treatment adopted there for every trivial complaint." Others argued that in former residents of India, the "tympanum is affected with the results of previous catarrh"; often as a result of the constant onslaught of fevers and infections. Children born in India were believed to be peculiarly vulnerable to deafness "with no visible cause" as they inched toward puberty.[15] While they disagreed on the causes, it was clear that aurists believed that India definitely "produced" deafness.

Varying from the colonial state somewhat, missionary discourse tended to focus on some elements of deaf experience as well as on highlighting the supposed callousness and barbarity of Indian attitudes toward corporeal difference. At a meeting of the Zenana Mission for the Deaf in Exeter, representatives from missionary-run deaf schools in India claimed that Indians believed that the deaf harbored "evil spirits" in consequence of actions in their past lives; women and children were often dispatched to work as beggars while the "stronger men were harnessed to the bullock cart."[16] Despite highlighting what they saw as Indian cruelty to the deaf, the Zenana missionaries went on to defend the colonial state's neglect of deaf education in the colony—and pointed out that only "30 per cent of the normal children went to school."[17] Such narratives were hardly uncommon and circulated often in the public sphere in the metropole, often framing appeals for funding for institutions for the deaf.[18] Clearly, there is a disjuncture between the colonial and missionary discourses on deafness in British India, a disjuncture that is perhaps explained by the ways in which the colonial state and missionaries perceived the deaf colonial subject. For the colonial state, the deaf colonial subject was best consigned to the care of private actors and philanthropy, while the missionary saw the deaf simultaneously as opportunities for proselytization as well as signifiers of Indian superstition, cruelty, and fatalism.

Additional evidence of the experiences of deaf historical subjects lies in the archival traces of schools for the deaf Indian child. By the early twentieth century, there were at least five schools established in British India by a variety of non-state agencies.[19] The schools were imagined as spaces where "science has come to the help of the deaf and dumb."[20] They were funded by various private charitable actors, including the Catholic and Protestant missionaries in addition to Indian self-advocates and activists; nevertheless, often they were provided with state sanction and some state grants, as well as from local philanthropy. The schools, however, were quite limited in their impact on deaf lives. In 1928, for instance, the Zenana mission, one of the most important missionary actors in deaf education, publicly claimed to be teaching 220 deaf Indian children out of the 50,000 "deaf-mutes" between the ages of five and fifteen.[21] In contemporary India, these deaf schools have become sites of "pan-Indian deaf experience" and are important spaces for constructing and communicating identities through sign language.[22] But in the nineteenth and first half of the twentieth centuries, there was little uniformity between the different deaf schools, all of which had vastly differing attitudes, processes, and systems for educating deaf students. For instance, the Calcutta School experimented with "symbolical finger languages," although it appears more attention was paid to lip-reading and oralism.[23] At the Palamcottah School for the deaf, teachers adapted British sign language to local vernacular or Tamil—although how effective this was may have been debatable. Tamil had more alphabets than English, and one British teacher, Florence Swainson, reported that she substituted "letters which are not in one language for extra ones in the other, and making a few of our own."[24]

"What Spectacles are for the Eyes": Devices for the Deaf

As evident from the previous section, extricating a sense of historical deaf experiences from the colonial archive can be challenging overall, as this was an archive that was shaped by colonial (and missionary) priorities.[25] However, contemporaneous newspapers can prove to be an antidote to the colonial archive. Published in English and in a range of vernacular languages across South Asia, these newspapers represented a range of perspectives. As rich the articles themselves are as sources, particularly since they reflect the perceptions and responses to law and policy often missing in the colonial archive, the newspapers also offer another relevant source: advertisements. Nestled in between newspaper reports, declarations from various state actors and agencies, announcements for bicycles, tonics, insurance agents, and cigarettes, a significant number of classifieds lauded the benefits of devices, technologies, nostrums, and remedies for everything from deafness to "debility," from leprosy to lameness. These products were targeted at bodies living with difference, bodies that had become weak and debilitated owing to chronic illness and bodies that lived with constant pain and weakness. These advertisements underscore the sense that the everyday corporeal experience in the nineteenth and early twentieth centuries was all too frequently marked by illness and impairment. They can also reveal reflections of prevailing social and cultural norms and perceptions around impairment and health. Scholars have already used advertisements from colonial newspapers to explore the growing industry of quack medicines and nostrums in the colonies, in addition to being a space where interconnected ideas of race, hygiene, and dominance were articulated and negotiated.[26] These advertisements should be read with a caveat, however, they present highly essentialized examples of perception and behavior but can nonetheless constitute extraordinarily rich sources they allow us to problematize and nuance the experience of deafness that is apparent in the colonial archive. These advertisements serve as both historical and ethnographic texts on the experience of and negotiations with disability.

The late nineteenth century was indeed a time when inventors and companies designed devices that purported to "cure" deafness, a trend that had begun in the previous century. As Turner and Withley pointed out, the Enlightenment saw the emergence of a thriving demand for medical technologies ranging from trusses to artificial limbs and machines that claimed to correct posture.[27] By the nineteenth century, companies and inventors began more actively targeting deaf customers through advertisements and selling a range of devices that made lavish promises about enabling the deaf to hear.[28] These designs were constructed and advertised as the natural result of applying science to the "problem" of deafness and these "scientific" devices designed for and available to the deaf in the European metropole and in the United States were also available to consumers in the colony of British India.[29]

In South Asia, companies that usually imported medical and surgical apparatus also advertised and sold devices for the deaf, often mediated through physicians, surgeons, and hospitals.[30] For instance, in Calcutta, the government-appointed Bathgate and Company sold ear trumpets, ear cornets, Toynbee tympanums, and conversation tubes alongside medical and surgical ear instruments.[31] Ear trumpets varied in their design and materials, but were intended to collect and carry amplified sound vibrations toward the inner ear.[32] The tube of the trumpet was often made of India-rubber, gutta-percha, or vulcanite, the funnel-shaped trumpet itself was often comprised of metals such as tin.[33] While some were worn on the head, other trumpets were designed to be hand-held and other designs placed the ivory tube of the elastic tube in the ear of the wearer with the other end held up to the mouth of the speaker. Ear cornets were small scroll-shaped metal tubes, which were inserted into the ear canal, with the flattened disc-like mouth seated on the ear. South Asian newspapers advertised bronzed ear cornets covered with silk through medical supplies companies for a cost of ten rupees.[34] Both the ear cornet and the ear trumpet were intended for the "partially deaf," rather than those who had been born deaf, or were completely deaf. The Toynbee artificial tympanum was manufactured with India-rubber and gutta percha between two delicate rings made of silver riveted together and attached to a thin silver wire.[35] Inserted into the ear, the artificial tympanum was intended as a substitute for a damaged or torn tympanum. South Asian newspapers also advertised conversation tubes which comprised a mouthpiece and earpiece connected with a flexible tube, and were used to teach deaf students intonation and pitch.[36]

Aside from these older devices, more complicated technologies were also sold and advertised by the latter half of the nineteenth century. Unlike the "clumsy, unsightly and frequently harmful devices as trumpets, horns, tubes, ear drums and fans," according to promoters this new generation of devices were to be more effective and more "scientific" than older devices.[37] One of the most widely acclaimed designs in this period was the audiophone. "Disgusted" with the "usual routine of ear-trumpets," the Chicago-based deaf inventor Richard Rhodes designed an entirely new device for hearing impaired persons. Rhodes claimed to have been inspired to create the audiophone when he realized that he could "hear" the ticking of his watch when he put it between his teeth.[38] Reported to resemble a "huge tongue hanging out of the mouth," the audiophone consisted of a hand-held disc of varnished and waterproof hardened rubber or thin pasteboard, which was held up to the teeth of the upper jaw.[39] The contact between this disc and the teeth of the wearer permitted them to pick up the vibrations of sounds from a distance. Advertisements for audiophones claimed to enable deaf-mutes to "distinguish musical sounds of some instruments and even vocal articulations."[40] Indeed, advertisements claimed the audiophone as so effective that "oral education" for the deaf student was shortened by its use. In India, companies like Bathgate imported and sold audiophones for around four rupees.[41] How deaf Indians or British consumers in the colony responded to the design of the audiophone in India remains elusive in the archive, although the advertisements in the metropole often included effusive and fulsome testimonials from users. There certainly appeared to be at least some demand for the device: for instance, an Indian theosophist CKM published a public appeal to American and European theosophists for "cheap and durable audiphones suitable to this country."[42] Regardless of the claims made by advertisements and testimonials, contemporary observers in the United States, United Kingdom, and India eventually condemned audiophones as an abject technological failure and instead recommended the older ear trumpets.[43]

At the beginning of the twentieth century, electricity was considered especially promising in alleviating deafness, with much of the experimentation conducted in the United States.[44] As another design explicitly advertised as restoring hearing to the deaf, the Stolz electrophone began to appear in American newspapers at the beginning of the twentieth century [Figure 4.1]. Vaunted as being a "new, scientific and practical" invention for the deaf or partially deaf, the Stolz electrophone claimed to be far superior to older technologies like the ear trumpets, horns, fans, speaking tubes, and "such old-fashioned and harmful things" and being as effective as a prosthetic ear.[45] The design comprised a "miniature type of telephonic apparatus" with a transmitter of globular carbon and an earpiece. The device itself was a light, black disc that fit snugly in the ear and weighted around twelve ounces[46]. It purported to magnify sound waves and transmit them to aural nerves, to overcome "the inner buzzing and roaring ear noises, but making all outer sounds distinct and clear."[47] In British India, it was imported and sold by the James Murray Company, which also advertised the Stolz electrophone as endowing "perfect hearing" in those "who have remained deaf for years" [Figure 4.1].[48] However, compared to the audiophone, the Stolz electrophone was remarkably expensive; in the United States the device cost around thirty-five dollars.[49]

Figure 4.1 Advertisement for the Stolz Electrophone in an Indian newspaper. Credit: From NewsBank, inc. and the Center for Research Libraries. All Rights Reserved.

With all of these technologies for the deaf, we know more about their producers and their designs than their users. Given that these were advertised in English-language newspapers, they were likely intended for a select, literate population; mostly private consumers purchased these technologies. While institutions for the deaf in the United States and the United Kingdom had experimented with a range of devices for those with hearing impairments, impelled by the late-nineteenth-century fascination with the possibilities of technology, no such practice was evident among the cash-strapped institutions for the deaf in the colonies.[50] We are left with little information available on how people with hearing impairments may have responded to these technologies in South Asia. It is fair to assume that access to these technologies was contingent on income, class, and physical access to these commodities and their markets. It is therefore difficult to assess how useful the Stolz electrophone or the audiphone actually were in transforming the experience of deafness or hearing impairment. At the same time, it does tell us about some of the possibilities for an individual living with a hearing impairment.

The Language of the Fingers: *Kar Pallavi Bhasha* as Adaptive Technology

Moving away from the material object to the signed language, this section will focus on the designs and systems of sign languages devised by deaf Indians themselves for their own purposes, which stands in stark contrast to the transnational commerce of the devices for the deaf. Worldwide, deaf communities have demonstrated a powerful propensity to develop their own iterations of sign language, which served as the primary languages in these populations. Sign language also served as significant substitutes for spoken language across the world. In North America, a non-verbal system of sign language had been common among the diverse, multilingual Native American communities that served to cut across communication barriers in trade, politics, and other negotiations.[51] In South Asia, too, indigenous systems of signs that were employed by both the hearing and the deaf had existed before the arrival of the British. This is hardly surprising given the linguistic diversity of the region. Orientalist observers noticed the existence of sign language among the merchants and traders in the bazaars of South Asia; similar systems were also noted in contemporaneous Iran.[52] This sign language was characteristic of the Muslim traders of a range of commodities including hides, leather, wool, grain, and fruit.[53] The sign for silence (*Angusht bi-sar-I dimagh zadan*) was conveyed when the right hand was closed into a fist with the exception of the forefinger which was placed with the middle joint touching the tip of the nose, with the fingertip placed on the left cheek, or with the fingertip placed on the nose, or on the closed lips. Another gesture used to signal silence was the biting of the lower lip. This tactile system of signs helped to negotiate and communicate in crowded environs between individuals who often did not speak the same language. As the principal of the Bombay Deaf School commented:

> It is no uncommon thing to see a couple of sedate-looking traders seated on the ground, each with his right hand concealed in his neighbor's capacious sleeve, and engaged to all appearance in squeezing each others' fingers. For a few minutes, they will remain in this position, one nudging the other occasionally, but without exchanging a single word, then arising they will separate and go their way … A couple of merchants will stand in the middle of a brawling, gesticulating crowd, by which they are surrounded and observed: one will raise the end of his long robe or turban, and under cover of this the pair will clasp hands and fingers as before.[54]

Records from missionary schools for the deaf often give the implicit and explicit impression that a "finger alphabet" in a regular structured form as it existed in the European metropole did not exist in South Asia. However, there is some evidence from the colonial archive that clearly complex and systematized versions of sign language had indeed existed in the region well before the Europeans introduced their versions of sign or finger language. In Bombay, for instance, the colonial state reported the existence of a system of signs that permitted communication and "conversation … in the narrow sphere open to poor people."[55] In Kathiawar, for instance, Rao Bahadur Gopali Desai informed the colonial state that the deaf-mute student was taught by signs and by pointing out articles and writing their names down on slates, although this was not consistently done.[56] Upon investigation by the Assistant Deputy Inspector, a deaf-mute student in a Surat school was found to be able to write out the alphabet and to associate written words to objects and fellow-pupils.[57] The system of signs utilized in this part of India was of long standing and had been in use for several generations by "indigenous masters."[58] Called *Kar Pallavi Bhasha,* the system of signs was based around eight signs that corresponded to a set of letters of the Gujarati language.

The first of these signs, *Adarsha*, was communicated by showing the open hand upright like a mirror. *Kamal* was communicated by forming the hand into the shape of a full-blown lotus flower. *Chakra* was communicated by raising the forefinger, turning it around like a wheel with all the other fingers remaining closed into a fist. *Tankar* was signed by holding the nail of the forefinger on the middle line of the thumb and jerking the forefinger rapidly in the opposite direction "just as an earthen pot or jack fruit is sounded with the fingers." *Talhastak* was communicated by folding the fingertips inward to meet the "place where the fingers rise from the palm" holding the palm upright. *Patra* was signaled when the hand was extended "open palmed across the body as if one were reading a letter." *Yachan* was communicated by holding the hand held forth "as if in begging." *Shatka*, the last class of signs, was signaled by raising the little finger while folding all the other fingers. After having used the sign denoting one of these six classes of letters, the signer conveyed which of the letters in each group he referred to by a simple system of secondary signs—for the first four letters within each class, the signer would touch the tip of the thumb to the lowest joint of each of the four fingers. The fifth letter was indicated by touching the top of the forefinger to the lowest joint of the thumb. The sixth letter was signaled to when the signer touched the top of the thumb to the palm. Eleven "air signs" or signs shaped into the left palm by the right hand were used to convey vowels that would connect consonants. Compound letters, which are not uncommon in many South Asian languages, were indicated by "sounding a fillip and then indicating the compound letters as above and then sounding a fillip to show that the compound is completed."[59]

While language more broadly and sign language in particular has been understood and interpreted as evidence of the human predisposition for communication it also needs to be examined as a cultural artifact "in that they reflect particular ways of behaving and doing things allowed by the same mind, and they vary systematically." Equally, although very different from mass-produced, imported designs like the audiphones, it is important to understand sign language as a designed system of signs and as a technological adaptation to the needs of everyday deaf lives.[60] For Mufwene, sign language should be understood as a technology in so far as it was comprised of signed physical units, was marked by the existence of "non-physical elements" such as specific rules and semantic units.[61] Working with Mufwene's conceptualization of sign language, I would argue that *Kar Pallavi Bhasha* should be interpreted as an indigenous technological adaptation to the need for communication within the deaf community. *Kar Pallavi Bhasha* clearly had a complex, multifaceted architecture and was a nuanced system that communicated information within and for deaf worlds. Furthermore, the complexity of *Kar Pallavi Bhasha* does provide a strong argument for both its longevity in the region and the strong possibility that the language was taught or communicated to successive generations of deaf Indians (at least in this region of the colony). Indeed, when serious attempts were made to explore the genealogies and structures of what is known as Indo-Pakistani Sign Language in the 1970s, it was found to be unrelated to French, Spanish, or American Sign Languages but was inflected to some degree by British Sign Language.[62] This suggests that the indigenous systems of signs used by the deaf were largely left untouched by the encounter with the colonial state and with missionaries.

Yet, the colonial establishment as well as the few existing providers of deaf education in the colony appears to have taken a rather dim view of such indigenous systems. Some reports from within the colonial administration suggest that such forms of communication by signs were neither systematic nor organized.[63] For example, in the first annual report of the Bombay Institution for Deaf-Mutes published in the *Madras Mail*, the governing committee commented on the condition of the "uninstructed deaf and dumb" in the country.[64] For the committee, the deaf were supposedly consigned to isolation, "cut off from social intercourse with their fellowmen, their minds remain almost a perfect blank" because they were "shut out from … a knowledge of (spoken) language."[65] The committee commented on indigenous sign language among the deaf in India and claimed that it was a "medium of some rude and imperfect signs" which facilitated some nonetheless was insufficient as a medium of communication. The reliance on sign language, the report continued, rendered the deaf completely isolated, "a burden on their families and … a charge on the community."[66] Further, the use of sign language was believed to also encourage nonverbal patterns or "dumbness or speechlessness."[67] Despite the colonial condemnations of *Kar Pallavi Bhasha*, it is clear that to those who knew the system of signs, it allowed for communication and possibly a sense of community and belonging.

Conclusions

Like other categories of corporeal difference, deafness has a tendency to be rather elusive both in histories of design and within the colonial archive. When mentioned in the latter, it was often equated with infectious diseases that were perceived to be threats to colonial order, commerce, or the bodies of colonizers themselves. When deafness is perceptible, the colonial/missionary narrative constructed the South Asian experience of deafness as being marked by apathy, fatalism, and neglect.[68] More importantly, the colonial state understood deafness as an Indian problem best solved by private actors and Indian charity rather than colonial intervention or legislation. Yet, this period also saw an active engagement with a range of sign language formats and experimentation with oralism in the deaf schools. This chapter looks outside these institutions and examines designs for the deaf transported from the metropole to the colony, and juxtaposes these designs against the indigenous innovations and designs embodied in the architecture of *Kar Pallavi Bhasha*. While devices for the deaf imported and sold in the colonial market were largely superfluous to deaf lives and deaf experiences, I would argue that *Kar Pallavi*

Bhasha should be understood as a more meaningful and impactful adaptation to deafness. The nineteenth-century emphasis on oralism and an increasing reliance on mass-produced devices produced in the West contributed to a disdain for sign language/finger language, especially among missionaries and advocates for the deaf. This preference allied to the general suspicion of indigenous knowledge and practices may together explain the relative neglect paid to systems like *Kar Pallavi Bhasha*. And yet, such languages may actually have outlived the oralism and/or sign systems that were introduced by the missionary deaf schools. Further, the story of *Kar Pallavi Bhasha* suggests that Indian deaf communities were indeed innovative and engaged.

Notes

1. *Cork Constitution,* Saturday, July 1, 1893, 3; *Belfast News-Letter,* Saturday, July 3, 1897, 8.
2. "The British Deaf and Dumb Association." *The Times*, July 27, 1899, 4.
3. Francis Maginn, "The Deaf in India." *Proceedings of the World's Congress of the Deaf and the Report of the Fourth Convention of the National Association of the Deaf, Volume 4* (Chicago, IL: 1893), 266.
4. *Liverpool Mercury*, Thursday, July 27, 1899, 8.
5. "Deaf Mutes in India." *Daily Inter Ocean*, December 6, 1896, 37.
6. David Arnold, *Everyday Technology: Machines and the Making of India's Modernity* (Chicago, IL: University of Chicago Press, 2013); Deepak Kumar, "Reconstructing India: Disunity in the Science and Technology for Development Discourse, 1900–1947," *Osiris* 15 (2000): 241–257; D.K. Lahiri Choudhury, *Telegraphic Imperialism: Crisis and Panic in the Indian Empire, c. 1830* (Basingstoke: Palgrave Macmillan, 2010).
7. Daniel R. Headrick, *The Tools of Empire: Technology and European Imperialism in the Nineteenth Century* (Oxford: Oxford University Press, 1981); David Arnold, *Science, Medicine and Technology in Colonial India* (Cambridge: Cambridge University Press, 2000).
8. W.C. Plowden, *Census of the N.W. Provinces, 1872, Vol 1: General Report* (Allahabad: North-Western Province's Government Press, 1873).
9. V.R. Thygarajaiyar, *Census of India, 1921, Volume XXIII, Part I: Report* (Bangalore: Government Press, 1923), 112.
10. W.H. Thompson, *Census of India 1921, Volume V: Bengal* (Calcutta: Bengal Secretariat Book Depot, 1923), 326. But, despite the enumerations of infirmity, the census was consistently derided as unsuitable to enumerate disability and the statistics continually called into question. This was particularly true for leprosy and insanity, as both categories were likely to be concealed.
11. E.A. Gait, *Report of the Census of India, 1901, Volume 6, Part I* (Calcutta: Bengal Secretariat Press, 1902), 284.
12. Ibid.

13 Murari S. Krishnamurthi Ayyar, *Census of India 1921, Volume XXV: Travancore* (Trivandrum: Government Press, 1922), 171.
14 W. Wright, "On the Causes and Treatment of Deafness," in *The Lancet London: A Journal of British and Foreign Medicine, MDCCCXXX–XXXI, Volume 2* (London: Mills, Jowett and Mills, MDCCXXXI), 493.
15 James Hinton, *The Questions of Aural Surgery* (London: Henry S. King, 1874), 289–290. Hinton had been the aural surgeon to Guy's Hospital.
16 *Exeter and Plymouth Gazette,* Saturday, November 24, 1928, 8.
17 Ibid.
18 Western Morning News, October 19, 1928, 2.
19 Church Missionary Archives, University of Birmingham Library, CEZ/G/EL 5/11, Mylapore, 1929–1939; Maginn, "The Deaf in India."
20 *Amrita Bazar Patrika*, August 5, 1911, 7.
21 *Exeter and Plymouth Gazette,* Saturday, November 24, 1928, 8.
22 Michele Ilana Friedner, *Valuing Deaf Worlds in Urban India* (New Brunswick, NJ: Rutgers University Press, 2010), 38–39.
23 *Amrita Bazar Patrika,* April 1, 1910, 4.
24 Irene H. Barnes, *Between Life and Death: The Story of CEZMS Medical Missions in India, China and Ceylon* (London: Marshall Brothers, 1901), 124.
25 *Amrita Bazar Patrika,* August 29, 1899, 7.
26 Srirupa Prasad, *Cultural Politics of Hygiene in India, 1890–1914: Contagions of Feeling* (New York: Springer, 2014); Anne McClintock, *Imperial Leather: Race, Gender and Sexuality in the Colonial Context* (New York: Routledge, 1995).
27 David M. Turner and Alun Withey, "Technologies of the Body: Polite Consumption and the Correction of Deformity in Eighteenth-Century England," *History* 99, no. 338 (December 2014), 775–796.
28 *Daily Herald*, July 16, 1899, 12.
29 Pat Kirkham, *The Gendered Object* (Manchester: Manchester University Press, 1996), 50–51; Jennifer Esmail, *Reading Victorian Deafness: Signs and Sounds in Victorian Literature and Culture* (Athens: Ohio University Press, 2013).
30 *The Pioneer*, April 6, 1886, 8.
31 Ibid.
32 Christopher A. Bayly, *Empire and Information: Intelligence Gathering and Social Communication in India, 1780–1870*, Cambridge: Cambridge University Press, 1999, 108. The ear trumpet became the unlikely pretext for intelligence gathering in Central Asia when the ruler of Kashgar requested the British government at Calcutta to send a hearing trumpet for his wife, who was deaf. The British saw this as an opportunity to send an "intelligent man" along with the trumpet to assess whether the granaries of Kashgar were supplying a mobilized Chinese army.
33 John Tully, "A Victorian Ecological Disaster: Imperialism, the Telegraph and Gutta-Percha," *The Journal of World History* 20, no. 4 (December 2009): 559–579. Although largely forgotten today, gutta-percha (the name derived from a Malay word for gum or

resin) is a natural plastic; a sap from the gum from the *taban* tree in Southeast Asia. Widely used in producing everything from furniture to boot soles to the telegraph to linings for water cisterns, gutta percha works were part and parcel of the landscape of industrializing England.

34 *The Pioneer,* September 15, 1869, 11.
35 Joseph Toynbee, *Artificial Membrana Tympani, in Cases of Deafness Dependent Upon Perforation or Destruction of the Natural Organ* (London: John Churchill, 1853).
36 Joseph Gordon, ed. *Education of Deaf Children: Evidence of EM Gallaudet and AG Bell, Presented to the Royal Commission of the United Kingdom on the Condition of the Blind, the Deaf and Dumb, etc*, Washington, DC: Volta Bureau, 1892), 120.
37 *Scientific American,* 158, 14 (April 4, 1908), 249.
38 *Ceylon Observer,* May 6, 1880, 4; *The Pioneer,* May 19, 1880, 1.
39 *The Essex Standard, West Suffolk Gazette and Eastern Counties' Advertiser,* Saturday, February 21, 1880, 3.
40 Ibid.
41 *The Pioneer,* February 10, 1887, 17; *The Audiphone: A New Invention that Enabled the Deaf to Hear through the Medium of the Teeth and Many of the Deaf and Dumb to Hear and Learn to Speak, Invented by Richard S Rhodes of Chicago*, Chicago, IL: Rhodes and McClure, 1880. The audiphone cost between 10 and 50 dollars in the United States.
42 *The Theosophist, Volume 7* (Madras: The Theosophist Society, 1886), 83.
43 *The Pioneer,* May 19, 1880, 1; Laurence Turnbull, "A Comparison between the Audiphone, Dentaphone, etc and the Various Forms of Ear-Trumpets for the Deaf," *Medical Times and Register* 10: 590–944; Jan Branson and Don Miller, *Damned for Their Difference: The Cultural Construction of Deaf People as Disabled* (Washington, DC: Gallaudet University Press, 2002).
44 "To Relieve the Deaf: What Electricity Promises," *Amrita Bazar Patrika*, May 6, 1901, 9.
45 *Popular Mechanics,* May 1908, 109.
46 *Colorado Springs Gazette,* March 22, 1908, 11.
47 Ibid.
48 *Amrita Bazar Patrika*, June 10, 1915, 1.
49 Jessica Ellen Sewell, *Women and the Everyday City: Public Space in San Francisco, 1890–1915* (Minneapolis: University of Minnesota Press, 2011), 45.
50 Margret A. Winzer, *The History of Special Education: From Isolation to Integration* (Washington, DC: Gallaudet University Press, 2002), 204. Phonoscopes, hearing aids, hearing tubes, audiphones, dentaphones and electrophones were bought for students, although most of them were later found largely useless.
51 Jeffrey E. Davis, *Hand Talk: Sign Language among American Indian Nations* (Cambridge: Cambridge University Press, 2010).
52 D.C. Phillott, "A Note on Sign-, Gesture-, Code- and Secret-Language etc. amongst the Persians," in *Journal and Proceedings of the Asiatic Society of Bengal, Vol 3* (Calcutta: Asiatic Society, 1907), 619–622.

53 T.A. Walsh, "The Sign Language of Mohammedan Traders," in *American Annals of the Deaf, Volume 33* (Washington, DC: The Convention of American Instructors of the Deaf, 1888), 194–196.
54 Ibid.
55 British Library, IOR/L/PJ/6/295, File 202. Letter from W. Lee-Warner, Secretary to Government, Bombay Educational Department to the Secretary to the Government of India, Home Department, October 4, 1890.
56 British Library, IOR/L/PJ/6/295, File 202. Letter from E. Giles to the Director of Public Instruction, Poona, July 7, 1890.
57 Ibid.
58 Ibid.
59 Ibid.
60 Douglas McArthur, "Le Langage considéré comme une technologie," *Cahiers de Lexicologie* 50 (1987), 157–164. Such conceptualizations of language as technology are by no means new—McArthur articulated that language could be considered a technology because it embodied a collection of tools and methods, produced through "human invention," produced and elaborated over time and adapting to circumstance.
61 Salikoko S. Mufwene, "The Evolution of Language as Technology: The Cultural Dimension," in *Beyond the Meme: Development and Structure in Cultural Evolution. Minnesota Studies in the Philosophy of Science*, ed. A.C. Love and W.C. Wimsatt. (Minneapolis: University of Minnesota Press, 2019).
62 M.J. Vashistha, M.J. Woodward and K. Wilson, "Sign Language in India: Regional Variation within the Deaf Population," Paper presented at the 5th International Congress of Applied Linguistics, Montreal, August 1978.
63 BL, IOR/L/PJ/6/295, File 202, Letter from T.B. Kirkham to the Director of Public Instruction, Poona, August 2, 1890.
64 *Madras Mail*, June 15, 1887, 5.
65 Ibid.
66 Ibid.
67 *Amrita Bazar Patrika*, August 5, 1911, 7.
68 Aparna Nair, "'They Shall See His Face': Blindness in British India, 1850–1950," *Medical History* 61, no.2 (April 2017): 181–199.

Bibliography:

Anonymous. *The Audiphone: A New Invention That Enabled the Deaf to Hear through the Medium of the Teeth and Many of the Deaf and Dumb to Hear and Learn to Speak, Invented by Richard S Rhodes of Chicago*. Chicago, IL: Rhodes and McClure, 1880.

Arnold, David. *Everyday Technology: Machines and the Making of India's Modernity*. Chicago, IL: University of Chicago Press, 2013.

Arnold, David. *Science, Medicine and Technology in Colonial India*. Cambridge: Cambridge University Press, 2000.

Ayyar, Murari S. Krishnamurthi. *Census of India 1921, Volume XXV: Travancore*. Trivandrum: Government Press, 1922.

Barnes, Irene H. *Between Life and Death: The Story of CEZMS Medical Missions in India, China and Ceylon*. London: Marshall Brothers, 1901.

Bayly, Christopher A. *Empire and Information: Intelligence Gathering and Social Communication in India, 1780–1870*. Cambridge: Cambridge University Press, 1999.

Branson, Jan and Don Miller. *Damned for Their Difference: The Cultural Construction of Deaf People as Disabled*, Washington, DC: Gallaudet University Press, 2002.

Choudhury, D.K. Lahiri. *Telegraphic Imperialism: Crisis and Panic in the Indian Empire, c. 1830*. Basingstoke: Palgrave Macmillan, 2010.

Davis, Jeffrey E. *Hand Talk: Sign Language among American Indian Nations*. Cambridge: Cambridge University Press, 2010.

Esmail, Jennifer. *Reading Victorian Deafness: Signs and Sounds in Victorian Literature and Culture*. Athens: Ohio University Press, 2013.

Friedner, Michele Ilana. *Valuing Deaf Worlds in Urban India*. New Brunswick, NJ: Rutgers University Press, 2010.

Gait, E. A. *Report of the Census of India, 1901, Volume 6, Part I*. Calcutta: Bengal Secretariat Press, 1902.

Gordon, Joseph, ed. *Education of Deaf Children: Evidence of EM Gallaudet and AG Bell, Presented to the Royal Commission of the United Kingdom on the Condition of the Blind, the Deaf and Dumb, etc*. Washington, DC: Volta Bureau, 1892.

Headrick, Daniel R. *The Tools of Empire: Technology and European Imperialism in the Nineteenth Century*. Oxford: Oxford University Press, 1981.

Hinton, James. *The Questions of Aural Surgery*. London: Henry S. King, 1874.

Kirkham, Pat. *The Gendered Object*. Manchester: Manchester University Press, 1996.

Kumar, Deepak. "Reconstructing India: Disunity in the Science and Technology for Development Discourse, 1900–1947." *Osiris* 15 (2000): 241–257.

Maginn, Francis. "The Deaf in India." *Proceedings of the World's Congress of the Deaf and the Report of the Fourth Convention of the National Association of the Deaf, Volume 4, Part*, Chicago, IL, 1893.

McArthur, Douglas. "Le Langage considéré comme une technologie." Cahiers de Lexicologie 50 (1987): 157–164.

McClintock, Anne. *Imperial Leather: Race, Gender and Sexuality in the Colonial Context*. New York: Routledge, 1995.

Mufwene, Salikoko S. "The Evolution of Language as Technology: The Cultural Dimension." In *Beyond the Meme: Development and Structure in Cultural Evolution. Minnesota Studies in the Philosophy of Science*, ed. A.C., Love and W.C. Wimsatt. Minneapolis: University of Minnesota Press, 2019.

Nair, Aparna. "'They Shall See His Face': Blindness in British India, 1850–1950." *Medical History* 61, no.2 (April 2017): 181–199.

Phillott, D.C. "A Note on Sign-, Gesture-, Code- and Secret-Language etc. amongst the Persians." In *Journal and Proceedings of the Asiatic Society of Bengal, Vol 3*, Calcutta: Asiatic Society, 1907.

Plowden, W.C. *Census of the N.W. Provinces, 1872, Vol 1: General Report*. Allahabad: North-Western Province's Government Press, 1873.

Prasad, Srirupa. *Cultural Politics of Hygiene in India, 1890–1914: Contagions of Feeling*. New York: Springer, 2014.

Sewell, Jessica Ellen. *Women and the Everyday City: Public Space in San Francisco, 1890–1915*. Minneapolis: University of Minnesota Press, 2011.

Thygarajaiyar, V.R. *Census of India, 1921, Volume XXIII, Part I: Report*. Bangalore: Government Press, 1923.

Thompson, W.H. *Census of India 1921, Volume V: Bengal*. Calcutta: Bengal Secretariat Book Depot, 1923.

Toynbee, Joseph. *Artificial Membrana Tympani, in Cases of Deafness Dependent Upon Perforation or Destruction of the Natural Organ*. London: John Churchill, 1853.

Tully, John. "A Victorian Ecological Disaster: Imperialism, the Telegraph and Gutta-Percha." *The Journal of World History* 20, no. 4 (December 2009): 559–579.

Turnbull, Laurence. "A Comparison between the Audiphone, Dentaphone, etc and the Various Forms of Ear-Trumpets for the Deaf." *Medical Times and Register* 10 (1880): 590–944.

Turner, David M. and Alun Withey. "Technologies of the Body: Polite Consumption and the Correction of Deformity in Eighteenth-Century England." *History* 99, no. 338 (December 2014): 775–796.

Vashistha, M.J., M.J. Woodward and >K Wilson. "Sign Language in India: Regional Variation within the Deaf Population." Paper presented at the 5th International Congress of Applied Linguistics, Montreal, August 1978.

Walsh, T.A. "The Sign Language of Mohammedan Traders." In *American Annals of the Deaf*, ed. Edward Allen Fay, 194–196. Washington, DC: The Convention of American Instructors of the Deaf, 1888.

Winzer, Margaret. A. *The History of Special Education: From Isolation to Integration*, Washington, DC: Gallaudet University Press, 2002.

Wright, W. "On the Causes and Treatment of Deafness." In *The Lancet London: A Journal of British and Foreign Medicine, MDCCCXXX–XXXI, Volume 2*. London: Mills, Jowett and Mills, MDCCXXXI.

Amrita Bazar Patrika, August 29, 1899, 7.*Amrita Bazar Patrika,* October 11, 1900.
Amrita Bazar Patrika, May 6, 1901, 9.
Amrita Bazar Patrika, August 5, 1911, 7.
Amrita Bazar Patrika, June 10, 1915, 1.
Amrita Bazar Patrika, August 5, 1911, 7.
Belfast News-Letter, Saturday, July 3, 1897, 8.
Ceylon Observer, May 6, 1880, 4.
Colorado Springs Gazette, March 22, 1908, 11.
Cork Constitution, Saturday, July 1, 1893, 3.
Daily Herald, July 16, 1899, 12.
Daily Inter Ocean, December 6, 1896, 37.
Liverpool Mercury, Thursday, July 27, 1899, 8.
Madras Mail, June 15, 1887, 5.
The Theosophist, Volume 7, (Madras: The Theosophist Society, 1886), 83.
Exeter and Plymouth Gazette, Saturday, November 24, 1928, 8.
The Essex Standard, West Suffolk Gazette and Eastern Counties' Advertiser, Saturday, February 21, 1880, 3.
The Pioneer, July 5, 1888.
The Pioneer, September 15, 1869, 11.

The Pioneer, February 10, 1887, 17.
The Pioneer, May 19, 1880, 1.
Popular Mechanics, May 1908, 109.
Scientific American, April 4, 1908. Vol XCVII, No. 14, 249.
The Times, July 27, 1899, 4.
Western Morning News, October 19, 1928, 2.
British Library, India Office Records, IOR/L/PJ/6/295, File 202.
Church Missionary Society Archives, Cadbury Library, University of Birmingham, CEZ/G/EL 5/11, Mylapore, 1929–1939.

Part 2 Disability and World-Making in the Twentieth Century

After Vic Finkelstein, a South African anti-Apartheid activist who used a wheelchair, was released from prison and moved to London in the late 1960s, he began imagining a world built for disabled people. In a speculative short story first published in 1975, Finkelstein depicted an "upside down world," a community organized for—and run by—wheelchair users. Some of the inhabitants would open stores, he imagined, while others organized schools. Some would be street cleaners while others ran the village transit system. Wheelchair-using architects would design features friendly to the village's inhabitants, including lower door lintels and ceilings. "The buildings and environment [would be] truly in tune with their needs," Finkelstein wrote, but this would not necessarily be a utopia. Non-disabled residents would find themselves out of place; they would knock their heads on ceilings and doors, getting bruised or more seriously injured. They would be outcasts, unable to use typical environments and excluded from jobs based on their bodily differences. After years on the margins, Finkelstein imagined, a group of these able-bodied disabled might recognize that they had never been consulted in the planning of this village. "They realised that there may be solutions to their problems which had never occurred to the wheelchair users," Finkelstein wrote.[1] Finkelstein used the parable to suggest the social meaning of disability, not determined by a person's bodily condition alone but amplified or lessened by design.

Finkelstein was among a generation of disabled activists to contest the medicalized model that had dominated the nineteenth and much of the twentieth centuries, in which disability was viewed as a pathology to be treated or eliminated by medical intervention. This new generation argued that disability was more than a physical or psychological condition, that it was a product of biases and beliefs in the broader society. The chapters in this part show how in the late twentieth and early twenty-first centuries, sites and products resembling Vic Finkelstein's vision emerged as designers and planners rethought the built environment with the daily life of disabled citizens in mind. Their definitions of disability and the best way to design in consideration of it differed, but they shared an understanding that design shapes society. In this way, it may be argued, design shapes the social experiences of disabled people.

Disability in the Modernist World

Vic Finkelstein's parable introduced the emerging idea of disability as a political status, and one that was embedded within the built environment. If the previous part presented examples of disabled people as consumers in early industrialization, the chapters here examine the era in which design was used to intervene in the position of disabled person as citizen. In schools, under veterans' policies, within social welfare programs, and in design manifestoes and philosophies, designers interpreted disability as a component of the designed world rather than as an individual bodily situation to be addressed through singular devices.

This shift can be linked to broader design industry changes. In the twentieth century, design was firmly established as a culturally powerful activity. Architects, urban planners, graphic designers, and a host of other specialists made over the industrialized world. From skyscrapers to potato peelers, modern lives were thoroughly designed. The studies in this part show disability as a part of what design theorist Anne-Marie Willis calls "the double movement of ontological designing"; in other words, how "we design our world, while our world acts back on us and designs us."[2] Efforts to develop and hone modern design both echoed deep-rooted ideas about human difference and re-shaped those ideas as well.

If the twentieth century was marked by an ever more organized and planned society, these programs of design and reform most often overlooked or actively excluded disabled people. By mid-century, design standards solidified the able-bodied, usually male figure, as the primary user of design, leaving disabled people as outsiders, unrecognized as present in homes, schools, or industry.[3] Medical and educational programs of the period emerged to shape the disabled experience specifically, creating a genre of architecture in the proliferation of specialized schools, medical institutions, and sanitaria.[4] Meanwhile, European models that linked built environment with human health were transported to former colonies, where notions of a "healthy" environment intermingled with racial ideologies of cleanliness and purity as well.[5]

Surveying the grim postwar landscape of bombed factories and impoverished cities, many designers agreed with the Milanese architect Ernesto Rogers, who in 1952 is said to proclaim this the moment to comprehensively redesign the postwar world, "dal cucchiaio alla città" (from the teaspoon to the city).[6] As the cases in this part reveal, many architects and communities also translated this social purpose of design into service for the greater inclusion of disabled people. In contrast to the normative tendency of much of twentieth-century design, these cases link alignments between the social visions of modern design to emerging arguments for disability rights and inclusion.

Making an Accessible World

The history of disability and design in the twentieth century is, in many ways, a policy history. Over the course of the century, disability was addressed through legislation on rehabilitation, social welfare, and civil rights, with approaches distinct to various Western nations. The social ambitions of accessible design have significant origins in the post–Second World War era, beginning with returning disabled veterans. Early government programs to support those injured in the War showed an overlap between patriotic beneficence and technological enthusiasm. Many countries were particularly insistent on the need for high-tech prosthetic limbs to suit returning heroes from military conflict. But initial changes for this population soon led to a broader agenda. In North America and Europe, government involvement in design encouraged widespread adoption of new standards, such as wheelchair ramps or specially designated parking spaces for disabled people.

Few works of design history have made a link between the twentieth-century focus on design as a social tool and the history of disability. But as Elizabeth Guffey explains, design was central to two divergent, design-led modes of social policy around disability that emerged after the Second World War. In the United States, accessible design was modest above all else, emphasizing integration in order to express the values of independence and "overcoming" one's disability. In many European countries, design was instead part of a larger social project and linked to the emerging welfare state. Guffey explains the implications of these two approaches in the work of British architect Selwyn Goldsmith, who first adopted, but then rejected the American model of integration and independence. Wanda Liebermann further teases out Guffey's implications, arguing that in European welfare states like the Netherlands, design was mobilized to rehabilitate both technology and society itself. Liebermann points specifically to the case of Het Dorp, an experimental planned village explicitly designed to accommodate disabled residents in the early 1960s. As a "village for invalids," Het Dorp inspired Vic Finkelstein's later utopian parable, but it also raised an equally problematic specter of segregation of disabled people by design.

These postwar Modernist efforts provide a backdrop to a rights-oriented reform of architecture in the mid to late twentieth century. The history of access is complex and commitments to inclusion have often been counter-balanced by backlash against changes to design standards.[7] A significant contribution has come from design experts who argued that the benefits of accessible design also extended to improvements to design more generally. American designers like Ronald Mace, a polio survivor, wheelchair user, and practicing architect, began to pattern their research and design proposals on a new premise: accessible design was best integrated into a general design strategy of usability, rather than as separate features.[8] Furthermore, Mace would argue, this research brought new value in a changing marketplace. Attention to aging and disability, he and his collaborators wrote, "may be the next frontier in design, one that will set apart competitors in upcoming decades."⁹ The impact of these ventures spread beyond the practically minded, easy-to-grip cutlery sets and the development of more comfortable cane-handles, and shaped the development of creative and market-oriented approaches to access.

While arguments over accessibility, universality, and inclusiveness shaped much of disability design discourse in the later twentieth century, other cases challenged the very definitions of disability and access. In this volume, Debra Parr introduces a less commonly acknowledged form of disability and chronic illness—the inability to breathe as a result of chemical substances in the air. Parr situates the "right to breathe" within a history of clean, flowing air as a Modernist architectural value. With changing medical and social definitions of chemical sensitivity, Modernism's sealed environments gain new and threatening implications. The very same strategies once seen as creating cleanliness now became the cause of exclusion and discomfort.

In other cases, design approaches acquire different meanings depending on how they were framed and who administered them. Kristoffer Whitney describes the design models of the National Technical Institute for the Deaf, founded in 1968 under a US government mandate. The Institute's sound- and sight-conscious spaces represented to its founders a fulfillment of the rights of deaf and hard of hearing students. But, coming at the same time as emerging Disability Rights and Deaf self-advocacy movements, the Institute's top-down approach foreclosed options for in design. In recent years, the design templates of DeafSpace use similar approaches to this earlier predecessor; with an emphasis on self-advocacy, however, the outcomes are quite distinct.

Taken together, these four studies show a range of approaches to access in the period from the 1940s to the 1970s. They show designers responding to local cultural and legislative contexts as they prioritized, in different measures, specific disability communities or a general sense of "access" or inclusion. In this part's final chapter, Elizabeth Guffey examines these arguments through a case of product design and marketing in Japan. The story of The Walking Bag, a mobility aid that resembles a wheeled suitcase that was designed in the 1990s and early 2000s, reveals clear cultural and market-based differences between the United States and Japan. As this case study suggests, the rules of disability and design continue to change. No single ethos or model gained dominance by the end of the twentieth century. And yet, taken together, they reveal the emergence of design as a key method and means of treating disability.

As a professional practice, design in the later twentieth century moved still further away from its earliest role as an aesthetically based activity dedicated to form-giving. Instead, design was employed increasingly as a broader strategy for creatively approaching innovation. As the scholar Richard Buchanan puts it, the focus of design in the late twentieth century was "no longer on material systems—systems of 'things'—but on human systems, the integration of information, physical artifacts, and interactions in environments of living, working, playing, and learning."¹⁰ In the society at large, design was increasingly seen as an agent of change, including within the disability community. The shifting models for addressing disability, ranging from more independence- and market-oriented solutions to social welfare and universalist approaches, created distinct styles and meanings for design in this period.

Notes

1. Vic Finkelstein, "To Deny or Not to Deny Disability," in *Handicap in a Social World: A Reader*, ed. Ann P. Brechin, Penny Liddiard, and John Swain, Repr, Set Book / Open University Press (Kent: Hodder and Stoughton, 1983).
2. Anne-Marie Willis, "Ontological Designing," *Design Philosophy Papers* 4, no. 2 (June 2006): 80, https://doi.org/10.2752/144871306X13966268131514
3. Sarah F. Rose, *No Right to Be Idle: The Invention of Disability, 1840s–1930s* (Chapel Hill: University of North Carolina Press, 2017); Aimi Hamraie, *Building Access: Universal Design and the Politics of Disability* (Minneapolis: University of Minnesota Press, 2017).
4. Margaret Campbell, "What Tuberculosis Did for Modernism: The Influence of a Curative Environment on Modernist Design and Architecture," *Medical History* 49, no. 4 (December 2005): 463–488.
5. Fabiola López-Durán, *Eugenics in the Garden: Transatlantic Architecture and the Crafting of Modernity* (Austin: University of Texas Press, 2018).
6. Deyan Sudjic, *The Language of Things: Understanding the World of Desirable Objects* (New York: Norton, 2009): 34–35.
7. Bess Williamson, *Accessible America: A History of Disability and Design* (New York: New York University Press, 2019), 129–146.
8. Aimi Hamraie, "Building Access, Universal Design and the Problem of 'Post-Disability' Ideology," *Design and Culture*, August 19, 2016, 1–25.
9. Molly Follette Story, James L. Mueller, and Ronald L. Mace, *The Universal Design File: Designing for People of All Ages and Abilities* (Raleigh, NC: Center for Universal Design, 1998), 3.
10. Richard Buchanan, "Design Research and the New Learning," *Design Issues* 17, no. 4 (2001): 12.

5 The Ideologies of Designing for Disability
ELIZABETH GUFFEY

Though trained as an architect, Selwyn Goldsmith is less known for any building than for his book, *Designing for the Disabled* (1963), the classic guide to access planning for buildings, facilities, and public spaces. Intended as a comprehensive manual, Goldsmith's was the first book to publish anthropometric studies of wheelchair users, describe door heights and ramp grades that optimized access, and many other features that would soon become part of building code in the UK and abroad. It quickly assumed the status of the primary sourcebook on the subject; it continues to inform design for disabled people to this day. But however much it has been praised for its "radical new vision," few commentators now realize that Goldsmith actually repudiated this seminal work several years after he first published it. This chapter explores the curious case of Goldsmith's shift, but also positions him–and *Designing for the Disabled*—as caught between changing medical and social mores and shifting political ideologies.

Goldsmith's text built on advances in medicine, procedures, and treatment of injuries that cut mortality rates during the Second World War. In the decades after, large numbers of disabled veterans joined more and more private citizens who benefited from medical advances and were surviving serious injuries, diseases, and life-changing conditions. *Designing for the Disabled* helped articulate a changed attitude toward physical impairment: thoughtful design could mitigate or even change the nature of disability.

As it turned out, he would later believe his writings had deeply political implications on an international scale. While Britain armed its disabled citizens with special provisions that marked their difference and gave them separate access, Goldsmith argued that the United States opted to mask difference with facilities that made all spaces accessible. Of these two approaches, he later argued, one was based on "compensation, special treatment" and a "pragmatism" that was deeply infused by the socialist ethos of many liberal democracies across Europe in the years following the Second World War. The other approach, which Goldsmith would come to identify with the United States, was a different, albeit "coherent design ideology." The latter stressed "enablement, equal treatment" and perhaps most tellingly "idealism."[1] The first edition of Goldsmith's book reflected what observers at the time called "the orthodox American approach."[2] But he revisited his own text in the next two editions, shifting their emphasis in order to reflect what he believed was a more British approach toward design for disability. In the end, he believed that research on the subject could be shaped by deep biases, resting as it did on deep "moral and ethical bases."[3]

A Book about Disabled People

Before Selwyn Goldsmith's seminal *Designing for the Disabled* there was virtually no guidance outside the United States for architects and designers interested in providing access for disabled people. *Designing for the Disabled* is thus a landmark; its modest subtitle, "A Manual of Technical Information," masks an ambitious philosophical platform. Disabled people, it argued, could manage independently if only architects and designers would begin working with them in mind. Goldsmith would later acknowledge the book's pioneering status: "From an academic base and in an academic fashion I had written a book about disabled people."[4]

Indeed, the book offers a groundbreaking series of anthropometric studies of wheelchair users, people on crutches and other mobility aids and advises how the needs of such people can be incorporated into mainstream design. To do this, it included a compendium of some 224 diagrams for designers to consult. These diagrams make clear that much of what passes for "disability" can actually be fixed by relatively easy to implement and thoughtful design, including constructing ramps, expanding door widths, and tweaking lavatories with higher toilet seats, a more accessible flushing handle, and support rails on either side of the toilet. As a technical guide, the book included a rigorously conceived approach toward building materials, the disposition of services like heating and lighting, and the space requirements necessary to properly operate assistive devices. Covering seemingly minor details, like the use of accessible clothing rails, as well as the measured specifications necessary to pivot or continuously move wheelchairs indoors, *Designing for the Disabled* was welcomed as an authoritative guide.

Selwyn Goldsmith's contribution to issues of access stemmed in part from his own experiences with disability. After studying architecture at Cambridge and then at University College London's Bartlett School of Architecture, Goldsmith contracted polio on a trip to Italy in 1956. For Goldsmith, polio was "not a tragedy," but a new calling. He went from designing "pigsties and cowsheds" and helping to plan industrial and commercial buildings in London to designing for disabled people.[5] In 1961, the Royal Institute of British Architects and a polio-based charity prodded him to write a comprehensive guidance manual for designers working for people with impairments similar to his own. *Designing for Disability* would be that project.

In retrospect, the book seems remarkable not only for pioneering efforts, but also for how quickly it was written. Yes, Goldsmith was an architect and himself disabled, but he had no expertise on the subject. Nevertheless, he completed the project in two years, relying in large part on the *American Standard Specifications for Making Buildings and Facilities Accessible to and Usable by the Physically*

Handicapped. First issued in 1961 under the auspices of the American National Standards Institute, the American report was based on research by Timothy Nugent, a US-based rehabilitation expert, who had spent more than a decade remaking the University of Illinois's campus into a kind of wheelchair "utopia."[6] As director of the university's Rehabilitation Education Center, Nugent conducted hundreds of studies to ensure that accommodations were helpful and consistent and used this research to oversee the smooth integration of carefully designed accessibility features around campus. As Goldsmith drew from Nugent's research in Illinois, he began to discover a deep ideological divide that would separate his approach from that of his American counterpart. But, he would argue, this rift was also shaped by larger national and international concerns.

A New Ideology of Design

The decades after the Second World War presented an opportunity to rebuild Europe's devastated built environment and, with it, to reconceptualize disability. Until the middle of the twentieth century, most disabled people lived severely circumscribed lives; the world was simply not designed with them in mind. As survival rates after serious injuries and disease improved and life expectancies extended, the goal to "restore" disabled people to some kind of "normalcy" began to seem more and more pressing. Where the focus in the years after the First World War remained narrowly bent on vocational and job-getting efforts, for instance, once hostilities ceased after the Second World War both Allied and Axis powers quickly moved not only to mend the bodies of their veterans, but to reintegrate them as fully as possible into society.[7] For the first time, European and North American governments undertook wide-ranging programs to "normalize" their wounded but still functioning citizens. But the ideologies were different. In war-ravaged Europe, the approach was part of a broader effort to reshape society through socialist, communitarian principles.

Although Goldsmith had little reflected on it before he began work on *Designing for Disability*, the UK was already developing its own distinctive culture of disability. By the late nineteenth and early twentieth centuries, the British government had assumed a significant role in caring for the special needs of disabled people, passing, for example, the Elementary Education (Blind and Deaf Children) Act in 1893 and the Blind Persons Act in 1920 (and requiring local authorities find appropriate services and employment for visually impaired people).[8] But it was only after the Second World War, when the left-leaning Labour Party was voted into office, did the government begin implementing sweeping changes meant to create a more equitable society.

While long-standing illness and physical impairment had previously been treated by individual doctors or simply ignored, the new National Health Ministry gradually came to require its own design culture built on medical interventions, rehabilitation, and the support of special facilities. From the beginning, social ministries and government bureaucrats agreed that care and assistive devices should be free. As a fundamental feature of the government's new service, the Ministry began developing and overseeing production of medical supplies. Thus, for example, in the late 1940s the National Health Service (NHS) developed its own standard issue wheelchairs.[9] These devices were provided free to all eligible wheelchair users, as were NHS-provided three-wheeled cars. The latter were designed to hold and store a folding NHS wheelchair in its back and seat a single disabled driver in the front. Marked by their unusual shape and painted a distinctive color of blue, their impact was mixed. On the one hand, these unique vehicles visibly distinguished and segregated disabled people, but also gave them special access to various facilities (they could park on the edge of soccer fields, for instance, when games were being played).

Significant as these provisions were, the NHS's approach to design sometimes enhanced access could also have the opposite effect, accentuating difference and further limiting ability. For almost four decades, the Invacar, for example, was issued free to mobility-impaired people; run on gasoline and capable of being driven on open highways, for most purposes it would be classified as a vehicle. Nevertheless, for administrative purposes the NHS categorized the car as a "prosthesis."[10] This categorization made it hard for disabled people to apply and receive other forms of transport assistance. Even as the Invacars filled many of the same transportation functions of a car, the category of "prosthesis" meant that NHS planners continued to look for transportation that took the shape of accommodations that allowed bodily augmentation. On the other hand, whole areas of architectural planning and construction were ignored. Neither the national government nor the NHS, for example, had much to do with regulating buildings or adapting housing to accommodate disabled people. Indeed, special hospitals and rehabilitation centers knew well the sizes (and clearance of) NHS-issued wheelchairs. Nevertheless, this information was not always passed on to government-funded hospital builders. In 1964, the medical journal *The Lancet* reported, for example, that it was common for disabled persons or their caregivers to encounter problems similar to that of a new orthopedic unit in the north of England. Although the government controlled the construction of new hospitals and also the design of most wheelchairs in use, the consulting room door was so narrow that standard issue wheelchairs could pass through the main entrance with only millimeters to spare.[11] On a larger level, this lack of guidance meant that most disabled people in Britain continued to live in a world that was not designed with them in mind.

While the British government established a welfare state with state-run medicine, the United States took a different tack. American politicians feared that large numbers of returning Second World War veterans might recreate the widely disparaged Civil War pension system, wherein large numbers of young men lived out their lives in soldiers' homes with no opportunity to reintegrate into society. Similar concerns fueled political efforts to "rehabilitate" injured or otherwise disabled citizens so they might achieve a degree of "normalcy" and live independent. In asserting this argument, they were also voicing a long-established principle in America shaped around ideas of useful disablement.[12] As a result, in the United States there was a larger emphasis on infrastructure and planning; furthermore, efforts meant to normalize injured veterans and other disabled people reached to the highest level of government.

Indeed, with this ideal of independence in mind, we see a radical approach toward disability—and design—develop in the 1950s. Congress itself formed the President's Committee on Employment of the handicapped in 1947. Largely based on Nugent's work at the University of Illinois (and federal funding of his program through the Veterans' Administration), his university-wide efforts came to the attention of this Committee. Largely motivated by the Illinois program, a subcommittee was formed to establish a set of national accessibility design standards. Eventually the group gained support from other nonprofits, including the American Institute of Architects. Believing in well-considered design and construction recommendations, these groups believed integration was achievable through the dissemination of clear and simple building standards. Issued in 1961, the American Standard Specifications were based on these recommendations; this was an industry-led effort amounting to a group of recommendations meant to make buildings and facilities accessible to and usable by the physically disabled. Based as they were on Timothy Nugent's work in Illinois over the previous decade, they slowly began to become law through local building codes.

But Nugent did more than set the pace for building and design protocols; he lived and breathed the American ethos of independence, believing that disabled people were no different from anyone else. Preaching a doctrine of self-reliance, Nugent wanted them to live "independently and without distinction."[13] But Nugent parted ways with his predecessors by pointing to the built environment as the principal source of disability. According to Nugent, steps, narrow doorways, and rough or uneven surfaces all were "barriers" to access.[14] By removing these thoughtless and debilitating barriers, he would argue, his disabled students could perform on an equal basis with non-disabled students. Providing "barrier-free architecture," Nugent argued, did not give special advantage to disabled people. Rather, it served to "neutralize" the effects of disability. In effect, planners were meant to simply provide the same kind of access that non-disabled people already enjoyed.[15]

Initially, Nugent's book of specifications was widely praised. Goldsmith found it so compelling that the first edition of *Designing for the Disabled* was largely cribbed from it. It was largely "a matter of plagiarizing," Goldsmith himself, would say "the few relevant publications that I could find and giving the material a coherent structure."[16] As it was:

> The preparation of the first edition of *Designing for the Disabled* was a straightforward task. It was facilitated by my having only a superficial appreciation of the subject, by there not being anyone who had tackled the topic previously, by there being few people in Britain who knew much about it, and by my ignorance of the techniques of scientific research.[17]

It was, he'd later note, largely including more specifically Nugent's recent work in the United States for the "American Standard Specifications." All Goldsmith had to do, he himself would later recall, was to give "the material a coherent structure."[18]

As it was, Goldsmith's first edition was so successful that he was almost immediately commissioned to write a second, expanded version. With this mandate, he decided to "sharpen" his research, namely, doing his own user studies.[19] With this in mind, Goldsmith selected the East Anglia town of Norwich as the ideal representative city in which to conduct his study. But what he found was nothing like what Nugent had described in his earlier work. And for Goldsmith, occupied as he was with Britain's emerging interest in the lot of disabled people with in the welfare state, the results were damning.

Toilet Troubles in Norwich

With a sharp and analytical mind, Goldsmith was a born researcher; but even as a disabled one, he had little considered the real-life situations behind the specifications and instructions he'd so recently borrowed for his own book. In the mid-sized city of Norwich, this changed. Goldsmith began surveying the needs of wheelchair users, disabled drivers, and the vision impaired. To do this work, he assumed the title of "Research Architect" for the Norwich Corporation, and partnered with the local Town Clerk, the City Architect, and its Chief Welfare Officer. Rather than study young and eager co-eds, as had Nugent, Goldsmith used the welfare rolls to seek out subjects. As a result, Goldsmith's sample skewed significantly older and was often economically disadvantaged. The stories these people told alarmed him.

Immediately, Goldsmith was struck by the social and physical isolation of Norwich's disabled residents. In fact, of the almost 300 people he initially interviewed, Goldsmith found that only six resembled Nugent's typical wheelchair user, that is people who were "able to go out and use public buildings independently."[20] Most required significant help to even leave home (Figure 5.1). Almost to a one, Goldsmith found that the people he interviewed had caregivers who helped them, not least with basic aspects of care like toileting. These wheelchair users were less concerned with ramps providing access to cinemas, restaurants, or churches than they were with finding accessible public toilets. This, he learned, was "one of the main deterrents to disabled people going out."[21]

Part of the problem was technical. Few wheelchair users were able to maneuver in cramped toilet stalls. And most, in any case, relied on caregivers like a spouse or family member to help them transfer between wheelchair and toilet. There was certainly no room for them both. What's more, single-sex washrooms prohibited disabled people from being accompanied by caregivers of the opposite sex. Normal caregiving arrangements didn't follow the cultural mores that shaped public conveniences.

A handful of memorable cases made the problem vivid for Goldsmith. One woman, for example, found it difficult to enter public toilets on her own, without her caregiving husband. When on holiday, she had to invite a (female) friend to join the couple solely to attend to her toileting needs.[22] While Nugent had focused on infrastructure that might allow disabled people independence, Goldsmith observed that many people needed care. Perhaps, then, the solution was not infrastructure, but rather a caring state.

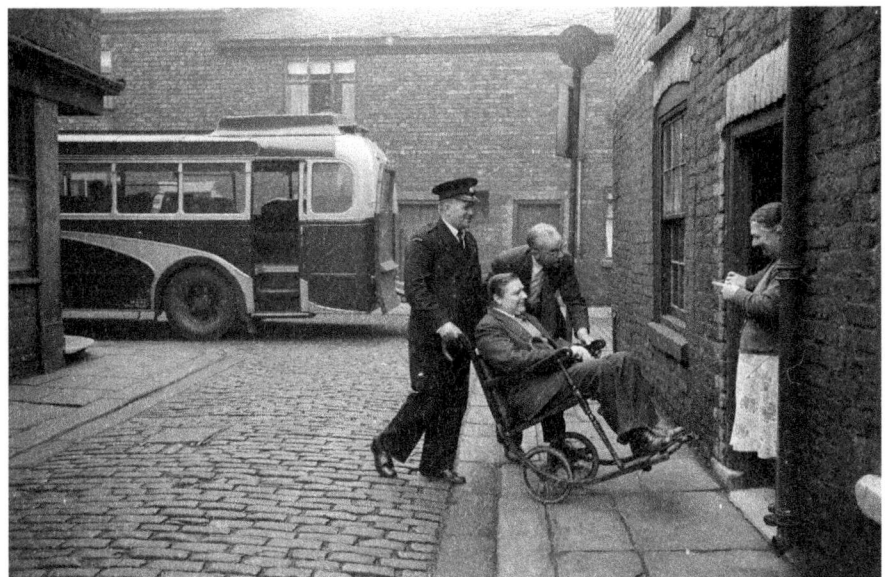

Figure 5.1 Harry Kerr. Goldsmith believed most wheelchair users required assistance leaving home (1956). Getty Images/Harry Kerr/Stringer.

From its three-wheeled cars to the wheelchairs provided by the government free of charge, the British system, Goldsmith would argue, demonstrated a "treat as different" approach that was fundamentally dissimilar to approach conceptualized in the United States. As Goldsmith would later say, "Tim Nugent was imbued with the firm moral values of Midwest America."[23] Nugent saw success for disabled people as deeply enmeshed with ideas of work, competition, and independence. At the University of Illinois, Goldsmith would later claim, Nugent "insisted that his handicapped students must be trained to compete equally with others for the rewards that America could bring; they must learn how to manage independently, and not be obliged to look to others to assist them to do what able-bodied people could do without personal help."[24] Goldsmith characterized this approach as "tough minded and demanding," and would eventually refer to the American attitude as mercilessly "treat as normal."[25] Goldsmith would argue that Nugent pushed the students in his rehabilitation program toward unrealistic goals; his ideas of complete independence were uncompromising and Nugent expected even the most severely disabled students be entirely independent in things like dressing, eating, and also toileting. "The discipline was apparent," Goldsmith observed. "If you miss the bus and don't get to your lecture, too bad—you won't make the same mistake again next time."[26] Most important, Nugent's study was skewed toward those who could meet his expectations. Those who could not adjust were turned down from the program, or subsequently were often forced to leave. With such specific standards, how could Nugent's findings be widely applied? The problem, Goldsmith insisted, was Nugent's method as well as his insistence on "a rigid independence criterion."[27]

The Problem with Independence?

In 1967, after completing his research in Norwich, Goldsmith thoroughly revised the second edition of *Designing for the Disabled*, rethinking specifications as well as the book's ethos. Goldsmith still believed that "architects design buildings to cater primarily for normal, able-bodied people, and concessions are rarely made for people who are not able-bodied."[28] But in a thirty-three-page commentary, he criticized the 1961 American Standard as "defective."[29] Implicitly, he challenged the previous publication's "unquestioned assumptions about the value of normality and independence."[30]

While American design standards were set to encourage independence, Goldsmith would argue, British standards could and should be different. In his view, "A criterion designed to guarantee maximum physical independence is not a critical necessity." Rather, it should provide for disabled people "more as a component of the overall social fabric" than as individual or independent entities.[31] Just before the publication of the second edition of *Designing for the Disabled*, Goldsmith felt it necessary to publicly explain why the ethos of the new book deliberately challenged the views expressed in the first edition. In "The Disabled: A Mistaken Policy?" an editorial published in the journal of the Royal Institute of British Architects (RIBA), Goldsmith explained his new position. The rhetoric around the American standards overemphasized the need to integrate disabled citizens into society so that they could work, compete, and gainfully contribute to society. Ultimately, Goldsmith argued, "The fundamental divergence on the issue of the evaluation of human worth is what ultimately isolates the philosophy of the American [approach] from the philosophy of Designing for the Disabled."[32]

But Goldsmith also questioned the practicality of many of the American recommendations. For example, he asked, how, "on a narrow and awkwardly graded site can the architect arrange a ramp that has a gradient not steeper then 1 in 12, has a 3 ft level platform at the top, a 6 ft straight clearance at the bottom, and level platforms at 30 ft intervals?" Similarly, "Is it realistic," he asked, to specify that "neither the internal depth nor width of a lift should ever be less than 5 ft?" Furthermore, Goldsmith took umbrage with the American insistence that accommodations be provided "without distinction." This, he adjured, "means that where such facilities are accessible and usable, they must not be identified as being convenient for people who use wheelchairs, since any admission by means of an identifying notice would draw attention to the differences and distinctions which are not supposed to exist."[33]

Once Goldsmith revised his opinions, he did not shy away from highlighting the differences that he perceived between these two approaches. He advanced the idea, for example, that public signage should accompany accommodations for disabled people. And in contrast to the American code's insistence that public toilets should have at least one stall dedicated to disabled people, he advocated for significantly larger, entirely separate toileting spaces for disabled people; rather than establishing a separate space within public restrooms, such segregated rooms could provide access as well to caregivers—even if they are of the opposite gender. Goldsmith's new design agenda was suffused with a new philosophy. As Goldsmith himself would later write, "imbued as I was with the social welfare ethos of England, the way to help disabled people had to be the 'for the disabled' way."[34]

The publication of Goldsmith's revision was contemporaneous with the 1964 election of a new and energetic Labour government. After thirteen years of Conservative rule, Prime Minister Harold Wilson led a charge to "refresh" the welfare state with a legislative agenda extending its reach to a variety of underprivileged or underrepresented groups. This new agenda opened the door for the widespread reception of Goldsmith's new approach. In fact, Goldsmith's text also brought this way of thinking to a whole generation of bureaucrats and government planners. *The Public Health Journal*, whose readers comprised a cross-section of government social workers, researchers, medical analysts, and other bureaucrats, claimed that new edition would be invaluable for local officials. "Mr. Goldsmith," the journal gushed enthusiastically, "has, in fact, put into the hands of the local authority's officers the means of solving most of the practical problems of daily living with which buildings confront both ambulant and the chair-bound disabled, and the philosophy of his approach is well in accord with 'modern thought' of rehabilitation."[35]

Goldsmith also introduced his evolving view of access more directly through the British Standard code of practice for architects. After Goldsmith published the first edition of *Designing for the Disabled*, Wycliffe Nobel, a consultant architect to the Central Council for the Disabled, approached the British Standards Institution to form a committee charged with shaping new building guidelines. Goldsmith was invited as the principal expert to draft specific material. Published in the same year as the second edition of *Designing for the Disabled*, the code drew heavily from Goldsmith's work. Though the guidelines (CP96 Access for the Disabled to Buildings) gave many general recommendations based on the 1961 American Standard A117.1, the British code departed from American strictures on several significant points. For example, Goldsmith introduced a model of public toilet reflecting his more "caring" belief that disabled people should benefit from special treatment. The CP96 toilet was separated from toilets available to the general population; one of these facilities had to be available in public spaces, was unisex and substantially larger than an American version. Essentially, they were designed to allow access not only to disabled people, but also to their caregivers.

More recently, the British government has moved away from a model of social welfare, but aspects of Goldsmith's design guidelines have survived. Though the specifications have been tweaked and altered somewhat—over time, the special toilets have become even larger—over 10,000 separate toilets for disabled people, for instance, remain in use across Britain today. Years after they were first installed, Goldsmith would proudly observe that, always "signposted at roadsides in towns and villages, they are scattered across urban and rural landscapes. In every public building ... there is at least one of them. In other buildings where there are public toilets, they have been fitted in. In or alongside historic buildings a place has been found for them. They have proliferated." "They are," he would declare, "an emblem of a caring society, of a society that is keen to help disabled people and likes to advertise how genuinely concerned it is to do so."[36]

Into the Mainstream

Goldsmith believed that design could change disabled people's circumstances—even their "disability" itself. But there was little precedent for how to realize such change. Goldsmith would always be proud of his studies, and his "unique resource of solid information and dates, not a medley of suppositions drawn from impressions, surmises, legend and mythology." Grounded as it was in scientific study, his approach—based on caring and segregation—was anything but neutral. And later, in the 1980s, he would come to disavow it.

When Selwyn Goldsmith ultimately issued a fourth and final version of *Designing for the Disabled* in 1997, he gave it a new subtitle, *The New Paradigm*, and issued a complete reappraisal of the American model. But he was rethinking his support of the welfare state approach as early as 1983. In an address to the American Environmental Design Research Association, Goldsmith asserted that "in the context of designing for the disabled we can discern that the self-help culture has a more practical approach than the social welfare culture."[37] This meant a reappraisal of the Invacar, the segregated toilets, and the other features of Britain's socially minded welfare culture. Prioritizing independence at all costs, for example, Goldsmith now argued that the American "self-help culture" "does not want special vehicles for the handicapped—it wants accessible bus and subway systems; it prefers for its public toilets for there to be a presumption of self-management."[38] In *Designing for the Disabled: The New Paradigm*, the book's fourth and final edition, Goldsmith went further. Here Goldsmith insisted that "America was bold where Britain, was cautious. America, the land of opportunities and civil rights, and a vision: from the start, from the day that the 1961 A 117.1 was launched, it was determined that its buildings could and should be made comprehensibly accessible to disabled people."[39] By 1997, when the book was finally published, Goldsmith had retired and was less active in British design circles. Many of his contemporaries had also retired—or died—and RIBA Publications, his earlier publisher, declined to issue this new edition. It was ultimately taken up by an entirely different publisher, Architectural Press.

Goldsmith was part of a burgeoning international barrier-free design movement that grew up in the years after the Second World War and this was a positive force for not only disabled people but all demographics. As Goldsmith himself would later put it, "there can be no dispute that conventionally designed buildings and facilities are inimical to disabled people, and that barrier-free environments must be beneficial" to all.[40] In spite of his changing opinions he helps us understand how approaches to designing for disability are intertwined with broader assumptions and practices. Even a seemingly transparent goal—providing a barrier-free environment—is more complex than what first meets the eye. By pegging these ideas to broader political agendas to design for disability, he proved that sensitivity to ideology is essential in understanding these practices. Above all, he made clear that design for disability is neither a simple nor a neutral practice.

Notes

1. Selwyn Goldsmith, "The Ideology of Designing for the Disabled," *Proceedings of the Fourteenth International Conference of the Environmental Design Research Association* (1983), 200.
2. Anonymous, "Times Diary," *The Times* (London), September 9, 1967, 10.
3. Goldsmith, "The Ideology of Designing for the Disabled," 198.
4. Selwyn Goldsmith, *Designing for the Disabled: The New Paradigm* (London: The Architectural Press, 1997), 22.
5. Ibid., 5.
6. Marshall Wall, *From Where I Sit, from Where You Stand: A Roll through Life* (Bloomington: AuthorHouse, 2007), 106.
7. See, for example, David Gerber, "Heroes and Misfits: The Troubled Social Reintegration of Disabled Veterans in the Best Years of Our Lives," in *Disabled Veterans in History*, ed. David Gerber, (Ann Arbor: University of Michigan Press, 2012).
8. Jameel Hampton, *Disability and the Welfare State in Britain* (Bristol: Policy Press, 2016), 34–35.
9. Brian Woods and Nick Watson, "In Pursuit of Standardization: The British Ministry of Health's Model 8F Wheelchair, 1948–1962." *Technology and Culture* 45, no. 3 (July 2004), 540–568.
10. Goldsmith, "The Ideology of Designing for the Disabled," 198.
11. Anonymous, "Designing for the Disabled," (book review) *The Lancet* 283, no. 7331(February 29, 1964), 484.
12. Sarah Rose, *No Right to Be Idle* (Chapel Hill: North Carolina State University Press, 2017).
13. Timothy Nugent, "A National Attack on Architectural Barriers," *New Building Research* (Fall, 1961), 59.
14. Ibid., 51.
15. Selwyn Goldsmith, *A Symbol for Disabled People* (London: RIBA, 1969), 76.
16. Goldsmith, *Designing for the Disabled: The New Paradigm*, 21.
17. Ibid., 38.
18. Ibid.
19. Leslie McIntyre, *Selwyn Goldsmith (1932–2011) and the Architectural Model of Disability: A Retrospective of the Man and the Model*, 2015, http://lesleymcintyre.com/the-selwyn-goldsmith-monograph/ (accessed February 15, 2017).
20. Goldsmith, *Designing for the Disabled: The New Paradigm*, 29.
21. Selwyn Goldsmith, P.J.R. B. Rostence Nicols, J. Angell, and L. Angell, "Designing a Public Convenience for the Disabled," *Rheumatology* 8, no. 8 (1966): 307.
22. Goldsmith, *Designing for the Disabled: The New Paradigm*, 42.
23. Ibid., 9.
24. Ibid.
25. Ibid., 39.
26. Ibid., 11.

27 Selwyn Goldsmith, "The Disabled: A Mistaken Policy," *RIBA Journal* (1967), 387.
28 Ibid.
29 Selwyn Goldsmith, *Designing for the Disabled* (London: RIBA, 1967).
30 Goldsmith, "The Disabled," 387.
31 Goldsmith, "The Ideology of Designing for the Disabled," 200.
32 Goldsmith, "The Disabled," 389.
33 Ibid., 388.
34 Goldsmith, *Designing for the Disabled: The New Paradigm*, 28.
35 Anonymous, "*Designing for the Disabled*," (book review) *Journal of Public Health* 82, no. 4 (1968): 192.
36 Goldsmith, *Designing for the Disabled: The New Paradigm*, 25.
37 Goldsmith, "The Ideology of Designing for the Disabled," 200.
38 Ibid.
39 Goldsmith, *Designing for the Disabled: The New Paradigm*, 90.
40 Goldsmith, "The Ideology of Designing for the Disabled," 199.

Bibliography

Anonymous. "Designing for the Disabled," *The Lancet* 283 no. 7331(1964), 484.
Anonymous. "Times Diary," *The Times*, (London), September 9, 1967, 10.
Gerber, David (ed). *Disabled Veterans in History*, Ann Arbor: University of Michigan Press, 2012.
Goldsmith, Selwyn. *Designing for the Disabled*. London: RIBA 1963.
Goldsmith, Selwyn, *Designing for the Disabled*. London: RIBA, 1967.
Goldsmith, Selwyn, *Designing for the Disabled: The New Paradigm*, London: Taylor & Francis, 1997.
Goldsmith, Selwyn, "The Ideology of Designing for the Disabled," *Proceedings of the Fourteenth International Conference of the Environmental Design Research Association* (1983), 198–214.
Goldsmith, Selwyn, Selwyn Goldsmith, P. J. R. Nicols, B. Rostence, J. Angell, and L. Angell, "Designing a Public Convenience for the Disabled," *Rheumatology*, 8 no. 8 (1966), 307–317.
Hampton, Jameel. *Disability and the Welfare State in Britain*, Bristol: Policy Press, 2016.
McIntyre, Leslie. *Selwyn Goldsmith (1932–2011) and the Architectural Model of Disability: A Retrospective of the Man and the Model* (2015) http://lesleymcintyre.com/the-selwyn-goldsmith-monograph/ (accessed 2/15/2017)
Nugent, Timothy. "A National Attack on Architectural Barriers," *New Building Research* (Fall, 1961), 51–66.
Rose, Sarah. *No Right to Be Idle*. Chapel Hill: North Carolina State University Press, 2017.
Wall, Marshall. *From Where I Sit, From Where You Stand: A Roll Through Life*. Bloomington: Author House, 2007.
Woods, Brian and Nick Watson, "In Pursuit of Standardization: The British Ministry of Health's Model 8F Wheelchair, 1948-1962." *Technology and Culture* 45 no. 3 (July 2004): 540–568.

6 Architecture, Science, and Disabled Citizenship

WANDA KATJA LIEBERMANN

Open Het Dorp

You have awakened something within us, within the people, namely, awareness of our fellow disabled citizens—not only those who will come and live in the Village but those living in our society.[1]

        Minister of Social Affairs Marga Klompé, November 23, 1962, *Open Het Dorp*

Although mostly forgotten now, in late November 1962, the Dutch people were captivated by the nation's original mass television spectacle, called *Open Het Dorp*. The object of this (first-ever) round-the-clock broadcast was soliciting funds to build a new residential community for 400 disabled people called Het Dorp (the Village) in Arnhem, in the eastern part of the Netherlands. The financial success of the telethon—21 million in total (57 million Euros in today's money)—was only one sign of the event's tremendous impact on postwar Dutch society. Indeed, *Open Het Dorp* and later television broadcasts about its development and occupation shaped cultural beliefs about disability, which occurred alongside debates about government welfare policy for disabled people. As significant, the cultural phenomenon of Het Dorp catalyzed a new national postwar identity which was entwined with the inclusion of disabled citizens into Dutch society. So influential was media coverage of Het Dorp that any meaningful analysis of Het Dorp's design must include the array of representations that brought it into being. Indeed, the influence of the ideas of citizenship, modern subjectivity, and normality embedded in these representations projected and reflected far beyond Het Dorp and disability.

    The Village was the invention of Dr. Arie Klapwijk, the director of the Johanna Foundation, a private secular charity founded in Arnhem in 1900 for the rehabilitation of disabled children and young adults.[2] His work there with young people with disabilities, and earlier with war veterans, convinced him that Dutch society had a responsibility to make spaces for them to live after completing their rehabilitation.[3] It was Klapwijk who enlisted the nascent technology of television and recruited celebrity television announcer Mies Bouwman to produce the telethon broadcast. Its moral and ideological message was that the creation of a self-sufficient village would for the first time extend modern Dutch society's rights and comforts to people with disabilities.

Imagining Dutch citizenship for disabled people was based on humanist concepts of the responsibilities and self-fulfillment of the liberal subject, a topic of intense political debate in the Netherlands at that time. While in pre-scientific times, disability was considered a sign of either an angered God or a divine gift, in the modern era, disability could be understood as a particular bodily lack, which could be compensated for by technological means. Het Dorp's very design would work on the body to make disabled citizens part of modern society.

The architect selected to design Het Dorp, Jaap Bakema, was the younger partner of the prominent Rotterdam firm Van den Broek and Bakema and a leading member of a group called Team 10 that opposed the orthodoxy of the dominant modernist architectural association, CIAM (Congrès International d'Architecture Moderne). His firm's considerable experience with large government housing and planning projects made it the clear choice among several Dutch architectural firms that had been inspired by the telethon to pledge their professional services. Bakema's belief that architecture should "arouse the needs of social justice, freedom and cooperation" aligned perfectly with the telethon's rhetoric.[4] Bakema himself developed the concept and drew sketches for this high-profile project. He presented the design in a broadcast called *Het Dorp van de Grond* (Het Dorp from the Ground), playing the role of architectural spokesperson. Media coverage like this showed the public how Het Dorp would combine architecture, modern science, and a new civic commitment to revalidate disabled Dutch citizens.

More than a half century later, one can see the product of these ideals along the Amsterdamseweg (Amsterdam Road), a ten-minute walk up from the Arnhem train station. Het Dorp's cluster of low-slung monolithic brick buildings, topped by yellow painted fascias, emerges below in a meadow with trees. The entrance to Het Dorp turns off the main road into a parking lot, edged by a few small shops, ending vehicular connection to the surrounding neighborhood. Its core consists of a commercial cluster bordering the Amsterdamseweg on one side and a brick-paved plaza in front of the main civic building, the Kerkelijk Kultureel Centrum (Church and Cultural Centre) on the other. Below, eight long red brick residential buildings extend down the slope to the site's lower periphery, bending here and there to form courts, creating intricate relationships between interior and open space.

Double Dutch Citizenship

Open Het Dorp's spectacle of secular spirituality was one of the first mass representations of disabled bodies in the Netherlands. As the title suggests, the broadcast introduced people with disabilities into civil discourse, defining a largely unrecognized group that lived mostly out of sight in private homes and institutions. Central to shaping the architecture of Het Dorp was how project proponents imagined people with disabilities. Throughout history, people with impairments have represented different things in different times and places, which determined how they were treated. Stiker's incisive *A History of Disability* traces the changing beliefs about and social conditions of disabled people from the Old Testament view of disability as the mark of human sin on the body, which the community must purge to ward off evil. By the early modern period, the rise of systems of charity made disabled people a source of salvation for the wealthy through good works.[5] The greatest transformation of the treatment of disabled persons began in the late eighteenth century with the introduction of the concept of rehabilitation, following the dramatic growth of scientific knowledge, development of professions, and industrial capitalism's reorganization of work and domestic space. The modern attitude toward disability is part of modernity's focus on the body as a site of improvement: modernity "offers the body as a lack, at the same time as it offers technological compensation."[6] With the advent of rehabilitation theories for disabled people came modern regimes and spaces for the isolation, treatment, and management of wayward bodies, as exemplified by Ebenezer Howard's utopian plan for the Garden Cities of Tomorrow, which located the Farm for Epileptics, Convalescent Homes, and Asylum for Blind and Deaf outside the Circle Railroad, among cow pastures and fruit farms.

Open Het Dorp succeeded by contrasting this special village with the tradition of isolating and marginalizing people with disabilities. The telethon, which featured Holland's most famous cabaret singers, bands, and comedians, performing in front of a live audience, was filmed at the newly opened Amsterdam RAI Convention Center. Shown on television and simulcast on the radio, it saturated Dutch airwaves. The Dutch term *televisie actie* (television action) accurately describes its improvisational and participatory character. People spontaneously organized local fundraisers and the intimate geography of the Netherlands made it possible for members of the public to attend the extraordinary event unfolding in Amsterdam. Groups lined up at the RAI stage to deliver their donations, often in traditional costumes of their trade or affiliation, like the "milkmaid" carrying metal buckets full of coins donated by a dairy farmers association.[7] As the telethon MCs pointed out repeatedly, participants represented all segments of Dutch society, unified by a single purpose: to build a village for their *invalide medeburgers* (disabled fellow citizens). In the aftermath Klapwijk received thousands of letters echoing sentiments like this man's: *Open Het Dorp* had given him "the rich feeling of being a Dutchman, that national feeling [he missed] so much."[8]

Joining television, the most modern of technologies, with nationalism in the creation of Het Dorp was key to modernizing Dutch society. *Open Het Dorp* and the subsequent decades-long media project on Het Dorp enlisted mass-society in material and affective investment in the project through which was constructed a new civic identity for the Dutch population. "Equating the television audience and the nation," Open Het Dorp cast the viewer as citizen and appealed to his sense of patriotism to play a role in the expansion of democracy through the inclusion of an excluded group into the state.[9] Participation in the telethon constituted citizenship as practice, not simply as membership status.[10] In the twenty-fifth anniversary broadcast, journalist Henk van der Meijden recalled: "You could call it mass psychosis, but this was mass psychosis for a good cause … That is why the entire country became one and that was a great success."[11] Meijden's reference to mass psychosis frames *Open Het Dorp* as the moral antidote to the mass enlistment of the public produced by earlier Nazi mass media techniques, and as a collective redemptive act at a time of heated debate about Dutch complicity in Nazi atrocities in the Netherlands.

In fact, the telethon symbolically produced a complicated double form of citizenship: a purified postwar Dutch citizen and disabled Dutch citizenship. People with disabilities were largely absent from the RAI stage. Instead, their story was presented in a documentary that opened the telethon, called Het Dorp Moet Er Komen (Het Dorp Must Come), which explained the plight of young people with disabilities.[12] The separation of physical and representational spaces of the RAI auditorium and the documentary demarcated the non-disabled contributor from the beneficiary of his generosity.[13] At the same time, the main argument for their inclusion was that despite their disabilities they were just like regular folk. Telethon images and other broadcasts featured young patients, prospective Het Dorp residents, engaged in a variety of physical activities and therapies, signaling the two related prerequisites for Het Dorp's residents, namely, their disabilities had to be "only" physical and not progressive.

Klapwik's provision of a founding constitution for Het Dorp, whose principles included, the right to privacy, the opportunity "to pursue useful occupations," and a "democratic right-of-say in our private and community lives," was predicated on a view of disabled villagers as capable of being self-governing subjects.[14] For the humanist ideals of the Dorp to be realized, the disabilities of its inhabitants should need only the prosthetic of the specially designed environment to restore autonomous subjectivity. Civic revalidation was only available to residents whose bodies were seen as responsive to rehabilitation.[15] People with intellectual or behavioral problems were (officially) excluded, as were those with progressive diseases, such as muscular dystrophy, because they contradicted the modernist teleology of progress through rehabilitation. To ensure the right population, prospective residents underwent a battery of medical exams and questionnaires designed to identify and eliminate people with mental, behavioral, and progressive infirmities from Het Dorp's resident pool.[16] A 1971 list of the medical diagnoses of residents appears to include only physical conditions, like cerebral palsy, polio, and spina bifida.[17] People diagnosed with developmental impairments were refused and instead sent to institutions like 's Koonings Jaght, founded in the 1920s, a few kilometers from Het Dorp.[18]

Rehabilitating Architecture

What will be the art of building an open society?

Jaap Bakema, quoted in Dirk van den Heuvel[19]

Het Dorp's rhetorical linkage of civic inclusion of people with disabilities with physically accessible environments rehearsed key political questions of this period. In the context of welfare state development, citizenship is characterized by the creation of social programs that involve the government directly in the well-being of the people through the provision of basic necessities, like housing and health care.[20] By the mid-twentieth century, citizen-building had joined rehabilitation as two parts of the same postwar political project in Europe, one in which modernist architects and urban designers played key roles. *Open Het Dorp* coincided with a drawn-out parliamentary debate in the Netherlands about how far social support systems should be extended.[21] Disabled people were the last group to receive benefits under a relatively slow-developing social welfare system that eventually included the General Act on Exceptional Medical Expenses (Algemene Wet Bijzondere Ziektekosten, or AWBZ) of 1968 and the 1976 Public Disability Act. These programs shifted support of disabled people from charity to the state, based on citizenship rather than on employment. Although *Open Het Dorp* predated these, it undoubtedly helped produce a kind of disability in the "image of honorable entitlement" without which "no decent welfare policy can emerge."[22]

The war raised doubts among architects about the adequacy of modern architecture to address the material and social needs of a democratic society and its citizens.[23] This was compounded by the postwar proliferation of state-sponsored technocratic housing developments which sparked criticism of the strict functionalism of powerful CIAM. Team 10 was an influential group of architects, led by Bakema and Alison and Peter Smithson, who in the late 1950s broke away from CIAM, based on a rejection of the universal application of functionalist and rationalist values it prescribed. Instead, they argued that architecture should respond to the individual through attention to the specific culture, identity, and meaning of a place, based on natural and social science research.[24,25] As his firm's leading intellectual figure, *Forum* editor, and prominent Team 10 voice, Bakema espoused a humanistic alternative against a political backdrop that included fascism's intolerance, the escalating Cold War, and technocratic government building programs.[26]

A 1968 broadcast, *Dialoog in Het Dorp*, explained that "the goal [of the Village] is to give these residents the feeling of belonging and not being an outsider of society."[27] Both housing and, with the advent of social assistance laws, flourishing health care architecture played important roles in the project of inclusion.[28] From hospitals and clinics to old people's homes, new typologies were developed, stimulated by new government programs. Drawing on new scientific theories from environmental behaviorism, social psychology, and ergonomics, architects such as Bakema devised new spaces tailored to user needs and tendencies, with the aim of bringing about socially harmonious and productive behaviors for the betterment of society.[29] Rehabilitation discourse, which was both medical and administrative, intersected with the social science orientation of Team 10 and with Bakema's ideas about architecture's social role "as a technology of healing," applied here to both the individual body and society as a whole.[30]

The new architecture made the architect an agent for interpreting the needs of users, which would be defined by new expertise, including that of the users themselves. The inclusive rhetoric of the *Open Het Dorp* broadcasts joined the empirical evidence that the participation of prospective residents brought to the design process with Bakema's psychological theories of space. From the start, a group of future residents served on several planning and design committees, whose ideas were publicized in an exhibition in the nearby town of Zeist.[31] They mostly influenced the design of the living units. Equating spatial privacy with the development of individual identity, Bakema believed that the nucleus of the personal unit would offer residents an interior life—for the first time, for many. Bakema's group collaborated with Klapwijk's team of patients and physiotherapists to determine space requirements such as the ideal bedroom and bathroom for a single person. This method was integrated into Bakema's usual design approach of proceeding from the interior outward, a strategy he infused with psychological concepts, which later became common in institutional design.[32] Building on an elder housing unit prototype, designers considered how to accommodate the residents' special ambulatory and dexterity needs as well as spatial requirements for caregivers. After developing ideas on paper, the architecture team constructed a full-scale model of a typical unit in a shed in Arnhem, probably in the Johanna Foundation workshop.[33] The result was a typical room, approximately 12 by 20 feet, containing a bathroom next to the entry, a bed and living area, and a small galley kitchen with large doors or windows opening onto verdant views (Figure 6.1).

Dirk van den Heuvel observes that "industrial and technological innovation was key in making the Western European welfare state a reality."[34] This line of thought might be extended further. At Het Dorp, careful design was essential to Het Dorp's larger vision of a wheelchair-accessible community, which owed a great debt to applied sciences. Irving Zola, an American sociologist who conducted research at Het Dorp in the early 1970s, called the village "a tribute to modern technology and what could be done to make life livable" for people with disabilities.[35] Disabled bodies offered an opportunity for technological intervention, framed as social progress by the contradictory terms of the telethon. Indeed, its liberal ideological foundations depended on the concept that careful design can eradicate disability by remaking the dependent disabled body in the image of the "autonomous and unitary male subject of modernity."[36] To that end, the design team combined and modified technologies to tailor the buildings to the inhabitants. Residential units included open kitchen undercounters, grab bars, roll-in showers, adapted toilets, and specially mounted fixtures geared to seated, wheeled residents. Roads without curbs and entrances without thresholds, steps, or stairs created continuous access. More sophisticated features, like automatic overhead door closers and radio transmitters integrated into building surfaces, enabled residents to manage interior environments, including curtains, lights, and television, through communication between wheelchair control consoles and architecture.

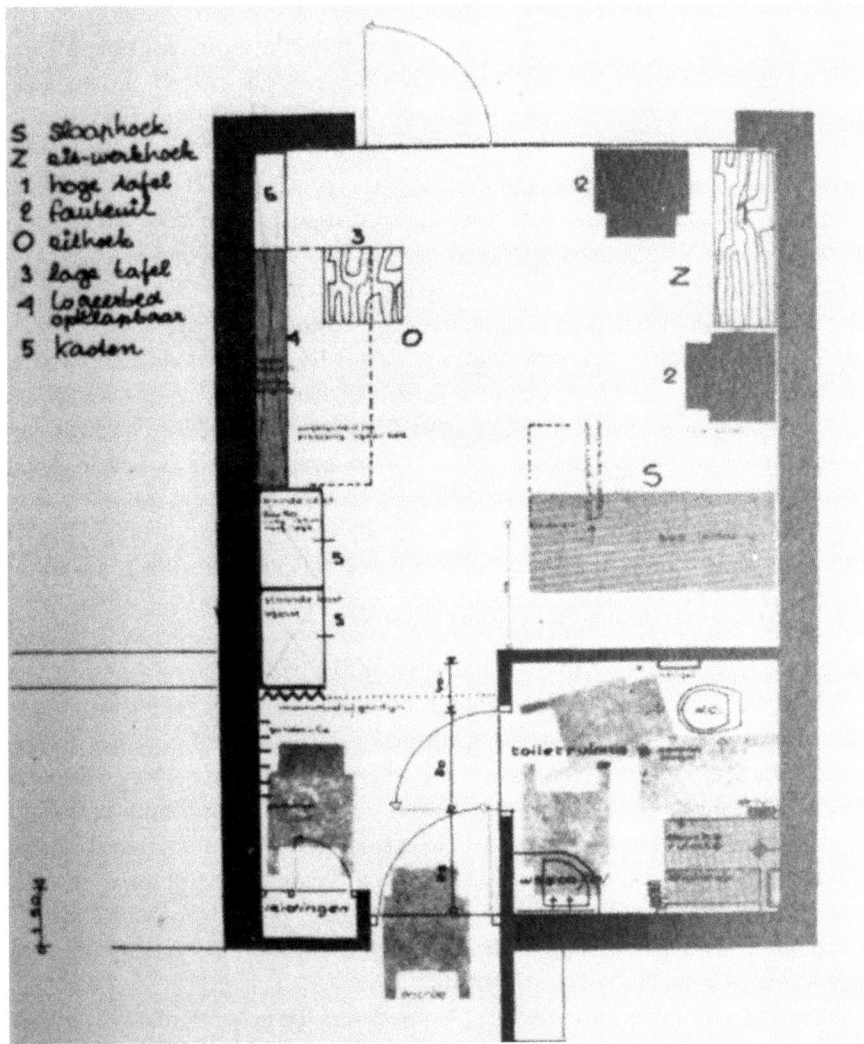

Figure 6.1 Typical original residential unit plan, with wheelchair stamp, Het Dorp, Arnhem, the Netherlands, Van den Broek and Bakema, 1963–1965.

Village as Citizen Technology

Technical solutions to problems are less painful than solutions that require political or social changes.[37]

(Rudi Volti, *Society and Technological Change*)

Klapwijk envisioned a community that would give disabled inhabitants "active democracy .... Now they can make their own decisions here in the Village about everything that happens to them."[38] Klapwijk said at another time: "If we can develop more means in the sense of modern technology, which would make the physically handicapped as independent as possible, … then we can turn 'making people happy' into a reality."[39] This was a radical break from the top-down order of the institutions of the past, and the discourse of self-governance, instead of paternalistic oversight, was the basis for several important symbolic and design decisions. To foster a vibrant democratic society, architects at this time, particularly Team 10 members, used a variety of sociospatial ideas and scales like the habitat, the street, and the core, to inform the design of buildings and urban environments like Van den Broek and Bakema's Kennemerland Regional Plan, 1957–9, and Bakema/Opbouw's Alexanderpolder expansion of Rotterdam.[40] The idea of a democratic community harmonized with Van den Broek and Bakema's strategy of decentralizing large developments into nonhierarchical polycentric communities, building on the neighborhood model (*wijk gedachte*), which was a particularly influential concept in postwar Dutch design circles. For Het Dorp, the neighborhood concept was realized through two related organizational ideas: the "street" as an independent social unit and the decentralized site plan, which responded to the terrain to produce a spatial order of nonhierarchical and varied spaces—decidedly anti-panoptic.

Perhaps the most consequential gift of the *Open Het Dorp* telethon was the anonymous contribution of a sixty-five-acre wooded parcel, in Arnhem, that would serve as the site for the project. The site's rugged topography—it rose ninety feet from end to end and was split by a ravine filled with mature trees—meant Bakema's main challenge at Het Dorp was developing a unified and poetic strategy for wheelchair mobility. The challenge of wheelchair access on this terrain was amplified by the desire to minimize dependence on elevators, which, during power failures, trapped vulnerable people on upper floors.[41] In addition, Bakema's theosophical belief that enlightenment is available through direct experience with nature spurred a design that enabled even wheelchair users to experience "living under the trees … living against the trees."[42] This meant preserving both trees and ground, because substantially cutting or filling the existing terrain would destroy "the cathedral" of the tree canopy as experienced from the ravine floor.[43]

Combining Bakema's environmental philosophy with the project's mobility requirements, the design team translated the neighborhood concept into long, low-rise buildings that follow the site downward from the Amsterdamseweg in a zigzag configuration. In order to create uninterrupted floor planes for wheelchair movement, Het Dorp's scheme fused Van den Broek and Bakema's typical segmented geometrical arrangement into continuous structures, or "stacked streets." Bakema oriented these in the direction of the slope instead of perpendicular to it, so that the buildings traverse a considerable elevation change, thereby providing direct entry at different exterior points. The stacked streets, or *wegen*, exploit and organize the sloping site. From top to bottom, the change in grade adds floor levels, or streets, making each story accessible from different points along the slope, so that "every floor was a ground floor."[44] Maintaining uniform rooflines across the site resulted in one-story structures framing intimate outdoor spaces on the upper end of the site, while buildings grow to three and four stories at the lower end of the site.

The concept of the street as a sociospatial unit, like neighborhood and habitat, derived in part from the growing influence of the social sciences in postwar architecture. Renewed interest in the street as a site of social vitality had inspired Alison and Peter Smithson's "streets-in-the-air" design for Golden Lane housing, which was presented at the 1953 CIAM conference at Aix-en-Provence, where it generated a great deal of discussion.[45] For Het Dorp, Bakema had floors and walls of his "stacked streets" finished in (donated) brick, simulating a historical Dutch streetscape, that wrapped the exterior of the building and continued into the interior. His idea was that the "internal streets have recesses [that] will look as if they give access to little houses," creating an inverted and diminished version of "regular" neighborhoods.[46] Living units let directly onto the streets, and units for live-in caregivers were located at the corners. Midway along the street, a common room called the *resto* serves as the main gathering point for meals and other activities, reproducing in miniature a node of collective living around a town square. Wheelchairs, "scoot mobiles," bicycles and kick scooters (used by young staff members to travel the streets), and electric recharging cable stands are located along the street.

The "street" design combined new technical and science-based ideas with Bakema's interpretations of how architecture should address the needs of people with disabilities, particularly wheelchair users. For example, strategically located curved corners responded to the turning radius of wheelchair locomotion, though this idea also derived from concepts of "natural movement patterns of the human occupants as they walked or rolled down the hallways," something that Joy Knoblauch notes was in the air for new healthcare institution design infused by social science methods.[47]

Unlike the open residential walkways or galleries of projects like the 1950s design for Golden Lane Housing, however, Het Dorp's "street" is an interior space. The ceiling measures only 2.2 meters (7 feet 3 inches) above the floor, based on a belief that the vantage point of wheelchair users demanded a lowered ceiling to reproduce "normal" visual and spatial experience.[48] Bakema's belief that wheelchair users were visually deprived by their limited vantage point prompted him to design streets with abrupt corners, which he believed would offer the mental stimulus of "shifting vistas."[49] But combined with multiple exits to stairs and the outside, these corners make the *wegen* hard to regulate. Moreover, upon completion of the first residential structure, brick floors proved to be too uneven for wheelchair locomotion, so they were soon refinished in linoleum, diminishing the intended outdoor feeling.

Nevertheless, influence of the street on Het Dorp's social structure and life is profound. Caregiving is organized by street, and until recently each had a "team leader" who managed the street staff. Resident-elected street presidents co-manage the street-level (*bewoners overleg*) meetings of the Village council. With the enactment of universal disability insurance, disability benefits began to be pooled for each street rather than allotted to the central administration or individual clients. Residents often live for decades in their original apartments, cementing their identification with their street, each of which has developed distinct rules and atmosphere. They refer to where they live exclusively by street name, such as Stroperweg and Vogelaarweg (Poacher Way and Birdwatcher Way), as if they were spatial entities separate from the building envelope, and in contrast to administrative buildings which are known by building names, such as Dorpsbrink (Village Green).

Modernizing as Normalizing

In this way, normalization describes a double movement: on the one hand homogenizing and aggregating individuals into a population, on the other distributing and identifying differences between them.

> Peter Cryle and Elizabeth Stephens, *Normality: A Critical Introduction*, 8

Throughout the broadcast the public repeatedly heard that Het Dorp would be a "real" village, signaling that Het Dorp was going to be a regular, albeit materially accommodated, community of civically engaged individuals. In the opening documentary of the *Open Het Dorp* telethon, its future inhabitants were presented simultaneously as *gewone mensen* (regular people) and *invalide medeburgers* (disabled fellow citizens). This complicated dialectic of normal and not-normal citizenship was reflected in the telethon's visual and spatial compartmentalization and of course in the village solution itself. Normal and normality are concepts that emerged in the postwar consciousness, with the advent of the "commercial use of anthropometric data."[50] This notion did not only force normative standards on subjects, but produced the "flexible body," one that proved adaptable to new conditions and change. Het Dorp's symbolic order depended on the social inclusion of disabled citizens on these "normal" terms. The telethon promised that the Village would enable people with disabilities to live independently, a vision which required an image of a particular disabled person, or type of disability, in an adapting and remediating relationship with architectural technologies. The idea being that the not-normal could be restored to normalcy and membership through (and only within) Het Dorp's design. That the Village was *not* "normal" was evident from a few basic facts. First, its genesis as a charitable initiative disclosed that it wasn't a regular residential community; if it had been, it would have received public funding under the Housing Act. Facilities like Het Dorp weren't state subsidized until the passage of AWBZ several years later. In addition, the land donated for the Village was already zoned for social purposes (*maatschappelijke doeleinden*), a designation that permitted only education- and care-related development.[51] The paradox was summed up by a remarkable statement that Irving Zola found in an early planning document: "Though, of course, formally and officially Het Dorp is a subsidized establishment for the treatment and nursing of physically handicapped persons, for the sake of its inmates, its character will avoid any resemblance, both in its architecture and in its organization to an institute."[52]

Media depictions of the residents as "normal" people doing familiar daily activities, like hosting coffee parties, attending council meetings, and taking smoking breaks

Figure 6.2 A resident applying lipstick, looking in an angled mirror, Van den Broek and Bakema, 1963–1965.

obscured this paradox. Always well-groomed and neatly dressed, their portrayal emphasized the conventionality of their appearance, behavior, and aspirations. In particular, enactments of stereotypical gender and labor roles normalized the residents. For example, an extended scene in the 1968 television special *Dialoog in Het Dorp* showed an attractive young woman carefully selecting, testing, and purchasing a lipstick in downtown Arnhem and then cut to a long close-up of her face reflected in her home bathroom mirror, mounted at the precise downward angle needed for her position in her wheelchair (Figure 6.2). In this scenario, adapted designs enable her to achieve typical feminine appearance within her own home. Along similar lines, project architect Ab Van der Vet explained in colorful prose in a 1971 journal interview that Het Dorp's residents were just like everyone else in their expectations of home: "someone just wants to be able scratch himself without being seen and go to bed with a woman without being heard."[53] Images like these linked domestic privacy, independence, gender conformity, and heterosexual desire with the normalized body.

Reforming disabled people into normal productive members of society through paid work was another theme of television broadcasts and publicity events. Some early residents did hold regular jobs outside Het Dorp such as in a local furniture factory[54]; others labored in the sheltered workshop located in a large building, the *werkplaats Heijenoord*, built for this purpose on the site's perimeter. Klapwijk and Bijleveld emphasized how specially modified work stations, such as looms adapted for foot operation, enabled residents to participate in the market economy. A law requiring that disabled bodies be capable of at minimum one third the productivity of a "normal" body to qualify for employment in the workshop meant that only a fraction of village residents worked there.[55] These failures led to the demolition in 1996 of the workshop. Zola and other critics regarded the sheltered workshop as a place where the gap between the "normal" bodies projected by the village and its real bodies was most evident. It also signaled the limits of a purely design solution within the larger social, economic, and political circumstances that village inhabitants faced.

Media broadcasts insisted that Het Dorp was a "real" village, understood in terms of both its self-sufficiency (and that of its inhabitants) and its integration with surrounding Arnhem. For example, the commercial core, which originally included a gas station, an office of the ANWB (similar to the American Automobile Association), a pub, a post office, a supermarket, and a hairdresser, served, in Bakema's terms, as "in-between" space linking public and private, new and old, and parts to the whole, something which Bakema argued was key to living in an open, heterogeneous society.[56] Dependent on customers from both Het Dorp and outside, the shops were designed to both buffer and foster encounters between inside and outside worlds, between disabled and able-bodied populations.[57] Concept diagrams show this space as mediating between *valide* and *invalide* populations, which required careful social engineering to overcome fear of and prejudice against disabled villagers, something W. P. Bijleveld, Het Dorp's first director (1966–78) compared to integrating black and white families in US residential neighborhoods.[58] At the same time, Het Dorp proponents and administrators pointed to these shared amenities, the Village's central location close to downtown Arnhem, and the lack of physical enclosure separating it from the surrounding neighborhoods as indicative of the Village's "realness," or normality. Yet, what differentiated this from Bakema's usual designs was that Het Dorp inverted the typical order. By design, the "familiar" was located outside Het Dorp and the "other" contained within.

The normal/not normal paradox mirrors the tension in postwar modern liberal states of the process of "creation and maintenance of a homogenous nation" while also bestowing civic status to groups on the basis of a differentiated identity.[59] Homogenization and differentiating operated at every scale of Village representation and design. Scenes of residents going about their daily activities in the halls and apartments of the village were a common feature of early Het Dorp media broadcasts. Images focused on the minutiae of the inhabitants' interactions with practical designs, like gliding through automatic doors and operating foot-pedal faucet controls. Film techniques, like long takes and replays, gave the Dutch public intimate glimpses into the ways that wheelchair users worked with designs that integrated building, wheelchair, and body. Portrayals suggested that the material environment, from lipstick to automatic door opener, enrolled the residents as normal members of a modern democratic society.

News coverage omitted or glossed over numerous important aspects of Het Dorp life and administration. For example, it was not widely known that Het Dorp also accommodated 400 day and live-in staff and that residents required medical services that were located off-site.[60] Het Dorp also included mandated marriage restrictions, the sheltered workshop (where residents did mindless, repetitive tasks for a pittance), and counseling against childbearing aimed at curtailing the reproduction of residents. These policies and patterns, which Mitchell and Snyder describe as part of the landscape of eugenics, lived alongside values and practices of emancipation and self-determination.[61] In the end, Het Dorp reveals a modernist design that embeds both liberal and eugenicist values, demonstrating that instead of standing in opposition, they are in many ways part of the same master narrative of modernity.

Conclusion

Het Dorp's symbolic potency rested on the concept of transforming disabled people into modern liberal subjects using architectural and industrial design combined with soft sciences in order to rehabilitate their bodies into an order of normal. Disability as a formalized classification is a kind of post-Enlightenment disqualification.[62] But the overarching village narrative was that healing the nation could be achieved by healing these "invalid" bodies, thereby requalifying them as citizens, through specific remediating relationship with architectural technologies. In the context of the public sorting out of the Dutch role as both victim and accomplice under Nazi occupation, maintaining the modern belief that social progress was achievable through design and technological transformation depended on two things. First, responding to evil war machinations, technology and society must be mutually rehabilitated by applying technology to a humane purpose. And second, Het Dorp had to be seen as a break with the (hidden) brutish history of isolating and murdering disabled persons. Instead, I have argued elsewhere, its modern spaces transparently displayed the disabled body, plugged into customized design solutions.[63]

These contradictions demand a more nuanced analysis, one in which the cultural power of normality is a highly contested and contingent concept. At Het Dorp, design produced both a disciplinary and a liberatory condition. That is to say, design was used to make villagers appear as both normal and not-normal at the same time. While it did not disrupt the binary of normal and not-normal, the Village attests to design's increasing role in the expanding inclusiveness of liberal democratic states.

Notes

1 The *Open Het Dorp* archive consists of eight broadcasts. Only around two hours of the original broadcast was preserved, including the closing ceremony, but several additional segments of the original telecast were included in later televised programs, such as the 25th Anniversary Program.

2   Wanda Katja Liebermann, "Humanizing Modernism? Jaap Bakema's Het Dorp, a Village for Disabled Citizens," *Journal of the Society of Architectural Historians* 75, no. 2 (2016): 158–159.
3   Irving Kenneth Zola, *Missing Pieces: A Chronicle of Living with a Disability* (Philadelphia, PA: Temple University Press, 1982), 9.
4   Francis Strauven, "The Dutch Contribution: Bakema and Van Eyck," *Rassegna* 14, no. 52 (December 1992): 51.
5   Henri-Jacques Stiker, *A History of Disability* (Ann Arbor: University of Michigan Press, 1999), 30, 87.
6   Tim Armstrong, *Modernism, Technology, and the Body: A Cultural Study* (Cambridge: Cambridge University Press, 1998), 3.
7   *Open Het Dorp: 26 en 27 November 1962*. Television program, AVRO.
8   Ibid.
9   Anna McCarthy, *The Citizen Machine: Governing by Television in 1950s America* (New York: New Press, 2010), 9.
10 Gershon Shafir, ed., *The Citizenship Debates: A Reader* (Minneapolis: University of Minnesota Press, 1998), 11.
11 Henk van der Meijden, *Open Het Dorp: 26 en 27 November 1962*, 25th Anniversary Program. He wrote something similar in an article, "Small People with Big hearts," soon after the telethon. He contextualized the telethon as a repudiation of the destructive "mass psychosis" roused by Nazi propaganda uses of media.
12 The documentary *Het Dorp Moet er Komen*, which opened the original telethon, exists today only in parts in some of the later programs.
13 Paul K. Longmore, "Conspicuous Contribution and American Cultural Dilemmas: Telethon Rituals of Cleansing and Renewal," in *The Body and Physical Difference: Discourses of Disability*, ed. David T. Mitchell and Sharon Snyder (Ann Arbor: University of Michigan Press, 1997), 134–160.
14 Zola, *Missing Pieces*, 10. The use of the first person, plural personal pronoun in this pronouncement formulated by Dr. Klapwijk and his colleagues, speaking in the voices of the residents sounds like a usurpation or introjection of agency.
15 See Helen Meekosha and Leanne Dowse, "Enabling Citizenship: Gender, Disability and Citizenship in Australia." *Feminist Review* 57, Citizenship: Pushing the Boundaries (Autumn 1997): 49–72, for a detailed discussion of traditional conceptions of citizenship for disabled people.
16 Zola, *Missing Pieces*. See also a description from a medical point of view in Metz, Willem. *Het Dorp: Menselijk Welzijn En Lichamelijk Gebrek* (Nijkerk, The Netherlands: Callenbach, 1970).
17 Zola provides a list of diagnoses of residents in his book, in Zola, *Missing Pieces,* 15.
18 Annemargreet Meurs, longtime Het Dorp managing psychologist, author interview, Het Dorp, The Netherlands, May 12, 2010.
19 Dirk van den Heuvel, "Towards an Open Society: The Unfinished Work of Jaap Bakema," in *Open: The Work of Jaap Bakema*, ed. Arjen Oosterman, Dirk van den Heuvel, and Brendan Cormier Venice Biennale Exhibit, Rotterdam: Het Nieuwe Instituut, 2014.

20 Kenny Cupers, *The Social Project: Housing Postwar France* (Minneapolis: University of Minnesota Press, 2014). See also James Holston, *Cities and Citizenship* (Durham, NC: Duke University Press, 1999).
21 Robert Henry Cox, *The Development of the Dutch Welfare State: From Workers' Insurance to Universal Entitlement* (Pittsburgh, PA: University of Pittsburgh Press, 1993), 114.
22 Shafir, *The Citizenship Debates,* 115.
23 Sarah Williams Goldhagen and Réjean Legault, "Introduction: Critical Themes of Postwar Modernism," in *Anxious Modernisms: Experimentation in Postwar Architectural Culture*, ed. Sarah Williams Goldhagen and Réjean Legault (Cambridge, MA: MIT Press, 2000), 13.
24 Max Risselada, Dirk van den Heuvel, and Architectuurinstituut Nederlands, *Team 10: 1953–81: In Search of a Utopia of the Present* (Rotterdam: NAi, 2005), 249.
25 CIAM's demise and Team 10's rise have been well documented by Eric Mumford and others. Eric Paul Mumford, *The CIAM Discourse on Urbanism, 1928–1960* (Cambridge, MA: MIT Press, 2000). Annie Pedret, *Team 10: An Archival History* (London and New York: Routledge, 2013); Risselada and Van den Heuvel, *Team 10*.
26 Earlier that year an exhibit of Van den Broek and Bakema's work titled "The Architecture of an Open Society" opened at the Rotterdam Museum Boymans-van Beuningen. Bakema frequently framed lectures in this period with the question, "what will be the art building an open society?" See Dirk van den Heuvel, "Towards an Open Society: The Unfinished Work of Jaap Bakema," Supplement to *Volume* #41, *Open: The Work of Jaap Bakema* (Venice Biennale Exhibit, 2014).
27 Henk Neijssel, the narrator, makes this statement near the beginning of the program. *Dialoog in Het Dorp*, AVRO, television broadcast, September 16, 1968.
28 Noor Mens and Cor Wagenaar, *Health Care Architecture in the Netherlands* (Rotterdam: NAi, 2010), 85–92.
29 Ibid., 86.
30 Joy Ruth Knoblauch, *Going Soft: Architecture and the Human Sciences in Search of New Institutional* Forms, *1963–1974*. PhD Dissertation, Princeton University, 2012, 47.
31 Zola, *Missing Pieces,* 32; J.F. Het Dorp resident, author interview, May 9, 2010.
32 Knoblauch, *Going Soft,* 19.
33 Frans Hooykaas, author interview, Rotterdam, The Netherlands, August 31, 2010. Hooykaas, van den Broek and Bakema employee from 1961 to 1990, was trained as an architect but worked largely as an illustrator, on a wide variety of projects in the office. His longtime position as Bakema's assistant brought him into close contact with Bakema, whom he accompanied on his travels to Team 10 and other meetings, and teaching assignments abroad. Hooykaas was a consultant to the 2014 "Open: The work of Jaap Bakema" Venice Biennale Exhibit, organized by the Jaap Bakema Study Centre based at Het Nieuwe Instituut in Rotterdam
34 Van den Heuvel, "The Open Society and Its Experiments," 140.
35 Zola, *Missing Pieces*, 97.
36 Bill Hughes, "Wounded/Monstrous/Abject: A Critique of the Disabled Body in the Sociological Imaginary," *Disability & Society* 24, no. 9 (2009): 402.

37 Rudi Volti, *Society and Technological Change*, 2nd ed. (New York: St. Martin's Press, 1992), 18.
38 *Open Het Dorp*, AVRO, television broadcast, May 30, 1970.
39 Arie Klapwijk, remarks in *Het Dorp kwam er*, AVRO, television broadcast, November 27, 1967.
40 Mumford, *The CIAM Discourse on Urbanism*, 206.
41 Hooykaas, author interview.
42 J.B. Bakema, *From Doorstep to City: A Story about People and Space* (Zeist, The Netherlands: Uitgeversmaatschappij W. de Haan N.V., 1964), 10.
43 Hooykaas, author interview.
44 Ibid.
45 Mumford, *The CIAM Discourse on Urbanism*, 235.
46 Het Dorp van de grond, AVRO, television broadcast, 1966 (no further date information available).
47 Knoblauch, *Going Soft,* 36.
48 *Dialoog in Het Dorp*. Also, Hooykaas, author interview.
49 Selwyn Goldsmith, "Het Dorp," *Architectural Review* 149, no. 4 (April 1971): 230.
50 Peter Cryle and Elizabeth Stephens, *Normality: A Critical Genealogy* (Chicago, IL, and London: University of Chicago Press, 2017), 354.
51 Hans Pepers, Siza Corporation director of property development, author email correspondence, follow-up to interview, March 5, 2012, Het Dorp, The Netherlands; Minke Geurts, Siza Corporation manager of development, email correspondence with author, December 10, 2012.
52 Zola, *Missing Pieces,* 27. The quote is not footnoted; I presume the translation is Zola's.
53 "Het Dorp: A Village for the Handicapped in Arnhem, Netherlands," *Plan: Maandblad voor ontwerp en omgeving*, 4 (1971): 57.
54 H.W., Het Dorp resident, author interview, Het Dorp, The Netherlands, March 4, 2012.
55 Zola, *Missing Pieces,* 29.
56 Van den Heuvel, "The Open Society and Its Experiments," 134.
57 Ibid.
58 W.P. Bijleveld, interview in "Het Dorp: A Village for the Handicapped in Arnhem, Netherlands," 56–57.
59 Shafir, *The Citizenship Debates*, 16, 18.
60 Zola, *Missing Pieces*, 156.
61 David Mitchell and Sharon Snyder, "The Eugenic Atlantic: Race, Disability, and the Making of an International Eugenic Science, 1800–1945," *Disability & Society* 18, no. 7 (2003): 846.
62 Ibid., 859.
63 Liebermann, Wanda Katja, "Rehabilitating the Invalid Body: Architecture and Citizenship in Jaap Bakema's Design for a Dutch Postwar Village for the Disabled," in *Architecture and the Body, Science and Culture*, ed. Kim Sexton (New York: Routledge, 2018), 196–216.

Bibliography

Armstrong, Tim. *Modernism, Technology, and the Body: A Cultural Study*. Cambridge: Cambridge University Press, 1998.

Bakema, Jacob Berend. *From Doorstep to City: A Story about People and Space*. Zeist, Netherlands: Uitgeversmaatschappij W. de Haan N.V., 1964.

Cox, Robert Henry. *The Development of the Dutch Welfare State: From Workers' Insurance to Universal Entitlement*. Pittsburgh: University of Pittsburgh Press, 1993.

Cryle, Peter, and Elizabeth Stephens. *Normality: A Critical Genealogy*. Chicago, IL: University of Chicago Press, 2017.

Cupers, Kenny. *The Social Project: Housing Postwar France*. Minneapolis: University of Minnesota Press, 2014.

"Dialoog in Het Dorp." Television program. AVRO, 1968.

Goldhagen, Sarah Williams, and Réjean Legault. "Introduction: Critical Themes of Postwar Modernism." In *Anxious Modernisms: Experimentation in Postwar Architectural Culture*, ed. Sarah Williams Goldhagen and Réjean Legault. Cambridge, MA: MIT Press, 2000.

Goldsmith, Selwyn. "Het Dorp." *Architectural Review* 149, no. 4 (1971): 227–236.

"Het Dorp: A Village for the Handicapped in Arnhem, Netherlands." *Plan: Maandblad voor ontwerp en omgeving* 4 (1971): 54–70.

"Het Dorp Kwam Er." Television program. AVRO, 1967.

"Het Dorp Van De Grond." Television program. AVRO, 1966.

Holston, James. *Cities and Citizenship*. Durham, NC: Duke University Press, 1999.

Hughes, Bill. "Wounded/Monstrous/Abject: A Critique of the Disabled Body in the Sociological Imaginary." *Disability & Society* 24, no. 9 (2009): 399–410.

Knoblauch, Joy Ruth. "Going Soft: Architecture and the Human Sciences in Search of New Institutional Forms, 1963–1974." PhD Dissertation, Princeton University, 2012.

Liebermann, Wanda Katja. "Humanizing Modernism? Jaap Bakema's Het Dorp, a Village for Disabled Citizens." *Journal of the Society of Architectural Historians* 75, no. 2 (2016): 158–81.

Liebermann, Wanda Katja. "Rehabilitating the Invalid Body: Architecture and Citizenship in Jaap Bakema's Design for a Dutch Postwar Village for the Disabled." *Architecture and the Body, Science and Culture*, ed. Kim Sexton, 196–216. New York: Routledge, 2018.

Longmore, Paul K. "Conspicuous Contribution and American Cultural Dilemmas: Telethon Rituals of Cleansing and Renewal." In *The Body and Physical Difference: Discourses of Disability*, ed. David T. Mitchell and Sharon Snyder, 134–60. Ann Arbor, MI: University of Michigan Press, 1997.

McCarthy, Anna. *The Citizen Machine: Governing by Television in 1950s America*. New York: New Press, 2010.

Meekosha, Helen, and Leanne Dowse. "Enabling Citizenship: Gender, Disability and Citizenship in Australia." *Feminist Review* 57, Citizenship: Pushing the Boundaries (1997): 49–72.

Metz, Willem. *Het Dorp: Menselijk Welzijn En Lichamelijk Gebrek*. Nijkerk, Netherlands: Callenbach, 1970.

Mitchell, David, and Sharon Snyder. "The Eugenic Atlantic: Race, Disability, and the Making of an International Eugenic Science, 1800–1945." *Disability & Society* 18, no. 7 (2003): 843–864.

Mumford, Eric Paul. *The CIAM Discourse on Urbanism, 1928–1960*. Cambridge, MA: MIT Press, 2000.

Mens, Noor. and Cor Wagenaar. *Health Care Architecture in the Netherlands*. Rotterdam: Het Nieuwe Instituut/NAi, 2010.

"Open Het Dorp: 26 en 27 November 1962." Television program. AVRO, 1962.

"Open Het Dorp: 26 En 27 November 1962, 25th Anniversary Program." Television program. AVRO, 1987.

Pedret, Annie. *Team 10: An Archival History*. London and New York: Routledge, 2013.

Risselada, Max, Dirk van den Heuvel, and Architectuurinstituut Nederlands. *Team 10: 1953–81: In Search of a Utopia of the Present*. Rotterdam: NAi, 2005.

Shafir, Gershon, ed. *The Citizenship Debates: A Reader*. Minneapolis: University of Minnesota Press, 1998.

Stiker, Henri-Jacques. *A History of Disability*. Ann Arbor, MI: University of Michigan Press, 1999.

Strauven, Francis. "The Dutch Contribution: Bakema and Van Eyck." *Rassegna* 14, no. 52 (1992): 48–57.

Van den Heuvel, Dirk. 'Towards an Open Society: The Unfinished Work of Jaap Bakema'. *Open: The Work of Jaap Bakema*, ed. Arjen Oosterman, Dirk van den Heuvel, and Brendan Cormier. Venice Biennale Exhibit, Rotterdam: Het Nieuwe Instituut (2014).

Volti, Rudi. *Society and Technological Change*. New York: St. Martin's Press, 1992.

Zola, Irving Kenneth. *Missing Pieces: A Chronicle of Living with a Disability*. Philadelphia, PA: Temple University Press, 1982.

7 Disability and Modern Chemical Sensitivities
DEBRA RILEY PARR

In the United States, the Clean Air Act of 1963 put forth the promise of a nationwide check on air pollution, in recognition of devastating regional impacts and the necessity to manage air quality on the largest scale possible. This legislation, with significant additions in 1970 and 1990, aimed to regulate specific sources of air pollution such as factories and automobiles, but also to ensure reductions in the overall levels of pollution in ambient, or open air. Prior to 1963, the Air Pollution Control Act of 1955 afforded federal resources for research concerning air pollution, but despite the word "control" in its title, this act did not authorize federal actions or programs to regulate air pollution.[1] Historians point to two critical events prompting the US Congress to begin grappling with deteriorating air quality: the 1948 Donora smog event that caused twenty deaths and respiratory problems for more than 6,000 people in Pennsylvania and the 1952 devastating smog tragedy in London that caused more than 3,000 deaths throughout the UK.[2]

The twentieth century made disability modern by designing more physically accessible buildings and better-functioning prosthetics; at the same time, this century also contributed to the expectation of clean, odor-free environments enabling all people to access clean air, to breathe freely. By the time that the Clean Air Act was passed, many designers, architects, and theorists had already addressed the desire for clean air, especially in response to the polluted air brought about by the Industrial Revolution of the nineteenth century. In *Towards a New Architecture,* Le Corbusier presents an argument for a modern architectural revolution and condemns the state of early-twentieth-century housing, writing, "The machine that we live in is an old coach full of tuberculosis."[3] He writes also that everyone realizes the need "of sun, of warmth, of pure air and clean floors."[4] Similarly, in the late 1920s, International Style architect Richard Neutra built the renowned Lovell Demonstration Health House, a modernist domestic space in the foothills of Los Angeles where the desire for healthful air circulation and hygiene determined design decisions as much as Neutra's innovative use of steel for framing the house.[5] Several decades later, sociologist Pierre Bourdieu notes in *Distinctions: A Social Critique of the Judgement of Taste* that the expectation of "no smell" firmly registers in the habitus of the bourgeoisie.[6] Reflecting the modern aspiration to sweep clean the past, the ideal of "no smell" suggests a deeply ingrained expectation to breathe freely and to encounter no obstructions to this bodily action.

As evidenced in these few examples, pure, clean, and unscented air became a conscious design ideal in the twentieth century, marking a stark value shift in comparison with the previous century. By the 1960s and 1970s, with mass actions, such as the first Earth Day on April 22, 1970, demanding a government response to environmental pollution, the formation of the Environmental Protection Agency in December 1970, and the passage of critical amendments to the 1963 Clean Air Act, a refocused attention to the right to breathe emerged, overlapping with the Disability Rights consciousness of the 1970s and subsequent decades. Historian Hsuan Hsu has argued that over the last two centuries far from being a universally accessible resource, air increasingly becomes a fraught site of political struggle given the uneven distribution of airborne pollutants and their uneven production of what Hsu describes as "contested geographies of health, productivity, and power."[7] The fight to ensure equal access to clean air is a modern—and ongoing—response to the very conditions brought about by modernity, including modern chemical sensitivities that make breathing difficult and precarious. The term "multiple chemical sensitivity" (MCS) emerged during the 1980s as a descriptor for a complex of symptoms in the work of Mark Cullen, a physician and professor of Occupational Medicine at Yale University.[8] These symptoms include a range of adverse reactions to airborne chemicals in the environment, including nasal congestion, headaches, fatigue, inability to concentrate, memory loss, among more lethal reactions such as seizures and anaphylaxis. For Cullen and others, MCS raises an urgent question: What is to be done when some populations can breathe freely while others inhale air that threatens their very lives?[9]

The Clean Air Act put forward a legal argument distinguishing the right to breathe as a fundamental human right, anterior to life, and now recognized and protected by international and national organizations.[10] The United Nations issued guidelines urging all governments to regulate and protect the air as a common, shared resource necessary for life.[11] From the time we are born until the time we die, we are collectively breathing and smelling the world around us with every breath. People with anosmia, an inability to detect odors, still inhale aromatic molecules, even if they remain undetected. Indeed, many airborne chemicals have no odor and cannot be detected by the olfactory system, but this fact hardly lessens the impact of their effects as they travel through the body. The argument here is that on the other end of the spectrum, people with sensitivities to what might be breathed in—detectable or not by the human olfactory system—must be guaranteed access to an environment free of impediments to breathing.

The association of bad air with disabling and sometimes deadly effects is hardly new, even if the understanding of what constitutes good or bad air has changed over time. Early medical practice theorized that deadly epidemics such as the bubonic plague were transmitted through urban miasmas breathed in while in the vicinity of those stricken with such diseases. In *The Foul and the Fragrant*, Alain Corbin charts the city of Paris's municipal acts and legislative responses to this powerful, if often erroneous, belief that bad odors were dangerous to humans. The hypothesis that the repugnant odors of the city contributed directly to the bad health of its inhabitants later proved to be false in the case of many communicable ailments, but the careful regulation of air that resulted from such ideas functioned as the beginning of the need to guarantee access to something none of us can live without.

This right to breathe gained urgency as modernity brought new technological advances, mass production, increasing reliance on petrochemicals, and innovation in the design and manufacturing of textiles and building materials. With the rise and expansion of modern industrialization, many of the molecules drawn into the body with each breath were often rife with toxic effects, and more intensely so in urban spaces. Despite the nose's great capacity to act as a filter, the breathing body in such environments becomes laden with unhealthy and often deadly particulates. As modernity reshaped the environment, pollutants inhaled through the nose attacked the body in the form of black lung, asthma, and other respiratory conditions. In 1869, George Miller Beard published a paper about the side effects of modern innovations such as "the steam engine, telegraph, printing press, and the higher education of women."[12] Notably, one of the side effects he pointed to was a condition he termed "neurasthenia." Fresh air was often the remedy for a diagnosis of this "nervous weakness"—and Beard along with other doctors of the period prescribed excursions to the country, away from the polluted cities in order for patients to breathe freely. In the nineteenth and twentieth centuries, the effects of air pollution in industrialized, coal-burning cities like London and Pittsburg became visibly dangerous, with particulates in the air often causing the environment to be thick with dark, noxious smogs.

A Contested Condition

However, what of the governance and regulation of the micro-environments of the contemporary work place, schools, and homes, many often tightly enclosed spaces with air controlled by powerful heating, ventilation, and air conditioning (HVAC) systems? The modern push described by Corbin to clear cities of stenches produced by humans, animals, and industrial activities prompted the design of new methods of waste management and early iterations of indoor ventilation systems. The contemporary goal of achieving healthy indoor air quality (IAQ) remains critical, often managed behind the scenes and invisible to inhabitants of most indoor spaces. Linda L. Nussbaumer in her research with regard to interior design, quoting the Environmental Protection Agency, notes: "One class of chemicals that triggers [MCS] symptoms is volatile organic compounds (VOC), which are 'compounds that vaporize (become gas) at room temperature.'"[13] Chronic exposure even to low levels of indoor pollution can produce a range of responses from the annoying and debilitating to the lethal.

The widely varying symptoms associated with MCS contribute to its status as a still contested condition. It is generally agreed that over the past seventy-five years, MCS has emerged as a bodily response to problematic air quality and to the increasing presence of chemicals in the air. One question still hovering over the medical diagnosis and treatment of MCS is whether this condition is physical or psychological, or a complex psychosomatic combination of responses to airborne toxins. Also in question is the status of MCS as a chronic illness or disability. Disability is defined as a "physical or mental impairment that substantially limits one of more of the 'major life activities' of the impaired individual."[14] The Americans with Disabilities Act defines "major life activities" as activities that the "average person" has no difficulty performing, such as "caring for oneself; performing manual tasks; walking; seeing; hearing; speaking; breathing; learning; and working."[15] With respect to the life activity off breathing, MCS overlaps with other diagnoses of ailments like asthma and allergies that limit the ability to breathe, but may not be classified as disabilities. Anthropologist of medicine and technology, Danya Glabau, writes of what she terms as the "hygienic sublime," in her analysis of food allergies that like MCS are also "difficult to understand and manage."[16] She acknowledges the struggle of achieving a level of purity that guarantees safety:

> Part of what is "sublime" about the hygienic sublime is its very status as an unattainable, yet deeply desired, state of affairs. The clean, volatile organic compound (VOC)-free and nut-free kitchen, the meticulously researched ingredient supply chain, the homegrown vegetables free of commingled grain or vegetable contaminants: these are the best expressions of the hygienic sublime. Seeking or convincingly performing the hygienic sublime has the power to instill feelings of responsibility and safety while reducing the risk of allergic reactions toward zero.[17]

MCS similarly prompts actions to mitigate complex environmental conditions that are almost impossible to manage at the level of the personal.

Comprising a range of disparate physical indicators, MCS was first recognized in 1945 as allergic toxemia, and in 1950, Illinois allergist Theron Randolph, founder of the Society of Clinical Ecology, proposed it as a distinct disease. Albert H. Donnay of MCS Referral and Resources, however, cites much earlier, suggestive literary descriptions of MCS in Edgar Allen Poe's stories from the nineteenth century, including "The Fall of the House of Usher" (1839) and "The Tell-Tale Heart" (1843).[18] The main characters of these narratives suffer from afflictions that seem produced by an atmosphere composed of a "pestilent and mystic vapor or gas, dull, sluggish, faintly discernible and leaden-hued."[19] Donnay speculates that Poe seems to be describing the toxic IAQ produced by illuminating gas, a noxious mix of coal, carbon monoxide, toluene, and other volatile organic compounds used to light interior spaces and capable of causing what Poe labels as "overacuteness of the senses."[20]

In his stories, Poe casts this condition as physical, not psychological, although the symptoms in the narratives present themselves in a confounding way, as they continue to do even today. Ellen Goudsmit's and Sandra Howes's critical evaluation of MCS provocation studies concludes that many "have overstated the role of psychological factors in the aetiology of MCS."[21] Albert Donnay, in his review of the literature, reports that "there are more than twice as many peer-reviewed articles, books, and book chapters that support an organic interpretation of MCS as compared to a psychogenic or iatrogenic view."[22]

A Disabling Condition?

While the Clean Air Act was passed in 1963 to limited effect, the 1990 signing of the Americans with Disabilities Act (ADA) has extended its implications. Recent legal interpretations of the ADA have begun to recognize MCS, also referred to as idiopathic environmental intolerance or environmental illness, as a physical condition warranting accommodations. These might include providing better ventilation systems and HEPA (high efficiency particulate air) filters, instituting no-fragrance policies, and using less toxic cleaning products, among others. However, legal claims are often denied as being unreasonable as a matter of law. Andrew K. Kelley offers an insightful review of failed cases, most of which interestingly involved the problem faced in the workplace by people sensitive to tobacco smoke.[23] His conclusion is that given the three separate titles of the ADA, many MCS claimants have found it impossible to meet the criteria laid out in the Act. They had difficulty demonstrating that they were disabled and also that the accommodation they sought was reasonable.[24] In 1997, however, the Social Security Administration of the United States issued a court memorandum officially recognizing MCS "as a medically determinable impairment" on an agency-wide basis, acknowledging that some people with MCS are too disabled to be meaningfully employed. For those with MCS who can and want to keep working, however, Kelley recommends claimants should focus on their *impaired ability to breathe*, not on an impaired ability to work:

> By focusing on an inability to breathe properly in the presence of odors found in the workplace, a plaintiff with MCS can claim that he or she is disabled ... By framing MCS properly as a condition which substantially limits the major life activity of breathing, a plaintiff with MCS can pass the critical initial barrier to an ADA claim.[25]

Nonetheless, even those claimants who won "reasonable" accommodations such as being provided with an air purifier, not sitting next to a smoker, or having access to a window, the right to breathe could only be fully guaranteed by passing legislation making it specifically illegal to smoke in the workplace. In this sense, second-hand smoke could be considered a modern production of disability and the anti-smoking legislation constitutes an important step in the ongoing struggle to assert that in addressing disability the environment must be redesigned rather than perceiving the individual with a disability as needing somehow to be "fixed."

Smoking is now illegal in most indoor spaces, but exposure to airborne chemicals, perfumes, and other fragrant materials remains a particular concern for those with MCS. According to recent research, 80 percent of those with MCS report sensitivities to fragrances, creating barriers that prevent access to air that is necessary for life. As discussed by Bess Williamson, access "holds the curious distinction of being seemingly easy to define and comprehend, but difficult to create."[26] It seems logical to create deliberately fragrance-free zones, as in the case of the city of Halifax, Nova Scotia, the University of California, Los Angeles, or as the public libraries in southern

California have done by forbidding the use of perfume or fragrance that might interfere with librarians' ability perform their duties.[27] Many conferences and other events presenting research on disability require that venues hosting them observe as much as possible a fragrance-free policy. The right to breathe air free of *any* fragrance is complicated, however, by several factors. First by their very nature, smells cannot be easily controlled or contained. Secondly, there is a considerable lack of understanding—even now in the twenty-first century—of how the human olfactory system works. Additionally, seemingly unlikely things like furniture, flooring, building materials, carpeting, printers, and many others that are not readily associated with fragrances are off-gassing into the environment. Off-gassing occurs when any material—solid or liquid—releases volatile organic compounds into the air, including toxic chemicals such as formaldehyde, chloroform, acetone, ozone, benzene, among many others. Moreover, as artist and scent scholar, Matt Morris, notes in his writing about olfactory art, the implementations of such anti-fragrance policies "are not neutral and often disadvantage workers whose cultural backgrounds are characterized by fragrant cuisines, religious practices, and home lives that are not easily appreciated or assimilated into mainstream (read: white) American social space. Indeed, the use of the concept 'freedom' from scent here is especially charged, enacted as it is alongside mounting xenophobia in the Unites States and abroad."[28] The policing of odor certainly has a long history in the establishment and maintenance of white supremacist tactics of identifying and excluding the other, and should be of concern. But, are these the odors being targeted by recent bans on fragrance in public spaces, or does fragrance prohibition primarily call into question the environmental risks of synthetically composed and manufactured products, such as perfume, soaps, laundry detergents, and fabric softeners that distribute airborne inhalants, aligning these fragrances not with the odors produced by cooking or the body but with toxic cigarette smoke that propelled the anti-smoking campaigns of the recent past?

Furthering the contested status of MCS, Michael Fallace and Richard Long argue that it should be excluded from the ADA on the grounds that it is simply too difficult to assess the condition in comparison to what they call "traditional" disabilities. They assert that providing accommodations can prove costly and ineffective as in the case of the "ecology house," designed and built by Kodama Architects in the late 1990s for the Department of Housing and Urban Development in Marin County, California. The housing project promised residents suffering from MCS a chemical-free environment.[29] According to Fallace and Long, this promise proved impossible to deliver. They cite this project as prompting a backlash against providing traditional accommodations like curbs and ramps. Additionally they point to intolerance toward fragrance prohibitions as in the case of a student at the University of Minnesota threatening to wear "a heavy dose of perfume" while attending classes as a protest to the ban.[30] Again, Andrew K. Kelley's emphasis on the legal power of asserting one's right to breathe reminds us that what is at stake here is breathing, having access to air free of contaminants and debilitating chemicals.

Recent European Union (EU) regulations banning traditional materials used in perfumery exacerbate the issues with fragrance bans, given that plants like oakmoss and animal excretions including musk extracted from the endangered muskdeer have been historically critical components in many accords, perfumed compositions of many natural and/or synthetic substances. The EU's primary concern with such materials, however, lies in the potential for contact allergies affecting the skin, not with the potential respiratory effects of airborne molecules like the banned atranaol and chloroatranol.[31] However, the Environmental Working Group (EWG) reports that while many popular perfumes, colognes, and body sprays contain trace amounts of natural essences, they also typically contain a dozen or more potentially hazardous synthetic chemicals, some of which are derived from petroleum. To protect trade secrets, makers are allowed to withhold fragrance ingredients, so consumers can't rely on labels to know what hazards may lurk inside a new bottle of perfume.[32] The Lung Association of Canada notes that scents are "usually made from a mixture of natural and man-made chemicals. A typical fragrance can contain between 100 to 350 ingredients. The problem with scented products is not so much the smell itself as the chemicals that produce the smell." The association cautions: "Even products labeled 'unscented' or 'fragrance-free' may actually contain fragrances used to mask the smell of certain ingredients. Health Canada has specific rules about how companies can use these words on their labels. According to its labeling regulations, 'fragrance free' or 'unscented' means that there have been no fragrances added to the cosmetic product, or that a masking agent has been added in order to hide the scents from the other ingredients in the cosmetic."[33] In 2017, Proctor & Gamble (P&G), a formidable corporation in the production of scented products, pledged more transparency in its use of fragrance. A press release on their website indicates that by 2019, the company would share online "all fragrance ingredients down to 0.01 percent for its entire product portfolio in the U.S. and Canada by the end of 2019, which includes more than 2000 fragranced products. P&G is the first company to commit to this level of fragrance ingredient detail across such a broad product portfolio."[34]

An Alert to Danger

As logical as it might be to restrict the use of fragrances and to make transparent the ingredients in such products however, I would like to situate the current debate about the uncertain status of MCS as a disability in the larger context of modern environmental degradation of the air and water. MCS seen in this context becomes a sign of the modern threat to the environment and of the imminent environmental collapse brought about by the anthropocenic industrialization of the planet. The United Nations 2019 report on the alarming rate at which species are becoming extinct confirms the ecological damage we face.[35] Our olfactory capacities, as under-educated and under-acknowledged as they may be, are at least widely credited with having the role of alerting humans to danger: the smells of rotten food or natural gas or fire function as clear warnings to be heeded. Indeed, the cultivation of one's sense of smell could be a critical survival skill in the face of further environmental ruin. Humans must learn to recognize the olfactory signs of this situation. Could the olfactory capacities of people with MCS which render them acutely incapacitated while inhaling chemical-laden air serve as a warning to us all about the state of the commons, the shared resource of air, along with water, which all of us depend upon to live? Political geographer Marijn Niewenhuis writes, in a provocative essay (entitled "A Right to Breathe"), of the pressing need to address the state's role in cutting off the breath of citizens, either through deadly police chokeholds or in the use of teargas to control unruly people. Eric Garner's final words as he suffered at the hands of the police resonate, "I can't breathe." The state, Niewenhuis argues, disciplines and punishes by such "police-sanctioned deprivation of air."[36] However, he goes on to extend this argument to a wider consideration of the modern state's complicity in creating the conditions by which air is polluted "with the toxic chemicals of 'progress' and 'development.'"[37] The US Center for Disease Control reports a significant rise in childhood asthma especially in urban environments and in under-resourced neighborhoods.[38] Modern technology can be seen as a boon, of course, to the production of important accommodations like amazingly designed prosthetics, concrete smoothness, digital interfaces, and air purifiers. However, along with these contributions to making disability modern, the effects of modernity with respect to environmental degradation are hardly salubrious, but rather can be seen (and smelled) as a cause of disability.

Niewenhuis writes, "I am not referring here only to the physiological and medical consequences of global warming, which of course beyond any rational doubt are lethal, but I am also referring to the pollution of the air more widely which makes breathing difficult."[39] In addressing the violent actions that impede the breathing subject's access to air, he also posits that air is more than a site of political struggle and must be seen as a "medium that unifies and overcomes difference. What makes bodies strong and intimate. I inhale the air you exhale. The air constitutes a politics that is radically democratic, free and equal. We constantly exchange the medium that makes us."[40] Ensuring access to clean air to those with MCS will accrue benefits to all beings, and needs to happen at the most planetary scope.

While the Clean Air Act represented a step forward and brought new force to these issues for the first time, its more recent implications remain fraught. To draw a definitive conclusion about MCS as a disability may be contentious and difficult. Access to clean, scent-free air remains a struggle in this contemporary moment where the impacts of industrialization and the dependence on petrochemicals manifest unevenly across the globe. Instituting and respecting fragrance bans constitute local, short-term remedies benefiting populations whose sensitivities are triggered by acute, proximate exposure to chemicals. However, given the chemical-laden environment that has been produced in the last two centuries, access to chemical and scent-free air cannot be guaranteed. This situation, far from the modern utopia of clean air, is especially true for populations living in geographies where the right to breathe is precarious and increasingly a concern of environmental activists. The work to achieve the modernist desire for clean air requires further research as well as contemporary commitments to design better, more widely available materials, to fight to protect the commons that supports all living beings, and to design environments that cease to produce *modern* chemical sensitivities. The urgency for action cannot be overstated.

Notes

1. For a clear outline of US legislation regarding air pollution, see https://www.epa.gov/clean-air-act-overview/evolution-clean-air-act
2. https://www.epaalumni.org/hcp/air.pdf
3. Le Corbusier, *Towards a New Architecture* (New York: Dover Publications, 1986), 277.
4. Ibid., 277.
5. Notably, Los Angeles at this time produced one-fifth of the US oil supply, and while air pollution did not become a major threat in the city until after the Second World War, many of the wells in production at the time Neutra designed the Lovell Health House are still in operation today or are capped and buried, and as City Lab notes are "prone to seeping toxic gases." See Emily Badger, "One of the Most Disturbing Maps of Los Angeles You Will Ever See," City Lab, June 18, 2013. https://www.citylab.com/life/2013/06/one-most-disturbing-maps-los-angeles-youll-ever-see/5933/
6. Pierre Bourdieu, *Distinctions: A Social Critique of the Judgement of Taste* (Cambridge, MA: Harvard University Press, 1984).
7. Hsuan Hsu, "Olfactory Art, Transcorporeality, and the Museum Environment," *Resilience: A Journal of Environmental Humanities* 4, no. 1 (Winter 2016): 1–24.
8. Mentioned in Linda L. Nussbaumer, "Multiple Chemical Sensitivity: The Controversy and Relation to Interior Design," *Journal of Interior Design* 30, no. 2 (2004), 51–65. See also, Mark R. Cullen, "Workers with Multiple Chemical Sensitivities," *Occupational Medicine State of the Art Reviews*, 1987.
9. For an overview of MCS, see https://health.gov/environment/mcs/I.htm
10. In the course of my research, I found much inspiration for the assertion that there is a right to breathe in an essay by Marijn Niewenhuis.
11. See, for example, the United Nations recently published 2018 messages from the *Emissions Gap Report* providing the scientific underpinning for the UN 2019 Climate Summit. http://wedocs.unep.org/bitstream/handle/20.500.11822/26896/EGR-KEYMESSAGES_2018.pdf?sequence=1&isAllowed=y
12. Albert H. Donnay, "On the Recognition of Multiple Chemical Sensitivity in Medical Literature and Government Policy," *International Journal of Toxicology* 18 (1999): 384.
13. Nussbaumer, "Multiple Chemical Sensitivity: The Controversy and Relation to Interior Design," np.
14. Andrew K. Kelley, "Sensitivity Training: Multiple Chemical Sensitivity and the ADA," *Boston College Environmental Affairs Law Review* 25, no. 2 (Winter 1998).
15. Ibid.
16. Danya Glabau, "The Purity Politics of Food Allergic Living." https://danyaglabau.com/2017/03/31/the-purity-politics-of-food-allergic-living/

17 Ibid.
18 Donnay, "On the Recognition of Multiple Chemical Sensitivity in Medical Literature and Government Policy," 383.
19 Ibid.
20 Ibid.
21 Ellen Goudsmit and Sandra Howes, "Is Multiple Chemical Sensitivity a Learned Response? A Critical Evaluation of Provocation Studies," *Journal of Nutritional and Environmental Medicine* 17, no. 3 (September 2008): 195.
22 Donnay, 385.
23 Kelley, "Sensitivity Training: Multiple Chemical Sensitivity and the ADA," np.
24 Ibid.
25 Ibid.
26 Bess Williamson, "Access," *Keywords for Disability Studies* (New York: New York University Press, 2015): 15..
27 Mike Reicher, "Newport Beach Approves New Library Rules," *Los Angeles Times*, July 11, 2012. http://www.latimes.com/tn-dpt-0712-library-20120711-story.html
28 Matt Morris, "Through Smoke and across Dissent: Power Plays with Perfumery," *The Seen* 1, no. 8 (April 2019): 126–132.
29 Ecology House website last updated 1999. http://www.tikvah.com/cc/eh/misstmt.html
30 Michael Fallace and Richard Long, "Why Multiple Chemical Sensitivity and Related Conditions Should Be Excluded from the Americans with Disabilities Act," *Labor Law Journal*, February (1997): 66–80.
31 Astrid Wendlandt and Pascale Denis, "EU Commission Propose Tighter Regulation of Perfume Ingredients," Reuters Market News (February 13, 2014). https://www.reuters.com/article/lk-perfume-eu/eu-commission-proposes-tighter-regulation-of-perfume-ingredients-idUSL5N0LI4BQ20140213
32 Roddy Scheer and Doug Moss, "Scent of Danger: Are There Toxic Ingredients in Perfumes and Colognes?," @Earthtalk, Scientific American, nd. https://www.scientificamerican.com/article/toxic-perfumes-and-colognes/
33 https://www.lung.ca/lung-health/air-quality/indoor-air-quality/scents
34 https://news.pg.com/press-release/pg-corporate-announcements/pg-expands-transparency-commitment-include-fragrance-ingred (August 30, 2017).
35 https://www.un.org/sustainabledevelopment/blog/2019/05/nature-decline-unprecedented-report/
36 Marijn Nieuwenhuis, "A Right to Breathe," *Critical Legal Thinking: Law and the Political* (January 19, 2015). http://criticallegalthinking.com/2015/01/19/right-breathe/
37 Marijn Nieuwenhuis, "The Terror in the Air," Open Democracy (December 21, 2014). https://www.opendemocracy.net/en/terror-in-air/
38 J.E. Moorman, L.J. Akinbami, C.M. Bailey, et al. "*National Surveillance of Asthma: United States*, 2001–2010. National Center for Health Statistics," *Vital Health Stat* 3, no. 35 (2012). http://cac.websitetesturl.com/wp-content/uploads/2014/05/CDC-National-Surveillance-2001-2010.pdf

39 Nieuwenhuis, https://www.opendemocracy.net/en/terror-in-air/
40 Nieuwenhuis, https://www.opendemocracy.net/en/terror-in-air/

Bibliography

Badger, Emily. "One of the Most Disturbing Maps of Los Angeles You Will Ever See." *City Lab*. June 18, 2013. https://www.citylab.com/life/2013/06/one-most-disturbing-maps-los-angeles-youll-ever-see/5933/

Bourdieu, Pierre. *Distinctions: A Social Critique of the Judgement of Taste*. Cambridge: Harvard University Press, 1984.

Cullen, Mark R. "Workers with Multiple Chemical Sensitivities." *Occupational Medicine State of the Art Reviews* 2, no. 4 (1989) Hanley & Belfus, Philadelphia, 655–662.

Donnay, Albert H. "On the Recognition of Multiple Chemical Sensitivity in Medical Literature and Government Policy." *International Journal of Toxicology* 18 (1999), 384.

Fallace, Michael and Richard Long. "Why Multiple Chemical Sensitivity and Related Conditions Should Be Excluded from the Americans with Disabilities Act." *Labor Law Journal* February (1997): 66–80.

Goudsmit, Ellen and Sandra Howes. "Is Multiple Chemical Sensitivity a Learned Response? A Critical Evaluation of Provocation Studies." *Journal of Nutritional and Environmental Medicine* 17, no. 3 (September 2008): 195.

Hsu, Hsuan. "Olfactory Art, Transcorporeality, and the Museum Environment." *Resilience: A Journal of Environmental Humanities* 4, no. 1 (Winter 2016), 1–24.

Kelley, Andrew K. "Sensitivity Training: Multiple Chemical Sensitivity and the ADA." *Boston College Environmental Affairs Law Review* 25, no. 2 (Winter 1998).

Le Corbusier. *Towards a New Architecture*. New York: Dover Publications, 1986.

Moorman, J.E., L.J. Akinbami, C.M. Bailey, et al. "*National Surveillance of Asthma: United States*, 2001–2010. National Center for Health Statistics." *Vital Health Stat* 3, no. 35 (2012). http://cac.websitetesturl.com/wp-content/uploads/2014/05/CDC-National-Surveillance-2001-2010.pdf

Morris, Matt. "Through Smoke and across Dissent: Power Plays with Perfumery." *The Seen* 1, no. 8 (April 2019): 126–132.

Nieuwenhuis, Marijn. "The Terror in the Air." *Open Democracy*. December 21, 2014. https://www.opendemocracy.net/en/terror-in-air/

Nieuwenhuis, Marijn. "A Right to Breathe." *Critical Legal Thinking: Law and the Political*. January 19, 2015. http://criticallegalthinking.com/2015/01/19/right-breathe/

Nussbaumer, Linda L. "Multiple Chemical Sensitivity: The Controversy and Relation to Interior Design." *Journal of Interior Design* 30, no. 2 (2004): 51–65.

Reicher, Mike. "Newport Beach Approves New Library Rules." *Los Angeles Times*. July 11, 2012. http://www.latimes.com/tn-dpt-0712-library-20120711-story.html

Scheer, Roddy and Doug Moss. "Scent of Danger: Are There Toxic Ingredients in Perfumes and Colognes?" @Earthtalk, Scientific American. nd. https://www.scientificamerican.com/article/toxic-perfumes-and-colognes/

Williamson, Bess. "*Access*." *Keywords for Disability Studies*. New York: New York University Press (2015).

8 Design for Deaf Education: Early History of the NTID
KRISTOFFER WHITNEY

Introduction

The National Technical Institute for the Deaf (NTID) is one of the colleges of the Rochester Institute of Technology (RIT) in Rochester, New York. Created by an Act of Congress and signed into law in 1965 by Lyndon B. Johnson, the Act was to "provide for the establishment and operation of a coeducational, postsecondary institute for technical education of persons who are deaf or hard of hearing." RIT was selected as the site for NTID in 1966, the first technical programs were offered through the college in 1969 using RIT facilities, ground was broken for an NTID campus in 1971, and the newly built NTID campus was dedicated in 1974. Today, NTID enrolls 1,300 students and boasts over 8,000 alumni.[1] This chapter focuses on the period between 1965 and 1975, in order to explore the design and construction of the original NTID campus: a single academic building (Lyndon B Johnson, or as it is known on campus—LBJ), a dormitory, and a dining commons. This decade sits at the crossroads of the civil rights movement, including disability rights, and major changes in deaf education. The case of NTID both indicates and allows us to interrogate, competing tensions between specialized versus integrated education for persons with disabilities, "universal" and "accessible" design strategies, and modes of communication chosen by and for the deaf community in pedagogical settings. History and sociology of science, geography, and science studies generally have long grappled with the meaning and power of space, place, and the design of the built environment.[2] NTID, as a "truth spot" designed and built with then-cutting-edge technology to be a source of "legitimate scientific knowledge" about education for persons who are deaf or hard of hearing, certainly lends itself to analysis through this tradition of scholarship.[3] But the design history of NTID, marked as it was by competing impulses and legal mandates to create spaces for deaf community and integration with the hearing world, is also fruitfully viewed through the lenses of disability studies in general and deaf studies in particular. Geographer Rob Kitchin, for example, has argued that "disability is spatially, as well as socially, constructed."[4] And disability studies scholar Russell Rosen has coined the term "sensescape model" to describe the ways in which "the spaces where deaf and hard of hearing people are found … are the sites where different institutions create and imprint their ideologies, practices and properties pertaining to their sensory notions of the deaf body onto brick-and-mortar spaces in the DeafWorld."[5] As I will show below, the design and construction of NTID was animated almost entirely by the notions of what (mostly hearing) educators decided that deaf bodies (and minds) needed.

The creation of NTID, situated as it was in time and space, compares and contrasts in interesting ways with more contemporary notions of what is referred to as DeafSpace. In order to make this comparison, it is useful to bring in several recent concepts from deaf studies. Like other disability studies scholars, those in deaf studies subscribe to a social definition of "disability":

> Most Deaf people would grant that there is little disability in an all-signing environment. It is only once there is no access to communication that the conditions of disability become evident. Thus, it is only within the contact zone between hearing and deaf worlds, between auditory and visual modalities, that the conditions of disability make themselves present .... It is here that hearing people enjoy systems of advantage and deaf persons systems of disadvantage.[6]

Furthermore,

> To many in the deaf community, being deaf has nothing to do with 'loss' but is, rather, a distinct way of being in the world, one that opens up perceptions, perspectives, and insights that are less common to the majority of hearing persons. The biological, social, and cultural implications of being deaf are not automatically defined simply by *loss* but could also be defined by *difference,* and, in some significant instances, as *gain*.[7]

Using this "Deaf Gain" as a formal framing device, Hansel Bauman has described "DeafSpace" and deaf architecture in similar terms:

> Many deaf people possess an acute architectural awareness and a sensitivity to the connection between personhood and the spaces they inhabit. These aptitudes, honed by daily experiences of isolation and physical barriers to communication and orientation, form a unique sensibility that stands to enhance the way architecture is conceived and constructed for deaf people and society at large. This is Deaf Gain for architecture ... —a complete work that goes beyond adapting buildings to meet the needs of deaf people to creating an aesthetic and meaning that emerge out of the ways deaf people inhabit and construct their spaces.[8]

As I describe below, the creation of NTID to a large extent—though not entirely—lacked the self-determination on the part of the deaf population that was to inhabit the campus to be considered DeafSpace, per se. However, when contrasted to the rest of the RIT campus or other mainstream academic contexts, and in sharp distinction to "universal design" in pedagogy, NTID was created to cater specifically to the educational and social needs of its imagined deaf and hard of hearing clientele.[9] The design of NTID therefore sits at an important historical crossroads of thinking about deaf education, deaf community, and the institutional aspects of "disability."

Designing for Deafness[10]

After President Johnson signed the 1965 NTID Act, a National Advisory Group was created to bring experts in deaf education and technical education together, and to begin the process of bringing NTID as an Act of Congress into being as a physical campus and institution. The National Advisory Group held their inaugural meeting on July 6 and 7, 1967, and that same year Hugh Stubbins and Associates out of Cambridge, Massachusetts, were tapped to design the NTID campus. The architectural firm was later awarded the interior design contract for the three buildings, as well. In consultation with RIT/NTID administration, the National Advisory Group, and the US Department of Health, Education, and Welfare (DHEW), the architects' design was meant to represent the cutting edge of both deaf education and education technology:

> A program was begun to orient the architects and several key personnel within RIT to the needs and requirements of deaf students as they relate to construction. This orientation included extensive reading; a series of site visits to a variety of educational settings within the United States and abroad dealing with both deaf and hearing students; attendance at numerous conferences; and lengthy discussions with NTID professional staff.[11]

While NTID students would be expected to integrate with their hearing peers on the rest of the RIT campus, the three NTID buildings were to be designed with these "needs and requirements of deaf students" in mind. By November of 1967, a "detailed program of spaces and areas" was sent to the architects and presented to the DHEW to detail the plans for "special (because of deafness) versus non-special spaces" on the future campus.[12] The conceptual underpinnings of these "special" spaces described in detail the perceived needs of future deaf students, and directly informed the staffing, design, and construction of NTID. In the sections to follow, drawing on early documents between RIT, the DHEW, and the architects, I detail both these broad concepts in deaf education and the way in which they were concretized into particular buildings.

The Vision

When designing the campus, and justifying the design to DHEW, RIT/NTID explicitly referenced the NTID Act and accompanying Congressional reports when outlining their vision for this "model Institute":

> NTID must plan and operate from the basic premise that tomorrow's problems for the deaf cannot be solved with yesterday's standards. To create the model, program planning and all construction planning should incorporate the most recent thinking available to make NTID exemplary throughout. All the documents mentioned above also suggest that NTID be a multi-purpose institute. As well as being an educational center, NTID should be 1) a service center to prepare

the deaf for full participation in community living; 2) a <u>training center</u> to assist in developing professional manpower to serve the deaf; and 3) <u>a research and demonstration center</u> to influence education of the deaf in general[13]

These four purposes, educating the deaf, providing social services to deaf students, training teachers of the deaf, and researching deaf education, would eventually occupy physical space in LBJ in the form of classrooms and offices, as well as clinical and research space. In addition, the "program philosophy" of NTID emphasized:

> This new opportunity in post-secondary education of deaf students being developed at RIT is unique in at least three respects: It emphasizes confidence that deaf students can progress to the semi-professional and professional levels in science, technology, and applied arts; it is the first national endeavor at the college level to educate deaf students within an academic environment that is primarily a hearing community; and The Agreement which relates RIT and DHEW is a unique arrangement for operating a government Institute free to participating students, through total support via federal funds for construction and operation, within a private institution of higher education.[14]

From the earliest planning documents, therefore, this "model" for postsecondary deaf education was meant to be a hybrid institution that not only devoted brick and mortar to a wide range of pedagogical, professional, and social services, but was also meant to join deaf and hearing worlds, as well as public and private endeavors. The components of this hybrid philosophy would translate directly into the design features of the campus.

"Special Services"

The RIT/NTID administration identified a number of "special services" that would require support across the Institute and student body. Two academic tracks were envisioned for incoming students. The first track, "vestibule students," was for those considered not yet ready for college-level work, requiring remedial education before going into the majors at NTID or RIT. The second, "diploma students," was for those ready to immediately begin study in the technical subjects at which the NTID curriculum was to excel, with the end goal of earning an Associates or Bachelors-level degree. Vestibule students were imagined to require more support services, but:

> It is expected that all vestibule students and many diploma program students will not be ready for large-scale integration with RIT hearing students and that they will require a very intensive regimen of special services and educational care, including speech, language, hearing, psychological, and sociological services. It is expected, too, that many other diploma students program and all degree students, though they will be integrated with RIT hearing students on a large scale, will need considerable support services of this same kind, including such things as interpreting, tutoring, and notetaking services.[15]

In addition to the needs identified for different types of students, a range of staff "specialists" were imagined to cater to their communication preferences, psychological needs, and employment requirements. "Admissions specialists" were to "be sufficiently proficient at manual communication ... to interview deaf applicants," "counseling specialists" were required because "deaf students in general have greater need for psychological services than their hearing counterparts," and "placement specialists" were needed because "there are both positive and negative aspects to hiring deaf employees and there are correspondingly 'good' and 'poor' jobs into which deaf employees may be placed ... Knowing the difference and selling the employer and employee on the difference requires a specialist."[16] In the following sections, I move from these overarching "special services" planned for the deaf student body to building-specific designs for the campus.

LBJ: The Building

LBJ was planned as the sole, NTID-specific academic building. As such, it not only housed classrooms, but office space to accommodate the personnel supplying the "special services" described above, research and training space to fulfill the vision of a "multi-purpose" institute, and specialized infrastructure to meet the needs of deaf students with an array of communication preferences. Early design criteria for the building included "semi-circular classrooms" (for clear sight lines between each student and the instructor), "communication systems" (e.g., text telephones or TTY, and the Vista Phone—an experimental video phone designed for NTID), "emergency signal systems" (e.g., fire alarms with strobe lights), "vibration and acoustic controls," "communication center resources" (e.g., observation/speech therapy rooms, audiology testing suites, and speech analysis and psychoacoustics laboratories), and "audio-visual resources" (e.g., a computer-aided learning center).[17]

The semi-circular, "clustered classrooms" were a particular point of pride for LBJ's designers. These rooms incorporated all of the criteria above: they were semi-circular for clear sight lines, insulated with acoustic controls, and outfitted with electronics for visual communication—including a central room from which images and film could be projected into each of four classrooms (Figure 8.1). They were, in and of themselves, seen as a model infrastructure for deaf education that would cut out all visual and auditory distraction:

> No windows were designed for the pie-shaped classrooms since any distraction would make the student lose more information than a typical hearing student—he must 'hear' with his eyes as well as see with them ... It is believed that providing the deaf with a specially designed learning environment will give them a better chance to succeed in the hearing world.[18]

The Institute was proud enough of these classrooms that NTID made the silhouette of the floor plan, in the four colors chosen for the interior of the building, into the logo for the building dedication on October 5, 1974 (Figure 8.2). This logo was used on the invitations to the dedication ceremony and the dedication program, was turned into name tags and lapel pins, and served as a backdrop for dedication speakers.

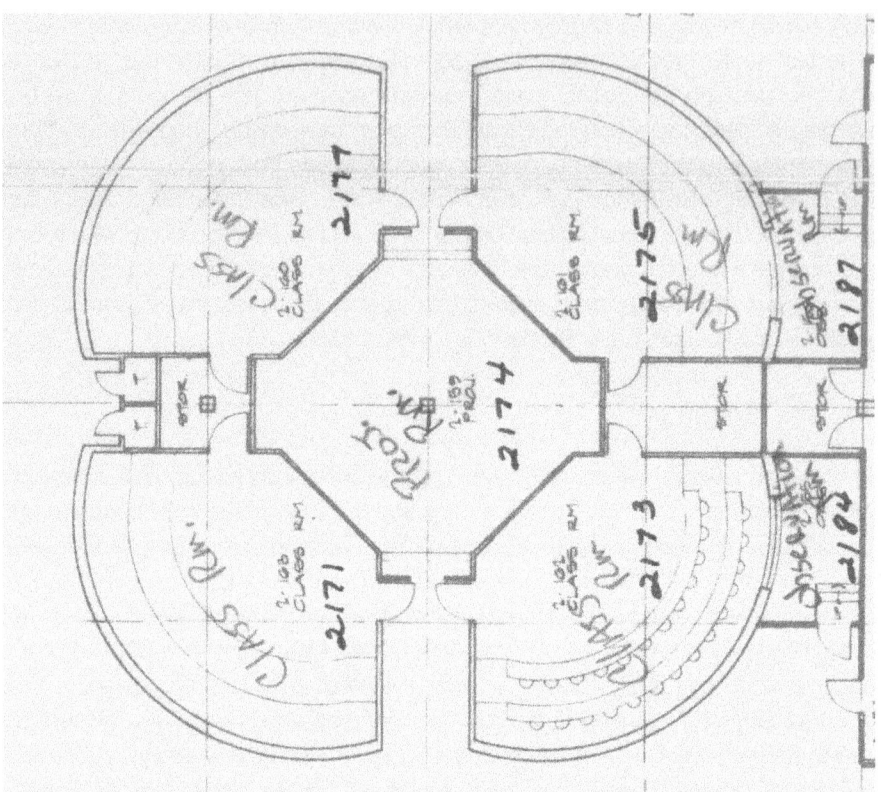

Figure 8.1 Close-up of the cluster classrooms from the floor plans. Courtesy of RIT/NTID Deaf Studies Archive, Rochester Institute of Technology.

Much of the technological infrastructure of the building was to enable so-called oralist approaches to deaf education, focused on residual hearing, lip-reading, and speech production:

> Since World War II technologic advances in electronic hearing aids have been put to use in the education of the deaf. Extensive use of these in classrooms, laboratories, shops and residence halls will maximize the educational attainments of NTID students. Sound control and sound isolation are essential to successful use of hearing aids by the deaf. Control of outside sounds, of reverberation of sound inside rooms, of vibration, and of lighting conditions is essential to successful hearing students. Such factors are achieved through soundproofing, air condition-core doors, replicated walls and concrete.[19]

This extended beyond the control and enhancement of sound, to include visual technologies. Consider, for example, this rationale for including a television and recording system in LBJ from a 1969 telecommunications plan:

> Magnification: … In teaching the deaf, this may well be a very important technique. For example, a television camera can be focused closely on an individual's

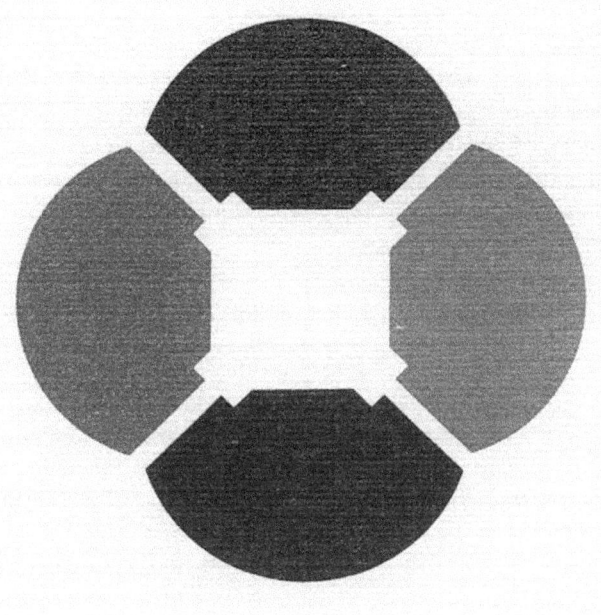

Figure 8.2 Cluster-classroom logo on the dedication program. Courtesy of RIT/NTID Deaf Studies Archive, Rochester Institute of Technology.

mouth and a large group of deaf students could observe the formation of various words and sounds and thus improve their lip-reading ability.[20]

NTID was also being designed, however, at a time when American Sign Language (ASL) was being reintroduced into deaf education and schools for the deaf after a century of suppression in favor of oralism. Take, for instance, the following list of "Special Facilities (related to Deafness)" planned for LBJ:

1. Special Facilities (related to Deafness)
    A.   Hearing & Speech
Deaf students may generally be required to have:
  1. Speech and language rehabilitation on a regular, continuing basis.
  2. Periodic pure tone audiologic evaluations.
  3. Special diagnostic audiologic evaluations.
  4. Periodic hearing aid evaluations.

5. Lipreading instruction.
6. Manual Communication instruction.
7. Auditory training.[21]

In this draft report on academic space requirements, "manual communication instruction" was circled with a line pointing to the title of the section, suggesting that "A. Hearing & Speech" be changed to "Hearing & Speech and Related Communication Skills." While the services and technologies designed for LBJ were skewed toward "language rehabilitation" and oral instruction, it is notable for the time that "manual communication" was included and that both sign language instruction and interpreting were to be provided.

One of the most prominent features of the LBJ design was a large auditorium theater. This, like the rest of the building and campus, had its own rationale and objectives:

> To provide special support services, within an institution of higher learning, which facilitate and encourage deaf students to achieve a high degree of personal, social and cultural development ... To stimulate social interaction and mutual understanding between the deaf and hearing students at RIT and for later community participation ... to expand the social-recreational needs of deaf students via visual means of entertainment ... to provide supplementary work-training projects in stage craft for deaf students ... to provide opportunities for the adult deaf community of greater Rochester to participate in all avenues of educational, cultural, and social enrichment at RIT.

And, like the rest of the building, these rationales and objectives for the theater translated into specific, deafness-related design features:

> A wide and <u>rounded</u> "apron" should be incorporated in the "thrust" stage. This architectural feature would resemble "a stage in the round" to some extent, making for better sight lines and closer intimacy required for deaf audiences ... the <u>back of each seat</u>, in the center section consisting of approximately 200 seats, should be equipped with a small "reading lamp" that would permit a deaf person to <u>read from the script of the play</u> while following the dialogue and action ... This permits <u>complete understanding and interpretation by deaf</u> audiences who need all possible visual aids for reinforcement and recall." (emphasis in original)[22]

If the staffing, structures, and technologies planned for the academic facilities in LBJ showcased the commingling of different audiological and visual forms of communication and pedagogy, the raison d'etre of the theater perhaps best encapsulated the hoped-for balance between space designed specifically for the deaf community and "interaction" with their hearing peers. This creative tension between integration and separation of the deaf and hearing communities at RIT/NTID was further elaborated in the design of the NTID dormitory and dining commons.

Dormitory and Dining Commons

For the dormitory, two different types of living quarters were envisioned, depending on the level of college preparation that students arrived with:

> The first type of living quarters is intended for all vestibule students and such diploma program students as are not ready for large scale integration with RIT hearing students ... They will require a more intensive regimen of sociological, psychological and educational care ... it is anticipated that [these] students will require and seek more time among themselves during this first real venture into the hearing world.[23]

It was for these "vestibule" students, considered less ready for the academic and social rigors of college, that the residence hall would include:

> Four faculty offices ... The primary users of these offices will be faculty members in the area of social sciences for the vestibule program. Social sciences cover the myriad of customs, mores and consumer knowledge which most hearing students have learned either through personal experience or vicariously. The deaf student, by virtue of his restricted environment and limited communications with the hearing world is relatively unfamiliar with this social milieu. By its very nature, this subject is better taught in the informal surroundings of the residence halls than in the academic classrooms since the residence halls more readily approximate home-life.[24]

Furthermore, the dormitories were to include "Faculty-Student Consultation Rooms," because in the minds of the educators and designers:

> Deaf students are not as worldly as the typical hearing college students. The typical deaf student is in fact, quite naïve. A major responsibility of NTID will be to encourage and facilitate a high degree of personal and social development among NTID students ... Though NTID has been conceived as an educational program which will seek maximum integration of deaf students with hearing students, it must be remembered 1) that not all deaf students will be comfortable with total integration, 2) that nearly all deaf students will need, from time to time, to be able to retreat from the pressures of integration, and 3) that the experience of other integrated education or vocational programs for the deaf have found that most deaf individuals feel and express the need for a place which they can call their own.[25]

The dining commons, envisioned as a cafeteria, but also as an all-purpose event space and student union in miniature, also reflected the complementary (or competing, depending on one's perspective) goals of integration and separation between deaf and hearing student populations on campus:

> The dining hall-commons facility will serve the deaf students as a multi-purpose facility ... They will be able to plan large or small social events such as banquets or parties, to which they may invite hearing students or not, as they choose. They will have a modest recreational area to which they can retreat if they feel the need

to relax from the pressures of having to communicate constantly with the hearing world ... A facility of the type discussed here will afford maximum opportunity for deaf students to socialize with other persons, both deaf and hearing, as they see fit.[26]

As with the tensions between oral and manual pedagogy and research reflected in the academic building, the design of these living spaces at NTID embodied different ideas and assumptions about the degree to which deaf students would or could be encouraged to build their own community and engage with the hearing population on campus. And as in the examples above, at times this was couched in patronizing tones about the amount of support "naïve" deaf students would need to develop socially, while at other times deaf students seemed empowered to create community and a "place which they can call their own," "as they see fit." Before these spaces could be constructed, however, NTID had to repeatedly justify their approach to deaf education to Washington.

Government Pushback on Special Services

For all of the federal support for NTID and its expansive vision, there was also significant pushback in the DHEW against the expense and space that NTID requested, often linked to the "special requirements" of deaf students described above. At a meeting on May 2, 1968, a DHEW deputy assistant secretary presented RIT representatives with a number of pointed questions comparing NTID's plans with what Gallaudet provides "their" deaf college students. Concerning the academic facilities, DHEW asked:

> Question 7. For fiscal year 1969, Gallaudet College expects to serve 1,171 students during the regular academic year. They have ... approximately 120 square feet per student. You request ... approximately 255 square feet per student for essentially these same functions. Why do you need over double the amount that Gallaudet requires?

> RIT's answer:
> The comparison upon which this question is based does not appear to be a fair one ....It is well known that Gallaudet has a speech and hearing center, a large auditorium, a large counseling center space, and a construction concept for a vast learning center. To make a fair total comparison the gross square footage of these facilities must be added to the Gallaudet figures.

> With regard to the dormitories, DHEW posed:
> Question 9. Consistently, RIT has requested that their dormitories and those at NTID be comparable. RIT has stated that it has 225 square feet per student for this function. However, RIT is requesting ... 275 square feet per student for NTID. Why?

> The answer:
> The NTID dorms are conceived to house special study carrels, faculty-student consultation rooms, and spaces to be used by counselors and by interns in

training … the per student space requirements are well within reason for deaf students.

And with respect to the building infrastructure:

Question 10. Why should we air condition NTID facilities when virtually none of the RIT facilities are air conditioned … ?

RIT:

The exclusion of noise from facilities for the deaf is imperative for best support to oral communication in this respect; air conditioning goes hand-in-hand with soundproofing.[27]

All of the "extra" space, in short, was required to meet the special needs of the deaf community (and, if one made the proper comparison, was on par with Gallaudet's facilities). By early summer, 1968, these answers had seemingly satisfied the DHEW, and the concept drawings were recommended for approval. This approval hit another roadblock on August 20, 1968, however, when the newly appointed assistant secretary for education at DHEW, Lynn Bartlett, sent a letter to RIT offering *qualified* approval of the concept drawings—a necessary step to proceed with construction—but pushed back on several design features, including "academic and other special facilities in the dormitories."[28] The president of RIT immediately wrote back in the negative, and penned a duplicate letter to the secretary of the office, stating that "Dr. Barlett's letter of August 20th places a whole series of qualifications upon the approval of our architectural concept studies and constitutes a rescinding of agreements already accomplished. This can only throw the NTID project into a new period of unwarranted delay. In the light of previous problems this is intolerable."[29] The founding director of NTID, Robert Frisina, explained the conflict to the National Advisory Group this way: "With regard to Dr. Bartlett's request that we should eliminate study carrels, seminar rooms and faculty offices in the dormitories, we emphatically cannot agree with him that these are duplicative and unnecessary. The placement of these rooms in the living quarters was by design, and considered essential to the program of educating deaf students NTID is to serve."[30]

Approval to proceed with construction, without the suggested modifications and caveats, would be given later that year, but government support continued to wax and wane in the years leading up to campus completion. RIT was notified in early 1969, for example, that the Nixon budget for fiscal year 1970 would "remove the construction funds for NTID buildings," but these funds were restored the following year by Congress.[31] The expansiveness of the NTID "Grand Experiment"—a multipurpose, deaf-centric campus with social services in academic buildings and academic support in ostensibly social spaces—gave formerly enthusiastic government supporters pause. In the end, however, LBJ, a residence hall, and a dining commons were built, dedicated on October 5, 1974, and adhered largely to the program philosophy and design concepts of NTID laid out from the very beginning.

Conclusion: NTID and DeafSpace

It would be anachronistic to consider the design of NTID an early example of DeafSpace, per se, as this contemporary design movement is envisioned as a bottom-up effort, taking its cues from the ways in which deaf people inhabit space. Rather, the creation of NTID was a top-down process in which largely hearing educators and professionals designed the campus *for*, as opposed to *with*, deaf peers and students. Nevertheless, NTID represents a historically unique time and place in deaf education, in which significant effort went into, among other things, creating spaces in which, among peers and without communication barriers, students could experience Deaf Gain, rather than hearing *loss* in higher education in science and technology.

It would also be inaccurate to portray NTID as solely a creation of hearing people. One deaf educator, Robert Panara, was appointed to the National Advisory Group and served as one of the founding faculty members at NTID. Though he was the sole deaf member of the NAG, the Institute slowly grew to incorporate a number of deaf educators, researchers, and professionals. As Panara himself wrote, in an undated essay titled "NTID—A fulfillment of the American Dream," "I am deeply appreciative of this opportunity … More important than this token courtesy, however, is the fact that the NTID has provided the opportunity for a good number of outstanding deaf persons to become an integral part of the institute and the community of educators at RIT." And just as he drew attention to the incongruity between the tokenism inherent in his position on the NAG and the opportunities for other deaf educators to follow, in this short essay he likewise identified the importance of NTID as a place for both deaf community and social integration:

> These guidelines and objectives [for NTID] stressed the urgency and need of a program that would provide for the technical education of the deaf at the postsecondary level so as to offer greater opportunities for employment and a wholesome social climate that would prepare them more fully to participate in the great mainstream of life … More than 300 deaf students are now integrated with the society of hearing peers and scholars numbering over 5,000 on this campus. They have accepted each other as equals and, collectively, they are working hard to overcome "the communication barrier", the "education gap", and all those remaining differences which might have isolated them into minority-majority groups had they not benefitted from the opportunity to serve as a model for all human involvement and endeavor.[32]

NTID was, and is, a hybrid institution that reflects the creative tensions and competing philosophies in deaf education in a post–civil-rights-movement historical landscape. Choices about modes of communication and instruction, as well as student integration and separation, were solidified in concrete, brick, and metal as the institute was designed and built. In contradistinction to "universal design," NTID was a highly specialized institution that benefited from broad, if fitful, support from the US government, as well as schools for the deaf from around the country. The Institute both relied upon, and obviated, deafness as a disability. And while NTID in these early years was initially, largely a place for the deaf built by the hearing, it laid the groundwork for subsequent modification and expansion toward the ideal of DeafSpace. In that sense, the "Grand Experiment" from "Dream to Reality" continues.[33]

Notes

1. For statistics on NTID enrollment, see http://www.ntid.rit.edu/numbers/; For a timeline of the creation of NTID, see http://www.ntid.rit.edu/history; for a local history commemorating the founding and development of NTID, see Harry G. Lang and Karen K. Conner, *From Dream to Reality: The National Technical Institute for the Deaf, A College of Rochester Institute of Technology* (Rochester, NY: Rochester Institute of Technology, 2001).
2. E.g. David N. Livingstone, *Putting Science in Its Place: Geographies of Scientific Knowledge* (Chicago, IL: University of Chicago Press, 2003); Thomas F. Gieryn, "A Space for Place in Sociology," *Annual Review of Sociology* 26 (2000): 463–496; Tim Cresswell, *Place: An Introduction*, 2nd ed. (Chichester, UK: Wiley Blackwell, 2015).
3. Thomas F. Gieryn, "Three Truth-Spots," *Journal of History of the Behavioral Sciences* 38, no. 2 (2002): 113–132.
4. Rob Kitchin, "'Out of Place', 'Knowing One's Place': Space, Power and the Exclusion of Disabled People," *Disability & Society*, 13, no. 3 (1998): 343–356.
5. Russell S. Rosen, "Geographies in the American DeafWorld as Institutional Constructions of the Deaf Body in Space: The Sensescape Model," *Disability & Society* 33, no. 1 (2018).
6. H-Dirksen L. Bauman, "Designing Deaf Babies and the Question of Disability," *Journal of Deaf Studies and Deaf Education* 10, no. 3 (Summer 2005): 314.
7. H-Dirksen L. Bauman and Joseph J. Murray, eds., *Deaf Gain: Raising the Stakes for Human Diversity* (Minneapolis: University of Minnesota Press, 2014), xv. Deaf Gain is a recent, positive reframing of the "disability" of deafness. Many in the signing deaf community consider themselves part of a linguistic minority, rather than disabled, citing the pioneering work of William Stokoe in gaining acceptance for American Sign Language as a complete language in its own right (see William C. Stokoe Jr, "Sign Language Structure: An Outline of the Visual Communication Systems of the American Deaf," reprinted in *Journal of Deaf Studies and Deaf Education* 10, no. 1 (2005 [1960]). From this perspective, the extent to which deaf persons are "disabled" depends, as with the social definition of disability above, upon their contact with "audism" in the hearing world (see Tom Humphries, "Communicating across Cultures [Deaf-Hearing] and Language Learning [Doctoral dissertation. Cincinnati, OH: Union Institute and University, 1977], p. 12).
8. Hansel Bauman, "DeafSpace," in *Deaf Gain*, ed. H-Dirksen L. Bauman and Joseph J. Murray, 375–400.
9. On the history of inclusion or "mainstreaming" in education for persons who are disabled, and the anomaly of schools for the deaf, see R. Osgood, *The History of Inclusion in the United States* (Washington, DC: Gallaudet University Press, 2005), chapter 7.

On space, pedagogy, and universal design see, for example, Jan Doolittle Wilson, "Reimagining Disability and Inclusive Education through Universal Design for Learning," *Disability Studies Quarterly* 37, no 2 (2017).

10 Unless otherwise noted, all primary source documents cited are located in the NTID Records collection, RIT/NTID Deaf Studies Archive, Rochester Institute of Technology, Rochester, New York.

11 "National Technical Institute for the Deaf: Construction Details" no author, no date; NTID Campus Construction Documents May 1967–October 1970, Folder 1; Construction/Williams, Box 89.

12 "NTID Construction History," January 18, 1971; NTID Construction, Folder 19; Box 74, Frisinia, Castle, VP's Office, Mr. Bayon.

13 "Attachment #B … a revision of the program of requirements" no author, undated; NTID Communications w/Hugh Stubbins and Associates, Folder 16; Box 89, Construction/Williams. Note that although this report is undated it is prefaced as a revision as "an outgrowth of a meeting held at RIT on July 12, 1968, by representatives of the Department of Health, Education and Welfare, the Rochester Institute of Technology, and the National Advisory Group for NTID."

14 "Program Philosophy," no author, no date; NTID Program Requirements and Philosophy—1968, Folder 1; Box 90.

15 "Program Philosophy," no author, no date; NTID Program Requirements and Philosophy—1968, Folder 1; Box 90.

16 "National Technical Institute for the Deaf; Space Requirements; Academic" November 1967, pages 3–6; NTID Miscellaneous Documents Folder 20; Box 90.

17 "Project Construct," no author, Draft 1, 3/5/73; NTID Program Requirements and Philosophy—1968 Folder 1; Box 90.

18 Teresa D. Bilyk, "H.E.W's Project for the Deaf to Open at R.I.T.," draft, April 13, 1973; NTID Correspondence with Frank C. Trentacosti, Folder 13; Box 90.

19 "Attachment #B … a revision of the program of requirements" no author, undated; NTID Communications w/Hugh Stubbins and Associates, Folder 16; Box 89, Construction/Williams.

20 Hugh Stubbins and Associates and Hubert Wilke, Inc., "Telecommunications Report & Budget: Part 1 of Phase 1," RIT/NTID, Rochester, New York, July 1969; NTID Campus Construction Documents May 1967–October 1970, Folder 1; Construction/Williams, Box 89.

21 "National Technical Institute for the Deaf; Space Requirements; Academic" no author, November 1967; NTID Miscellaneous Documents, Folder 20; Box 90.

22 "Auditorium-Laboratory Theatre," October 1967; NTID Campus Construction Documents May 1967–October 1970, Folder 1; Box 89, Construction/Williams.

23 "Construction Program," no author, no date; NTID Program Requirements and Philosophy—1968, Folder 1; Box 90.

24 "Residence Hall Concept (Special Facilities)," no author, no date; NTID Construction Concepts and Proposals, Folder 10; Box 90.

25 "Construction Program," no author, no date; NTID Program Requirements and Philosophy—1968, Folder 1; Box 90.
26 "Construction Program," no author, no date; NTID Program Requirements and Philosophy—1968, Folder 1; Box 90.
27 "Attachment #2 Responses to the eleven questions presented by Mr. Bruce Cardwell DHEW Deputy Assistant Secretary, Budget to Dr. Paul Miller and RIT Representatives at the meeting of May 2, 1968," no author, no date; NTID Program Requirements and Philosophy—1968, Folder 1; Box 90.
28 Lynn Bartlett, Assistant Secretary for Education, Department of Health, Education, and Welfare to Mark Ellingson, President, Rochester Institute of Technology, August 20, 1968; NTID Camus Details, Folder 4; Box 90.
29 Mark Ellingson, President, Rochester Institute of Technology to Wilbur J. Cohen, Secretary, Office of Education, Department of Health, Education, and Welfare, August 28, 1968; NTID Camus Details, Folder 4; Box 90.
30 Robert Frisina, memorandum to National Advisory Group, August 30, 1968; NTID Camus Details, Folder 4; Box 90.
31 "NTID Construction History" no author, January 18, 1971; NTID Construction, Folder 19; Frisina, Castle, VP's office, Mr. Bayon, Box 74.
32 Robert Panara, "NTID—A Fulfillment of the American Dream," undated; NTID Campus Construction Documents January 1971–March 1972, Folder 2; Box 89 Construction/Williams.
33 Harry G. Lang and Karen K. Conner, *From Dream to Reality*.

Bibliography

Bauman, H-Dirksen L. "Designing Deaf Babies and the Question of Disability." *Journal of Deaf Studies and Deaf Education* 10, no. 3 (Summer 2005).
Bauman, H-Dirksen L. and Joseph J. Murray, eds. *Deaf Gain: Raising the Stakes for HumanDiversity*. Minneapolis: University of Minnesota Press, 2014.
Bauman, Hansel. "DeafSpace." In *Deaf Gain Deaf Gain: Raising the Stakes for Human Diversity*, ed. H-Dirksen L. Bauman and Joseph J. Murray, 375–400. Minneapolis: University of Minnesota Press, 2014.
Cresswell, Tim. *Place: An Introduction*. 2nd ed. Chichester, UK: Wiley Blackwell, 2015.
Gieryn, Thomas F. "A Space for Place in Sociology." *Annual Review of Sociology* 26 (2000): 463–496.
Gieryn, Thomas F. "Three Truth-Spots." *Journal of History of the Behavioral Sciences* 38, no. 2 (2002): 113–132.
Humphries, Tom. "Communicating across Cultures (Deaf-Hearing) and Language Learning." Doctoral dissertation. Cincinnati, OH: Union Institute and University,1977.
Kitchin, Rob. "'Out of Place', 'Knowing One's Place': Space, Power and the Exclusion of Disabled People." *Disability & Society* 13, no. 3 (1998): 343–356.
Lang, Harry G. and Karen K. Conner. *From Dream to Reality: The National Technical Institute for the Deaf, A College of Rochester Institute of Technology*. Rochester, NY: Rochester Institute of Technology, 2001.

Livingstone, David N. *Putting Science in Its Place: Geographies of Scientific Knowledge*. Chicago, IL: University of Chicago Press, 2003.

Osgood, R. *The History of Inclusion in the United States*. Washington, DC: Gallaudet University Press, 2005.

Rosen, Russell S. "Geographies in the American DeafWorld as institutional constructions of the deaf body in space: the sensescape model." *Disability & Society* 33, no. 1 (2018).

Stokoe Jr., William C. "Sign Language Structure: An Outline of the Visual Communication Systems of the American Deaf." Reprinted in *Journal of Deaf Studies and Deaf Education* 10, no. 1 (2005 [1960]).

Wilson, Jan Doolittle. "Reimagining Disability and Inclusive Education through Universal Design for Learning." *Disability Studies Quarterly* 37, no 2 (2017).

9 Designing the Japanese Walking Bag

ELIZABETH GUFFEY

First introduced on the Japanese market in 1995, the Swany Bag functions as a kind of rolling cane. Relatively small and lightweight, the device looks like a soft suitcase with a gently curved handle. It rolls on wheels that pivot 360 degrees, allowing the bag to function like a gliding handrail. This case study of the Swany Bag developed by Etsuo Miyoshi explores a design innovation that grew in response to Japan's cultural reception of physical difference and a growing national awareness of disability. Ultimately, the Swany Bag's development reveals changes in Japanese attitudes toward the latter as disability has become less hidden and more in public view.

I use the Swany Bag as an assistive device in my own day-to-day life. As a disabled person who walks slowly, stops often to rest, and has uncertain balance, I've found that it provides support, but is also more supple and responsive to relatively fine-tuned movements than other devices currently available to people whose bodies look and move like mine. As it is, those of us with mobility impairments often lament the limited range, scope, and function of assistive devices, such as canes, crutches, walkers, and wheelchairs. Indeed, I first encountered the Swany Bag not through a medical supplier but rather at a local travel store, where its flexible ingenuity immediately caught my attention. Smaller and more maneuverable than a walker or wheelchair, the rolling support opened new possibilities to me. Mounted onto its frame is a small fabric bag big and strong enough to carry a load of books or several bags of groceries. And yet, I've discovered that the Swany Bag also carries within it an implicit tension. Styled to look like a small overnight suitcase rather than a medical device, it appears to belong in an airport or an upscale hotel lobby. Of course there are many places where—whether for security or decorum—luggage is not welcome. In restaurants, the maître d' will often stare at it quizzically, and then offer to store it for me in a distant cloakroom. Taxi drivers and hotel bell hops routinely lunge for the bag, hoping to help by taking it away from me. Guards and security officers routinely stop me when entering institutions like museums and banks. And casual passersby often ask me if I'm a tourist—in my home town. More often than not, when I explain that it is an assistive device, I get only blank stares in return.

I wish to thank Mr Etsuo Miyoshi for his assistance in my research for this chapter. Additionally, I am also grateful to Noriko Okada for her assistance with translating the original Japanese texts and sources used in this research.

I say this less to complain, than to clarify: the Swany Bag's design does not announce its use, nor does its form divulge its function. Over time, I've come to realize that this appearance is no accident: for the Swany Bag, disguise is a strategic feature. Designed by a disabled person for other disabled people in Japan, its creator understood intimately the "inconveniences" they face.[1] The Swany Bag is hiding in plain sight.

"Getting Used to Being around Disabled People"

Etsuo Miyoshi, creator of the Swany Bag, was never an activist nor a scholar, but still grew up knowing much about being disabled in Japan. Miyoshi contracted polio when he was six months old and has since walked with weakness on the right side of his body. He would later recount how he was repeatedly judged an unsuitable candidate for marriage and felt so estranged from society that he even considered suicide.[2] His experience of alienation is shared by many disabled people across the world, but it also reflects his Japanese culture. As recently as 1998, a best-selling autobiography by Hirotada Ototake, a sports journalist and educator born without arms and legs, could confidently assert that "you don't come across many disabled people in the streets or on the trains in Japan."[3] For Ototake, this lack of visibility— what he called "familiarity"—is a common theme. Although Japan has no fewer or more disabled people than other countries its size, its disabled population has traditionally kept out of sight. "With so few opportunities for contact," wrote Ototake, "it may be close to impossible for most Japanese to get used to being around disabled people."[4]

Like most societies the world over, Japan has a complex relationship with disability. Longer histories of Japanese practices, customs, and ideas suggest that disabled people inhabited a carefully hewn niche in a complex and subtle social hierarchy. Traditional Japanese social structures, coupled with a sense of familial stigma, meant that disabled people often lived their lives out of public view.[5] Some families believed that a disabled child would have been better off not being born at all. Only after the Second World War did aspects of this situation slowly begin to change. Parents, advocates, and sociologists began to argue that disabled people would benefit from living in larger institutions that could provide special medical and caregiving services. By the early 1970s, some observers and disabled people themselves began to argue that this newer system —which was largely modeled on Western medical approaches to disability—left residents open to abuse and medical neglect. Few disabled people, meanwhile, were emerging into everyday society. At one facility, residents were only allowed to leave the premises once every three months, and then only when their parents wrote a special request for this to happen.[6] Where once they lived within a network of family support, disabled people are now isolated from their families–even as they continued to live lives out of public view.

The question of disability–and visibility—was a key issue in Japan's early home-grown activism. Aoi Shiba no Kai (The Green Grass Club), formed in 1957 by a group of people with cerebral palsy, faced a particularly galvanizing moment with the 1970 case of a young mother killing her disabled, two-year-old daughter. The incident drew nationwide attention, and the mother received such widespread public sympathy that the local prosecutor's office considered dropping its criminal case against the woman. With the slogan "Mothers Do Not Kill," Aoi Shiba no Kai mounted a successful counter-petition campaign and the case went to trial.[7] Using this first national public discussion of infanticide and disability as a point of departure, members of Aoi Shiba no Kai then began to draw attention to how disabled people were treated in Japanese society. In late 1970 Hiroshi Yokota, a member of Aoi Shiba's executive committee, published a four-point platform suggesting that the position of disabled people in society was marginal at best. Claiming that Japanese society not only rejected them but continued to accept a dangerous line of reasoning that favored infanticide when faced with physical or mental impairment, Yokota described disabled people as living "an existence which should not exist."[8] Aoi Shiba asserted its public presence by mounting sit-ins and marches; thus it performed the radical act of resistance simply by drawing attention to members' existence.

In Japan, many observers point to the United Nations 1981 declaration of the International Year of Disabled Persons as a turning point;[9] international attention and growing ties to activists in the United States and Europe helped push new laws and policy goals in terms of access and the built environment. The 1994 Heart Building Law, for example, recommended accessibility features in public buildings, including hospitals, department stores, and cinemas as well as meeting spaces. Alternately, the Project for Building Barrier-Free Cities, an initiative established by the Ministry of Health and Welfare in 2000, led to a series of legislative acts to ensure the construction of elevators, ramps, curb cuts, accessible public toilets, and other features as part of the built environment. As in other parts of the world, however, these new projects and legislation did not necessarily annul centuries of stigma and invisibility.

The social marginality of Japan's disabled people has been the subject of academic studies and popular accounts alike.[10] Most focus on how slowly social change has occurred. More than a decade after Japan's first access laws were passed, a 2007 article in the English-language *The Japan Times* observed, "We see more station elevators, wheelchair-accessible toilets and buses with passenger lifts nowadays. Such facilities are visible, but many people hardly ever encounter those who use them—let alone anyone with non-physical disabilities."[11] Part of a critical series on disability in Japan, the article highlighted issues involving public awareness. Noting the "vacant elevators and seldom-used toilets," *The Japan Times* observed that "according to Japanese government statistics, one in twenty people in Japan has a physical or mental disability." But, as *The Japan Times* demanded, "where are they?" Cutting to the bottom line, they asked, "Is 'Disability' still a dirty word in Japan?"[12]

Etsuo Miyoshi was part of a generation in which a small number of disabled people were emerging as major public figures. In the 1990s, autobiographer Hirotada Ototake and Minoru Murata, a lawyer, began writing frankly about their experiences living as disabled people in Japan. Murata's *The Town and the Wheelchair* (1994) recounts his own encounters while navigating his wheelchair through Tokyo.[13] Although he notes how few people have had contact with a wheelchair, he also describes his own hesitancy to ask for help. When he does so, Murata observes, it causes acute embarrassment; most people are so unfamiliar with the device, they don't know what to do.[14] As *The Japan Times* notes, "Most Japanese quite likely live their whole lives without ever interacting with their disabled fellow citizens."[15] Hirotada Ototake, who titled his best-selling autobiography *No One's Perfect*, spent his career building a carefully honed public persona based on cheerful resilience in the face of adversity. In some ways he became the most public face of Japanese disability. Etsuo Miyoshi, meanwhile, maintained a lower public profile. Through the early 1990s Miyoshi rarely drew attention to his own disability, nor to his status as a polio survivor. Instead, he used his intimate knowledge of disability to develop a new design– the quietly unassuming Swany Bag.

A New Approach

As he would repeatedly tell journalists, sales teams, and disabled people themselves, Etsuo Miyoshi drew from his own profoundly personal experiences to design the Swany Bag. Miyoshi's work at his family's glove-making firm, Swany, required him to travel frequently and carry product samples with him. On an especially exhausting sales trip to New York in 1967, Miyoshi bought a wheeled trunk fitted with rolling casters.[16] Not only did the trunk hold his sales samples but, he would later recall, he also noticed that the bag facilitated his walking, offering support just as effective as that of a cane. He began taking the case everywhere, leaving it empty for personal travel. As helpful as he found the wheeled trunk, however, it remained big and bulky. It was difficult to maneuver the thing in and out of taxis or up and down stairs.[17] Miyoshi began considering a new type of assistive device—a bag that functions like "a movable handrail."[18] But, as Miyoshi later stressed, Swany also "changed the role of the bag from being pulled to being pushed and supporting."[19] It was a new approach toward a mobility device, but also represented a larger change of mindset within Japanese disability culture.

This change came slowly and—in spite of Miyoshi's novel design—it would take another two decades, and an atmosphere of crisis, before Miyoshi began designing the Swany Bag in earnest. Like many Japanese companies in the 1990s, Swany suffered from the deep recession that has sometimes been dubbed Japan's Lost Decade. At the same time, Japan faced a more existential threat as the nation moved from a high birth to death ratio to a low birth to death ratio. Demographers recognized that these longevity rates threatened to shrink the work force and lower productivity still further.[20] For his part, Etsuo Miyoshi realized that as the Japanese populace grew older, so too would the ranks of disabled people. Once part of a stigmatized minority, by the early 1990s Miyoshi found himself in an unusual position—part of a growing demographic. At Swany, Miyoshi persuaded the company's executives that a new product designed for Japan's changing population might resuscitate sales in the midst of economic recession. As Shugei Isei, the original head of Swany's new Bag division, confirmed, "We thought it'd be good not only for polio survivors but also the old."[21] Taking advantage of government support and low-interest loans, the company poured money into developing the Swany Bag. And yet, when Swany introduced the Bag in 1995, the idea of marketing a consumer product to disabled people was still quite novel.

Swany was hardly alone in noticing Japan's need to begin designing for an aging (or disabled) population; the growth of this demographic proved one reason for the 1999 founding of the Kyoyo-hin Foundation. This nonprofit organization traced its roots to the beginning of the decade, when Yasuyuki Hoshikawa of the Japanese toymaker TOMY started an informal reading and study group meant to fill a need unmet by Japanese manufacturers. Hoshikawa initially focused his efforts on the design of toys for disabled children, and the group was often referred to as the "E&C" or "Enjoyment and Creation" Project. Aiming to make more playthings accessible, Hoshikawa began collaborating with industrial designers, disability advocates, and representatives from nonprofit organizations like the Japan Braille Library. By the mid-1990s, however, Japan's rapidly aging population was reaching a critical mass and the goals of the "E&C" Project began to receive more and more attention. As this happened, Hoshikawa and others began to expand its mission.

As the E&C Project grew, it began to align itself with principles of "Universal Design" as developed in the United States and Europe.[22] Although it initially developed separately, Hoshikawa and other proponents of the E&C Project took a major step toward the Universal Design movement when they reorganized and renamed themselves the Kyoyo-hin Foundation in 1999. This name change emphasized the concept of "kyoyo," a Japanese word that translates as "commonly useable" and mirrors the term "universal" in English. To reinforce this parallel, a 2001 White Paper published by the Kyoyo-hin Foundation explained the difference between Universal Design and kyoyo design as little more than a matter "of perspective."[23] While the Swany Bag was not developed in close coordination with these ideas, by the late 1990s Etsuo Miyoshi's approach toward disability had brought him to a similar place. Both Swany and the E&C Project realized that Japan's population was aging and the need for accommodations was rapidly growing. As Miyoshi would later realize, "My goal was what kyoyo-hin is. Therefore, [Swany and the E&C Project] were overlapped from the beginning."[24] Any yet, for both groups finding this demographic required some rethinking.

While Universal Design had received considerable attention in the design world of the 1980s and 1990s, by the time the Swany Bag was introduced to the public in 1995 the emerging concept of kyoyo-hin was still little known. Throughout the 1990s, for instance, industry groups like the Brewers Association of Japan, the Association for Electric Home Appliances, and the Japan Cosmetic Industry Association adjusted wrapping and packing at the urging of the E&C Project; these changes included printing the word "beer" in Braille on beer cans and reconfiguring shampoo bottles with specifically uneven surfaces to distinguish them from hair conditioners. But these efforts remained relatively low profile.

As Miyoshi and Swany quickly discovered, in a country where people with similar disabilities were still largely invisible, there was no conventional path for marketing a product designed for them and their needs. With no established infrastructure for selling, nor any national habit of buying accessible design, Swany found itself adrift. The Kyoyo-hin Foundation also struggled to see its products reach the consumer base it had targeted. By 2001 the national organization lamented how activity on the "distribution front" had been "lagging" for some years.[25] But at Swany this difficulty translated into a very real problem. The Swany Bag, Miyoshi would later note, proved "ten times harder to sell than to develop."[26]

By and for Disabled People

Encouraged by his brother Asao, at the family-run business Etsuo Miyoshi built on his own experience as a polio survivor to develop a product for Japan's underserved but emerging consumer base of elderly and disabled people. Introduced in 1995 as a boxy-looking trunk set on four rotating casters, the Bag's design continued to be modified over the next few years. Soon, Miyoshi worked to change the bag's design, making it smaller and more stylish, while also changing its handle. Throughout this process, however, Miyoshi's early confidence in his personal judgment was clear. He fervently believed that there was "a huge market that was invisible to healthy people."[27] As Miyoshi would later recall in Swany publicity materials, "I was convinced that my own needs would be applicable to all people with weak legs."[28] While he may have understood the needs of these hidden consumers, trying to find that consumer base—and what they wanted—was more difficult.

The first Swany Bag challenged the company to bring Miyoshi's ideas to this emerging larger consumer base. Because its primary product was gloves, the company had no ties to the luggage industry but also struggled to find a clear marketing message or audience—disabled or otherwise. Recalling those early years, Miyoshi and Swany looked for "any place where customers are, rather than following a marketing strategy."[29] In the next few years the company mounted a series of promotions aimed at gaining broader visibility; these ranged from simple giveaways to the first customers responding to ads,[30] to sending representatives to provide visitors with free use of Swany bags at regional agricultural shows.[31]

With no marketing template to follow, Swany also began to promote the Bag in the national press. When it was first launched in 1995, Swany's earliest publicity introduced the device as "Easy Swany," a travel bag useful for both businessmen and young people.[32] Foreign and domestic travel continued as a principle focus in advertising for years to come. By the next year, a more extensive advertising campaign dwelled on the rigors of travel. "Taking trips overseas is fun but also a lot of work," one advertisement insisted, but "for people who feel this way, the glove maker Swany developed the Easy Swany suitcase".[33] Although this advertising copy emphasized the Bag's general ease of handling, there was little direct information about its disabled maker, nor their primary function as an assistive device for mobility impaired people. While also briefly explaining Miyoshi's early childhood bout with polio, for example, stressed it could make "your way home with a heap of souvenirs easier."[34] Nevertheless, even as the Bag was simultaneously being marketed as "Easy Swany" and the "Stick-Bag" (often in the same densely written advertising copy), sales continued to be disappointing. By the end of 1998, the company had poured tens of millions of yen into the product and found almost 400 distributors, and yet Swany was "on the brink."[35]

Although Miyoshi clearly believed that "it is impossible to survive a market without understanding the inconvenience of people with disabilities,"[36] it was only around 2000, with financial failure looming, that Swany began to clearly refocus its marketing tactics (and Miyoshi chose to make his personal "mission" clearer).[37] At his insistence, the company developed a marketing campaign that addressed disabled consumers directly; Miyoshi himself began communicating his own deep understanding of disability itself.[38] Shirking social stigma, Miyoshi began appearing in advertising campaigns that not only mentioned, but actually dwelled his personal story, his experiences with disability since childhood, and also his work life. Typical of these stories is a February 2001 article published in Sankei Shinbun and accompanied by a publicity photograph introducing the designer standing in front of a display of Swany snow gloves. Neatly dressed in a business suit while leaning on a Swany Bag, the executive is featured prominently.[39]

Miyoshi's presence—as well as his confident sense of personal well-being even while disabled—began being prioritized in advertising and promotional pieces (Figure 9.1). Soon special in-store displays featured life-size pictures of Miyoshi, and each bag was tagged with a picture of Miyoshi himself leaning on a bag. The advertising and promotional copy prominently featured Miyoshi's simple and direct

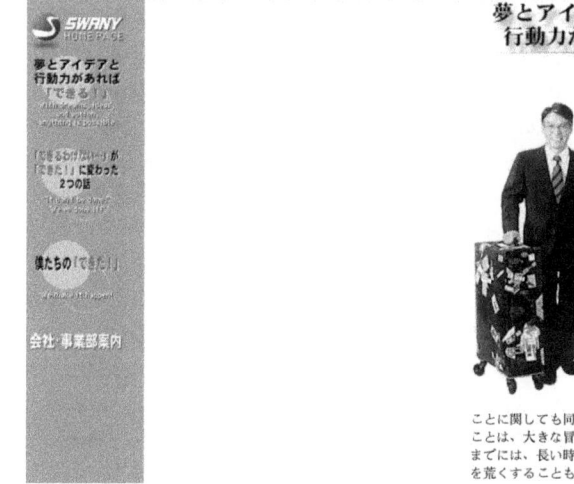

Figure 9.1 SWANY promotional website 2001. Permission Etsuo Miyoshi.

statement: "I am suffering from the after effects of polio. I've traveled around the globe a hundred times, but all the while I kept wondering how I could make my bag lighter; finally, I designed a bag I can lean on to walk."[40] Not only did Miyoshi look at ease, but his accounts of easy travel to foreign countries made his disability seem like a manageable thing; clearly the Swany Bag helped ensure that his post-polio impairments would not interfere with his day-to-day life. Indeed, Swany's candid, even explicit, advertising took the very opposite stance of the deliberately modest and unobtrusive bag itself. Rather than eliciting embarrassment, Miyoshi's appeal proved not only affirming, but also provided the model of a successful disabled man who many consumers might even be able to identify with. As Shuji Isei, then head of Swany's Bag division, explained to a journalist in 1999, "we already have sticks or canes or walkers for elderly or lightly disabled people to use, however especially for men they have psychological difficulty in using these things."[41] Whether Miyoshi's own presence addressed male discomfort explicitly remains unclear. But, with the benefit of hindsight several years later, Miyoshi himself judged the new approach a real accomplishment; looking backward some three years later, he firmly believed his "real experience" could successfully "move people."[42]

This shift in marketing yielded rapid changes. The advertisements featuring Miyoshi himself almost immediately attracted attention to Swany's sales displays. Even better, salespeople also reported that, once shoppers "finished reading the tag," the bags seemed to sell themselves.[43] Within a few months, the company's Bag division began meeting its sales targets and even started to grow.[44] Miyoshi insisted that "I had to tell them of my experience and thoughts directly."[45] This new marketing, Miyoshi would later observe, "is how it started to get on track."[46]

But Miyoshi also tried to build his reach and connection with individual disabled customers. To even better accommodate users, Swany also distributed a blank, self-addressed postcard with each bag so that users could provide them with feedback, and the company incorporated these responses into later designs. For example, people reported that the Swany Bag had a tendency to glide away if the user let go; the company added a small brake to its wheeled mechanism. A removable "leash" was also added so that the user could strap one end to themselves and the other to the bag. Other customers noted that, following Japanese social mores, a rolling suitcase was often unwelcome in traditional interiors; later bags were developed to be detachable from their steel frames—the wheeled rolling mechanism could be left outside, and the fabric bag itself carried on in. Other consumers claimed that, when tired, they would sit on their Bag; some subsequent models began to incorporate a folding seat, with a collapsible camp stool locked into the back of the bag, into their design.

But Swany's user feedback also alluded to perceptions of disability and fears of marginalization in Japanese culture. Users consistently praised the Bag's relatively small size, for instance, while suggesting that the Bag could be even less obtrusive. Too often, consumers wrote, "in a quiet residential area, the sound of the casters is loud." While noise pollution can reach unmanageable proportions in dense neighborhoods, this response revealed a somewhat more complex problem.[47] Of course, loud wheels might disrupt a quiet street. But the sound might also draw attention to the Bag's user, rendering both user and Bag more visible. Swany quickly responded by redesigning its rotating casters to make almost no sound at all.

While much of the customer feedback to Swany followed this line of thinking and was quite practical, many of these replies revealed the thoughts and perspectives of disabled people. Customers frequently wrote to thank Swany for providing them with a new sense of freedom. People now felt that they could go about their daily lives in a way that was previously unimaginable. Acknowledging the social pressure that forces many people to try and keep their disabilities hidden, Miyoshi himself observed that "it takes courage to use a cane for the first time, as people see it and notice the disability. This can be a very painful thing."[48] As one customer wrote Swany, before purchasing the Bag, "I was embarrassed to use a cane," but now, "I cannot wait to go for a walk."[49] Another memorable postcard was sent by a son whose mother "refused to use a walker. I bought her the Bag and she is so happy she uses it every day."[50] Still another noted, "I am uncomfortable pushing a walker but I don't feel like that when I use an Easy Swany."[51] Even more personally, another insisted, "with the walking Bag, I feel like someone is holding my hand and walking with me."[52]

Hiding in Plain Sight

As a disabled person, when I first encountered the Swany Bag in the luggage section of an American travel store's catalog, I was both perplexed and intrigued. It was strikingly different from all other glossy photographs in that company's mail-order catalog. The Bag's American advertising featured a photo of the smiling Miyoshi leaning on a bag and an English text of his personal narrative. I could easily relate to Miyoshi's account of his physical exhaustion while traveling and his need for extra support while walking and standing. This small, lightweight bag to lean on made perfect sense to me; I wondered why nobody else had thought of this.

Over time, I have come to recognize that the Swany Bag is itself a traveler, migrating between cultural contexts and expectations. And this may explain why Swany's success with the design in Japan has been hard to duplicate abroad. Like the Japanese Heart Building Law, the 1990 Americans with Disabilities Act mandated infrastructural changes that fostered the growth of mobile wheeled bags in the United States. But the growing accessibility of American built environments also enabled the quick growth of Swany's competitors. Within two years of the Swany Bag's introduction in the United States, Denver-based Samsonite introduced its four-wheel "spinner" luggage. The spinners featured gliding, rotating wheels similar to Swany's, and advertisements touted the new product line with the phrase "Four wheels. Zero effort."

Nevertheless, not all pieces of luggage are made alike. While these newer bags have eased many travelers' trips, they lack the Swany Bag's robust steel frame, smoother rolling wheels and specially constructed handle. In fact, I only came to appreciate the deep innovations of Miyoshi's design when I accidentally purchased a similar, four-wheeled American-made bag. While the latter bag appeared similar and featured four swiveling wheels at its base, I barely left home before recognizing its deficiencies. The American bag had noisy wheels. Worse still, its spindly handle collapsed each time I shifted my weight and leaned on it. I retired this inexpensive version immediately.

When Etsuo Miyoshi introduced the Swany Bag in Japan, he announced his desire to create a new remake of the traditional stick or cane. The Swany Bag's particular properties reflect its designer's own personal and cultural understanding of disability. Deftly designed as an upscale accoutrement, it both corroborates—and undercuts–his culture's principle of invisibility. In the United States, meanwhile, the Bag presents a significant alternative to the largely functional, utilitarian appearance of assistive devices on the market. Indeed, the Walking Bag so closely resembles ordinary luggage that Swany never carved out a unique market identity and eventually ceased selling the device in the United States entirely. Designed by a disabled person for other disabled people in Japan, it had trouble translating its use and purpose overseas. Perhaps ironically, in the United States at least, the assistive device disguised to look like a piece of luggage has been overtaken by its own disguise.

Notes

1. Anonymous, "Prime Person: Syōgai ga kizukasete kureta kenjyōsya niha mienai shijyō 障害」が気付かせてくれた健常者には見えない市場" [A market that is invisible for healthy people but my disability has me see it]. *Business Kagawa* ビジネス香川, August 1, 2009, http://bn.bk-web.jp/2009/0801/person.php (accessed August 25, 2019).
2. Etsuo Miyoshi, "Hokou kara gengo no bariafurī he 歩行から言語のバリアフリーへ" [My Mission for Barrier-free Living, from Walking to Language], speech given at Kagawa Prefecural Social Welfare Convention, Sunport Takamatsu (2009). Accessed October 20, 2017. http://www.swany.co.jp/miyoshi/index01.html
3. Hirotada Ototake (trans Gerry Harcourt), *No One's Perfect* (Kodansha, 2003), 215.
4. Ibid., 216.
5. Katharina C. Heyer, *Rights Enabled: The Disability Revolution, from the US, to Germany and Japan, to the United Nations* (Michigan: University of Michigan Press, 2015), 129.
6. Reiko Hayashi and Masako Okuhira. "The Disability Rights Movement in Japan: Past and Future," *Disability & Society* 16, no. 6 (2001): 861.
7. Ibid., 862.
8. Osamu Nagase, "Difference, Equality, and Disabled People: Disability Rights and Disability Culture." Master's Thesis (The Hague, The Netherlands: Institute of Social Studies, 1995).
9. Kyoyo-hin Foundation. *Kyoyo-hin White Paper 2001*, accessed December 2, 2018. https://web.archive.org/web/20010222054827/http://kyoyohin.org/eng/index.html
10. Carolyn S. Stevens, *Disability in Japan* (New York: Taylor and Francis, 2013); Maho Suzuki, "Disability Studies in Japan: An Introduction," *Disability Studies Quarterly* 28, no. 3 (2008), accessed September 20, 2018. www.dsq-sds.org/article/view/115/115

11 Tomoko Otake, "Is 'Disability' Still a Dirty Word in Japan?," *The Japan Times* (August 26, 2006).
12 Ibid.
13 Murata, Minoru, *The Town as Seen from the Wheelchair* (Iwanamijuniashinsho) (Shinsho, 1994).
14 Ibid., 33–34.
15 Otake, op cit.
16 Anonymous, "Prime Person," op cit.
17 Ibid.
18 Etsuo Miyoshi, "Hokou kara gengo no bariafurī he 歩行から言語のバリアフリーへ" [My Mission for Barrier-free Living, from Walking to Language], op cit.
19 Etsuo Miyoshi, personal communication with author, June 2019.
20 Japan Aging Research Center (JARC). *Aging in Japan*. (Tokyo: JARC, 1996).
21 Shuji Isei, interview with author, October 2017.
22 Kyoyo-hin Foundation, op cit.
23 Ibid.
24 Etsuo Miyoshi, personal communication with author, June 2019.
25 Kyoyo-hin Foundation, op cit.
26 Anonymous, "Prime Person," op cit.
27 Shikoku Keizai Sangyōshō 四国経済産業省 [Shikoku Bureau of Economy, Trade and Industry] "Sekai kyōtsū, monozukuri ha hitozukuri 世界共通、ものづくりは人づくり"[Common World-Wide: Manufacturing Makes People], *Shikoku Bito* 四国びと, January 28, 2014. Accessed October 23,2017. https://www.shikoku.meti.go.jp/shikokubito/interview/47/index.html
28 Chūshō Kigyō Chō 中小企業庁 [The Small and Medium Enterprise Agency], "Karada wo sasae, tsue nimo tsukaeru 'wōkingu baggu' 株式会社スワニー:身体を支え、杖にも使える「ウォーキングバッグ」" [Swany Corporation Press Release: "Walking Bag" That Supports the Body But Can Be Used as a Cane], *Genki na monodukuri: Chūshō Kigyō 300 Sha 2007*元気なモノ作り:中小企業300社 2007, May 29, 2007. Accessed December 3, 2017. https://www.chusho.meti.go.jp/keiei/sapoin/monozukuri300cha19fy/7shikoku/37kagawa/37kagawa_03.pdf
29 Etsuo Miyoshi, personal communication with author, June 2019.
30 Anonymous, "Jyō hō Hiroba 情報ひろば:Idō youi na atache case wo purezento 移動容易なアタッシェケースをプレゼント" [Information Square: Movable atache case giving away] *Sankei Shinbun* 産経新聞, July 16, 1996.
31 Anonymous, "Kaijyō sansaku asisuto shimasu: Tsue, Isu ni naru baggu otoshiyorira ni kashidashi 会場散策アシストします　つえ、いすになるバッグ　お年寄りに貸し出し" [We will assist your strolling the fair: lending bags that serves as canes and chairs for elderly people]. *Sankei Shinbun* 産経新聞, March 10, 2000.
32 "Tebukuro no Suwanī ga Toranku 手袋のスワニーがトランク" [Glove maker Swany launches a bag business], *Nikkei Sangyō Shinbun* 日経産業新聞, June 19, 1995.
33 Yoko Sotokawa 外川洋子, "Syōhin Wocchingu 商品ウォッチング" [Product Watching], *Nikkei Ryutsu Shinbun* 日経流通新聞, June 22, 1996.

34 Ibid.
35 Anonymous, "Prime Person," op cit.
36 Ibid.
37 Etsuo Miyoshi, "Hokou kara gengo no bariafurī he 歩行から言語のバリアフリーへ" [My Mission for Barrier-free Living, from Walking to Language], op cit.
38 Ibid.
39 Anonymous, "Genki desu: Chu, Shikoku no kigyō ka" [I am fine: Entrepreneurs in Chugoku and Shikoku region], *Sankei Shinbun* 産経新聞, February 8, 2001.
40 Etsuo Miyoshi, "Hokou kara gengo no bariafurī he 歩行から言語のバリアフリーへ" [My Mission for Barrier-free Living, from Walking to Language], op cit.
41 Anonymous, "Fukuramu Sirubā Bijinesu: Kakusya no senryaku wo saguru 膨らむシルバービジネス：各社の戦略を探る" [Expanding Silver Business: Exploring a company's strategy], *Ryūtsu Sābisu Shinbun* ゆめ　ひと　企業, March 19, 2000.
42 Anonymous, "Yume Hito Kigyō: Suwanī 生産性新聞" [Dream, Person, Enterprise: Swany], *Seisansei Shinbun* 生産性新聞, March 25, 2003.
43 Anonymous, "Prime Person," op cit.
44 Ibid.
45 Tatsuya Tamaki 玉木達也, "Tomoni—Syōkoku Taimu Monogatari 5: Kishi kaisei no PR ともに 小国大夢物語5：起死回生のPR" [Together—Small Country, Large Dream 5: PR to revive], Mainichi Shinbun Kagawa July 20, 2016. Accessed August 12, 2017. https://mainichi.jp/articles/20160720/ddl/k37/040/340000c
46 Etsuo Miyoshi, personal communication with author, June 2019.
47 Anonymous, "Prime Person," op cit.
48 Ibid.
49 Etsuo Miyoshi, "Hokou kara gengo no bariafurii he 歩行から言語のバリアフリーへ" [My Mission for Barrier-free Living, from Walking to Language], op cit.
50 Ibid.
51 "Yume Hito Kigyō: Suwanī ゆめ　ひと　企業" [Dream, Person, Enterprise: Swany], op cit.
52 Anonymous, "Prime Person," op cit.

Bibliography

Anonymous. "Fukuramu Sirubā Bijinesu: Kakusya no senryaku wo saguru 膨らむシルバービジネス：各社の戦略を探る" [Expanding Silver Business: Exploring a company's strategy]. *Ryūtsu Sābisu Shinbun* 流通サービス新聞. March 19, 2000.

Anonymous. "Genki desu: Chu, Shikoku no kigyō ka" [I am fine: Entrepreneurs in Chugoku and Shikoku region]. *Sankei Shinbun* 流通サービス新聞. February 8, 2001.

Anonymous. "Jyō hō Hiroba 情報ひろば :Idō youi na atache case wo purezento移動容易なアタッシェ ケースをプレゼント" [Information Square: Movable attache case giving away]. *Sankei Shinbun* 産経新聞. July 16, 1996.

Anonymous. "Kaijō sansaku asisuto shimasu: Tsue, Isu ni naru baggu otoshiyorira ni kashidashi 会場散 策アシストします　つえ、いすになるバッグ　お年寄りらに貸し出し" [We will assist your strolling the fair: lending bags that serves as canes and chairs for elderly people]. *Sankei Shinbun* 産経新聞. March 10, 2000.

Anonymous. "Prime Person: Syōgai ga kizukasete kureta kenjyōsya niha mienai shijyō 障害」が気付 かせてくれた健常者には見えない市場" [A market that is invisible for healthy people but my disability has me see it]. *Business Kagawa* ビジネス香川. August 1, 2009.

Anonymous. "Tebukuro no Suwanī ga Toranku 手袋のスワニーがトランク" [Glove maker Swany launches a bag business]. *Nikkei Sangyō Shinbun* 日経産業新聞. June 19, 1995.

Anonymous. "Yume Hito Kigyō: Suwanī ゆめ ひと 企業" [Dream, Person, Enterprise: Swany]. *Seisansei Shinbun* 生産性新聞. March 25, 2003.

Chūshō Kigyō Chō 中小企業庁 [The Small and Medium Enterprise Agency], "Karada wo sasae, tsue nimo tsukaeru 'wōkingu baggu' 株式会社スワニー：身体を支え、杖にも使える「ウォーキングバッグ」" [Swany Corporation Press Release: "Walking Bag" That Supports the Body but Can Be Used as a Cane]. *Genki na monodukuri: Chūshō Kigyō 300 Sha 2007* 元気なモノ作り：中小企業300社 2007. May 29, 2007.

Hayashi, Reiko and Masako Okuhira. "The Disability Rights Movement in Japan: Past and Future," *Disability & Society* 16, no. 6 (2001), 855–869.

Heyer, Katharina C. *Rights Enabled: The Disability Revolution, from the US, to Germany and Japan, to the United Nations*. Michigan: University of Michigan Press, 2015.

Isei, Shuji. interview with author. October, 2017.

Japan Aging Research Center (JARC). *Aging in Japan*. Tokyo: JARC, 1996.

Kyoyo-hin Foundation. *Kyoyo-hin White Paper 2001*. Tokyo: Kyoyo-hin Foundation, 2001.

Miyoshi, Etsuo, "Hokou kara gengo no bariafurī he 歩行から言語のバリアフリーへ" [My Mission for Barrier-free Living, from Walking to Language]. speech given at Kagawa Prefecural Social Welfare Convention, Sunport Takamatsu (2009).

Miyoshi, Etsuo. personal communication with author, June 2019.

Murata, Minoru, Kurumaisu Kara Mita Machi [The Town as Seen from the Wheelchair]. Tokyo: Iwanami Junia Shinsho, 1994.

Otake, Tomoko, "Is 'Disability' Still a Dirty Word in Japan?" *The Japan Times* (August 26, 2006).

Ototake, Hirotada (trans Gerry Harcourt). *No One's Perfect*. New York: Kodansha USA, 2003.

Nagase, Osamu, "Difference, Equality, and Disabled People: Disability Rights and Disability Culture." Master's Thesis (The Hague, The Netherlands: Institute of Social Studies, 1995).

Shikoku Keizai Sangyōshō 四国経済産業省 [Shikoku Bureau of Economy, Trade and Industry] "Sekai kyōtsū, monozukuri ha hitozukuri 世界共通、ものづくりは人づく" [Common World-Wide: Manufacturing Makes People]. *Shikoku Bito* 四国びと. January 28, 2014.

Sotokawa, Yoko. 外川洋子, "Syōhin Wocchingu 商品ウォッチング" [Product Watching]. *Nikkei Ryutsu Shinbun* 日経流通新聞. June 22, 1996.

Stevens, Carolyn S. *Disability in Japan*. New York: Taylor and Francis, 2013.

Suzuki, Maho. "Disability Studies in Japan: An Introduction." *Disability Studies Quarterly* 28, no. 3 (2008)

Tamaki, Tatsuya, 玉木達也, "Tomoni—Syōkoku Taimu Monogatari 5: Kishi kaisei no PR に 小国大夢物語5：起死回生のPR" [Together—Small Country, Large Dream 5: PR to revive]. Mainichi Shinbun Kagawa. July 20, 2016.

Part 3 Making Disability Digital

In December 2018, a new Tokyo café opened with an unusual wait staff: robots. But perhaps even more disorienting, customers quickly learned that the robots were not what they seemed. Instead of being powered by Artificial Intelligence or some other kind of cutting-edge automation, the robots were actually avatars operated remotely by people with disabilities who were working from their homes. As the robots in question shuffled around the café on previously established paths, mingled with customers, and even served orders, their controllers worked off-site. Using wireless audio and video links, the robots' disabled controllers connected digitally via tablets or computers. The goal, according to the CEO of the lab behind this project, was to "enable physical work and social participation" for disabled people.[1] Like these robots, emerging technologies—and especially those in the digital space—suggest new ways for disabled people to operate both online and in the material world. Developments like the robot café foreground technological designs but also bring the design model of disability into the twenty-first century. In looking at the last several decades of digital history, this part's chapters ask, just who is really being served?

The advent of the personal computer in the 1970s coincided with the emergence of organized disability rights movements in Europe and the United States. Many US Disability Rights advocates of the period noted the potential of computers as useful tools for disabled people if made affordable, adaptable, and open to shared information. With the flourishing of the personal computing industry, disabled people have often been early adopters of digital tools, with or without the mediation of doctors and the medical profession.[2] Nor do these designs evolve directly from official policies or regulatory laws meant to effect social and economic equality. Using methods that embrace the individual distinctiveness of users rather than seeking generalized "universal" solutions, many digital tools offer the possibility of more customized interfaces and options than analog mass-production.

At the same time, the utopian dreams of computer scientists that promised social change through digital design often fall short. In Tokyo, despite the active participation of disabled workers in the robot café, the press greeted grand opening with language of charity, not independence. Just how design and technology engage disability begs new and emerging questions around context, use, and agency. The chapters in this part reveal the complexity of the design model of disability as it evolves in the digital age.

Uneasy Positions

With the rapid adoption of digital interfaces into health care, emergency services, and education, not to mention consumer electronics, disabled users occupy an uneasy position. Like Tokyo's robot café, some of these designs hold promise, but also highlight older ways of thinking about disability. In this volume, Jennifer Kaufmann-Buhler reminds us that desktop computers have been celebrated for their power and efficiency, but the introduction of computers into office work in the 1980s also created new categories of disability and injury out of a combination of new forms of hardware and the interaction between these hardware devices. Kaufman-Buhler suggests that monitors, keyboards, and other devices designed for computer work were never intended to be used in conjunction with older office furniture. Moreover, the majority of employees using computers in this era were low-level workers; they had little choice over their office furniture arrangements or the hardware that was installed for them to use.

While digital interfaces might be uncomfortable or even cause disablement, other technologies might supplant uneasy interactions such as the basic and fundamental human need to ask for help.[3] Elizabeth Ellcessor traces the marketing and media coverage of the personal emergency response systems, or PERS, which were wearable devices targeted to elderly people living at home, possibly in need of emergency assistance but unable to reach the phone. While rarely acknowledged as technologically advanced, Ellcessor argues, these devices were predecessors to mobile smart technologies in terms of being embedded in social, infrastructural, and intimate contexts. These devices were, in fact, "high tech" in their time, linking emergency call services with land lines and a small pendant-style wearable, but their marketing emphasized that they could replace the care-taking once undertaken within families. Thus they appealed to not only elderly people who felt at risk living on their own, but also the adult children who would or could not care for their aging parents.

In contrast, Bess Williamson's chapter on recent experiments in 3D printing in prosthetic limbs describes a scenario where design is not only seen as mitigating disability, but in this case disability is used to market designed products. Whether presented as a fashionable prosthetic leg or a crowd-funded printed hand made for humanitarian reasons, Williamson argues, the 3D-printed limb continues to assure us that design can solve the "problem" of disability, benefiting society at large. In this sense, these limbs, like the LifeAlert systems before them, reveal ways in which digital design is marshaled for social goals within a disability-conscious society.

The final chapter of the volume turns scholarly attention back on the study of the history of disability and design itself. Using the digital tools of humanities scholarship,

Jaipreet Virdi describes how new technologies are reshaping the practices of collecting, exhibiting, and interpreting artifacts of disability history. Because disability is so often hidden in the historical record, Virdi argues digital tools from social media, ranging from hashtags to online exhibitions, are particularly useful for their ability to cut across institutional collecting practices. However, she also suggests the need for critical consideration of new online projects, as they may replicate existing biases. And perhaps this opens a newer chapter in our understanding of the design model of disability. Here, it may be argued, the role of users in shaping the meaning and form of "disability things" can be newly discovered. Historians and other digitally adept scholars can now link technological histories to the populations that they aimed to serve.

These chapters build on historical scholarship in digital design and technology to reveal the ways in which digital technologies fit into existing design categories, be they of work, aging, or design itself as a cultural phenomenon. The design model of disability, like the digital technologies that allow it to flourish, is socially embedded. Even as it requires social and wired infrastructures, it forces us to reconsider our existing positions, reconsidering what design can do and for whom.

Notes

1 "Café Opens with Robot Waiters Remotely Controlled by People with Disabilities," *The Japan Times*, November 26, 2018 https://www.japantimes.co.jp/news/2018/11/26/national/cafe-opens-robot-waiters-remotely-controlled-people-disabilities/#.XT3AX5NKg_U
2 Elizabeth R Petrick, *Making Computers Accessible: Disability Rights and Digital Technology* (Baltimore, MD: Johns Hopkins University Press, 2015).
3 Early regulations for access emphasized that people should not need to ask for help to access spaces such as library stacks. Richard K Scotch, *From Good Will to Civil Rights: Transforming Federal Disability Policy*. 2nd ed. (Philadelphia, PA: Temple University Press, 2001), 73–74.

Bibliography

Petrick, Elizabeth R. *Making Computers Accessible: Disability Rights and Digital Technology*. Baltimore, MD: Johns Hopkins University Press, 2015.
Scotch, Richard K. *From Good Will to Civil Rights: Transforming Federal Disability Policy*. 2nd ed. Philadelphia, PA: Temple University Press, 2001.

10 The Politics and Logistics of Ergonomic Design
JENNIFER KAUFMANN-BUHLER

While the topic of ergonomics is not always included in disability studies, it is similarly concerned with the fit between diverse bodies and the design of spaces and things. Inadequately researched and ill-conceived design can—and often does—fail to take users' bodies into account. Design can cause users pain and even lead to disablement. In the context of work and the workplace, poorly designed equipment, tools, and spaces are not only a hindrance to their effective and efficient usage, they can also be a hazard to the bodies that use them.

As computers became increasingly common features in American offices in the late 1970s and early 1980s, intensive computer or VDT (video display terminal or visual display terminal) users began reporting increasing vision problems as well as significant musculoskeletal issues that were directly related to their intensive computer usage. Ergonomics research at that time focused on the mismatch between the design of the traditional paper-based office and the new technology, which required new furniture, new lighting, and new ways of working. Experts in the field often described the ideal computer workstation as one that would seamlessly integrate the new technology and fit the physical needs of the worker.[1] This idealized vision of the computer terminal, office furniture, and computer-user fitting together like a series of interlocking puzzle pieces, though idealized in the literature on ergonomics, was difficult to achieve in practice because of the enormous variation in computer design, furniture design, and users' bodies. For equipment manufacturers and employers, this ideal was economically and logistically impossible; meanwhile for workers, this misfit between the technology and office design created physical strain on their bodies as they struggled to work long hours using equipment (both furniture and technology) that were ill-suited to the task.

There has been significant work in the history of computing on the design of computer technology, the evolution of the form and aesthetics of computers and computer peripherals, and the issue of accessibility in computer design.[2] In addition, a number of design and architectural historians have examined the role of ergonomics, human factors, and accessibility in architecture and design.[3] There is also significant work on the political debates and policies related specifically to workplace hazards and injuries, as well as research on the social aspects of computer usage at work.[4] Building on this previous scholarship, this chapter examines the material, political, and social challenges associated with the adoption and implementation of ergonomics in office and computer design in the late twentieth century.

I argue that the messy and uncoordinated adoption of personal computers in American offices resulted in a perpetual mismatch between the technology, the workspace, and computer users. As ergonomic policies developed through the 1980s, the recommendations and practices focused almost entirely on adapting office design, office workers, and organizations to the needs of the computer, not adapting the computer to the needs of offices, workers, and organizations. Ultimately, the competing and often contradictory priorities and concerns of manufacturers, organizations, and workers resulted in a patchy ergonomic landscape that offered few protections for workers' health, safety, and well-being.

Mismatched Offices, Technology, and Bodies

The chronic mismatch between office design, office technology, and worker's bodies has its roots in the idiosyncratic manner in which personal computers first arrived in American offices. Through the 1960s and 1970s, public and private organizations invested enormous resources in large centralized mainframe computers, and elaborate automation systems in order to increase organizational efficiency and productivity. These large computing systems required enormous planning and coordination, and because of their size and power needs were generally siloed away from regular office areas in a dedicated space designed to meet the unique spatial and electrical requirements of these machines.[5] Through the late 1970s, personal computers were typically thought of as novelty objects that would never be appropriate for the large-scale needs of business. Even as late as 1984, IBM continued to insist internally that the future of corporate computing was the centralized mainframe not the personal computer.[6]

Yet as many public and private organizations were investing vast sums on the acquisition and implementation of centralized computing and office automation systems through the 1970s, the personal computer revolution (or end-user computing) was already underway. Early personal computers were marketed primarily to a domestic consumer, but by the late 1970s many computer manufacturers were extolling the benefits and possibilities of the personal computer in the office, and many offices within public and private organizations began acquiring these new machines.[7] In contrast to the intensive planning required for the acquisition and installation of mainframe computers and data processing equipment, personal computers were relatively inexpensive and easy to set up and so they were often acquired in a "grass roots" fashion by individuals at the department level.[8] The low cost of personal computers meant that even in federal agencies with very strict purchasing rules, individual units were often able to purchase computers without any oversight or formal permission.[9] Perhaps even more surprising is the fact that in both large federal agencies and privately owned corporations, it was typical for individual units to purchase their computers from mail order or retail outlets like Radio Shack or ComputerLand rather than buying in large quantities direct from the major computer manufacturers.[10] As a result, these new machines were often purchased in a piecemeal manner within both government and corporate offices generally without coordination, planning, or oversight by the larger organization. This lack of coordination and planning along with the diverse offerings of personal computers (numerous makes and models, competing software, and operating systems) meant that both public and private organizations often had a number of different types of computers within their offices.

This diversity of computer equipment within organizations was made even more complicated by the fact that computer design from the late 1970s through the late 1980s varied enormously, even among computers by the same manufacturer. For example, Radio Shack's TRS-80/Tandy computers featured multiple different models and forms in various combinations. In just one 1985 catalog they have examples of a model with all the components separated, two that featured a monitor and CPU (central processing unit) combination with a separate keyboard, an "all in one" model with CPU, monitor, and keyboard in one unit, and a keyboard with CPU combined with a separate monitor.[11] This is significant because it reveals the complex landscape of computer equipment at the time. Even within a single company selling just one line of computers there were enormous differences among the various types of equipment available.

As this miscellany of computers and other VDTs like word processors were cropping up in large and small, public and private organizations, American offices and office furniture were still designed primarily for processing paperwork. The desks, chairs, and lighting were all optimized around the traditional paper-based office. Furniture (even the new systems furniture) often had fixed height work surfaces and chairs had minimal adjustment capability.[12] In addition to the problems with the design of the furniture, the lighting overhead was intentionally bright and direct and windows were often uncovered to maximize the amount of sunlight in the office.[13] Thus, as personal computers began to appear in offices in the late 1970s, they were being used in workspaces that were never designed with such machines in mind. Once purchased, the new personal computer was often set up on a conventional table or desk in the office without much consideration for whether the arrangement was convenient or comfortable for users or even appropriate in size or shape for the machine itself.[14]

In studies on the ergonomics of VDT usage in both public and privately owned organizations, researchers found that tables used with computer equipment were typically too high, too low, or had inadequate desk space for the necessary monitor, CPU, keyboard, and supporting materials. Further, it was not uncommon for a stray office side chair or secretarial chair to be placed at the computer without consideration for the well-being or comfort of the operator.[15] Not only were these types of chairs insufficient in terms of upper back support, but also they were not adequately adjusted (or adjustable) to users.[16] Even workers using chairs that could have given some modest lower back support were often not aware of how to adjust the chair to optimally support their back.[17] The lack of adjustability in the chairs, desks, and tables along with the inadequate space for the equipment left computers users in a variety of contorted positions struggling to find a comfortable position to work.

Steven Sauter's manual on VDT usage features images of computer users sitting in ill-adjusted (or non-adjustable) chairs, hunched over keyboards, stretched awkwardly across overly high and/or deep tables, or physically straining their necks to type and see the screen or nearby supporting documents.[18] Similar types of images and examples are also featured in the 1985 report, *Automation of America's Offices*, again with workers in various states of discomfort using computers on inadequate desks and sitting in uncomfortable or unsupportive chairs.[19]

In addition to problems with the furniture, glare on computer monitors was another frequent office design challenge of the late 1970s and early 1980s. The bright overhead lights that were well suited for working with paper would often reflect off of the curving VDT screen resulting in headaches and eyestrain, especially for regular computer users. As a result of this glare, workers were often adjusting and contorting their bodies in all manner of ways in order to adequately see the screen exacerbating musculoskeletal issues.[20] Recommendations for reducing glare included using after-market filters for monitors which could enhance readability, as well as adding special louvres to overhead lights, purchasing window treatments and positioning terminals away from light sources such as windows.[21] In this way, the "bright lights" ideal for handling paperwork needed to be reduced in order to optimize computer-based work. Yet, workers using computers often needed to look at paper as well, so task lighting at the individual workstation was recommended to ensure a well-lit work surface without producing glare.[22]

In the 1970s and 1980s there was a great deal of uncertainty and controversy regarding the short-term and potential long-term consequences of computer usage on workers' bodies. In fact, one of the biggest public health debates at the time revolved around fears of computer radiation and the possible long-term consequences of that radiation on workers' bodies.[23] Meanwhile, most of the documented health issues arose from the use of these poorly designed workstations, with their inflexible furniture and equipment and poor lighting, which created significant physical problems for workers as they struggled to adjust their bodies in order to compensate for the lack of adjustment in the environment. Perhaps unsurprisingly to us today, the most widely reported problems associated with VDT usage were musculoskeletal ones, particularly in the upper and lower back, neck, and shoulders with some users also reporting significant pain in their arms, wrists, and hands.[24] Because the furniture and equipment were often not adjustable in design, workers were unable to adapt the surrounding workspace when they started to feel aches and pains during the work day, exacerbating the problem. Workers also reported visual discomfort with multiple studies finding workers with headaches, light sensitivity, blurred vision, eye strain, double vision, and visual fatigue following intensive use of computer equipment.[25] Some workers in intensive (and highly repetitive) VDT jobs also reported high levels of stress, anxiety, and depression which sometimes also manifest in a number of psychosomatic issues including gastro-intestinal as well as heart and blood pressure problems.[26]

Although all of these kinds of problems were common complaints and worries among VDT users, they were not considered "medically detectable" (resulting in a clear biological change to the body) so they were often dismissed when workers tried to make an injury claim for worker's compensation.[27] Cumulative physical stress through continued intensive computer usage however could over time create chronic conditions that had a lasting impact on workers' bodies. Perhaps the most widely reported repetitive stress disorder (and the one most easily confirmed by doctors) was carpal tunnel syndrome in which the nerves of the wrist are compressed against the carpal ligament creating numbness, weakness, and tingling in the hands and wrists that could create significant discomfort and chronic pain for workers. Left untreated and unaddressed, workers with carpal tunnel sometimes required surgery to repair the underlying nerve damage.[28] These kinds of health conditions could become debilitating, even severely limiting workers' ability to do their jobs, and also hindering their ability to perform ordinary domestic activities.

Reports on many of these health problems often emphasized how the worker's own working habits, preexisting conditions, and even after-work activities could aggravate problems of physical stress associated with computer usage. It was found, for example, that workers who used bifocals (which are optimized for looking down to read) were often tilting their head upwards in order to be able to read the computer screen.[29] In addition to vision issues, obesity, diabetes, pregnancy, preexisting back problems, a worker's diet, high heels, constrictive clothing, and poor posture could all increase the strain of VDT work on a worker's body.[30] In worker's compensation cases, workers who spent time after work watching TV or engaging in other types of activities that might cause similar injury were often used to dismiss the claim.[31] Emphasizing the importance of these diverse variables on an individual worker's experience and their relative pain or discomfort served to shift the blame of the issue to the worker rather than placing it on the technology.

Organizations could also be at fault for some of the problems especially in failing to allow adequate breaks from VDT work throughout the day. In VDT-intensive jobs, workers were sometimes expected to work continuously with very few breaks. This kind of organizational culture that demanded constant productivity and efficiency was viewed as a significant part of the problem. Ergonomic guidelines strongly recommended that organizations provide workers with ample breaks from computer usage, job rotation, and other opportunities to move and stretch during the work day so that they would not experience excessive physical fatigue as well as stress.[32]

Everything but the Computer

With all of the blame going around, what about the design of the computer itself? The formal ergonomic studies on VDT usage typically treated the design of the computer as a fixed element that could not easily be changed, and instead focused on making changes to the larger workspace, the worker, and the organization to better support the use of these new devices. Many of the ergonomic recommendations in the early 1980s indicated a preference for a detachable keyboard wherever possible to allow workers to situate the screen and keyboard for optimum typing and viewing height respectively, but this was often couched as a recommendation not a requirement.[33]

In fact, the problem of standardization and regulation of computer design was not just a technological issue, but it was also a deeply political one. At the time, other countries including Germany, Norway, Sweden, Great Britain, France, and Japan had begun developing and implementing standards and regulations surrounding the design and use of computers in workplaces. Some of these regulations focused on protecting the worker by mandating breaks, for example, and others had very specific technical requirements for the design of computers specifying keyboard design and even monitor specifications.[34] In the United States, there were six congressional hearings in the early 1980s to debate whether any standards or regulations should be imposed around VDT usage in American offices.[35] Representatives from the unions, computer manufacturers, office furniture manufacturers, doctors, and organizations all appeared before congress to discuss the possible risks associated with VDT use as well as whether regulation would be warranted.

In a 1985 congressional hearing a number of union representatives gave testimony documenting the thousands of worker complaints related to VDT usage, advocated strongly for regulation on the design and use of VDTs in the workplace, and argued for the development of protections to ensure the health, safety, and well-being of workers using computers.[36] In their response to these complaints at that same hearing, representatives of CBEMA (Computer and Business Equipment Manufacturers Association) along with BIFMA (Business and Institutional Furniture Manufacturers Association) and organizational groups like the Newspaper Publishers' Association argued strongly against any such regulation insisting that the problems workers were experiencing were not an issue of health and safety, but rather a matter of "comfort."[37] In this way, the provision of equipment (both technology and furniture) that would alleviate physical problems was treated not as a critical health and safety requirement, but rather as a frill intended to merely make the workplace "comfortable" not safe. The real physical issues workers experienced were thus reframed by industry as temporary and generally harmless. BIFMA, CBEMA, and other American industry representatives further argued that any effort to regulate and standardize technology or furniture in the United States would ultimately stymie innovation. They insisted that any regulation would be an expensive burden to the manufacturers and their customers, and that the marketplace itself would drive the adoption of ergonomic technology and furniture.[38] They also argued that any regulation would "force" an employer to invest in unnecessary equipment and force a worker whose workspace and chair were comfortable to adopt a potentially less comfortable "ergonomic" workstation out of obligation to comply rather than necessity or desire for change.[39] Instead, these industry groups advocated for "voluntary" or "self-regulation."[40]

Ultimately the industry groups won; the Health and Safety Subcommittee for the House of Representatives decided in 1985 that "rather than impose legislatively developed and mandated standards and/or rules and regulations, employers and employees are in the best position to determine what is best in each individual workplace so as to reduce complaints due primarily to ergonomic factors."[41] The phrasing of this statement is very revealing. Not only does it imply the political position that "regulations" of any kind would be a hindrance to business, but it also suggests that workers' health concerns were trivial "ergonomic issues" and not structural and physical problems tied to the use of VDT equipment itself. While some state and local governments (Wisconsin, Maine, California, Massachusetts, New Mexico, and Colorado) chose to create their own standards, there was no national regulation to ensure the protection of VDT users, and many of those regional regulations were ultimately struck down in the courts.[42]

Thus, instead of protecting workers from physical harm, the US government protected industry from the harm of potential regulation and oversight. While the hearings included the testimony of union leaders who represented literally thousands of workers, in evaluating the potential "risks" associated with VDT usage members of congress gave the voices and perspectives of industry leaders greater weight. Historian of technology, Langdon Winner, argues that the framing of a new technology as a "risk" implies that there are benefits as well as potential costs associated with the use or adoption of the technology, but those costs and benefits are not borne equally by all parties.[43] In the case of office automation and VDT usage, organizations benefited significantly from the increased efficiency, productivity, and cost savings associated with the new equipment, while workers bore the bulk of the "costs" in the form of physical pain and long-term health consequences such as carpal tunnel and other forms of chronic health problems.

Competing Constraints

By siding with the needs of business over the well-being of workers, the Health and Safety Subcommittee assumed that the market would ultimately ensure appropriate protection for workers. Yet that logic ignored the complex and often-competing priorities that informed the design, acquisition, and use of computer equipment and furniture in this era.

For designers and manufacturers of technology, the process of designing and producing new equipment was often limited by numerous other constraints that might interfere with ergonomic goals. In industrial designer Richard Hollerith's papers and drawings for an Interdata CRT (cathode-ray tube) from the mid-1970s, there is evidence that he was using an array of standard components by different manufacturers (CRT tubes, ports, and disk drives) and accommodating some specific manufacturing guidelines (e.g., using the "existing" base of a previous model). The numerous iterations of his design with adjustments in angles and components along with cryptic notes to check with certain individuals or units on various details suggest a complicated negotiation process in which these competing technical and manufacturing limitations were informing his design choices. Though Richard Hollerith was deeply committed to human factors and universal design, and was certainly thinking about the human–computer interaction in his design for Interdata (using the Henry Dreyfuss's male and female human factor charts to assess appropriate dimensions and angles), he was still under significant pressure to balance his interest in usability with these other kinds of manufacturing and technological limitations.[44] Though just one example, it suggests the layers of complexity and the competing constraints embedded in the design and manufacture process of computers which may have been part of the industry's motivation in strongly resisting federal, state, and local ergonomic regulation.

Similarly, furniture designers and manufacturers often struggled to accommodate diverse installations, uses, and equipment types. For example, Knoll's Hannah systems line included a special VDT corner designed to support the deep CRT-style monitor in 1983, but it was at a fixed height and did not include a keyboard tray or split surface at optimum typing height in the regular specs for the VDT workstation.[45] By the late 1980s, a keyboard tray was an available accessory in the Hannah line, but only if the VDT corner had originally been installed in a very particular way to allow the keyboard tray to be mounted properly.[46] Further although the keyboard tray was available with two different depths (to support thick and thin keyboards), if the "thick" keyboard option was selected there would not be sufficient clearance underneath the desk for the worker's legs.[47] The evolution of VDT furniture and accessories reflects the diverse form factors of computers at the time, and the challenge furniture manufacturers faced in designing around so many different equipment configurations. Simply managing their own system of furniture components in relation to the computer equipment could produce a design solution that was ill-suited to the body of the VDT worker.

For organizations, the conflicting information related to ergonomics along with the lack of regulation meant that they were often making decisions through the lens of their own economic, spatial, technological, and social constraints. Different computer models, competing operating systems, and diverse software types meant that ergonomic issues were just one variable among many different attributes that companies were weighing in their evaluation of new equipment, and compared to the technical requirements, ergonomic issues were often a fairly low priority. In other words, while it is unlikely that a company would have chosen an ergonomic machine that was not well suited to their technical needs, it is very likely they would have purchased a computer that met their technical needs but was not "ergonomic" in its design. The lack of federal regulation over ergonomics issues also meant that ergonomic policy was very localized to a particular organization and in some cases even a particular office within an organization.

Further, decisions about ergonomics made by organizations were informed by a number of practical and economic concerns. For example, the State of Wisconsin was one of a few state governments in the 1980s to develop a formal ergonomics policy for state workers, yet their policy was shaped largely by the economic and spatial restrictions of the time. Purchasing special VDT furniture was expensive and also space intensive at a time when the State had recently instituted measures to strategically reduce overhead costs and space usage in all agencies. In implementing their policy, they therefore focused on replacing furniture only for "high stress positions" or for "employees with documentable special needs."[48] In private organizations the implementation of ergonomics was similarly messy and complicated, and often constrained by organizational challenges in the 1980s and 1990s. A 1985 survey of Data Processing Management Association members found that 84 percent of the top corporate information processing executives were in corporations that did not have an ergonomics policy in place. While many of the respondents indicated that they thought ergonomics was important only a third of the respondents believed there were health hazards associated with computer usage. A substantial number of the respondents also indicated that management was generally reluctant to invest in "ergonomic enhancements" for workers due to budget constraints.[49]

For workers, these various structural constraints in terms of the design and acquisition of both technology and furniture could create a harmful working environment. An article in the *New York Times* from 1990 describes a tax collecting office in Trenton, New Jersey, in which a large group of clerks were seated at simple tables with chairs with only minimal adjustment (seat height and tilt) using sixteen-year-old computer terminals that could not be tilted, turned, raised, or lowered causing workers to shift and hunch their bodies uncomfortably through full work days in which they were typing a minimum of 10,000 keystrokes an hour. According to the article, a survey conducted of the 118 workers in that tax office found that 81–82 percent had hand, wrist, or shoulder pain. A number of the workers also had diagnosed tendinitis, cysts, or carpal tunnel. The article reports that some workers were reluctant to seek any accommodations for fear that they might lose their jobs.[50] Workers were thus negotiating fixed equipment that could not be adjusted or changed, and fixed (or minimally adjustable) furniture that was not well designed for the equipment and not well suited to the user's own body. In addition, workers were also under significant social and economic constraints. Some workers may have feared reprisal or demotion as a result of requesting special accommodations. Most importantly, workers that were intensive VDT users were frequently the most vulnerable to discrimination as a result of their gender, race, and social class.[51] These marginalized workers had the least power to challenge unfair policies and may have been less able to risk losing their job than more privileged workers in more flexible or autonomous jobs.

"Standard" Equipment and Exceptional Bodies

By the early 1990s, new computer terminal design consolidated around a fairly consistent form factor of all separate components: a monitor, a keyboard, a mouse, and a CPU. In his article "The (In)Difference Engine" from 2000, design historian Paul Atkinson describes the evolution of computer design from the space-age idealism to the ubiquitous "boring beige boxes" that became common in the late twentieth century.[52] In addition, the 1990s was also an era of much greater oversight and regulation in both private and public organizations through dedicated IT departments which took over the acquisition and maintenance of personal computers. As part of their role, IT departments were often implementing organizational policies and purchasing standard computer equipment intended to work with a set array of software selected for use across the organization.[53] Thus, in contrast to the miscellany of equipment characteristic of office of the 1970s and 1980s, computer equipment became increasingly standardized in offices.

The most ergonomically robust piece of equipment available to office workers since the 1980s has typically been the office chair. As discussed above, buying new desks and other furniture was often prohibitively expensive, instead companies began investing in "ergonomic" chairs as a way of lowering their own insurance rates by reducing back and neck injuries.[54] All of the major furniture manufacturers developed lines of ergonomic chairs designed for computer workstation usage; Knoll's Diffrient, Steelcase's Sensor, and Herman Miller's Equa were some of the major highly adjustable chairs from the 1980s.[55] Drawing on Henry Dreyfuss's *Measure of Man* charts published in 1960 and Niels Diffrient's *Humanscale* published in 1974, the designers of these office chairs typically relied on a range of average human dimensions (height, weight, proportion, and ability) as the basis of their design including the angle, shape, and dimensions of the seat; the overall height adjustment; the position of the arms; and the angle, placement, shape, and adjustability (tilt) of the back.[56] Though these types of averages were commonly used in industrial design in the late twentieth century as a way of integrating human factors, they were nonetheless problematic because they did not reflect a real human body, but rather a statistical fabrication derived from many diverse (and divergent) bodies.[57] Even with very high levels of adjustability, the emphasis in design practice on these kinds of standards meant that workers whose bodies did not conform to "average" dimensions, proportions, and abilities would still struggle to find a suitable adjustment for their bodies.

To address the unique needs of these non-average bodies, other types of "ergonomic" equipment became special items ordered and used to support the needs of workers whose bodies did not conform to the standard equipment. These specially designed accessories were intended to meet various challenges including disability, injury (like carpal tunnel), age-related body changes (e.g., for vision issues, musculoskeletal problems), unusual body dimensions (height, weight, width, and proportions that were outside the "average" range), or even just a simple case of left-handedness. Specially designed desks and chairs, wrist, palm, and arm rests and supports, adjustable keyboard trays, alternative keyboard designs, alternative mouse designs (including left-handed, vertical, large sized, and small sized), foot rests, document holders, monitor stands, screen magnifiers, and screen filters were all designed to make the "standard" equipment adaptable to diverse bodies.[58] As noted above, the ability to obtain these kinds of accommodations was typically tied to organizational culture and internal ergonomic policies (that may or may not have existed), and often dependent on a worker's own self-advocacy. Some organizations encouraged workers to seek these accommodations and made it easy to request such items to make the workstation more comfortable to the user.[59] In other cases, receiving accommodation was stricter requiring a documented health problem that could be specifically attributed to computer usage.[60]

In his very last days in office, President Bill Clinton signed a substantive OSHA bill that would have instituted ergonomic protections for 102 million workers and prevented as many as 460,000 injuries a year. According to a report in the *New York Times* from November of 2000, these were the "most far reaching set of labor regulations" that had ever been put in place in the United States. Hailed by union leaders as a major victory for workers, the new rules would have offered substantial protections for workers in all types of jobs in the United States including office workers and would have required businesses to invest substantial resources in evaluating and updating their workplaces to meet the new law.[61] In March of 2001, just a few months after his inauguration, President George W. Bush repealed the law arguing that it would inhibit business growth.[62] Once again, worker health and safety were treated as expendable in the face of economic expediency.

The landscape of ergonomic policy for office workers in the United States remains unregulated even today. Because this issue continues to be handled at a very local level within individual organizations, individual offices, and even under the supervision of individual managers, workers may have very different accommodations available to them. Underneath this problem is a deeper issue of equity in which workers' bodies are treated as adaptable and disposable, while technology and furniture are treated as fixed and "standard." In negotiating the numerous constraints that shaped ergonomic policy in the United States, workers' physical health and well-being was just one variable among a number of competing priorities. Ultimately, economic, technological, material, and political concerns continue to be privileged over creating a safe workplace for workers.

Notes

1. William Pulgram and Richard Stonis, *Designing the Automated Office: A Guide for Architects, Interior Designers, Space Planners, and Facility Managers* (New York: Whitney Library of Design, 1984), 118.
2. Paul Atkinson, "Man in a Briefcase: The Social Construction of the Laptop Computer and the Emergence of a Type Form," *Journal of Design History* 18, no. 2 (2005); Paul Atkinson, "The Best Laid Plans of Mice and Men: The Computer Mouse in the History of Computing," *Design Issues* 23, no. 3 (2007); Paul Atkinson, *Computer* (London: Reaktion Books, 2010); Elizabeth Petrick, *Making Computers Accessible: Disability Right and Digital Technology* (Baltimore, MD: Johns Hopkins University Press, 2015).
3. John Harwood, "The Interface: Ergonomics and the Aesthetics of Survival," in *Governing By Design: Architecture, Economy, and Politics in the Twentieth Century* ed. Aggregate (Pittsburgh: University of Pittsburgh Press, 2012); Bess Williamson, "Getting a Grip: Disability in American Industrial Design of the Late Twentieth Century," *Winterthur Portfolio* 46, no. 4 (2012); Barbara Penner, "Design Safety: Ergonomics in the Bathroom," in *Use Matters an Alternative History of Architecture*, ed. Kenny Cupers (New York: Routledge, 2013); Paul Emmons and Andreea Mhalache, "Architectural

Handbooks and the User Experience," in *Use Matters an Alternative History of Architecture*, ed. Kenny Cupers (New York: Routledge, 2013).

4 Vernon Mogensen, *Office Politics: Computers, Labor, and the Fight for Safety and Health* (New Brunswick, NJ: Rutgers University Press, 1996); Roger Horowitz, "'That Was a Dirty Job!': Technology and Workplace Hazards in Meatpacking over the Long Twentieth Century," *Labor: Studies in Working-Class History of the Americas* 5, no. 2 (2008); Shoshana Zuboff, *In the Age of the Smart Machine* (New York: Basic Books, 1988); Marco Diani, "The Social Design of Office Automation," *Design Issues* 3, no. 2 (1986); AnnMarie Brennan, "Olivetti: A Work of Art in the Age of Immaterial Labour," *Journal of Design History* 28, no. 3 (2015); Thomas Haigh, "Remembering the Origins of Word Processing and Office Automation," *IEEE Annals of the History of Computing* 28, no. 4 (2006).

5 Paul Atkinson, "Room with a VDU: The Development of the 'Glass House' in the Corporate Workplace," *Interiors: Design, Architecture and Culture* 5, no. 1 (2014).

6 Apple Computers, Annual Report 1984, p 1. Computer history museum archive, Jim Armstrong's papers, Box 5 Folder 19.

7 Atkinson, *Computer*, 88–91.

8 Office of Technology Assessment U.S. Congress, *Automation of America's Offices* (Washington, DC: U.S. Government Printing Office, 1985), 114.

9 Myron Hecht, *Microcomputers: Introduction to Features and Uses* (Washington, DC: Institute for Computer Sciences and Technology, National Bureau of Standards, 1984), 4–5.

10 Ibid., 4, 102–103. Tim Davis, "Information Technology and White-Collar Productivity," *The Executive* 5, no. 1 (1991): 58.

11 Radio Shack, catalog RSC-12, 1985. Trade Catalog available at archive.org.

12 US Congress, *Automation of America's Offices* 152–153; Steven Shute and Steven Starr, "Effects of Adjustable Furniture on VDT Users," *Human Factors: The Journal of Human Factors* 26, no. 2 (1984).

13 William Murray, "Potential Health Hazards of Video Display Terminals," ed. National Institute for Occupational Safety and Health (Cincinnati, OH: 1981).

14 Shute and Starr, "Effects of Adjustable Furniture on VDT Users," 158–159; U.S. Congress, *Automation of America's Offices*, 152; Timothy Springer, "Does Ergonomics Make Good Business Sense?," *Facilities Design and Management* 11, no. 7 (1992): 69.

15 Steven Sauter, L. John Chapman, and Sheri J. Knutson, *Improving VDT Work: Causes and Control of Health Concerns in VDT Use* (Madison: Department of Preventative Medicine, University of Wisconsin, 1985), 14; Murray, Potential Health Hazards, 25.

16 Subcommittee on Health and Safety, Committee on Education and Labor, "OSHA Oversight—Video Display Terminals in the Workplace," (Washington, DC: US, 1984), 31.

17 Sauter, Chapman, and Knutson, *Improving VDT Work*, 14.

18 Ibid., 18–25.

19 US Congress, *Automation of America's Offices*, 143.

20 Sauter, Chapman, and Knutson, *Improving VDT Work*, 50.

21　US Congress, *Automation of America's Offices*, 153; Etienne Grandjean, *Ergonomics in Computerized Offices* (New York: Taylor & Francis, 1987), 53.
22　US Congress, *Automation of America's Offices*, 143; Grandjean, *Ergonomics in Computerized Offices,* 54.
23　Karen Nussbaum and Judith Gregory, "Race against Time: Automation of the Office: An Analysis of the Trends in Office Automation and the Impact on the Office Workforce," *Office Technology and People* 1, no. 2/3 (1982): 225; US Congress, *Automation of America's Offices*, 146–148.
24　US Congress, *Automation of America's Offices*, 142–143.
25　Ibid., 146–156; Panel on Impact of Video Viewing on Vision of Workers, "Video Displays, Work, and Vision," ed. National Research Council (Washington, DC: National Academy Press, 1983), 21–22; Grandjean, *Ergonomics in Computerized Offices,* 55–61.
26　U.S. Congress, *Automation of America's Offices*, 142–143; Grandjean, *Ergonomics in Computerized Offices,* 184–185; Heidi Hartmann, Robert Kraut, and Louise Tilly, *Computer Chips and Paper Clips* (Washington, DC: National Academy Press, 1986), 134–135.
27　US Congress, *Automation of America's Offices*, 156.
28　Mogensen, *Office Politics,* 14; Women's Bureau, *Women and Office Automation: Issues for the Decade* (Washington, DC: Department of Labor, 1985), 27.
29　Subcommittee on Health and Safety, "OSHA Oversight—Video Display Terminals in the Workplace," 1984, 201–202.
30　Sauter, Chapman, and Knutson, *Improving VDT Work,* 25, 31, 36; Steven Sauter and Sheri J. Knutson, "Ergonomic Evaluation of VDT Workplaces in New York State Departments of Taxation and Motor Vehicles," (Cincinnati, OH: US Department of Health and Human Services, 1984), 15.
31　US Congress, *Automation of America's Offices*, 156.
32　Grandjean, *Ergonomics in Computerized Offices,* 190. Gail E. Brooks, "How Have Unions Address the Issue of VDT Users' Health and Safety," *Labor Law Journal* 37, no. 9 (1986): 670.
33　Sauter, Chapman, and Knutson, *Improving VDT Work,* 16.
34　Subcommittee on Health and Safety, "OSHA Oversight—Video Display Terminals in the Workplace," 1984, 118, 161,169; U.S. Congress, 20.
35　Mogensen, *Office Politics,* 67.
36　Subcommittee on Health and Safety, Committee on Education and Labor, "A Staff Report on the Oversight of OSHA with Respect to Video Display Terminals in the Workplace" (Washington, DC: US GPO, 1985), 32–34.
37　Subcommittee on Health and Safety, "A Staff Report on the Oversight of OSHA with Respect to Video Display Terminals in the Workplace," 1985, 20–21, 27, 43–46, 58–60.
38　Subcommittee on Health and Safety, "OSHA Oversight—Video Display Terminals in the Workplace," 1984, 114–115.
39　Ibid., 304–306.
40　Ibid., 114–115.

41   Subcommittee on Health and Safety, "A Staff Report on the Oversight of OSHA with Respect to Video Display Terminals in the Workplace," 1985, 2–3.
42   Laura Pincus, "Legal Liability for the Health Hazards Resulting from the Use of Video Display Terminals: Who Must Pay?" *Computer/Law Journal* 11, no. 1 (1991): 135, 165.
43   Langdon Winner, *The Whale and the Reactor: A Search for Limits in the Age of High Technology* (Chicago, IL: Chicago University Press, 1986), 149.
44   Interdata CRT, keyboard layout, 1976, MD-6 Folder 103, Richard Hollerith papers (Accession 2054), Hagley Museum and Library.
45   Knoll, *Furniture Price List*, 1983, trade catalog, Hagley Museum and Library.
46   Knoll, *Hannah Desk System Price List*, 1989, trade catalog, Hagley Museum and Library.
47   Ibid.
48   Ergonomic Policy (undated), Department of Administration Secretary Subject File, Box 52 Folder 17, Wisconsin Historical Society.
49   "Ergonomics Not in Corporate Policies," *Data Processing* 27, no 4 (1985): 47.
50   Peter Kilborn, "Hazards at the Keyboard," *New York Times*, June 24, 1990.
51   US Congress, *Automation of America's Offices*, 23.
52   Paul Atkinson, "The (in)Difference Engine: Explaining the Disappearance of Diversity in the Design of the Personal Computer," *Journal of Design History* 13, no. 1 (2000).
53   Davis, "Information Technology and White-Collar Productivity," 57.
54   Jonathan Olivares, *A Taxonomy of Office Chairs* (New York: Phaidon Press, 2011), 23.
55   Ibid., 48–61.
56   Ibid., 21–22.
57   Williamson, Getting a Grip, 216; Herman Miller, *Office Workers and the Computer: Reconciling the Demands of Technology and the Needs of People* (Zeeland, MI: Herman Miller, 1991), 9–10.
58   MISCO catalog, 1989, 28–45; Ali-Med, *Ergonomics*, 2008, HJ28–HJ75; General Services Administration, *GSA Supply Catalog*, 2001, 269–271.
59   Jane Wollman, "Selecting a Desk for a Computer," *New York Times*, June 30, 1983.
60   Kilborn, "Hazards at the Keyboard."
61   Steven Greenhouse, "Battle Lines Drawn Over Ergonomic Rules," *New York Times*, November 18, 2000.
62   Steven Greenhouse, "Rules' Repeal Heightens Workplace Safety Battle," *New York Times*, March 12, 2001.

Bibliography

Ali-Med. *Ergonomics*. 2008. Trade Catalog from the Hagley Museum and Library.
Atkinson, Paul. "The (in)Difference Engine: Explaining the Disappearance of Diversity in the Design of the Personal Computer." *Journal of Design History* 13, no. 1 (2000): 59–72.
Atkinson, Paul. "Man in a Briefcase: The Social Construction of the Laptop Computer and the Emergence of a Type Form." *Journal of Design History* 18, no. 2 (2005): 191–205.
Atkinson, Paul. "The Best Laid Plans of Mice and Men: The Computer Mouse in the History of Computing." *Design Issues* 23, no. 3 (2007): 46–61.

Atkinson, Paul. *Computer*. London: Reaktion Books, 2010.
Atkinson, Paul. "Room with a VDU: The Development of the 'Glass House' in the Corporate Workplace." *Interiors: Design, Architecture and Culture* 5, no. 1 (2014): 89–115.
Brennan, AnnMarie. "Olivetti: A Work of Art in the Age of Immaterial Labour." *Journal of Design History* 28, no. 3 (2015): 235–253.
Brooks, Gail E. "How Have Unions Addressed the Issue of VDT Users' Health and Safety." *Labor Law Journal* 37, no. 9 (1986): 668–675.
Bureau, Women's. *Women and Office Automation: Issues for the Decade*. Washington, DC: Department of Labor, 1985.
Davis, Tim. "Information Technology and White-Collar Productivity." *The Executive* 5, no. 1 (February 1991): 55–67.
Diani, Marco. "The Social Design of Office Automation." *Design Issues* 3, no. 2 (Autumn 1986): 73–82.
Emmons, Paul, and Andreea Mhalache. "Architectural Handbooks and the User Experience." In *Use Matters an Alternative History of Architecture*, ed. Kenny Cupers, 35–50. New York: Routledge, 2013.
"Ergonomics Not in Corporate Policies." *Data Processing* 27, no. 4 (1985): 47.
General Services Administration. *GSA Supply Catalog*. 2001. Trade Catalog from the HathiTrust.
Grandjean, Etienne. *Ergonomics in Computerized Offices*. New York: Taylor & Francis, 1987.
Greenhouse, Steven. "Battle Lines Drawn over Ergonomic Rules." *New York Times*. November 18, 2000.
Greenhouse, Steven. "Rules' Repeal Heightens Workplace Safety Battle." *New York Times*. March 12, 2001.
Haigh, Thomas. "Remembering the Origins of Word Processing and Office Automation." *IEEE Annals of the History of Computing* 28, no. 4 (October–December 2006): 6–31.
Hartmann, Heidi, Robert Kraut, and Louise Tilly. *Computer Chips and Paper Clips*. Washington, DC: National Academy Press, 1986.
Harwood, John. "The Interface: Ergonomics and the Aesthetics of Survival." In *Governing by Design: Architecture, Economy and Politics in the Twentieth Century*, ed. Aggregate, p 70–92. Pittsburgh, PA: University of Pittsburgh Press, 2012.
Hecht, Myron. *Microcomputers: Introduction to Features and Uses*. Washington, DC: Institute for Computer Sciences and Technology, National Bureau of Standards, 1984.
Herman, Miller. *Office Workers and the Computer: Reconciling the Demands of Technology and the Needs of People*. Pamphlet from the Hagley Museum and Library. Zeeland, MI: Herman Miller, 1991.
Horowitz, Roger. "'That Was a Dirty Job!': Technology and Workplace Hazards in Meatpacking over the Long Twentieth Century." *Labor: Studies in Working-Class History of the Americas* 5, no. 2 (2008): 13–25.
Knoll. *Furniture Price List*. 1983. Trade Catalog from the Hagley Museum and Library.
Knoll. *Hannah Desk System Price List*. 1989 Knoll Office Binder (1990). Trade Catalog from the Hagley Museum and Library.
Kilborn, Peter. "Hazards at the Keyboard." *New York Times*. June 24, 1990.
MISCO. *Misco: Your International Source for Computer Supplies and Accessories*. 1989. Trade Catalog from the Hagley Museum and Library.

Mogensen, Vernon. *Office Politics: Computers, Labor, and the Fight for Safety and Health*. New Brunswick, NJ: Rutgers University Press, 1996.

Murray, William. "Potential Health Hazards of Video Display Terminals," ed. National Institute for Occupational Safety and Health. Cincinnati, OH: US Government Printing Office, 1981.

Nussbaum, Karen, and Judith Gregory. "Race against Time: Automation of the Office: An Analysis of the Trends in Office Automation and the Impact on the Office Workforce." *Office Technology and People* 1, no. 2/3 (1982): 197–236.

Olivares, Jonathan. *A Taxonomy of Office Chairs*. New York: Phaidon Press, 2011.

Panel on Impact of Video Viewing on Vision of Workers. "Video Displays, Work, and Vision," ed. National Research Council. Washington, DC: National Academy Press, 1983.

Penner, Barbara. "Design Safety: Ergonomics in the Bathroom." In *Use Matters an Alternative History of Architecture*, ed. Kenny Cupers, 153–168. New York: Routledge, 2013.

Petrick, Elizabeth. *Making Computers Accessible: Disability Right and Digital Technology*. Baltimore, MD: Johns Hopkins University Press, 2015.

Pincus, Laura. 1991. "Legal Liability for the Health Hazards Resulting from the Use of Video Display Terminals: Who Must Pay?" *Computer/Law Journal* 11, no. 1: 131–171.

Pulgram, William, and Richard Stonis. *Designing the Automated Office: A Guide for Architects, Interior Designers, Space Planners, and Facility Managers*. New York: Whitney Library of Design, 1984.

Radio Shack. Catalog RSC-12. 1985. Trade catalog available from archive.org.

Sauter, Steven, and Sheri J. Knutson. "Ergonomic Evaluation of VDT Workplaces in New York State Departments of Taxation and Motor Vehicles." Cincinnati, OH: US Department of Health and Human Services, 1984.

Sauter, Steven, L. John Chapman, and Sheri J. Knutson. *Improving VDT Work: Causes and Control of Health Concerns in VDT Use*. Madison: Department of Preventative Medicine, University of Wisconsin, 1985.

Shute, Steven, and Steven Starr. "Effects of Adjustable Furniture on VDT Users." *Human Factors: The Journal of Human Factors* 26, no. 2 (1984): 157–170.

Springer, Timothy. "Does Ergonomics Make Good Business Sense?" *Facilities Design and Management* 11, no. 7 (July 1992): 46.

Subcommittee on Health and Safety, Committee on Education and Labor. *OSHA Oversight—Video Display Terminals in the Workplace*. Washington, DC: US GPO, 1984.

Subcommittee on Health and Safety, Committee on Education and Labor. *A Staff Report on the Oversight of OSHA with Respect to Video Display Terminals in the Workplace*. Washington, DC: US GPO, 1985.

U.S. Congress, Office of Technology Assessment. *Automation of America's Offices*. Washington, DC: US Government Printing Office, 1985.

Williamson, Bess. "Getting a Grip: Disability in American Industrial Design of the Late Twentieth Century." *Winterthur Portfolio* 46, no. 4 (2012): 213–236.

Winner, Langdon. *The Whale and the Reactor: A Search for Limits in the Age of High Technology*. Chicago, IL: Chicago University Press, 1986.

Wollman, Jane. "Selecting a Desk for a Computer." *New York Times*. June 30, 1983.

Zuboff, Shoshana. *In the Age of the Smart Machine*. New York: Basic Books, 1988.

11 Designing Emergency Access: Lifeline & LifeCall
ELIZABETH ELLCESSOR

Heavily marketed on television during the 1980s and 1990s, personal emergency response systems (PERS) are best remembered today for one particular, widely disseminated 1989 LifeCall advertisement. In it, the elderly Mrs. Fletcher falls to the floor, presses the mobile radio panic button that she wears around her neck, and cries, "I've fallen, and I can't get up!" This chapter traces the history and design of the PERS as a form of emergency media and communications. Issued by manufacturers such as Lifeline (now Philips Lifeline) and LifeCall (now Life Alert), these systems used the landline telephone system as an alert technology, enabling people to easily summon help when needed. They were primarily used by women in their seventies and eighties, often living alone, as a means of ensuring safety while preserving a degree of independence not understood to be possible in assisted living or similar arrangements.[1]

This chapter explores the design, development, and diffusion of the PERS with particular attention to themes of aging, debility, and social isolation in its cultural footprint. I draw upon patent literatures, applied medical literatures, popular press, and the infamous advertising campaign. Notably, I do not have access to the hardware (pendant and/or panic button) that users would have worn in order to have continuous, mobile access to the emergency response system in their home. Like telephone handsets of an earlier era,[2] these physical devices were considered the property of the companies involved and have not had robust subsequent lives in resale markets, garage sales, or other secondary markets. Thus, as with many histories of design, I rely upon a corpus of artifacts that reflect the discourses and material conditions that surrounded these technologies.

Simultaneously, I also aim to flag something less tangible but even more pervasive. Many of these designs encouraged users to rely on newer technologies rather than older or more dispersed forms of emergency communication. They were developed to actively protect and ensure a particular form of safety for their elderly or disabled users, even as their cultural circulation minimized these issues and privileged campier, humorous takes on the PERS. The PERS presaged the development of mobile smart technologies marketed to a mainstream audience today, and its largely forgotten history provides a useful reminder of how design for disability may innovate broadly desirable technologies.

Designing Emergency Access

In this section, I explore three of the earliest patents in PERS design, held by Lifeline Systems, Inc. Each marks important steps in the development of these systems, and each also highlights a thematic element that is relevant to emergency media and communications more broadly: the historical PERS was *social*, *infrastructural*, and *intimate*.

The invention of the PERS is usually attributed to Andrew Dibner, a former professor of psychology at Boston University and the founder of Lifeline Systems, Inc.[3] Dibner's 1976 patent for a PERS described the invention as "an automatic telephone alarm," which would dial preset numbers to send an alarm.[4] This early iteration proposed that "If the owner shows his healthy capability through daily use of the telephone the present invention would keep a silent vigil; but in the event that the telephone is not used for 24 hours, or for a selected shorter time, possibly indicating an incapability of the owner, the device automatically sounds an alarm, or in some versions calls a prerecorded number or numbers giving emergency messages."[5] This structure, in which the technology would automatically act in the absence of user initiation, is a *passive* form of alarm. There is no need for an individual to recognize the problem, remember necessary actions, and complete a series of steps to summon aid. Often, passive alarms are preferred when possible, as they eliminate these hurdles and may facilitate quick response.

The taken-for-granted foundation of this design, of course, is that daily—or at least regular—use of a landline telephone is a demonstration of "healthy capacity" and normative part of daily life. In fact, 1975 marked an all-time high in landline telephone service, with 95 percent of American households having service.[6] With few alternatives for synchronous interpersonal communication, regular telephone use thus may have seemed a reliable indication of a user's well-being. Yet, as Dibner's patent dramatically stated, "old or infirm people who live alone fear their becoming incapacitated, being unable to summon help, and perhaps expiring or suffering irremediable damage because they may not be found for days."[7] This description invokes a relatively isolated elderly audience, and one can imagine that many people living alone and feeling such concerns may not have robust social networks maintained via telephone. Yet, this design promised that in the case that the telephone was not used and the alarm was sounded, the device would call a "prerecorded number or numbers." It did not indicate that these would be the phone numbers of a police, medical, or monitoring service; in fact, early literature about how to use a PERS often suggested that these preset numbers be the means of contacting family or neighbors, who could then initiate a physical check on the user at their home.[8]

The foundations of the PERS, it seems, included reliance on a supportive social network. These included not only close ties, such as family members, but relatively looser ties of geography and acquaintance (neighbors) that were nonetheless central to community strength.[9] Historically, emergency response was a matter of social interaction before, or instead of, professional intervention.[10] Care of elderly or disabled individuals was also a social, and largely domestic, phenomenon. As family organizations changed in the last half of the twentieth century, moving away from cohabitation or proximity, more elderly people aged in relative isolation. The PERS offered to mitigate such separations and technologically enable care over distance. Alerting neighbors or family members was a core function of the PERS, implying that responsibility for the health and safety of the PERS user was shared between community members and technological infrastructure. Together, the user, the call center, and the social network would ensure proper handling of emergencies.

In 1977, Dibner and Lifeline Systems, Inc. received another patent, titled "Closed-Loop Emergency Alarm and Response System." This patent encompassed the full infrastructure that would become foundational to personal emergency response systems: "A PERS has three components: a small radio *transmitter* (a help button carried or worn by the user); a *console* connected to the user's telephone; and an *emergency response center* that monitors calls."[11] The 1977 patent introduced the design as "a closed-loop system for monitoring the condition of a person in a residence."[12] This system is illustrated in Figure 11.1, which includes "a portable radio transmitter panic unit with a button" (#21 in the figure), the local telephone handset and hardware, the public infrastructure of telephone lines, a monitoring station with a transceiver and an individual receiving messages, an ambulance being dispatched,

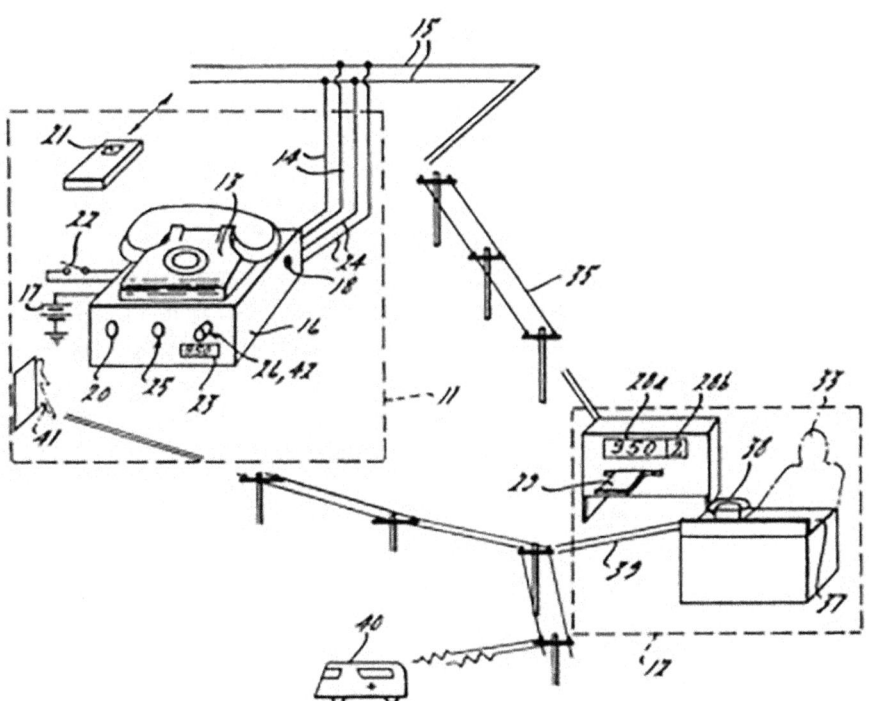

Figure 11.1 Illustration of the full system, from "Closed-Loop Emergency Alarm and Response System," US patent, 1977.

and an individual entering the user's home. The patent describes each numbered element of this illustration, human, technological, and procedural. The patent illustration indicates an "Information directory" (#37) that "includes data on emergency responders who are available for each user of the service. Responders may be neighbors, relatives, friends, or representatives of housing projects, social agencies, churches, police or fire departments who have previously indicated their availability to proceed to a residence from which an emergency alarm has been emitted."[13]

The invention illustrated in Figure 11.1 is not so much a designed artifact as it is a designed *infrastructure*. Infrastructure is a material network of connections and standards that supports routinized activities. Geoffrey Bowker and Susan Leigh Star define standards as "any set of agreed-upon rules" that span communities, time, and distance[14]; these rules, often assemblages of laws, technical norms, and industry lore, are an abstracted form of infrastructure that (in turn) may actualize particular arrangements of material, human, and ideological resources. Infrastructure is thus neither natural nor neutral, but must be learned and put into practice by a range of stakeholders and institutions. The diagram seen in Figure 11.1 is a map of one such infrastructure, layered atop of the telephone network, and encompassing technologies, the human components are necessary to the completion of its circuit; monitoring center employees enact procedures, and responders make contact with the PERS user. Architect Keller Easterling has argued that "infrastructure is now the overt point of contact and access between us all—the rules governing the space of every day life"[15]; this is as true of technologically mediated space as it is of our infrastructural physical environments. The potentialities and procedures of infrastructure guide and delimit our interactions, particularly in moments of emergency.

Where the 1977 patent hinted at the possibility of a remote device, a 1985 patent also held by Lifeline Systems, Inc. established a radio transmitting device "which can be worn on the wrist or suspended from a neck chain to provide immediate access in the event of an emergency condition and without interfering with the normal day-to-day activities of the wearer."[16] Often referred to as a pendant, the transmitter was a thick square, with a single button centrally placed (see Figure 11.2). As seen in advertising, a PERS button was usually worn on a cord around the neck, as a kind of protective jewelry.

The patent for the transmitting device illustrated a third dimension of the PERS that is relevant to contemporary emergency and medical apps and hardware: intimacy. Users were invited to take up intimate relationships with these devices, wearing them on their bodies at all times. One of the most common points of failure for the PERS was when someone forgot or chose not to wear or carry their transmitter; its efficacy was premised on its mobility and omnipresence. The 1982 patent described the transmitter—to be worn on a necklace or bracelet—as "sufficiently small, lightweight and impervious to water such that it is easily worn during all usual home activities without impediment."[17] Suggested in this description is that the device could accompany the wearer throughout the home, including in the bath or shower, a place where many falls occur.[18] On the one hand, we might consider these

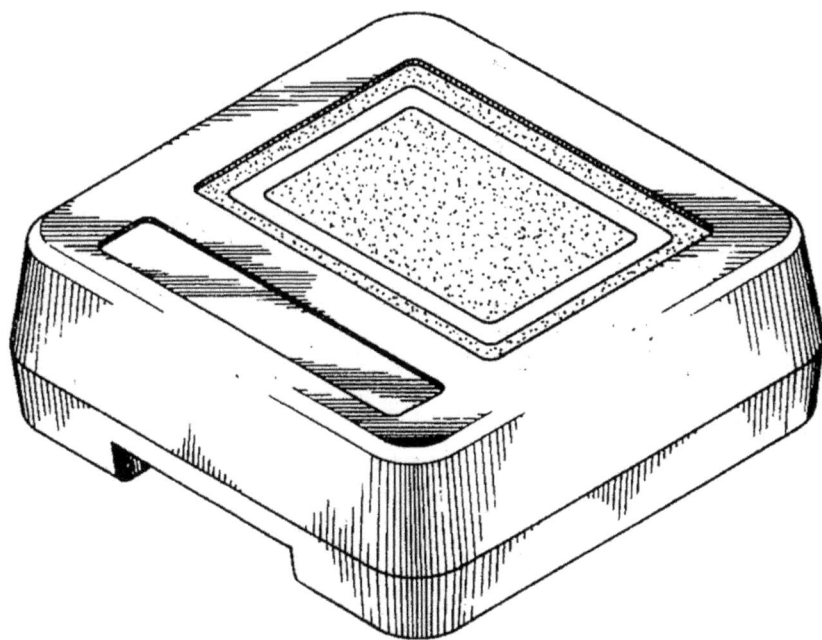

Figure 11.2 An "ornamental design" for the alarm transmitter, from a 1985 Lifeline US patent; current designs are quite similar in shape and simplicity.

designs to be substitutes for live-in servants, medical personnel, or family who at one time would have regularly attended to the well-being of aged or disabled people; the technology does not replace these caregivers or other social contact, but can call them if needed. But the bathroom, of course, is rarely a space connected with sociality. As a site of profound intimacy, nakedness, waste, and dirt, incorporating the PERS into this space, and associated activities, demonstrates a level of intimacy with the device (and potentially with those who would answer a call for help) that is worthy of attention.

In interviews with Eileen J. Porter, a scholar of gerontological nursing, several elderly women who used a PERS declared that "this thing is always around my neck."[19] From this experience of continual co-presence, Porter argues that these technologies be understood not as providing more traditional "live-in help" but instead is designed to be a "live-on helper."[20] Seen this way, we can begin to imagine the *pervasive* presence of this technology in users' experiences. Living-*on*, and the device-to-skin contact that it implies, facilitates an understanding of the PERS' basic design as an extension of the body. The beige plastic of the PERS, similar to that often used in hearing aids, is deliberately unfashionable. As argued by design scholar Graham Pullin, "Medical-looking devices are molded from pink plastic in an attempt to camoflage [sic] them against the skin,"[21] minimizing evidence of bodily differences that assistive technologies might reveal.

This analysis of the *design* of the PERS emphasizes its social, infrastructural, and intimate dimensions. Through this technology, users are potentially empowered to connect to an always-available, robust support system that could allow them to live more independently despite risks associated with aging or debility. In the following section, I turn to the *popular reception* of these devices; I look to how these devices circulated in popular culture, beyond their intended audiences, and how such circulation worked against the potentially empowering and useful innovations of the PERS.

Cultural Circulation of Personal Emergency Response Systems

As noted at the beginning of this chapter, PERS devices have been immortalized through a series of television commercials aired by LifeCall beginning in the late 1980s.[22] Often identified by a catchphrase—"I've fallen, and I can't get up!"—these commercials are well known among US adults who watched late-night, local, or cable television during the 1990s. These were low-budget ads,[23] aired in relatively affordable slots on cable and late at night, featuring several vignettes of elderly individuals using the LifeCall system in staged homes. Intended to communicate real-life scenarios, these commercials quickly permeated popular culture.

The best-known vignette was that of "Mrs. Fletcher," played by Edith Fore, who, as it happened, had experienced a similar fall in her own home before becoming the face of LifeCall.[24] A contemporary article in *USA Today* vividly described the action: "You've seen the ad. A little old lady takes a tumble, pushes a LifeCall emergency medical device and squawks for help. The response: 'We'll be right there, Mrs. Fletcher.'"[25] A more recent article emphasized the physicality of the performance, in which Mrs. Fletcher "lay sprawled on her bathroom floor, walker toppled, unable to recover from a fall."[26]

The PERS, like any cultural artifact, was subject to differing interpretations by varied audiences. Among its target audience, many viewers may have deeply identified with "Mrs Fletcher" and her situation. Simultaneously, however, "I've fallen, and I can't get up" took on a life of its own in a youthful popular culture. According to reporting in *USA Today,* "College kids, natch, were first to turn it into a kvetch phrase for distress."[27] The use of "natch" links the phrase to other kinds of youth culture and slang, further naturalizing the idea that a commercial aimed at the elderly was being taken up by a broader culture that was often unattuned to social and economic changes, a population that was rapidly growing older, and the stresses associated with aging, debility, and dependence in the late twentieth century. Instead, *The Atlanta Journal & Constitution* relayed that Mrs. Fore's dramatic line has saturated every corner of the culture. An American can hardly slip in public anymore without hearing a co-worker or bystander repeat it. *Life magazine* pronounced it "the statement of the year." Two rap songs incorporate it. Comedians, radio deejays, and TV talk-show hosts repeat it constantly.

Even critics of President Bush have used it whenever his popularity dips: "He's fallen in the polls, and he can't get up." Madonna has used it onstage like a modern-day

Mae West, lying down and cooing: "I've fallen, and I can't get up. But now that I'm down here ..."[28]

The expansion of this catch phrase from late-night, low-budget commercials targeted at elderly women to a broader popular culture may be understood in terms of what John Fiske referred to as the "textually disrespectful" discrimination of popular culture.[29] Popular culture (like the people who create it) often takes advantage of "elements of the oppositional, the evasive, the scandalous, the offensive, the vulgar, the resistant,"[30] picking up and reusing, recontextualizing, or otherwise putting a particular twist on the offerings of mass culture. In picking up on the camp delivery and banality of Mrs. Fletcher's line, the popular culture of late-twentieth-century America reveled in an irreverence toward age, debility, and assistive (or medical) technology.

Though Fiske offers the pleasures of the popular as a resource for political resistance, it is hard not to see the popular circulation of Mrs. Fletcher's plea as, in part, a repudiation of age and disability. Television advertisements have generally targeted audiences perceived as valuable; adults between 18 and 49; ads that address populations outside of that group are often found in cheaper morning or late-night time slots, on less-popular cable channels or specific programming that skews toward an older audience. The context of cable television in the late twentieth century, however, formed a perfect storm in which advertisements such as this one were being presented to audiences for late-night television, generally a youthful (even specifically collegiate) audience.[31] The intrusion of products and services aimed at disabled or otherwise marginalized audiences in mainstream spaces can provoke a disorientation that is ameliorated through humor.[32] The pleasures of the popular, when applied to these contexts, become somewhat difficult to accept. Rather than broadening the scope of who, and what, is part of popular culture, such humorous appropriations of accessibility features seem to suggest a retrenchment of normative subject positions.

The tension between the pleasures of popular irreverence and the possibility of strengthening cultural exclusion is evident in some responses from the time. The same *USA Today* article quoted from above posits: "What's so funny? It's not the age; it's the situation."[33] This brief framing offers a putative defense against charges of agism or mean-spiritedness, and the article quotes representatives of LifeCall and the American Association of Retired Persons (AARP) getting in on the fun, and "having a good time with it." What of Fore? LifeCall representatives claimed to be "doing our best to protect her from the media."[34] Yet, months later, an article was illustrated with a photo of Fore signing autographs at a "fall-off" held in an Atlanta mall.[35] These examples might demonstrate that there was a need for advocates for the PERS to accept, and participate in, the widespread mockery of the device and its users. But why? Mockery of the PERS and its users would seem to discourage usage and alienate a target audience, as these "catchy" ads could "cast a stigma that kept many from adopting the devices."[36]

This perspective, however, assumes that the end users (like the fictional Mrs. Fletcher) were the target audience for the PERS marketing. While they were certainly one important audience, in the following section I argue that the PERS was also a *surveillance technology* marketed directly to the children and caregivers of those people who would wear the devices and be monitored by the call center. The design itself relies on a structure of benevolent social and (more troubling) bureaucratic surveillance of elderly or disabled people; this system was foundational to the way that the PERS was marketed, sold, and employed.

Independence, Security, and Surveillance

The commercials, the catch-phrase, and their popular parodies created broad awareness of the PERS. A 1989 letter to the editor took this ambient awareness as a given: "Radio and television commercials have made almost everyone aware of the LifeCall concept."[37] Aware, and amused—the irreverent popular responses were widely circulated, while sincere uses and perspectives were not part of the mainstream media conversation. This imbalance further marginalized experiences of debility and aging, allowed some audiences to be both desirous of and distanced from these surveillant technologies.

It seems evident from both academic and popular literatures that the PERS companies were also attempting to reach out to adult children or caretakers who served the elderly. In 1990, Lee Norrgard of the AARP stated that "these systems give confidence to older people and confidence to their middle-aged children."[38] More recently, a popular press article about PERS technologies quoted Sandy Markwood, CEO of the National Association of Area Agencies on Aging, as saying that "a lot of calls come from the caregivers asking what would happen to Mom or Dad if they fell …. These devices provide a sense of relief for them."[39] The *confidence* and *relief* invoked in such statements are likely meant to reassure adult children that a PERS could ease their feelings of worry or unease technologically.

Advocates of PERS technologies regularly invoked "independence" and "security" as rationales for adopting the devices. A second 1985 Lifeline patent asserted that "the system is primarily intended for the elderly, infirm, or incapacitated who are living alone and who, in the event of illness or injury, might be unable to summon assistance and thereby suffer further harm as a result of inattention. The availability of this system will permit the aging and infirm to *live independently without this fear.*"[40] The goal of an independent, fearless life is made central to this rationale. Independence, as a value of normative adult life, is upheld here as a benchmark that those positioned as "elderly, infirm, or incapacitated" (or disabled) ought to aspire to. Fearlessness, or the oft-invoked "security," is similarly valued as necessary for maintenance of that independence. There is some evidence that these goals were at least partially realized; a review of a PERS program published in 1993 indicated "anecdotal reports that users felt secure."[41]

The inverse of these discourses, however, was present in the very structure of the design itself. As argued by many scholars of surveillance, "security" is a routine justification for increasingly invasive and far-reaching forms of information collection and use.[42] David Lyon asserts that surveillance is often "practiced with a view to enhancing ... health or safety."[43] This was true of the PERS, as well. Its very design enabled the constant possibility of social surveillance and relied upon the sharing of personal information via bureaucratic surveillance, all in the interest of promoting or preserving the end user's well-being.

The social surveillance enabled by a PERS is evident in the infrastructural diagram seen earlier (Figure 11.1). The image of the worker at the monitoring center and the neighbor entering the home indicates that these systems transform a personal health crises into a social event. Over time, the social group that could be notified of emergency grew even wider: "Prompt dispatching of the proper paramedic, police or fire personnel and notification to the victim's family and physician, as well as or instead of neighbors, insures that the right kind of assistance will be there as quickly as possible."[44] The social network described in PERS patents includes emergency personnel, as well as those who will be notified—without the express consent of the user. This ability to notify friends or, more often, family was presented as a benefit of a PERS: "911 doesn't have the capacity to call your daughter, too."[45] This social surveillance was often conceived of as benevolent, desired, and a means of maintaining family ties and robust information networks. However, this might not always be true. Feminist surveillance studies draw attention to how domestic violence, for instance, alters dynamics of privacy and surveillance[46]; the automatic notification in a health crisis is a site where social surveillance might become malign.

By its very design, the ever-presence and drawbacks of such social surveillance means that the PERS "might be more of a relief to family members and health care providers than it is to the older person."[47] Automatic notifications, for instance, might ease the worries and guilt of adult children living far from elderly parents. By contrast, Porter found that the eight women she interviewed were often startled by hearing a stranger's voice in their homes after accidentally activating the call button.[48] A more dramatic case was recounted in 1992, when San Francisco emergency personnel "pounded on the front door and again received no answer. They then forced their way into the house, where they found a frightened woman alone in bed, hiding under the covers from the 'intruders.'"[49] She had accidentally triggered the signal on her alarm, and was surprised by the unintended response. Such intrusions, in addition to being startling, could easily foster a sense of ever-present surveillance that *precludes* achievement of the independence hailed by PERS advocates.

Additionally, use of a PERS entails an exceptional, and possibly uncomfortable, level of bureaucratic surveillance. Where a typical call to 9-1-1 might involve sharing some personal health information, use of a PERS involved the creation of a data file on each end user. Individuals' health information, the contact information of their friends, family members, and doctors, their closest hospital, their address, and other material would be part of this file, which was maintained by the PERS and its monitoring center. Such records form an undoubtedly rich source for institutional ethnography as a means of understanding a circuit of surveillant practices.[50] In the case of the PERS, an institutional ethnography would highlight the processes of "bureaucratic disclosure"[51] by which PERS users share their personal and health information in a process that both justifies and shapes future services. That data body would lie in wait for an alarm, at which point it could be used by staff at the monitoring center to make a number of crucial decisions. The data practices employed with such files have proven nearly impossible to identify; thus I can only suggest the "security" associated with use of a PERS did not necessarily extend to the security of private and/or medical data. The identification of emergency contacts brought them into this web of surveillance as well, positioning them as responsible actors in the PERS surveillance circuit.

Surveillance by design has, of course, been of concern to many scholars of contemporary apps, wearable devices, and other health management technologies. My contention in drawing out these examples is that such surveillance is not new; it was built in to earlier forms of emergency monitoring, as were themes of the social, infrastructural, and intimate. Surveillance, however, appears to be the *end goal* of the PERS; it is a way of coping with aging and debility. But it also offers more agential discourses which are deployed in limited ways to "convince" end users to submit to the monitoring that might be more desired by others in their lives.

Conclusion

I conclude with the ending words of a 1991 overview of the PERS industry:

> It is not inconceivable that the time may come when everyone has his or her own portable PERS unit that they wear at all times so that, at any given moment, a central monitoring station can know where they are and what they're doing, and can send help right away, whether they need it or not. Relax. It's only a joke … now.[52]

While these concerns may have been masked as a joke then, they are rapidly becoming a reality. Indeed, the easy conflation of health, ability, and surveillance have not disappeared. Instead, such pervasive monitoring—and its more recent incorporation into heavily marketed designs—are only becoming increasingly common.

In some ways, this chapter might even be seen as a prehistory of the wearables, apps, and health management technologies now erupting out of Silicon Valley. Newer technologies like the Apple Watch (Series 3), for example, have only expanded the currency of wearable monitors. These more recent designs downplay the possibility of elderly, disabled, or otherwise marginalized groups might desire or be served by this kind of technology. Advertisements for the Series 3 feature images of young, active bodies, and emphasize use of the devices for strenuous exercise, constant white-collar work, and commercial entertainment. Furthermore, when official descriptions of the Series 3 do address "health," they do so not in terms of medical data or emergency communications, but in terms of apps to promote mindfulness, quality sleep, and weight loss.[53] The ambitions of these newer technologies are being recontextualized as innovative means of self-knowledge and security. In some ways, what is new is not the capacity, or even the characteristic themes or surveillant dynamics. The mass diffusion of this technology through emerging designs being offered to broader audiences is new, as is the resultant invisibility of possible elderly, infirm, or disabled users.

In this shift from elderly and disabled users and needs, we might observe what media and disability scholar Mara Mills terms an "assistive pretext," or "the resourcing of disability within technoscience."[54] She details the process by which deafness and assistive technologies were mined for technological innovations, and then abandoned for more profitable endeavors in audio technologies. Using the PERS as an example, we may also speak against the universalizing tendencies of much technocultural discourse, which presumes an able-bodied, youthful, affluent, and technologically savvy user. Reclaiming the assistive precursors and overlooked users of media technologies is a means by which to counteract the pathological novelty of digital media industries.

But such an analysis is also a way to produce "access-knowledge"[55] about the classifications, experiences, and material contexts experienced by people who are elderly, disabled, or both. A history of PERS products suggests an emerging belief that design can mitigate or even eradicate some of the most challenging problems with aging and debility. And finally, it is a method by which to advocate for a technoculture that learns from its past and treats seriously the technologies, gaps, and user experiences therein.

Notes

1. Robinson, "Lifeline services—An Industry Still Defining Its Own Identity," *Ageing International* 18, no. 1 (1991): 43.
2. Harry G. Lang, *A Phone of Our Own: The Deaf Insurrection against Ma Bell* (Washington, DC: Gallaudet University Press, 2000).
3. Robinson, "Lifeline services—An Industry Still Defining Its Own Identity," 43.
4. Andrew S. Dibner, Automatic Telephone Alarm System, US3989900A, filed November 4, 1974, and issued November 2, 1976, 1.
5. Dibner, Automatic Telephone Alarm System, 1.
6. "Statistical Abstract of the United States" (Washington, DC: US Census Bureau, 1999), 885, https://www.census.gov/library/publications/1999/compendia/statab/119ed.html
7. Dibner, Automatic Telephone Alarm System, 1.
8. Mariel Garza, "Help … I've Fallen and I Can't Get Up," *Journal of Emergency Medical Services* 17, no. 5 (May 1992): 13–18.
9. Mark Granovetter, "The Strength of Weak Ties: A Network Theory Revisited," *Sociological Theory* 1 (1983): 201–233.
10. Joshua Reeves, *Citizen Spies: The Long Rise of America's Surveillance Society* (New York: New York University Press, 2017).
11. "FTC Facts for Consumers: Personal Emergency Response Systems," 1. Emphasis original.

12 Andrew S. Dibner, Closed-Loop Emergency Alarm and Response System, US4064368A, filed June 7, 1976, and issued December 20, 1977, 1.
13 Dibner, Closed-Loop Emergency Alarm and Response System, 4.
14 Geoffrey C. Bowker and Susan Leigh Star, *Sorting Things Out: Classification and Its Consequences* (Cambridge, MA: MIT Press, 2000), 14.
15 Keller Easterling, *Extrastatecraft: The Power of Infrastructure Space* (London; New York: Verso, 2014), 11.
16 Eric L. LaWhite and Patrick G. Phillipps, Portable transmitter for emergency alarm system having watertight enclosure, US4491970A, filed December 30, 1982, and issued January 1, 1985, 1, https://patents.google.com/patent/US4491970
17 LaWhite and Phillipps, Portable transmitter, 4.
18 Falls were, and remain, a significant risk for elderly people living at home and in hospitals and assisted living facilities. See Christine T. Cigolle et al., "The Epidemiologic Data on Falls, 1998–2010: More Older Americans Report Falling," *JAMA Internal Medicine* 175, no. 3 (March 1, 2015): 443–445.
19 Eileen J. Porter, "Moments of Apprehension in the Midst of a Certainty: Some Frail Older Widows' Lives with a Personal Emergency Response System," *Qualitative Health Research* 13, no. 9 (November 1, 2003): 1321.
20 Ibid.
21 Graham Pullin, *Design Meets Disability* (Cambridge, MA: MIT Press, 2009), 15.
22 There is significant confusion in popular press and academic literature about the identities of specific PERS companies. Lifeline is now Phillips Lifeline, and the LifeCall company referenced by press from the 1980s and 1990s appears to now be affiliated with Life Alert Emergency Systems, which claims ownership of the classic catchphrase. A company called LifeCall Medical Alert exists, and boasts over forty years of service, but its relationship to the prior LifeCall is unclear. See: "LIFE ALERT Official Website—I've Fallen and I Can't Get Up!®," accessed April 16, 2018, http://www.lifealert.com/; "FallAlertTM Medical Alert Systems Emergency Response Systems," *LifeCall Medical Alert Systems* (blog), accessed April 16, 2018, https://www.lifecall.com/about/
23 The low budget can be inferred from the commercial's aesthetic, but is supported by reports that actress Edith Fore was paid $1000 and no residuals. See Jubera, "Falling for Mrs. Fletcher: Pathetic Plea from Older Lady in TV Ad Who Can't Get Up Pushes Right Button with Fans," *The Atlanta Journal and Constitution* (February 8, 1991), sec. Features.
24 Jubera, "Falling for Mrs. Fletcher."
25 Elizabeth Snead, "Stumbling onto a Hip New Catch Phrase," *USA Today*, October 2, 1990, sec. Life.
26 Patrick Verel, "Calling for Help Devices Help Seniors, Disabled in Case of an Emergency," *The Augusta Chronicle*, January 11, 2005, sec. Your Life.
27 Snead, "Stumbling onto a Hip New Catch Phrase."
28 Jubera, "Falling for Mrs. Fletcher."
29 John Fiske, *Understanding Popular Culture*, 2nd ed. (London; New York: Routledge, 2010), 151.

30 Fiske, *Understanding Popular Culture,* 127.
31 David J. Atkin, "Adoption of Cable amidst a Multimedia Environment," *Telematics and Informatics* 10, no. 1 (December 1, 1993): 51–58; Jonathan Gray and Amanda D. Lotz, *Television Studies* (Cambridge: Polity, 2011).
32 Elsewhere, I've written about the visibility of American Sign Language interpreters in weather related public announcements, and the subsequent redeployment of these videos and images in memes, *Saturday Night Live,* and breathless popular press articles. See Elizabeth Ellcessor, "Is There a Sign for That? Media, American Sign Language Interpretation, and the Paradox of Visibility," *Perspectives* 23, no. 4 (October 2, 2015): 586–98.
33 Snead, "Stumbling onto a Hip New Catch Phrase."
34 Ibid.
35 Jubera, "Falling for Mrs. Fletcher."
36 Sam Wood, "Philly-Based Medical Guardian Targets 'Massive' Market among Elderly for Personal Alarms," *Philly.com*, February 2, 2018, http://www.philly.com/philly/business/philly-company-targets-massive-market-in-personal-alarms-20180202.html. Obviously, many elderly and disabled users did purchase PERS devices and monitoring plans, and many likely did identify with the fears presented in the LifeCall advertisement. However, this audience, and their interpretation of the advertisements as cautionary tales, was largely invisible in popular conversations about the PERS. The campy, youth-driven popular culture narrative dominated media coverage, and thus I am working from an archive from which the elderly and disabled were largely excluded. Again, this speaks to a devaluing of those people as audiences, consumers, and participants in the culture of the PERS devices.
37 Donald Deixel, "'Are You O.K.?' Plan Is Good but Too Little," *New York Times*, August 13, 1989, sec. 12WC.
38 Barry Meier, "Concerns Grow about Marketing of Medical Alert Systems," *The New York Times*, July 14, 1990, sec. Style.
39 Verel, "Calling for Help."
40 L. Dennis Shapiro, Personal alarm system, US4524243A, filed July 7, 1983, and issued June 18, 1985. Emphasis mine.
41 Porter, "Moments of Apprehension in the Midst of a Certainty," 922.
42 Mark Andrejevic, "Interactive (In)security," *Cultural Studies* 20, no. 4–5 (July 1, 2006): 441–458; Simone Browne, *Dark Matters: On the Surveillance of Blackness* (Durham, NC: Duke University Press Books, 2015); Rachel E. Dubrofsky and Shoshana Amielle Magnet, eds., *Feminist Surveillance Studies* (Durham, NC: Duke University Press Books, 2015); Kelly A. Gates, *Our Biometric Future: Facial Recognition Technology and the Culture of Surveillance* (New York: New York University Press, 2011); David Lyon, *Surveillance after September 11*, 1st ed. (Malden, MA: Polity, 2003).
43 Lyon David, "Technology vs 'terrorism': Circuits of City Surveillance since September 11th," *International Journal of Urban and Regional Research* 27, no. 3 (October 13, 2003): 673.
44 Deixel, "'Are You O.K.?' Plan Is Good but Too Little."

45 Verel, "Calling for Help."
46 Dubrofsky and Magnet, *Feminist Surveillance Studies*.
47 Porter, "Moments of Apprehension in the Midst of a Certainty," 1319.
48 Ibid.
49 Garza, "Help … I've Fallen and I Can't Get Up," 13.
50 Kevin T. Walby, "Institutional Ethnography and Surveillance Studies: An Outline for Inquiry," *Surveillance & Society* 3, no. 2/3 (September 1, 2002), https://ojs.library.queensu.ca/index.php/surveillance-and-society/article/view/3498
51 Stephanie L. Kerschbaum, Laura T. Eisenman, and James M. Jones, *Negotiating Disability: Disclosure and Higher Education* (Ann Arbor, MI: University of Michigan Press, 2017).
52 Robinson, "Lifeline services—An Industry Still Defining Its Own Identity," 47.
53 "Apple Watch Series 3," Apple, accessed April 16, 2018, https://www.apple.com/apple-watch-series-3/
54 Mara Mills, "Deaf Jam: From Inscription to Reproduction to Information," *Social Text* 28, no. 1_102 (March 1, 2010): 39.
55 Aimi Hamraie, *Building Access: Universal Design and the Politics of Disability*, 1st ed. (Minneapolis: University of Minnesota Press, 2017).

Bibliography

Andrejevic, Mark. "Interactive (In)security." *Cultural Studies* 20, no. 4–5 (July 1, 2006): 441–458. https://doi.org/10.1080/09502380600708838

"Apple Watch Series 3." Apple. Accessed April 16, 2018. https://www.apple.com/apple-watch-series-3/

Atkin, David J. "Adoption of Cable amidst a Multimedia Environment." *Telematics and Informatics* 10, no. 1 (December 1, 1993): 51–58. https://doi.org/10.1016/0736-5853(93)90017-X

Bowker, Geoffrey C., and Susan Leigh Star. *Sorting Things Out: Classification and Its Consequences*. Cambridge, MA: MIT Press, 2000.

Browne, Simone. *Dark Matters: On the Surveillance of Blackness*. Durham, NC: Duke University Press Books, 2015.

Cigolle, Christine T., Jinkyung Ha, Lillian C. Min, Pearl G. Lee, Tanya R. Gure, Neil B. Alexander, and Caroline S. Blaum. "The Epidemiologic Data on Falls, 1998–2010: More Older Americans Report Falling." *JAMA Internal Medicine* 175, no. 3 (March 1, 2015): 443–445. https://doi.org/10.1001/jamainternmed.2014.7533

Deixel, Donald. "'Are You O.K.?' Plan Is Good but Too Little." *New York Times*. August 13, 1989, sec. 12WC.

Dibner, Andrew S. Automatic Telephone Alarm System. US3989900A, filed November 4, 1974, and issued November 2, 1976.

Dibner, Andrew S. Closed-Loop Emergency Alarm and Response System. US4064368A, filed June 7, 1976, and issued December 20, 1977.

Dubrofsky, Rachel E., and Shoshana Amielle Magnet, eds. *Feminist Surveillance Studies*. Durham, NC: Duke University Press Books, 2015.

Easterling, Keller. *Extrastatecraft: The Power of Infrastructure Space*. London; New York: Verso, 2014.

Ellcessor, Elizabeth. "Is There a Sign for That? Media, American Sign Language Interpretation, and the Paradox of Visibility." *Perspectives* 23, no. 4 (October 2, 2015): 586–598. https://doi.org/10.1080/0907676X.2015.1056814

"FallAlert™ Medical Alert Systems Emergency Response Systems." *LifeCall Medical Alert Systems* (blog). Accessed April 16, 2018. https://www.lifecall.com/about/

Fiske, John. *Understanding Popular Culture*. 2nd ed. London and New York: Routledge, 2010.

"FTC Facts for Consumers: Personal Emergency Response Systems." Federal Trade Commission, March 2001.

Garza, Mariel. "Help… I've Fallen and I Can't Get Up." *Journal of Emergency Medical Services* 17, no. 5 (May 1992): 13–18.

Gates, Kelly A. *Our Biometric Future: Facial Recognition Technology and the Culture of Surveillance*. New York: New York University Press, 2011.

Granovetter, Mark. "The Strength of Weak Ties: A Network Theory Revisited." *Sociological Theory* 1 (1983): 201–233.

Gray, Jonathan, and Amanda D. Lotz. *Television Studies*. Cambridge: Polity, 2011.

Hamraie, Aimi. *Building Access: Universal Design and the Politics of Disability*. 1st ed. Minneapolis: University of Minnesota Press, 2017.

Jubera, Drew. "Falling for Mrs. Fletcher: Pathetic Plea from Older Lady in TV Ad Who Can't Get Up Pushes Right Button with Fans." *The Atlanta Journal and Constitution*. February 8, 1991, sec. Features.

Kerschbaum, Stephanie L., Laura T. Eisenman, and James M. Jones. *Negotiating Disability: Disclosure and Higher Education*. Ann Arbor: University of Michigan Press, 2017.

Lang, Harry G. *A Phone of Our Own: The Deaf Insurrection against Ma Bell*. Washington DC: Gallaudet University Press, 2000.

LaWhite, Eric L., and Patrick G. Phillipps. Portable transmitter for emergency alarm system having watertight enclosure. US4491970A, filed December 30, 1982, and issued January 1, 1985. https://patents.google.com/patent/US4491970

"LIFE ALERT Official Website—I've Fallen and I Can't Get Up!®." Accessed April 16, 2018. http://www.lifealert.com/

Lyon, David. *Surveillance after September 11*. 1st ed. Malden, MA: Polity, 2003.

Lyon David. "Technology vs 'terrorism': Circuits of City Surveillance since September 11th." *International Journal of Urban and Regional Research* 27, no. 3 (October 13, 2003): 666–678. https://doi.org/10.1111/1468-2427.00473

MacDonald, John B. Portable emergency alarm transmitter. United States USD277465S, filed January 10, 1983, and issued February 5, 1985.

Meier, Barry. "Concerns Grow about Marketing of Medical Alert Systems." *New York Times*. July 14, 1990, sec. Style.

Mills, Mara. "Deaf Jam: From Inscription to Reproduction to Information." *Social Text* 28, no. 1_102 (March 1, 2010): 35–58. https://doi.org/10.1215/01642472-2009-059

Porter, Eileen J. "Moments of Apprehension in the Midst of a Certainty: Some Frail Older Widows' Lives with a Personal Emergency Response System." *Qualitative Health Research* 13, no. 9 (November 1, 2003): 1311–1323. https://doi.org/10.1177/1049732303253340

Pullin, Graham. *Design Meets Disability*. Cambridge, MA: MIT Press, 2009.

Reeves, Joshua. *Citizen Spies: The Long Rise of America's Surveillance Society*. New York: New York University Press, 2017.

Robinson, Barry. "Lifeline Services—An Industry Still Defining Its Own Identity." *Ageing International* 18, no. 1 (1991): 42–47. https://doi.org/10.1007/BF03004301

Shapiro, L. Dennis. Personal alarm system. US4524243A, filed July 7, 1983, and issued June 18, 1985.

Snead, Elizabeth. "Stumbling onto a Hip New Catch Phrase." *USA Today*. October 2, 1990. sec. Life.

"Statistical Abstract of the United States." Washington, DC: US Census Bureau, 1999. https://www.census.gov/library/publications/1999/compendia/statab/119ed.html

Verel, Patrick. "Calling for Help Devices Help Seniors, Disabled in Case of an Emergency." *The Augusta Chronicle*. January 11, 2005, sec. Your Life.

Walby, Kevin T. "Institutional Ethnography and Surveillance Studies: An Outline for Inquiry." *Surveillance & Society* 3, no. 2/3 (September 1, 2002). https://ojs.library.queensu.ca/index.php/surveillance-and-society/article/view/3498

Wood, Sam. "Philly-Based Medical Guardian Targets 'Massive' Market among Elderly for Personal Alarms." *Philly.com*. February 2, 2018. http://www.philly.com/philly/business/philly-company-targets-massive-market-in-personal-alarms-20180202.html

12 3D-Printed Prosthetics and the Uses of Design
BESS WILLIAMSON

In November of 2018, Design Museum Boston (DMB) presented a preview of their exhibition *Bespoke Bodies: The Design and Craft of Prosthetics*, before its opening in 2019. This pop-up installation was housed inside a shipping container and placed in Boston's City Hall Plaza. Part of HUBweek, a corporate and university-sponsored celebration of "where art, science, and technology meet," the exhibition included a number of opportunities for interaction with prosthetic limbs. Exhibits ranged from harness-operated "split-hook" arms (the most common and widespread limb design for over a century), to newer technologies such as myoelectric limbs that respond to a muscle sensor. Further displays included legs fitted with computer controls that respond to changes in terrain, along with decorative covers etched with tattoo-like floral forms made by 3D printers. Throughout the exhibit, hands-on and virtual-reality experiences intermingled with displays of prosthetic limbs. Many of the limbs on show represented current manufacturers and service providers such as the Hanger Clinic, one of the sponsors of the exhibition. As a whole, the exhibition tied its temporary status to the theme of flexible, responsive design: a public performance of new design ideas, all coded under the idea of the "bespoke."

The *Bespoke Bodies* pop-up evoked many of the tropes of twenty-first-century design culture. The Design Museum, with branches in multiple US cities, models itself on the fast-changing and mobile aspects of contemporary design culture by organizing exhibitions in public spaces with no permanent collection or static home. This approach suggests the possibility of digital services and technologies supplanting bricks-and-mortar institutions and long timelines of design and production. The focus on disability technologies, too, was in keeping with a contemporary focus on personalization as a key feature of digital design. In highlighting non-normative bodies, the exhibition emphasized how digital production technologies might succeed where mass production fails—particularly in the areas of custom fit and sizing, most clearly evoked by the clothes tailoring term "bespoke." While *Bespoke Bodies* included many disabled people themselves, as both makers and wearers of prosthetic limbs, the exhibition also pointed outward toward the benefit of digital technologies for nondisabled viewers. As Julie Passanante Elman writes in a study of personal data-monitoring devices such as FitBit, disabled bodies are often represented within broader publicity campaigns as a marker of the "uniqueness" of the technology and the promise of personalized data measurement, regardless of whether these technologies are actually usable by disabled people.[1] In the case of *Bespoke Bodies*, the exhibition deployed disabled bodies and disability technologies to represent the generalized message of design's social worth.

Bespoke Bodies' approach to these ideas is the latest in a long history of media, exhibitions, and producers using disability technologies, especially prosthetics, to indicate a social purpose for design and technology. Prosthetic limbs have been a part of discussions of the future of technology since at least the nineteenth century, when prosthetics took a prominent place in World Fairs and exhibitions, and were included in not only medical but also military and anthropological displays.[2] Particularly in times of wartime recovery, these devices presented the possibility that technology might serve a veteran population perceived as unequivocally deserving.[3] In fact, perhaps the most distinctive aspect of the recent iterations of high-tech prosthetics is the relative absence of what David Serlin calls "patriotic gore," or the attention to injuries suffered in wartime to evoke the strength of the nation.[4] This newer digital generation of prosthetics promoters instead brings a new focus on the aesthetic possibilities of customized and small-batch production. When brought to bear on the bodies of disabled people, these characteristics are framed as a social good and of greater urgency than mere fashion or whimsy.

This chapter examines a range of design projects and events that established a discourse around digital production of prosthetics in the 2010s. The DMB exhibition is only the latest among projects that present digital customization in terms of two main, and interlinked, themes: aesthetic style and humanitarian good. For consumer-focused ventures such as Bespoke Innovations, a custom prosthetic limb-making company unrelated to the *Bespoke Bodies* exhibition, personal style was the public veneer for technologies of individual bodily scanning and fitting. In a very different approach, Enabling the Future (ETF), a nonprofit, volunteer-driven organization that generated low-cost prosthetic devices, presented 'crowd' production as a means of leapfrogging existing barriers in the global field of prosthetics. In both cases, design and technical innovation brought forth genuinely novel prosthetic designs, many of which were and are beloved by their wearers. In so doing, I argue, they also objectified the disabled body as inherently experimental (and open to being experimented upon). The focus on this specific object as a product of digital production, moreover, overlooks the role of disabled people in designing or selecting their own technologies. Thus, while the 3D-printed limb suggests ambitious new arrangements on the production end, it leaves in place existing expectations that disabled people are recipients of design change, rather than change-makers themselves.

Prosthetics as Design Experiment: Bespoke Innovations

Recent digital projects reflect a long history of prosthetic limbs being used to represent technological experimentation and progress in modern Western design history. Governments have touted technological improvements for those who have lost limbs on the battlefield in the aftermath of every modern war from Napoleon to the War on Terror.[5] Images in paint, prose, and film have elaborated upon the fascinating ideal of technology that can not only replace, but also enhance the human body.[6] In foundational texts of postmodern critical theory, writers from Roland Barthes to Donna Haraway have used the prosthesis as a metaphor for the ways that technologies attach to human life.[7] In contrast to this rich visual and theoretical field, however, actual prosthetic limb wearers have generally rejected these metaphors as vastly oversimplifying the lived experience of fit and function in prosthetic limbs.[8] Cultural imaginings of prosthetics tend to detach the limbs from the bodies that wear them, leaving out the arduous, uncomfortable, and expensive processes of fitting, adjustment, repair, and maintenance.[9]

For more recent digitally produced limbs, touches of fashion further extend the prosthetic metaphor to cast design as a human service. The term "bespoke" indicates individually made to order, or "spoken for" rather than produced in multiples for a generalized consumer.[10] Like many terms of modern craft, it finds its origins in the industrial era of the nineteenth century as ready-made goods were increasingly available. The term is most commonly found in fashion, specifically men's tailoring or shoemaking, where craft techniques allow for the work to be constructed for individual body measurements. Unlike "couture"—a term available only to the most elite makers of clothing—bespoke suggests craftsmanship as a form of customer service, producing clothing and accessories that are well-made for everyday use.

In digital prosthetics projects, the term "bespoke" lends an air of the fashionable to the realm of assistive devices. In fact, the "bespoke" nature of these limbs is not a new aspect of the prosthetics industry. Even if parts are mass-produced, the process of fitting a prosthetic limb involves individual measurement and production of sockets, straps, or other components, and typically involves multiple visits, not unlike bespoke clothes-tailoring.[11] This is part of what makes prosthetics expensive; past attempts to produce standardized limbs as a cost- or labor-saving method have largely failed due to the urgency of this individual fitting process.[12] Still, new technologies aim to improve this fitting process, as well as to offer new opportunities for personalized styling.

Prosthetic limb projects of the last decade have continued to emphasize the element of personal style, now as a visible proof of the technical benefits of 3D printing. Because 3D-printed products are made one at a time, they allow for individualization beyond the model of mass production in which processes such as mold-making or die-cutting make identical multiples cost-effective. With 3D printing, individual components of a limb, such as the "fairings" or outer cover, can be made with shape, patterns, or colors customized for each wearer, and altered with digital modeling software before each new print. Bespoke Innovations, a company founded in 2010 by industrial designer Scott Summit and Dr. Ken Trauner, used a patented scanning technique to capture the shape of an intact leg in order to determine a form for the prosthetic fairing. Bespoke Fairings were made with a range of patterns and surfaces. Using the algorithmic possibilities of digital design, many featured repeating,

Figure 12.1 "Deborah" wearing Bespoke Fairings, bespokeinnovations.com (archived). Courtesy of Scott Summit.

geometric patterns, whether lace-like for a woman named Deborah who wanted a "limb designed to be seen," or a soccer-ball-like hexagon pattern for James, an athlete. The plastic printed fairing could also be overlaid with other materials, such as chromed metal or wood veneer.[13]

For Bespoke Innovations, the decorative surfaces of the fairings represented a design shift toward individualization for the body. Summit designated customization as the "fundamental tenet" of a new form of design that resisted the idea of a mass audience—something he described as designing for "a person" rather than "people."[14] Publicity images (Figure 12.1) played up these customized surfaces as a core design element, particularly with a series of photo shoots that posed a woman wearing a variety of Bespoke options while perched on the edge of chairs designed by mid-century design stars Charles and Ray Eames. With these chairs, the company links their prosthetics not only to the idea of bespoke clothing but also to designer furniture. The curve of the white plastic fiberglass chair above the warmer tone of wood leg expresses the Eames' delight in industrial forms born of twentieth-century Modernism, but also suggests the ways that technology can take the shape of a body. Recalling that choice, Summit mentioned his own affection for mid-century Modernist design and added that the curves of the chairs offered an "overall sensuality" to the image of the company.[15]

Posing his models in Eames chairs, Summit was also aware of Charles and Ray Eames' Second World War-era leg splints, developed in military research as an alternative to metal models.[16] It is unclear whether the Eames' splints were ever used (like much design research of the period, the War ended just as the splints were produced), but the slim, flexible plywood splints with tailoring-like darts are widely reproduced in design history publications. They are featured in Graham Pullin's *Design Meets Disability*, a 2009 book that argued for the benefit of fashion and high-design aesthetics for assistive technologies.[17] Pullin describes the Eames leg splint as a rare notable work in the history of design for disability and cites its appeal "not because of its medical purpose but as good design on any terms."[18] Perching the wearer of Bespoke Fairings on the work of these notable designers linked the company's prosthetics design to larger design values of form and function in the industrial age.

In addition to its reality as a company that produced customized limb fairings for $3,000–5,000 each, Bespoke Innovations was also part of the speculative discourse on the future of body technology and 3D printing of the early 2010s. When the limbs were included in the Museum of Art and Design's 2014 exhibition *Out of Hand*, they were presented along with an array of other works that merged body and technology to create new forms.[19] One of the principal images used for the exhibition was of Richard Dupont's sculpture *In Direction*, a figurative work that uses data from scans of the artist's own body to produce a distorted "melting" body shape. Several works in the exhibition centered on digital alterations of the body, seeming to suggest that this morphism was a distinctive quality of the medium. Even the name of the exhibition seems to play on the double meaning of eliminating the artist's hand and creating something beyond the natural body. In the context of this exhibition, Bespoke's limbs become a part of the futuristic speculation about the possible body.

With widespread press coverage and inclusion in exhibitions such as *Out of Hand* and the reopening of the Cooper-Hewitt National Design Museum in 2014, Bespoke's prosthetic covers stood in for the promises of 3D printing beyond their immediate application. Their algorithmic patterns projected a future of customization without compromise, visible in striking designs as well as applied to bodies immediately recognizable as "different." The media success and eventual sale of Bespoke Innovations also aligns with a broader tech-world strategy of producing a niche product and selling to a larger, mainstream company. Even as Bespoke limbs appeared in art and design exhibitions in 2014, the company had already been sold to 3D Systems, a maker of 3D printers.[20] The company acquired all of Summit's patents and designs, and incorporated a number of the company's designers into divisions of their larger firm; Summit has now left, and the company retains Bespoke's patents along with a portfolio of other assistive-technology investments.

In the case of Bespoke Innovations, the short-lived, highly visible lifespan of its designs contributed to the sense of disabled bodies as a test site for future technologies. As digital-production scholars Matt Ratto and Robert Ree point out, "customization" in digital culture often amounts to big promises that—in reality–deliver more incremental outcomes.[21] Rarely do these changes provide significant changes in product design. Instead, actual results are most often reflected in choices such as finishes and colors that are provided at the end of the production process. Indeed, with Bespoke Fairings, the limb covers could take on designs that are either flashy or elegantly discreet, but they did not change the underlying technology of a prosthetic, nor would a limb feel different to the wearer. Design and tech media claims that Bespoke was creating "prosthetic limbs" (rather than limb covers) that "fit comfortably" misstated the contribution of digital technology, especially when they linked these models to the potential for 3D printing to create customized consumer products for other markets.[22]

After much media coverage in its early years, Bespoke Innovations was little mentioned as it was sold to 3D Systems. Instead, design magazines, museums, and blogs tend to focus on product rollouts rather than their long-term lifespans. Addressing an audience assumed to be nondisabled or non-amputees, public coverage of this application of 3-D printing remained focused on the future of technology rather than the present state of prosthetics.

Enabling Humanitarian Design

If Bespoke Innovations called on the language of fashion and Modernist design for its interventions into prosthetics, Enabling the Future (ETF), a nonprofit organization that operated from 2013 to 2016, presented its work through the figure of an engineer and superhero: Iron Man. ETF gained its greatest public visibility through a viral YouTube video created in 2014 by the Collective Project, a Microsoft-owned innovation fund that supported the organization. The video depicted a meeting between the actor Robert Downey Jr, in character as Tony Stark, the engineer who develops his own robotic Iron Man suit in the Marvel Avengers franchise, and Alex Pring, a seven-year-old who was born with a foreshortened right forearm and partial hand. In the video, Downey Jr presents a star-struck Pring with a customized limb styled after the Iron Man bionic suit. In a charming encounter, the two banter about the arm, with Downey in character greeting Alex and the researchers as "fellow bionic experts." Downey shows his own Iron Man costume arm with its light malfunctioning—calling it a "technical glitch"—and notes that Pring's arm works better at a fraction of the price.[23]

The YouTube video presented a staged, dramatic story of the young boy receiving the custom limb, but this was far from Pring's first prosthetic arm. By the time this video was aired, Pring had been working with Albert Manero, an engineering graduate student at the University of Central Florida, on the "Limbitless Arm" project for about a year (Manero is also visible in the video as one of the "bionics experts" who were the recipients of Collective Project funding).[24] With an ETF model as the starting-point, Manero and his team developed a battery-powered, 3D-printed prosthetic arm that uses an Arduino processor to move prosthetic fingers and wrist.

ETF's 3D-printed prosthetics project reflected some of the same enthusiasm over digital technology and culture as did Bespoke Innovations, additionally magnified through the lens of humanitarianism. The group was organized around the principle of open sharing of design information across the world and among experts, amateurs, and limb-wearers themselves. The organization was founded in 2013 by Richard Van As, a South African carpenter, and Ivan Owen, an American theater prop designer, after Van As lost fingers in a work injury. Van As found Owen through online posts about steampunk puppet hands, and the pair developed a 3D-printed version together. With the growing availability of affordable desktop 3D printers such as Makerbots and readily available software, the two sought to share and produce these limbs through a network of volunteers. John Schull, an engineer and professor at Rochester Institute of Technology, joined the team as their mapper, using Google tools to match requests for hands with volunteers with access to 3D printers. By 2015, the organization reported more than 7,000 volunteers, and garnered significant attention, including grants and capital funding from tech companies including Google, AutoDesk, and Microsoft (who runs the Collective Project).[26]

ETF, like other 3D-printed prosthetics projects, emphasized the benefits of 3D printing for avoiding the pitfalls of mass production. Standard prosthetic limbs tend to be very expensive and poorly suited to the growing bodies of children. The ETF devices, however, could be easily sized using the scale tools in a 3D modeling program, and printing costs are minimal (although the time commitment of printing and assembling the more than thirty-part devices could be significant).[27] Produced by volunteers and distributed for free, they also avoided the time and trials required for approval as a consumer or medical device. In keeping with the appeal of disruption in digital design culture, this lack of expert interference was promoted as a feature, not a bug, leaving the production fully in the hands of ETF's network of "teachers, students, engineers, scientists, medical professionals, tinkerers, designers, parents, children, scout troops, artists, philanthropists, dreamers, coders, makers and every day people who just want to make a difference."[28]

From ETF's standpoint, the volunteer network and do-it-yourself making was a significant outcome in itself. The organization describes its crowdsourcing approach to production as a kind of global science project that teaches participants about the possibilities of technology. Their website and videos emphasized that the project benefited those who made the limbs as much as the individuals who received them. The project was often framed in educational terms, as an approach to STEM (science, technology, engineering, and math) fields that got students, scout troupes, and other volunteer groups "excited about using their math and design skills for something that will benefit the world." As ETF promoted the project, they emphasized how volunteers could become "a part of something amazing."[29] Moreover, they used available open-source technology sites to distribute the plans, joining a larger movement of 3D-printing enthusiasts. The sharing platform Thingiverse allowed ETF to distribute ready-to-print design files that each user could edit, for example to scale the parts to match measurements of a person's hands. ETF's website showed people making a wide range

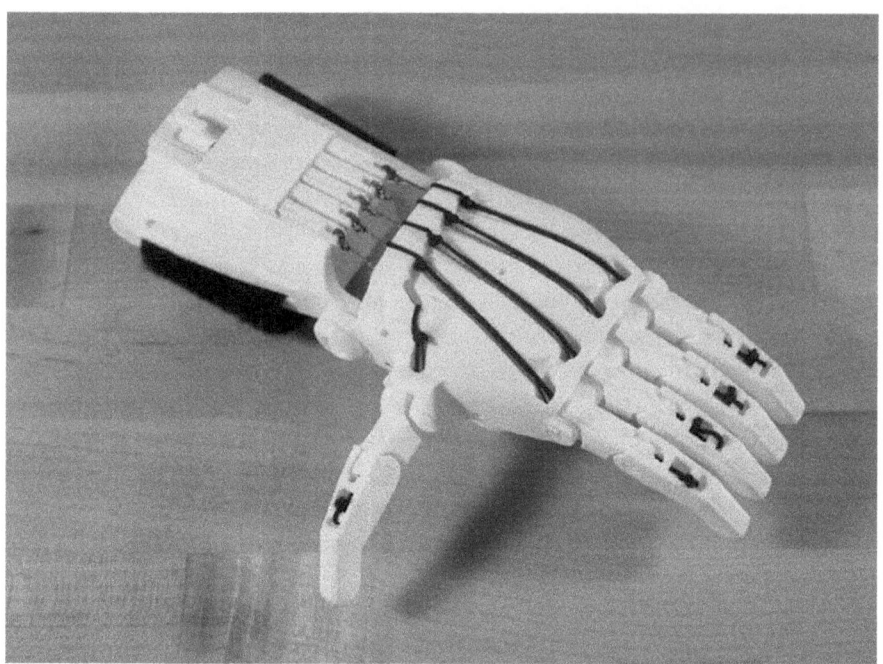

Figure 12.2 "Raptor Reloaded by e-NABLE," 3D-printed hand prosthesis with elastic components, 2014. Thingiverse.com.

of creative alterations, most frequently producing brightly colored hands for children, including superhero or Disney character colors.[30] ETF's use of Thingiverse also means that the limb project lives on past the life of the organization; the files can still be downloaded and these designs produced even as the organization is less active.

One aspect of ETF's limb-production project that goes little discussed on its extensive website and in media coverage is its design choice of upper-limb prosthetics, with a particular focus on wrist and hand devices. In contrast to the Limbitless arm that Alex Pring modeled, which included a full forearm and battery-powered wrist, most of the hands made through ETF's volunteer network were shorter, lower-arm devices, such as the basic "Raptor Reloaded" and "Phoenix" models (Figure 12.2). In these arms, elastic-tied fingers snap open and closed when the user pushes against the "palm" of the device, meaning that they cannot be operated by people with more substantial arm differences and do not require the complex assembly and programming of an Arduino device. The group does not explain why it has remained entirely dedicated to the development and sharing of arm-based prosthetics, which represent a minority of all prosthetics, let alone assistive devices more broadly.[31] While the organization's origin story in Van As's injury clarifies this choice somewhat, it is also in keeping with a historical attention to the upper limb prosthesis as a highly visible site of technological development.[32]

ETF's claims to addressing a significant global need were questionable, as well, considering that the limbs they produced were quite limited in functionality. Given the need for volunteer-printed limbs to be relatively simple in design, ETF did not produce limbs for people who have less than a functioning forearm. Thus, while their website abounds with images of excited children donning their hands, ETF has produced an outcome more like a toy than a functional replacement for an arm or hand. A study of children using ETF arms found that, in a group of eleven users aged three to seventeen, only three reported wearing the limbs for more than two hours a day. The most common use of the limbs was "just for fun," while school and sports were the least-commonly reported uses.[33] This "just for fun" response is in itself a strong design outcome—few assistive technologies introduce fun and playfulness as a key design element—but it differs from ETF's emphasis on technological breakthrough.

The recent dissolution of ETF reveals conflicts between the ideal of a crowdsourced, 3D-printed arm and the reality of varied needs for limbs and other devices. As the organization grew in 2015 and 2016, and obtained multi-hundred-thousand-dollar grants, several of the fundamental problems in its product and process grew as well. Grants from Google, Autodesk, and other private foundations funded technical development of the limbs and online network. However, even as this support grew, the organization confronted the limitations of their lower-arm model to serve a larger, particularly global audience. In areas of the world struck by natural and industrial disasters, or war, the demand for prosthetics was more likely for full-arm models rather than the hand- and wrist-devices that ETF could most easily make.[34] In 2016, the three founders of ETF left the organization in a split over the fundamental question: Was this an organization that made prosthetic limbs or a volunteer network of 3D designers and printers?[35] The Enabling Community Foundation refocused its efforts in a new venture called LimbForge that aims to produce affordable and medically certified, but not crowd-printed or free limbs. E-Nable, the volunteer network, became a distinct organization that, as of 2020, still pursues prosthetic limb projects and research, although on a reduced scale and with less publicity than when ETF began the project.

Like Bespoke Innovations, ETF's rise and eventual shift in direction reveal some of the limitations of modern media attention to technological innovation, especially when it involves disability applications. Enthusiasm for visible evidence of the positive contributions of these technologies becomes a driver for production, instrumentalizing disabled people's bodies for an overall positive message, with little follow-up on these subjects' lives. The carefully crafted public images and viral videos of these projects simplify or obscure the reality of their production. With a narrow focus on prosthetic arms and hands, rather than a broader category of tools disabled people may want or need, the company maintains a focus on the makers of the products and the moment of provision, rather than a longer-term lifespan of technology.

Missing Makers

Returning to the Design Museum's *Bespoke Bodies* pop-up, the public exhibition of 3D-printed and other high-tech limbs used prosthetics to represent the benefits of design innovation. The Design Museum's mission statement asserts in no uncertain terms the benefit of design change to bring about social improvement: "design has the power to make our everyday lives more comfortable, more efficient, more exciting, more rewarding, more … better."[36] By making an exhibition on prosthetics as a major part of its public outing in Boston, the organization assumes the general public's consensus on the beneficence of technology when it is applied to disabled bodies. The emphasis on prosthetics as an inherently positive form of technological innovation echoes what Ashley Shew calls "technoableism," or the sense that "using technologies to restore physical abilities is the key to addressing disability—and that disabled bodies are inferior when they are not properly equipped with those technologies."[37] Addressing disability always and necessarily through technology, Shew writes, reflects "a failure of imagination" given the many ways disabled people may *or may not* benefit from technology.

Missing in this discourse is the disabled person as a contributor to design, rather than simply its recipient. Prosthetic limb wearers themselves document a wide variation in the extent and habits of wearing limbs; we might consider adoption or rejection as a form of design choice in itself. Some always wear limbs, some rarely do; others change limbs often and see the cover as a fashion accessory and a source of play and expression.[38] Many users report social pressure to wear a limb and that their choices are at least partly shaped by the desire to show themselves to be willing participants in ideas of bodily normalcy.[39] Others reject that pressure by wearing no limb at all, or wearing surprising and notable decorations such as rhinestones applied to a prosthetic wrist, or more elaborate, sculptural works.[40]

The questions around the use and function of 3D-printed limbs in these much-covered projects relate to broader debates about the representation of disabled people as designers or makers. ETF highlighted some examples of users-as-makers, including founder Richard Van As, who produced their own prosthetics as well as limbs for others. But for the most part, these projects followed a convention of "designing for disability" in which disabled people are the recipients rather than makers of design work. In this sense, the digital era has not proved to be a harbinger of improved access for disabled people to design methods and tools. As a number of disability advocates and designers have noted, the spaces and equipment of the "maker" movement are often inaccessible. Sites are often in semi-industrial spaces, with little attention to comfort or access, and many major 3D modeling software programs do not include features such as voice controls. Truly creating works from scratch can require a level of modeling and printer operation that goes beyond the amateur production of Thingiverse-ready files.[41] This aspect of maker culture, however, gets much less attention than these higher-profile prosthetics projects.

From "bespoke" limb decorations to crowdsourced printed limbs, these recent intersections of digital production and prosthetics show how deeply embedded the image of the disabled body is within contemporary digital design and technology cultures. For technologies whose practical applications are not entirely clear to a broader public, disability applications provide visible and tangible examples along with an assurance of overall social good. The notions of customization, innovation, and other buzzwords indicating advancements of technology are transformed from vague business or design terms to inherently positive developments in part because they act on disabled bodies. In these cases, the theme of progress is insistent, as these cultural objects and events emphasize the value of improving both bodies and technologies. The disabled body, specifically the amputee or limb-different body, seems to be an incomplete body in need of aesthetic and functional completion. Likewise, these technologies are seen as works-in-progress, glimpses of the future still left to be completed.

In all this, the actual benefits to disabled people are often minimized in favor of a larger insistence on technological progress. The rapid organizational changes that came to both Bespoke Innovations and ETF, too, reveal the accelerated pace of a digital economy where rapid funding and media attention lead to corporate buy-outs, reshuffling, or outright failure. In these aspects, the digital prosthetic represents a vision of the future "both too large and not large enough," as Ratto and Rhee have suggested—simultaneously grandiose in its promises of innovation and often too small in its estimation of the vast cultural and technological changes that are required to alter a major human service such as rehabilitation technology.[42] We must ask, after decades of technological optimism embodied in the prosthetic limb, what modern society, and disabled people specifically, lose when disability is continuously proffered as a test case for design change.

Notes

1. Julie Passanante Elman, "'Find Your Fit': Wearable Technology and the Cultural Politics of Disability," *New Media & Society* 20, no. 10 (2018): 3761–3762
2. Julie K. Brown, *Health and Medicine on Display: International Expositions in the United States, 1876–1904* (Cambridge, MA: MIT Press, 2009), 160–161.
3. Beth Linker, *War's Waste: Rehabilitation in World War I America* (Chicago, IL: University of Chicago Press, 2011); David Harley Serlin, *Replaceable You: Engineering the Body in Postwar America* (Chicago, IL : University of Chicago Press, 2004).
4. Serlin, *Replaceable You*.
5. Linker, *War's Waste*; Ibid.
6. Elspeth Brown, "The Prosthetics of Management: Time Motion Study, Photography, and the Industrialized Body in World War I America," in *Artificial Parts, Practical Lives: Modern Histories of Prosthetics*, ed. Katherine Ott, David Serlin, and Stephen Mihm (New York: New York University Press, 2002), 249–281; Vivian Sobchack, "A Leg to Stand On: Prosthetics, Metaphor, and Materiality," in *The Object Reader*, ed. Fiona Candlin and Rayford Guins (New York: Routledge, 2009); Amanda Cachia, "The (Narrative) Prosthesis Re-Fitted," *Journal of Literary & Cultural Disability Studies* 9, no. 3 (October 1, 2015): 247–264, https://doi.org/10.3828/jlcds.2015.21

7. Alison Kafer, *Feminist, Queer, Crip* (Bloomington: Indiana University Press, 2013).
8. Sobchack, "A Leg to Stand On"; Serlin, *Replaceable You*; Steven Kurzman, "'There's No Language for This': Communication and Alignment in Contemporary Prosthetics," in *Artificial Parts, Practical Lives: Modern Histories of Prosthetics*, ed. Katherine Ott, David Serlin, and Stephen Mihm (New York: New York University Press, 2002), 227–248.
9. Katherine Ott, "The Sum of Its Parts: An Introduction to Modern Histories of Prosthetics," in *Artificial Parts, Practical Lives: Modern Histories of Prosthetics*, ed. Katherine Ott, David Serlin, and Stephen Mihm (New York: New York University Press, 2002), 6.
10. Alison Matthews David, "Tailoring," in *The Berg Companion to Fashion*, ed. Valerie Steele (Oxford: Bloomsbury Academic, 2010), https://www-bloomsburyfashioncentral-com
11. Sobchack, "A Leg to Stand On," 288–289; Kurzman, "There's No Language for This."
12. Beth Linker details one such attempt to make standardized limbs after the First World War, in which paperboard legs were found to be uncomfortable and unstable. Linker, *War's Waste*, 98–119.
13. "Bespoke Prosthetic Fairings: The Art of Personalized Medicine with Industrial 3D Printing," 3D Systems, accessed February 5, 2019, https://www.3dsystems.com/learning-center/case-studies/bespoke-prosthetic-fairings-art-personalized-medicine. Author: Charlie Sorrel Gear, "Bespoke Innovations Makes Beautiful, Custom Prosthetic Legs," *WIRED*, accessed January 12, 2017, https://www.wired.com/2010/12/bespoke-designs-makes-beautiful-custom-prosthetic-legs/
14. Scott Summit, "Designing with the Body," *Innovation: The Journal of the Industrial Designers Society of America* 31, no. 2 (Summer 2012), 10.
15. Scott Summit, Email correspondence with author, January 4, 2019.
16. Ibid.
17. Graham Pullin, *Design Meets Disability* (Cambridge, MA: MIT Press, 2009).
18. Pullin, *Design Meets Disability,* xi.
19. Ronald T. Labaco, ed., *Out of Hand: Materializing the Postdigital* (London: Black Dog Publishing for the Museum of Arts and Design, New York, 2013).
20. admin, "3D Systems Acquires Bespoke Innovations," Text, 3D Systems, May 24, 2012, http://www.3dsystems.com/press-releases/3d-systems-acquires-bespoke-innovations
21. Matt Ratto and Robert Ree, "Materializing Information: 3D Printing and Social Change," *First Monday* 17, no. 7 (June 27, 2012), http://firstmonday.org/ojs/index.php/fm/article/view/3968
22. Kathleen Maher, "From Digital to Real, and Back Again," *Computer Graphics World* 34, no. 6 (June 2011): 30.
23. "Robert Downey Jr. Presents Child with 'Iron Man' Arm—CNN.Com," *CNN*, accessed October 16, 2015, http://www.cnn.com/2015/03/12/health/robert-downey-jr-robotic-arm-irpt-feat/index.html
24. Zenaida Gonzalez Kotala, "Fulfilling a 6-Year-Old's Dream: UCF Students Design and Build Him an Arm," UCF News—University of Central Florida Articles—Orlando, FL News, accessed August 12, 2015, http://today.ucf.edu/fulfilling-6-year-olds-dream-ucf-students-design-build-arm/

25. "The Limbitless Arm," *Enabling the Future* (blog), accessed August 11, 2015, http://enablingthefuture.org/upper-limb-prosthetics/the-limbitless-arm/
26. "ABOUT US," *Enabling the Future* (blog), January 15, 2014, http://enablingthefuture.org/about/
27. "Raptor Reloaded by E-NABLE by e-NABLE," Thingiverse.com, December 17, 2014, https://www.thingiverse.com/thing:596966
28. "ABOUT US."
29. "ABOUT US."
30. "ABOUT US."
31. For example, in 2013 lower-limb surgical amputations were ten times more common than upper-limb surgeries. Adoption rates of upper-limb prosthetics are also lower than that for lower-limb devices. Engineering National Academies of Sciences et al., *Upper-Extremity Prostheses* (National Academies Press [US], 2017), https://www.ncbi.nlm.nih.gov/books/NBK453290/; Katherine A. Raichle et al., "Prosthesis Use in Persons with Lower- and Upper-Limb Amputation," *Journal of Rehabilitation Research and Development* 45, no. 7 (2008): 961–972.
32. The historian Beth Linker has noted that in the First World War era, for example, upper-limb prosthetics were overrepresented in photographs of rehabilitation; I have found the same in my studies of post–Second World War prosthetic limb research. Beth Linker, "Shooting Disabled Soldiers: Medicine and Photography in World War I America," *Journal of the History of Medicine and Allied Sciences* 66, no. 3 (2010): 313–346; Bess Williamson, *Accessible America: A History of Disability and Design* (New York: New York University Press, 2019), 21–26.
33. Jorge Zuniga et al., "Cyborg Beast: A Low-Cost 3d-Printed Prosthetic Hand for Children with Upper-Limb Differences," *BMC Research Notes* 8, no. 1 (January 2015): 155–171, https://doi.org/10.1186/s13104-015-0971-9
34. Michael Molitch-Hou, "Enable Community Foundation Gets Personal with 3D-Printed Prosthetics," August 19, 2016, https://www.engineering.com/3DPrinting/3DPrintingArticles/ArticleID/12857/Enable-Community-Foundation-Gets-Personal-with-3D-Printed-Prosthetics.aspx; John Schull, "E-NABLE at 4 and 10,000: Now What Do We Do?—E-NABLE.Org," July 29, 2017, http://e-nable.org/2017/07/29/e-nable-at-4-and-10000/
35. Schull, "E-NABLE at 4 and 10,000: Now What Do We Do?—E-NABLE.Org."
36. "Mission," Design Museum Foundation, accessed November 15, 2018, https://designmuseumfoundation.org/mission/
37. Ashley Shew, "Different Ways of Moving through the World," *Logic Magazine*, no. 5 (Fall 2018): 207.
38. A few examples of amputees' own reflections on variety and personal choice include Sobchack, "A Leg to Stand On"; *Aimee Mullins: My 12 Pairs of Legs*, 2009, http://www.ted.com/talks/aimee_mullins_prosthetic_aesthetics.html; Cynthia L. Bennett et al., "An Intimate Laboratory?: Prostheses as a Tool for Experimenting with Identity and Normalcy," in *Proceedings of the 2016 CHI Conference on Human Factors in Computing Systems—CHI '16* (the 2016 CHI Conference, Santa Clara, CA: ACM Press,

2016), 1745–56, https://doi.org/10.1145/2858036.2858564; Mallory Kay Nelson, Ashley Shew, and Bethany Stevens, "Transmobility: Possibilities in Cyborg (Cripborg) Bodies," *Catalyst: Feminism, Theory, Technoscience* 5, no. 1 (Spring 2019): 1–20.
39 Rosemarie Garland Thomson, *Staring: How We Look* (Oxford: Oxford University Press, 2009), 128–131.
40 Bennett et al., "An Intimate Laboratory?," 6; *Aimee Mullins: My 12 Pairs of Legs*.
41 Emeline Brulé, "Five Years of Do-It-Yourself Design of Educational Aids for Youth with Visual Impairments" (CHI 2018, Montreal, Quebec, April 21–26).
42 Ratto and Ree, "Materializing Information."

Bibliography

"ABOUT US." *Enabling The Future* (blog). January 15, 2014. http://enablingthefuture.org/about/

admin. "3D Systems Acquires Bespoke Innovations." Text. 3D Systems. May 24, 2012. http://www.3dsystems.com/press-releases/3d-systems-acquires-bespoke-innovations

Aimee Mullins: My 12 Pairs of Legs. 2009. http://www.ted.com/talks/aimee_mullins_prosthetic_aesthetics.html

Bennett, Cynthia L., Keting Cen, Katherine M. Steele, and Daniela K. Rosner. "An Intimate Laboratory?: Prostheses as a Tool for Experimenting with Identity and Normalcy." In *Proceedings of the 2016 CHI Conference on Human Factors in Computing Systems—CHI '16*, 1745–56. Santa Clara, CA: ACM Press, 2016. https://doi.org/10.1145/2858036.2858564

"Bespoke Prosthetic Fairings: The Art of Personalized Medicine with Industrial 3D Printing." 3D Systems. Accessed February 5, 2019. /learning-center/case-studies/bespoke-prosthetic-fairings-art-personalized-medicine

Brown, Elspeth. "The Prosthetics of Management: Time Motion Study, Photography, and the Industrialized Body in World War I America." In *Artificial Parts, Practical Lives: Modern Histories of Prosthetics*, ed. Katherine Ott, David Serlin, and Stephen Mihm, 249–281. New York: New York University Press, 2002.

Brown, Julie K. *Health and Medicine on Display: International Expositions in the United States, 1876–1904*. Cambridge, MA: MIT Press, 2009.

Brulé, Emeline. "Five Years of Do-It-Yourself Design of Educational Aids for Youth with Visual Impairments." (Unpublished paper, April 2018).

Cachia, Amanda. "The (Narrative) Prosthesis Re-Fitted." *Journal of Literary & Cultural Disability Studies* 9, no. 3 (October 1, 2015): 247–264. https://doi.org/10.3828/jlcds.2015.21

David, Alison Matthews. "Tailoring." In *The Berg Companion to Fashion*, ed. Valerie Steele. Oxford: Bloomsbury Academic, 2010. https://www-bloomsburyfashioncentral-com

Gear, Author: Charlie Sorrel. "Bespoke Innovations Makes Beautiful, Custom Prosthetic Legs." *WIRED*. Accessed January 12, 2017. https://www.wired.com/2010/12/bespoke-designs-makes-beautiful-custom-prosthetic-legs/

Kafer, Alison. *Feminist, Queer, Crip*. Bloomington: Indiana University Press, 2013.

Kotala, Zenaida Gonzalez. "Fulfilling a 6-Year-Old's Dream: UCF Students Design and Build Him an Arm." *UCF News—University of Central Florida Articles—Orlando, FL News*. Accessed August 12, 2015. http://today.ucf.edu/fulfilling-6-year-olds-dream-ucf-students-design-build-arm/

Kurzman, Steven. "'There's No Language for This': Communication and Alignment in Contemporary Prosthetics." In *Artificial Parts, Practical Lives: Modern Histories of Prosthetics*, ed. Katherine Ott, David Serlin, and Stephen Mihm, 227–248. New York: New York University Press, 2002.

Labaco, Ronald T., ed. *Out of Hand: Materializing the Postdigital*. London: Black Dog Publishing for the Museum of Arts and Design, New York, 2013.

"The Limbitless Arm." *Enabling The Future* (blog). Accessed August 11, 2015. http://enablingthefuture.org/upper-limb-prosthetics/the-limbitless-arm/

Linker, Beth. "Shooting Disabled Soldiers: Medicine and Photography in World War I America." *Journal of the History of Medicine and Allied Sciences* 66, no. 3 (2010): 313–346.

Linker, Beth. *War's Waste: Rehabilitation in World War I America*. Chicago, IL: University of Chicago Press, 2011.

Maher, Kathleen. "From Digital to Real, and Back Again." *Computer Graphics World* 34, no. 6 (June 2011): 28–31.

"Mission." Design Museum Foundation. Accessed November 15, 2018. https://designmuseumfoundation.org/mission/

Molitch-Hou, Michael. "Enable Community Foundation Gets Personal with 3D-Printed Prosthetics." August 19, 2016. https://www.engineeringcom/3DPrinting/3DPrintingArticles/ArticleID/12857/Enable-Community-Foundation-Gets-Personal-with-3D-Printed-Prosthetics.aspx

National Academies of Sciences, Engineering, Health and Medicine Division, Board on Health Care Services, Committee on the Use of Selected Assistive Products and Technologies in Eliminating or Reducing the Effects of Impairments, Jennifer Lalitha Flaubert, Carol Mason Spicer, and Alan M. Jette. *Upper-Extremity Prostheses*. Washington, DC: National Academies Press (US), 2017. https://www.ncbi.nlm.nih.gov/books/NBK453290/

Nelson, Mallory Kay, Ashley Shew, and Bethany Stevens. "Transmobility: Possibilities in Cyborg (Cripborg) Bodies." *Catalyst: Feminism, Theory, Technoscience* 5, no. 1 (Spring 2019): 1–20.

Ott, Katherine. "The Sum of Its Parts: An Introduction to Modern Histories of Prosthetics." In *Artificial Parts, Practical Lives: Modern Histories of Prosthetics*, ed. Katherine Ott, David Serlin, and Stephen Mihm, 1–43. New York: New York University Press, 2002.

Pullin, Graham. *Design Meets Disability*. Cambridge, MA: MIT Press, 2009.

Raichle, Katherine A., Marisol A. Hanley, Ivan Molton, Nancy J. Kadel, Kellye Campbell, Emily Phelps, Dawn Ehde, and Douglas G. Smith. "Prosthesis Use in Persons with Lower- and Upper-Limb Amputation." *Journal of Rehabilitation Research and Development* 45, no. 7 (2008): 961–972.

"Raptor Reloaded by E-NABLE by e-NABLE." Thingiverse.com. December 17, 2014. https://www.thingiverse.com/thing:596966

Ratto, Matt, and Robert Ree. "Materializing Information: 3D Printing and Social Change." *First Monday* 17, no. 7 (June 27, 2012). http://firstmonday.org/ojs/index.php/fm/article/view/3968

"Robert Downey Jr. Presents Child with 'Iron Man' Arm—CNN.Com." *CNN*. Accessed October 16, 2015. http://www.cnn.com/2015/03/12/health/robert-downey-jr-robotic-arm-irpt-feat/index.html

Schull, John. "E-NABLE at 4 and 10, 000:Now What Do We Do?—E-NABLE.Org." July 29, 2017. http://e-nable.org/2017/07/29/e-nable-at-4-and-10000/

Serlin, David Harley. *Replaceable You: Engineering the Body in Postwar America*. Chicago, IL: University of Chicago Press, 2004.

Shew, Ashley. "Different Ways of Moving through, the World." *Logic Magazine*, no. 5 (Fall 2018): 207–213.

Sobchack, Vivian. "A Leg to Stand On: Prosthetics, Metaphor, and Materiality." In *The Object Reader*, ed. Fiona Candlin and Rayford Guins. New York: Routledge, 2009.

Summit, Scott. "Designing with the Body." *Innovation: The Journal of the Industrial Designers Society of America* 31, no. 2 (Summer 2012): 10–11.

Thomson, Rosemarie Garland. *Staring: How We Look*. Oxford: Oxford University Press, 2009.

Williamson, Bess. *Accessible America: A History of Disability and Design*. New York: New York University Press, 2019.

Zuniga, Jorge, Dimitrios Katsavelis, Jean Peck, John Stollberg, Marc Petrykowski, Adam Carson, and Cristina Fernandez. "Cyborg Beast: A Low-Cost 3d-Printed Prosthetic Hand for Children with Upper-Limb Differences." *BMC Research Notes* 8, no. 1 (January 2015): 155–171. https://doi.org/10.1186/s13104-015-0971-9

13 Materializing User Identities & Digital Humanities

JAIPREET VIRDI

Both the artifacts owned and used by people with disabilities and those that are used upon them or that are encountered in life create possibilities, impose limits, assert political and ideological positions, and shape identity.

—**Katherine Ott (2014)**[1]

On July 15, 2015, the Smithsonian's National Museum of American History, together with the Kennedy Center's Office of VSA and Accessibility, and the US National Archives launched a Twitter initiative titled #DisabilityStories.[2] In honor of the twenty-fifth anniversary of the Americans with Disabilities Act and the fortieth anniversary of the VSA, citizens across the nation—and even globally—were invited to share stories, photographs, art, and technologies that captured their individual lived experiences with disabilities.[3] As Erin Blasco asserts, the main message of the initiative was to stress that #DisabilityStories "are everywhere—including some unexpected places—and they're important."[4] The result was a large conversation, generating between 7,800 and 8,900 tweets sent using the hashtag with 76.7 million impressions on Twitter.[5] Stories included the history of curb cuts, Blind Tom's performance at the White House, Krysta Morlan's Waterbike, prosthetics, ASL/BSL histories, iron lungs, adaptive gear, and personal modifications to wheelchairs. #DisabilityStories also signified a larger trend of using social media to connect to otherwise overlooked or invisible stories in disability history. The people who contributed, as Ellis and Kent emphasize, also ended up participating in conservations that could identify new types of disability narratives.[6] Social media in turn blurred boundaries of knowledge between specialists and non-specialists, forming dialogues and offering mutually beneficial exchange of expertise.[7]

The #DisabilityStories initiative additionally signified how digital humanities can foster different approaches to public disability history, a task that can be challenging for historians unfamiliar with digital scholarship. Knoblauch and Tomes remark that much of the anxieties "stems from a concern that the new digital forms of scholarship will undercut the quality and legitimacy of the older print forms."[8] Digital tools can be used to create new forms of knowledge, accessibility, and inclusion without diluting traditional academic scholarship. For disability history in particular, these tools also enable collections and stories to become accessible to broader audiences. Online exhibits, for example, often take into consideration the need to move away from entrenched historical assumptions and push inclusion beyond simple access and into content beyond stereotypical interpretations of disability.[9] Such content includes not only the complicated intertwining of disability and the medical model, but also the struggle to include materials about overlooked disabilities: the disabled veteran, the maimed, gender, and racial issues, and even medicalized objects.

As evidenced by the growth of multiple online exhibits and open-access institutional projects, digital humanities provide an accessible platform for engaging with disability scholarship and investigating how disability can reveal crucial aspects of broader historical and contemporary issues—projects such as Ryerson University's *Out from Under: Disability, History and Things to Remember*, (www.ryerson.ca/ofu), a collaboration with students, scholars, and alumni focusing on connecting hidden histories of disability with significant milestones in Canadian history. Since 2000, several digital collections were launched with a breadth of themes encapsulating the myriad experiences of disability: *Disability & Industrial Society* (www.dis-ind-soc.org.uk), housed at Swansea University and directed by David Turner and the late Anne Borsay; *Nineteenth-Century Disability: Cultures & Contexts* (www.nineteenthcenturydisability.org), an annotated collection of primary sources on the lives of Victorian individuals with disabilities; and the *Disability History Museum* (www.disabilitymuseum.org), a virtual project with over 3,000 primary source documents and images for fostering educational forums and teaching lessons. Traditional bricks-and-mortar museums also include virtual exhibits, including the Museum of disABILITY (www.museumofdisability.org) in Buffalo which is dedicated to advancing the lived experiences of people with disabilities, and the Smithsonian National Museum of American History's *EveryBody: An Artefact History of Disability* (www.everybody.si.edu).

These projects certainly reflect Douglas Baynton's frequently cited dictum that "disability is everywhere in history" and that disability is a collective experience as much as an individual one. It is also an experience that is intricately bonded with technology, tools, and machines of social interaction, as Katherine Ott's work has shown.[10] Indeed, #DisabilityStories revealed only a fraction of these technologies and tools: wheelchairs with activism stickers, Nike's zip-up "Freedom" sneakers, 3D-printed prosthetics, custom-made sports equipment, trade technologies, and corsets for spinal support. The breadth of these technologies as used by people with disabilities is not proportionately displayed in digital humanities projects or virtual collections. *EveryBody* contains the only virtual exhibit outlining the cultural history of disability through artifacts, but it is limited in scope and object narratives are not central stories; rather, artifacts are used to convey broader themes in cultural, political, medical, and economic histories. Perhaps seeking to fulfil this gap, Carleton University in Ottawa launched *A Wheelchair History of Disability in Canada* (www.mobilityhistories.ca). Collaborating with the Canada Science and Technology Museum and guided by curator David Pantalony, this student-created project concentrates on the wheelchair as an approach to uncover relationships between technology, social attitudes, and the goals of the user. Though focusing on a single artifact, the Carleton project lacks full consideration of user narratives, especially how users modified technologies to bring them into better alignment with the reading of their bodies.[11] This may be due to the object itself in question—the wheelchair—which tends to encapsulate passive representations of impairment and ability. A ubiquitous symbol of disability, the wheelchair is also a large object whose presence in museum collections is usually commanding, especially in war exhibits.

Seventeen years ago, Katherine Ott, David Serlin, and Stephen Mihm's seminal anthology, *Artificial Parts, Practical Lives* (2002), outlined how users were more willing participants in prostheses industries than had been previously uncovered in historical records. Users were involved in design and manufacturing stages, from giving feedback to engineers upgrading myoelectric limbs, nudging design discourse, or making personal adjustments to their prosthetics. Since then, there has been a steady increase in scholarship focusing on users and disability technologies within interstitial spaces among different disciplines, including material culture, design history, medical history, the history of science, and patenting histories.[12] These studies work from a close examination of "impairment" as a historically changing category, presenting case studies on how medical practitioners, engineers, designers, and users attempted to shape disability through prostheses and other technologies. The complexity of these analyses, moreover, outlines the necessity of moving away from a "diagnostic-centric" perspective of disability and away from the medical model that focuses on the need to "fix" impairment—while, of course, recognizing the complicated distinctions that intertwine medicine and disability, given that the medical model of disability remains an arduous hurdle for the material culture of disability.[13]

But what of the objects themselves? How do we use objects to reveal the construction of disability identities and the nuances involved in materializing user-narratives of disability experiences with technology? As scholars of material culture known all too well, object biographies—especially of neglected artifacts—can dictate patterns in larger historical trends. These objects can convey meaningful interactions with the world, but the meanings themselves also emerge and change continuously, oftentimes challenging the curating of disability artifacts in both museum collections and digital humanities projects, especially since there are many disability technologies that tend to be conspicuously absent in histories of material culture. Prosthetics and assistive technologies tend to garner curiosity and make best-of lists on the internet, but they are only one aspect of the lived experience of disability—albeit one that is intricately tied to a medical framework. What of rehabilitation therapy tools or occupational therapy art? Adjustments made for women or children, or to accomplish work or identify gender? Where do autism communication technologies or mental health tools fit? Or crafted devices rather than commercialized ones? The consideration of these objects in a collection will certainly inscribe a richer, more complex history of disability and the stories of users.

Collecting and Curating

Encouraged by the #DisabilityStories initiative and the growing scholarship on the material history of disability, in 2015 I began a project to identify and catalogue the material history of disability in Canada with the eventual goal of launching a new digital humanities site. Anchored at Brock University in St. Catharines, Ontario, the project, entitled *Objects of Disability*, concentrated on bringing forth the "invisible" within museum and archival collections, the narratives of objects that were not considered relevant for exhibition, or the users whose histories have been misappropriated. I spent several months visiting these institutions, collaborating with curators and archivists to identify artifacts that were used or created by persons with disabilities, in order to build a database that would serve as a repository for my research and future scholars interested in the topic as well. Currently, the database contains nearly 400 artifacts and photographs of people using their objects of disability, located across thirty-five different institutions. These objects range from nineteenth-century invalid cups, assorted prostheses, snowshoes used by indigenous people in Northern Canada, crafted wheelchairs, therapeutic art, and personalized adjustments to commercialized products.

I define "objects of disability" as technological tools that individuals autonomously attached to their bodies to increase their sensory and/or physical experiences with the world. Since the 1990s, scholars have shifted away from the old disability studies model that equated disability with "deviance" and portrayed individuals with disabilities as passive recipients of officially sanctioned medical treatments. The new model of disability, however, uses disability as an analytical tool for examining how "normality" varied according to different cultural, legislative or civic frameworks, and how such norms guided or defined the experiences and lives of persons with disabilities.[14] Focusing on the material culture of objects of disability enables us to observe and analyze how the ascendancy of the idea of "normal" in the late nineteenth century was embodied through the technologies and devices, to camouflage, limit, or "normalize" body parts.[15] The same analysis, however, can also reveal how people with disabilities challenged the (often medicalized) norm signified by their objects to obtain power for themselves, or at least govern the system of oppression embedded upon their bodies.

Rather than simply amassing a collection, I sought to uncover not only variations of physical and mental disabilities, but also the contexts of inclusion and identity that would lend weight to understanding disability history through material culture. What can the study of these artifacts reveal about the construction of user identity and design preference through object permanence? Design, in particular, can highlight the agency of disabled persons and the way they rejected prevailing conceptions of "normalcy"—including, for instance, how they drew attention to their technologies instead of camouflaging them—providing an alternative to contemporary approaches to include art school approaches to design, as Graham Pullin has suggested.[16] As artifacts of culture, the materiality of these objects can highlight the varied ways disability has been (re-)defined. They are more than tools to "fix" or "normalize" an impairment: they are objects for navigating (sometimes literally) and engaging with challenges of usability and adaptation.

Approaching individuals with disabilities as agents of design, I examined objects of disability under three frameworks. The first, *material design*: How did factors such as cost, functionality, or aesthetics motivate the selection, creation, or personal modification of devices?[17] What worked and what didn't? How did users experiment with different materials—if at all—to improve the proficiency of their designs? Secondly, *innovations in design*: What counted as "good design" and under what standards were these designs considered to be appropriate? For example, scholars have examined how designs for the hip joint of the artificial hip frequently changed alongside surgical innovations; "good design" reflected the contexts of a commercial environment and profitability as well as design functionality.[18] And third, *degrees of normalcy*: What can the design of these objects tell us about the social and medical conceptions of "normalcy" in Canadian history, including how physical or mental disability was perceived and, if at all, accepted? How did governmental assistance, medical diagnosis, and costs guide the selection of objects of disability?[19] To what extent do objects of disability designed by people with disability actually incorporate expectations of "normalcy" in their design and use? Examining how these artifacts were modified to forge personal identities—of personality, preference, and even medical diagnosis—can further serve as historical evidence for lived experiences of disability where no other evidence exists. The personal, in other words, becomes a vital counterweight to patronizing state- and physician-centered narratives that frequently overburden disability narratives.

Crafting User Narratives

"The objects that people with disabilities are forced to live with," writes Tobin Siebers "—prostheses, wheelchairs, braces, and other devices—are viewed not as potential sources of pain but as marvelous examples of the plasticity of the human form or as devices of empowerment."[20] Drawing on the social model of disability, we can craft user narratives of artifacts through the material culture of design and modification. In so doing, people with disabilities are cast not just as users, but as agents of technological change, suggesting both how they managed their daily lives and broader cultural and political exclusion, allowing us to conceptualize how users shaped their relationship to their object(s).[21]

The design of the wheelchair, for example, is well known for its response to disability politics especially after the Second World War when the technology was reframed from a cumbersome machine designed primarily to transport a patient, to "powerful tools of personal mobility" that were inspired by the Everest & Jennings foldable wheelchair. Woods and Watson argue that the 1950s were particularly notable for the "transformation in the form, function, and meaning of wheelchairs," leading to the design of the folding transit/general-purpose wheelchair that in part coincided with a greater cultural reliance on the automobile, the introduction of antibiotics, and the creation of lightweight materials.[22] Frustrated, with poorly designed chairs, people with disabilities demanded more inclusive designs (e.g., the joystick model) or else came up with their own innovations to reflect their own activities (e.g., Marilyn Hamilton's "Quickie' chair").[23] In many instances, user-designed wheelchairs are heralded as examples of empowerment and ideal design for maximum independence.

Yet, as Penny Wolfson has shown, prior to the mass-production of wheelchairs, users often relied on their own craftsmanship or that of others to shape the device for their own needs, subtly interplaying between the user and the object.[24] Wheelchairs could be made by adding cart wheels on dining or library chairs, by screwing rolling castors to rocking chairs, or repurposing motorcycle engines to hand-cranked wheelchairs.[25] While most nineteenth-century wheelchairs were manufactured by patent furniture makers prizing comfort, adaptability, and mobility, users also repurposed from household furniture.[26] These wheelchairs not only transformed how the user relied on the tool in the build environment—as well as the challenges of navigating on unpaved streets or streets without curb cuts—but they additionally reveal variants of identity construction that are embodied on the object itself. An early-twentieth-century wheelchair with three wheels housed at the Wellington County Museum, for example, contains a hint of embarrassment over the design, corrected by a grey fabric upholstered over the entire wheelchair to more closely resemble a library chair. With a steel bar affixed on the backside of the chair, there was little indication that the wheelchair was designed for full autonomy and mobility; like the Bath wheelchairs and late-nineteenth-century wicker chairs, these were designed for "invalids," especially the elderly whose weakened constitution left them with little upper body strength to propel themselves. Hand-cranked wheelchairs or dog-drawn carts, on the other hand, suggest a user desirous of personal freedom and mobility.[27]

The inclusion of crafted additions to the wheelchairs—home-sewn cushions, crocheted blankets or feet mats, and trinkets attached to spokes—further suggests the personalized relationship between user and technology. Wheelchairs were used as tools of personal mobility, but they also incorporated aspects of the user's personality; the merging of the chair and the person offering us insight into experiences of disability that were not always negative or exclusive. Other objects of disability afford similar analyses.

Amelia Woods, a deaf woman who resided at her sister's farm in Hazeldean, near Ottawa during the 1880s, left behind a legacy in the form of a personalized object. Woods relied on a conversation tube—a flexible mechanical hearing aid flared at the mouthpiece (for the speaker) and narrowed to an earpiece (for the listener)—seemingly carrying it around the farm to use when necessary (Figure 12.1). Depending on the length, these devices can be bulky to carry; I've come across many that are dented with severe wear and tear, but Wood's model was clearly cherished. There is little damage, save for a few tears by the earpiece, likely from bending when inserting into the ear canal. The care is probably more likely attributed to Wood's creation of a black drawstring bag, delicately woven and ornately beaded, for storing the

Figure 13.1a Amelia Woods's conversation tube pouch. Courtesy of Ken Seiling Waterloo Region Museum (1970.006.001).

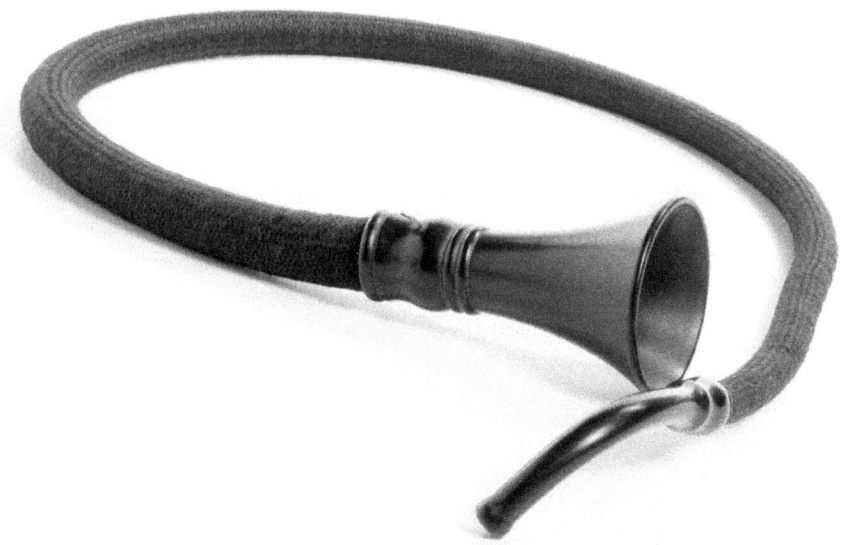

Figure 13.1b Amelia Woods's conversation tube. Courtesy of Ken Seiling Waterloo Region Museum (1970.007.001).

conversation tube and carrying it around when not in use. Here, the material design of the device becomes part of her body, the cotton strings serving to close the bag and drape it on her wrist or tied on her skirt, separate, but yet also still a necessary part of her body. The bag itself is an unusual example of user adaptation, clearly revealing how the conversation tube was valued, for nineteenth-century hearing trumpets were not usually sold or purchased with bags.[28]

The story of Andrew Gawley (1869–1961) of Meaford, Ontario, provides another example of the merging of users and their objects of disability. In 1885 at the age of sixteen, while working at the buzz saw at a local sawmill in Bruce Peninsula, Gawley had an accident resulting in both his hands being badly mangled.[29] Despite the severity of his injuries, it took a week's travel by boat to arrive to the nearest hospital in Owen Sound; after the surgeon amputated both of Gawley's hands up to his forearms, the hospital provided him with prosthetics, which Gawley deemed insufficient because they were designed to work with one regular hand—poorly designed and useless for an individual who lost both hands. At Gawley's request, the local blacksmith constructed simple wooden prosthetic hands allowing Gawley to hold a pencil and design his more functional and personalized hands to be self-sufficient. With assistance from his blind father, Gawley eventually built the prosthetics he would become famous for: hands made of cast iron and steel with five additional points of grip and strength. Teaching himself to use the grips—the "fingers" as he called them—Gawley eventually managed to learn aspects of "normal living": eating with a knife and fork, building toys for local children, working on a farm, a munitions factory, and later at his bicycle repair shop (Figure 12.2). He even made arms for injured soldiers and for civilians requesting them. And during the 1930s, he traveled with *Ripley's Believe It or Not!* billed as "The Man with the Steel Hands," demonstrating how he used his hands for daily activities, even lifting a 250lb Ford engine block for publicity photos.[30] In his hometown of Meaford, Gawley's story is inspiring, if not legendary. The prosthetics remain a cherished artifact housed at the Meaford Museum and in 2014, Gawley's life was celebrated in a local stage play.

Gawley's life is a remarkable story of self-sufficiency and "overcoming." It is also a story of a man whose prosthetic hands often overshadowed his own identity. "You don't realize what wonderful instruments your hands are," he expressed in an interview. "When you think of the things your hand can do, you never come to an end."[31] Even his autograph cards were "written by *my steel hand*" before they were signed by his own name.[32] It is a separation of sorts, between the two, the man and the prosthetic, yet the two remain adjoined, connected by their dependence—a symbiotic bond between user and object. For Gawley, the creation of his outfitted, visible identity—being independent and self-sufficient—and his designing, crafting, and making of his steel hands served to materialize that identity. They are not "normal" hands in appearance, but in their use, they become imbedded with meaning only by Gawley's insistence, by his physical encounters with the world.

Emily DePoy and Stephen Gibson question why there has been a failure to recognize prostheses and assistive devices as part of one's outfitted, visible

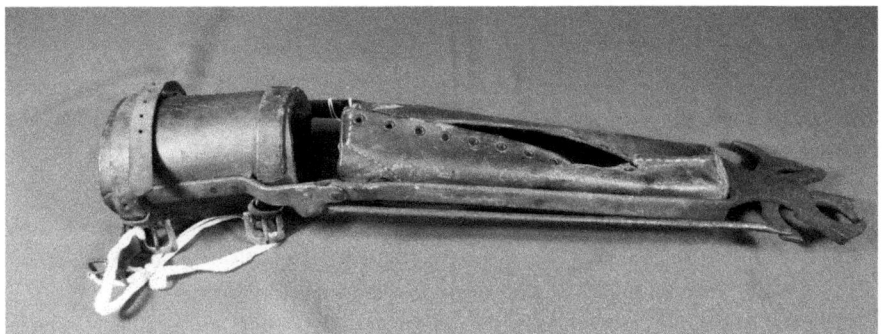

Figure 13.2 Andrew Gawley's prosthesis. Grey Roots Museum and Archives collection, object ID 1973.100.001.

identity, especially given the range of styles and prices historically available to users.[33] Prosthetic technologies have certainly transformed lives, especially for those who experienced impairment resulting from trauma, war, or accidents, as in Gawley's case. Yet many users remain frustrated with certain features of their prostheses, including affordability, functionality, and corporate monopolization and often take on their own modifications of their objects.[34] While disability and design have focused on how prostheses were constructed to respond to and shape social and environmental contexts—acknowledging of course, that not all prosthetic "fixes" are representative of the whole range of users—few have historicized how users engaged with their prosthetics address challenges of usability and adaptation. Gawley's various prosthetics suggest an identity that is designed through the material, welded through the steel hands to reconfigure not just physical interactions with the world, but also expectations about disabled bodies. We also see most assuredly that people with disabilities were "too busy living to be restrained by our post-structuralist worries over the cultural contingencies of what they did or who they were," as Ott has remarked.[35] From the steel hands, on the other hand, we perceive the centrality of disability experience within history, the physical manifestation of human endeavors that mirror larger historical patterns. The hands—the prosthetics—are tangible evidence of one man's lived experience with disability: the rough shaping of the curved grips, the tattered straps, and the softening of worn leather. They give us insight into the materiality of disability, perhaps—if not in Gawley's case, then certainly in others—serving as the only remaining evidence of such experience.

Methodological Issues

Searching for objects of disability does pose several methodological challenges, least of which is the simple identification of objects in collections. I began my research by contacting curators and archives of local institutions, providing an overview of the project and inquiring about the collections; most replies redirected me to online databases and advice for searching with historically contingent keywords (e.g., "imbecile," "deaf and dumb," "idiot"). Some curators, however, offered a copy of the collections database so I could browse and select relevant objects I would be interested in examining; others invited me to browse through the warehouse. The first challenge of course was the online database themselves. Despite remarkable advances in collections management and keyword tracking, sometimes the lack of proper keywords tends to overlook valuable artifacts of disability. Searching for "prosthetic," for example, did not always garner a result; searching for "leg," "limb," or "arm," however, resulted in far too many results to browse through.

This is not to say valuable artifacts of disability are overlooked. Indeed, most objects were actually placed within medical collections, revealing once again, the blurred boundaries between disability and medicine. As Nicole Belolan has argued, early Americans managed mobility disabilities by improvising household objects, often involving medical practitioners make living easier.[36] This raises a broader issue: To what extent does disability unravel itself from medicine? Nowhere is this more problematic than in psychiatric collections and objects of mental disability. As Ott asserts, how cognitive disability "is portrayed (or not portrayed) is directly related to core cultural values."[37] To fully encompass the range of cognitive disabilities, we need to move away from stereotypical interpretations of disability. The London Museum in Southern Ontario, for example, has an artifact: a glass jar filled nearly to the brim with small metal objects—nails, screws, bed springs, etc.—2,533 items that were surgically extracted from a woman's stomach in 1927.[38] The woman, Annie Hobson, was a patient at the Ontario Hospital and had a history of "manic-depressive insanity" with suicidal tendencies. The artifact certainly is (perhaps rightly so?) a medical curiosity, but given that records reveal the woman's history of mental illness, is it not an object of mental health as well?

Negotiating this boundary between medicine and disability can be an enervative process, especially when encountering histories of institutional abuse and horrific conditions faced by patients. Such objects can also reveal the cultural contingencies and politics involved in how objects with sensitive histories can be displayed for educational purposes or maintained in a collection. One collection, extracted from a former psychiatric hospital after it shut down, contains both instruments of invasive therapies and occupational therapy and crafts made by patients.[39] Several objects from this collection are displayed in a small exhibit in the hospital; the exhibit, however, limits the medical history and glorifies the patient art. The abhorrent treatments enforced on patients are reduced to two to three primary objects: a strap-on chair, a Utica crib, and a straightjacket—otherwise stereotypical representations of a psychiatric hospital. On the one hand, this strategy spotlights the patients rather than demonizing them or the treatments; on the other hand, by hiding the medical objects (and yes, literally, for most the medical collection is locked away in the basement), an important history is surely concealed.

Examining objects of disability for historical basis of design also incorporates the traditional goal of medical design to compensate for disability as discreetly as possible. Most twentieth-century lower-leg prosthetics, for instance, were modeled from pink plastic in attempts to camouflage against the skin, especially models that were supplied by hospitals or rehabilitation centers. These prosthetics were not designed to project a particular image—i.e., draw attention to the leg—but about not projecting *any* image whatsoever. It was meant to go unnoticed, the pink color disappearing into the skin, and of course, raising more questions about non-white users. Examining the political and cultural features embodied into the object, however, does not necessarily reveal any significant status of the object or any pivotal markers of design trajectory; sometimes objects are just ordinary objects, their value is not in what they can tell us about historical conceptions of disability, but rather, the simple, if not common, lives of the user—sometimes not in an object, but proudly worn and captured in a photograph, revealing more about feelings and attitudes than about the materiality of the artifact.

Of course, in selecting objects for my database, I am also curating and defining what disability means. How many eyeglasses do I include before it becomes redundant? Are different canes varied representations of disability or simply another type of mobility aid?[40] Staying focused on my primary goal offers guidance for what objects are included: personal modifications of wheelchairs; the use of crochet as therapy; reflections of normative identities; clues of gendering. By positioning these objects of disability as emissaries of culture and personhood, we can obtain insight into identity politics by uncovering varied representations of disability as marked-on artifacts. At the Centre for Addiction and Mental Health in Toronto, for instance, there is a strange-looking object that was nearly thrown out. It is a wheelbarrow, made entirely out of scrap pieces of metal and wood welded together, scavenged from garbage cans, dumping grounds, and other odd places by Larry, a patient at the former Ontario Hospital between 1938 and 1940. There is no other record of this patient, not even the reasons for his admission or his motivation for building the wheelbarrow; nor is there any evidence it was used for occupational therapy or constructed for farm work on the hospital grounds. Whether this wheelbarrow was constructed as self-therapy, art, or another function, it serves an important purpose: it is solid evidence of Larry's existence.

Toward the Future

Disability has always been central to our lives. From debates about qualifications of democratic citizenship, to the ravages of war, improvement of medical technologies, and controversies of access to accommodations, disability has been present in virtually all aspects of history. People have grappled with issues of disability in both their personal lives and the public arena, and nowhere do we see this more than in the things they used, the things they made, and the things they left behind. "Disability," Lennard Davis reminds us, "is not an object—a woman with a cane—but a social process that intimately involves everyone who has a body and lives in the world of senses."[41] The materiality of objects, however, can highlight the varied ways disability has been defined, but the reliance of medical technologies to enhance sensory and physical difference in disabled bodies often rests on an invisible logic of ableism. By trusting medical experts to fix bodies, such technologies often restrict the autonomy of people with disabilities, whose bodies thus become stigmatized. This historical context is crucial, lest medical experts and prosthetic designers recapitulate abelist representations of differences in contemporary public policy.

By paying greater attention to users, *Objects of Disability* highlights their importance as historical actors, and how both medical and non-medical practice and design influenced the creation of prosthetics and assistive technologies. Examining historical objects of disability and user designs can provide us with a more nuanced understanding of the relationship between material culture and disability history, including how acceptance and adjustment of a prosthesis represent a commitment to productive citizenship, as Ott has argued.[42] Rather than looking at these artifacts as symbols of exclusion, we can examine them to obtain insight into the identity politics and daily lives of persons with disabilities, uncovering varying representations of disability by users.

Nor should we assume the meanings of objects are static and embedded within their materiality. As museum curators know all too well, exhibiting the evolving trends of design and innovation in prosthetics is a powerful way to demonstrate how ideas about technology, design, and disability have transformed in response to cultural, political, and social measures. Thus, it is imperative that museums and digital humanities navigate accessibility within broader historical contexts, incorporating stories and voices of people with disabilities.[43] Otherwise, key experiences of disability are lost, or otherwise stereotypically narrowed to a single artifact, as is the case of the Canada War Museum in Ottawa which, in 2016 when I visited the museum, only had a single exhibit reference to disability—the exhibition of a prosthetic limb.

The challenge going forward is to recapitulate this transformation while still revitalizing the narratives of users who incorporated these artifacts as aspects of their identity and for navigating their built environment. *Objects of Disability* remains an ongoing project, as I am aiming to launch the database online (www.objectsofdisability.omeka.net) with interactive features for scholars to examine both the artifacts and the narrative of users, including 3D software to offer tactile interactions with the objects. It is imperative that the project takes into account the ways people with disabilities use digital resources, invoking new tactile interfaces for maximum accessibility—audio, ASL, large format text, screen reading software—in short, incorporating aspects of universal design and of course, making it open access. Such a site itself becomes an artifact, woven with the stories of objects it features, with the eventual goal of deepening our understanding of the material history of disability.

Acknowledgments

This project was funded by a Social Sciences and Humanities Research Council Postdoctoral Fellowship. I am grateful to the Department of History and the Humanities Research Institute at Brock University, Elizabeth Neswald, Daniel Samson, Jessica Clark, and Geoff Bil for encouragement and advice on the project's direction, and to all the archivists, curators, and museum volunteers who made this project worthwhile. Special thanks to David Sharron (Brock Library Special Collections & Archives), John Court (Centre for Addition and Mental Health), Stacy McLennan (Waterloo Regional Museum), and Jody Seeley (Meaford Museum). Earlier versions of this paper were presented at the *Making Modern Disability: Histories of Disability, Design and Technology* conference at Hagley Museum and Library, the 2017 American Association of the History of Medicine meeting, and at *(Im)Material Culture: Health History Collections in a Digital Era* symposium at the University of Toronto. Thanks to the audience for their remarks, and to Bess Williamson, Caroline Leiffers, Cara Fallon, Beth Linker, and Erich Weidenhammer for their reflections.

Notes

1 Katherine Ott, "Disability Things: Material Culture and American Disability History, 1700–2010," in *Disability Histories*, ed. Susan Burch and Michael Rembis (Chicago: University of Illinois Press, 2014), 119.
2 The VSA ("Very Special Arts") is an international organization on arts and disability.
3 Erin Blasco, "Share #DisabilityStories on Wednesday July 15," *The National Museum of American History Blog*, July 8, 2015, accessed October 24, 2017, http://americanhistory.si.edu/blog/share-disabilitystories-wednesday-july-15.
4 Erin Blasco, "So, how did #DisabilityStories go? Reporting on a big, lively, hashtag-based conversation/jamboree on Twitter," *Medium*, July 29, 2015, accessed January 5, 2018, https://medium.com/@erinblasco/so-how-did-disabilitystories-go-f65082aed5ea.
5 Ibid. Twitter "impressions" are responses to tweets sent by an account that generates interactions or replies from others; as defined by Twitter Analytics, it is the best indication of how well a tweet is being engaged by the audience.
6 Katie Ellis and Mike Kent, *Disability and Social Media: Global Perspectives* (New York: Routledge, 2017), 3.
7 On social media and disability see Jaipreet Virdi [as Virdi-Dhesi], "Dialogues on Disability: Social Media as Platforms for Scholarship," *Medical History* 58, no. 4 (October 2014): 628–631.
8 Heidi Knoblauch and Nancy Tomes, "The History of Medicine in the Digital Age," *Bulletin of the History of Medicine* 88, no. 4 (2014): 730–733.
9 Katherine Ott, "Disability and the Practice of Public History: An Introduction," *The Public Historian* 27, no. 2 (Spring 2005): 9–24; "Prosthetics," in *Keywords in Disability Studies*, ed. Rachel Adams, Benjamin Reiss, and David Serlin (New York: New York University Press, 2015): 140–143; "The Sum of Its Parts: An Introduction to Modern Histories of Prosthetics," in *Artificial Parts, Practical Lives: Modern Histories of Prosthetics*, ed. Katherine Ott, David Serlin, and Stephen Mihm (New York: New York University Press, 2002), 1–42; "Collective Bodies: What Museums Do for Disability Studies," in *Re-Presenting Disability: Activism and Agency in the Museum*, ed. Richard Sandell, Jocelyn Dodd, and Rosemarie Garland-Thomson (New York and London: Routledge, 2010), 269–279; Ott, "Disability Things."

10 Ott, "Disability Things," 120.
11 On users and modification of assistive technologies see Stuart Blume, *The Artificial Ear: Cochlear Implants and the Culture of Deafness* (New Brunswick, NJ, and London: Rutgers University Press, 2010).
12 Katherine Feo, "Invisibility: Memory, Masks and Masculinities in the Great War," *Journal of Design History* 20 (2007): 17–27; Beth Linker, *War's Waste: Rehabilitation in World War I America* (Chicago, IL: University of Chicago Press, 2011; David Serlin, *Replacable You: Engineering the Body in Postwar America* (Chicago, IL: University of Chicago Press, 2004); Mara Mills, "Hearing Aids and the History of Electronics Miniaturization," *IEEE Annals of the History of Computing* 11 (2011): 24–44; Jan Eric Olsén, "Vicariates of the Eye: Blindness, Sense Substitution, and Writing Devices in the Nineteenth Century," *Mosaic Journal* 46, no. 3 (2013): 75–91; Nick Watson and Brian Woods, "The Origins and Early Development of Special/Adaptive Wheelchair Seating," *Social History of Medicine* 18 (2005): 459–474; Carsten Timmermann and Julie Anderson, *Devices and Designs: Medical Technologies in Historical Perspective* (New York: Palgrave Macmillan, 2006); Marquard Smith and Joanne Morra. eds., *The Prosthetic Impulse: From a Posthuman Present to a Biocultural Future* (Cambridge, MA, and London: MIT Press, 2006); Vanessa Warne, "'To Invest a Cripple with Peculiar Interest': Artificial Legs and Upper Class Amputees at Mid-Century," *Victorian Review* 35, no. 2 (2009): 83–100; Bess Williamson, "Getting a Grip: Disability in American Industrial Design of the Late Twentieth Century," *Winterthur Portfolio* 46, no. 4 (2010): 213–236; David Serlin, "On Walkers and Wheelchairs: Disabling the Narratives of Urban Modernity," *Radical History Review* 114 (2012): 19–28; Claire L. Jones, ed., *Rethinking Modern Prostheses in Anglo-American Commodity Cultures, 1820–1939* (Manchester: Manchester University Press, 2017).
13 Katherine Ott, "Disability and Disability Studies," in *Material Culture in America: Understanding Everyday Life*, ed. Helen Sheumaker and Shirley Teresa Wajda (Santa Barbara, CA: ABC-CLIO, 2008); Geoffrey Reaume, "Disability History in Canada: Present Work in the Field and Future Prospects," *Canadian Journal of Disability Studies* 1, no. 1 (2012): 35–81; Beth Linker, "On the Borderland of Medical and Disability History: A Survey of the Fields," *Bulletin of the History of Medicine* 87, no. 4 (2013): 499–535.
14 Paul K. Longmore and Lauri Urmansky, eds., *The New Disability History: American Perspectives* (New York: New York University Press, 2001); Tanya Tichkosky and Rod Michalko. eds., *Rethinking Normalcy: A Disability Studies Reader* (Toronto: Canadian Scholars Press, 2009); Kim Nielsen, *A Disability History of the United States* (Boston, MA: Beacon Press, 2012); Susan Schweik, *The Ugly Laws: Disability in Public* (New York: New York University Press, 2010).
15 On the ascendancy of the "normal" see Lennard J. Davis, *Enforcing Normalcy: Disability, Deafness and the Body* (London: Verso Press, 1995); Douglas Baynton, *Forbidden Signs: American Culture and the Campaign against Sign Language* (Chicago, IL: University of Chicago Press, 1996); Anna Creadick, *Perfectly Average: The Pursuit of Normalcy in Postwar America* (Amherst & Boston, MA: University of Massachusetts Press, 2010).

16 Graham Pullin, *Design Meets Disability* (Cambridge, MA: MIT Press, 2009).
17 For instance, see Mary Tremblay, "Going Back to Civvy Street: A Historical Account of the Impact of the Everest and Jennings Wheelchair for Canadian World War II Veterans with Spinal Cord Injury," *Disability and Society* 11, no. 2 (1996): 149–169; Edward Slavishak, "Artificial Limbs and Industrial Workers' Bodies in Turn-of-the-Century Pittsburgh," *Journal of Social History* 37, no. 2 (2003): 365–388; Marcia J. Scherer, *Living in the State of Stuck: How Assistive Technology Impacts the Lives of People with Disabilities* (Cambridge, MA: Brookline Books, 2000).
18 Alex Faulkner, "Casing the Joint: The Material Development of Artificial Hips," in *Artificial Parts, Practical Lives*, 199–206; Julie Anderson, Francis Neary, and John V. Pickstone, *Surgeons, Manufacturers and Patients: A Transatlantic History of Total Hip Replacement* (Basingstoke: Palgrave Macmillan, 2007).
19 For a contemporary example, the Ontario Assistive Devices Program contributes up to 75 percent of the cost of assistive technologies. With regard to hearing aids, the program allocates a fixed amount determined by age and the audiologist's report; for individuals with limited income, sometimes the selection of hearing aids covered by the program is not always suitable for their own needs and interactions with the hearing world. Available choices, moreover, are not necessarily an improvement in technological design. Individuals used to analog hearing aids, for instance, frequently found it difficult to adjust to the newer digital aids, which required an audiologist to connect the user to a computer to adjust sound decibel and frequency. Not only does this drastically limit user autonomy, but the experience of hearing is thus determined by a computer and the audiologist's "reading," rather than the user's subjective experience.
20 Tobin Siebers, "Disability in Theory: From Social Constructionism to the New Realism of the Body," in *The Disability Studies Reader*, ed. Lennard Davis (New York and London: Routledge, 2006), 177.
21 Nelly Oudshoorn and Trevor Pinch, "How Users and Non-Users Matter," in *How Users Matter: The Co-Construction of Users and Technology*, ed. Nelly Oudshoorn and Trevor Pinch (Cambridge, MA: MIT Press, 2003), 1–25; 11.
22 Brian Woods and Nick Watson, "In Pursuit of Standardization: The British Ministry of Health's Model 8F Wheelchair, 1948–1962," *Technology and Culture* 45, no. 3 (2004): 540–568.
23 Joseph P. Shapiro, "The Screaming Neon Wheelchair," in *No Pity: People with Disabilities Forging a New Civil Rights Movement* (New York: Three Rivers Press, 1994), 211–236.
24 Penny Lynne Wolfson, "Enwheeled: Two Centuries of Wheelchair Design, from Furniture to Film," MA Thesis, Cooper-Hewitt, National Design Museum, Smithsonian Institution and Parsons the New School for Design (2014). See also Wolfson's chapter in this volume.
25 Rocking chair, Grey Roots Museum & Archives (1964.066.001); Commercial wheelchair-type motorcycle with engine, model "Argson Stanley" (1920), Canada Science and Technology Museum (1975.0514.001).
26 Wolfson, "Enwheeled," 33.
27 Photograph of a man in a hand-cranked wheelchair at a railway station, *c.* 1896, Library and Archives Canada MIKAN 2399464; Photograph of man in a dog-drawn cart at

CNE, *c.* 1950s, City of Toronto Archives, Fonds 1257 Alexandra Studio, Series 1057, Item 5737.
28 Graeme Gooday and Karen Sayer, "Purchase, Use, and Adaptation: Interpreting 'Patented' Aids to the Deaf in Victorian Britain," in *Rethinking Modern Prostheses*, 41.
29 Courtesy of Meaford Museum Archives.
30 Of course, Gawley's participation in a traveling troupe raises broader discussions of disability and the "sideshow freakshow" that scholars have examined in depth. See Robert Bogdan, *Freak Show: Presenting Human Oddities for Amusement and Profit* (Chicago, IL: University of Chicago Press, 1990); Rosemarie Garland-Thomson, *Freakery: Cultural Spectacles of the Extraordinary Body* (New York: New York University Press, 1996).
31 Meaford Museum Archives.
32 Meaford Museum Archives.
33 Elizabeth DePoy and Stephen Gilson, *Branding and Designing Disability: Reconceptualising Disability Studies* (Abingdon, Oxon: Routledge, 2014).
34 Claire L. Jones, "Modern Prostheses in Anglo-American Commodity Cultures: An Introduction," in *Rethinking Modern Prostheses*, 1.
35 Ott, "The Sum of Its Parts," 3.
36 Nicole Belolan, "'Confined to Crutches': James Logan and the Material Culture of Disability in Early America," *Pennsylvania Legacies* 17, no. 2 (2017): 6–11. See also Belolan's chapter in this volume.
37 Ott, "Disability and the Practice of Public History," 13.
38 For an overview of Annie Hobson's case see S.G. Chalk and H.O. Foucar, "Foreign Bodies in the Stomach: Report of a Case in Which More Than Two Thousand Five Hundred Foreign Bodies Were Found," *Archives of Surgery* 16, no. 2 (February 1928): 494–500.
39 Occupational therapy can be viewed as a later form of the craft revival movements of the nineteenth and early twentieth-centuries that aimed to promote and sell objects made by the poor and disabled living in institutions. While these objects contributed to female emancipation, they also reveal the high degree of skills females learned within these institutions. See Vivienne Richmond, "Crafting Inclusion for 'Invalid' Women: The Girls' Friendly Society Central Needlework Depôt, 1899–1947," in *Craft, Community and the Material Culture of Place and Politics, 19th–20th Century*, ed. Janice Helland, Beverly Lemire and Alena Buis (London and New York: Routledge, 2014), 161–176.
40 See Cara Fallon's chapter in this volume.
41 Davis, *Enforcing Normalcy*, 2.
42 Ott, "The Sum of Its Parts," 24.
43 In 2014, for instance, actor and activist Mat Fraser exhibited "Cabinet of Curiosities: How Disability Was Kept in a Box," critically analyzing the way disability artifacts were exhibited in museum collections, and the way medicine undermined or eliminated user voices. See Wellcome Trust, "Mat Fraser's Cabinet of Curiosities: How Disability Was Kept in a Box" (January 27, 2014), https://blog.wellcome.ac.uk/2014/01/27/cabinet-of-curiosities-how-disability-was-kept-in-a-box/A complete video of Fraser's talk is available here (without closed captioning), https://vimeo.com/110346267

Bibliography

Adams, Rachel, Benjamin Reiss, and David Serlin, eds. *Keywords in Disability Studies*. New York: New York University Press, 2015.

Blume, Stuart. *The Artificial Ear: Cochlear Implants and the Culture of Deafness*. New Brunswick, NJ, and London: Rutgers University Press, 2010.

Burch, Susan and Michael Rembis. *Disability Histories*. Chicago: University of Illinois Press, 2014.

Davis, Lennard. *Enforcing Normalcy: Disability, Deafness and the Body*. London: Verso Press, 1995.

Ellis, Katie and Mike Kent. *Disability and Social Media: Global Perspectives*. New York: Routledge, 2017.

Jones, Claire L., ed. *Rethinking Modern Prostheses in Anglo-American Commodity Cultures, 1820–1939*. Manchester: Manchester University Press, 2017.

Knoblauch, Heidi and Nancy Tomes. "The History of Medicine in the Digital Age." *Bulletin of the History of Medicine* 88, no. 4 (2014): 730–733.

Linker, Beth. "On the Borderland of Medical and Disability History: A Survey of the Fields." *Bulletin of the History of Medicine* 87, no. 4 (2013): 499–535.

Longmore, Paul and Lauri Urmansky, eds. *The New Disability History: American Perspectives*. New York: New York University Press, 2001.

Ott, Katherine. "Disability and the Practice of Public History: An Introduction." *The Public Historian* 27, no. 2 (2005): 9–24.

Ott, Katherine, David Serlin, and Stephen Mihm, eds. *Artificial Parts, Practical Lives: Modern Histories of Prosthetics*. New York: New York University Press, 2002.

Oudshoorn, Nelly and Trevor Pinch, eds. *How Users Matter: The Co-Construction of Users and Technology*. Cambridge, MA: MIT Press, 2003.

Pullin, Graham. *Design Meets Disability*. Cambridge, MA, and London: MIT Press, 2009.

Reaume, Geoffrey. "Disability History in Canada: Present Work in the Field and Future Prospects." *Canadian Journal of Disability Studies* 1, no. 1 (2012): 35–81.

Sandell, Richard, Jocelyn Dodd, and Rosemarie Garland-Thomson, eds. *Re-Presenting Disability: Activism and Agency in the Museum*. New York: Routledge, 2010.

Shapiro, Joseph P. *No Pity: People with Disabilities Forging a New Civil Rights Movement*. New York: Three Rivers Press, 1994.

Sheumaker, Helen and Shirley Teresa Wajda, eds. *Material Culture in America: Understanding Everyday Life*. Santa Barbara, CA: ABC-CLIO, 2008.

Siebers, Tobin. "Disability in Theory: From Social Constructionism to the New Realism of the Body." In *The Disability Studies Reader*, ed. Lennard Davis. New York and London: Routledge, 2006.

Wolfson, Penny Lynn. "Enwheeled: Two Centuries of Wheelchair Design, from Furniture to Film." MA Thesis, Cooper-Hewit, National Design Museum, Smithsonian Institution and Parsons the New School for Design, 2014.

Woods, Brian and Nick Watson. "In Pursuit of Standardization: The British Ministry of Health's Model 8F Wheelchair, 1948–1962." *Technology and Culture* 45, no. 3 (2004): 540–568.

Index

Note Locators with letter 'n' refer to notes.

A.A. Marks Company 61–71
AAC (Augmentative and Alternative Communication) 7
accessible design/accessibility 2, 6, 8, 20, 97–9, 101, 103, 105, 106, 108–110, 116–17, 118, 120, 131–2, 143, 161, 163, 164, 167, 177, 199, 225, 226, 236
Act of Congress 143, 145
Adams, John Quincy 56 n.13
adaptive devices 1, 4, 7, 8, 84–7, 225
advertisements 22, 23, 27, 46, 61, 62–3, 65, 68, 81–4, 109, 164–7, 193, 196, 199, 202, 205 n.36
aesthetics 2, 65, 98, 144, 177, 210, 213, 219, 229
agency 6, 29, 79, 126 n.14, 132, 135, 174, 228
aging 58 n.65
    accessible design 97–8, 163, 174, 175, 193
    associated risks 198
    and impairment 43–54, 97–8, 202, 203
    and stigma 44, 200
airborne chemicals/pollutants 131–9
Air Pollution Control Act 131
air purifiers 135, 138
allergies 134, 137
Almanack 22
American Association of Retired Persons (AARP) 198, 200
American National Standards Institute 103
    Specifications for Making Buildings and Facilities Accessible to and Usable by the Physically Handicapped 102–3, 105
American Sign Language (ASL) 87, 149, 155 n.7, 205 n.32, 225, 236

Americans with Disabilities Act (ADA) 2, 7, 134, 135, 167, 225
anaphylaxis 132
anosmia 132
anti-air pollution 131–9
    Donora smog event 131
    EPA governance and regulation 132, 133
    EU regulations 137
    fragrance bans 135–7
    London smog tragedy 131
    MCS disability/condition 132–9
    modern architectural revolution 131–2
    United Nations guidelines 132
anti-smoking 135–6
Aoi Shiba no Kai (The Green Grass Club) 160–1
Apple Watch (Series 3) 202
architecture
    avant-garde 2
    for deaf people 86, 87, 143–55
    for disabled people 105, 113–25
    Modernist 96–7
    role of ergonomics 177–87
Arduino device 216
arthritis 15, 53, 54. *See also* gout
Artificial Intelligence 173
artificial limbs. *See* prosthetics
Artificial Parts, Practical Lives (Ott, Serlin, and Mihm) 226
assistive technologies 1, 7, 15, 20, 102, 103, 159, 162, 164–5, 168, 197, 199, 203, 211, 213, 216–17, 227, 232–3, 236
asthma 133, 134, 138
Asylum for Blind and Deaf 115
Atkinson, Paul 185
Atlanta Journal & Constitution, The 198
Attfield, Judy 2–3

audiphone/electrophone 16, 78, 83, 84, 86
AutoDesk 215, 217

back problems 181
Bakema, Jaap 114, 116, 117–24, 127 n.33
barrier-free design 7, 105, 110, 161
Barthes, Roland 211
Bartlett, Lynn 153
Bathgate and Company 82, 83
bath wheelchairs 230
Bauman, Hansel 144
Baynton, Douglas 226
Beard, George Miller 133
bed chairs 19, 20, 25, 34 n.60
bedsteads 19, 20
Belliger, Cassius 22
Belolan, Nicole 15, 19–28, 234
bespoke
    digital prosthetics 211–14
    terminology 211
Bespoke Bodies: The Design and Craft of Prosthetics 209, 217–18
Bespoke Fairings 211–14
Bespoke Innovations 210–14, 215, 217, 219
BIFMA (Business and Institutional Furniture Manufacturers Association) 182
bifocals 181
Bijleveld, W. P. 124
biomedicine 78, 80
Blasco, Erin 225
blindness 4, 79
Blind Persons Act 103
Blind Tom 225
Blount, Walter 54
Boardman, Elijah 27
"body work" 32 n.41
Bombay Deaf School 85
Bombay Institution for Deaf-Mutes 87
Borsay, Anne 226
Bourdieu, Pierre 131
Bouwman, Mies 113
Bowker, Geoffrey 196
Braille 15, 163
British Deaf and Dumb Association 77
British Sign Language (BSL) 81, 87, 225
British Standards Institution 109
Brooks, Preston 47
Brown, Mary Eleanor 52
bubonic plague 132
Buchanan, Richard 98
Buchwald, Edith 52, 53

Burling, Thomas 25
Bush, George W. 187, 198

Canada Science and Technology Museum 226
caregiving 20, 104, 106–8, 118, 121, 160, 197, 200
Carleton project 226–7
carpal tunnel syndrome 181, 183, 185, 186
CBEMA (Computer and Business Equipment Manufacturers Association) 182
Cederstrom, Philip 52
Center for Disease Control and Prevention 21, 138
Centre for Addiction and Mental Health, Toronto 235
cerebral palsy 116, 161
Chandler, James 62, 69–70
chemical sensitivities. *See* multiple chemical sensitivity (MCS)
CIAM (Congrès International d'Architecture Moderne) 114, 117, 121
City Lab 139 n.5
civil rights 2, 97, 110, 143, 154
class 2, 16, 46, 49, 51, 79, 84, 185
clean air 98, 131, 132, 138–9
Clean Air Act 131, 132, 135, 138
Clinton, Bill 187
clothing 27–8, 181, 211, 212
clothing rails 102
Collection of Receipts. For the Use of the Poor (Wesley) 21
Collective Project 214, 215
Comba, Alessandro 62, 66–9
Comfort in the Gout (Rowlandson) 24–5, 27
computers
    accessibility in design 177
    health and safety standards and guidelines 182–7
    office design challenges 178–80
    related health problems 177, 180–1, 185
    role of ergonomics 177, 181–7
    as useful tool for disabled people 173–4
concentration problems 132
concept drawings 153
Convalescent Homes 115
conversation tube 82, 230–2
conversation tube pouch 230–1
Cooper-Hewitt National Design Museum 213
Corbin, Alain 132, 133
Covalt, Donald 52, 53

CP96 toilet 109
CPU (central processing unit) 179, 185
crip technoscience 6
crochet 230, 235
crutches 24, 43, 49, 52–3, 69, 70, 102, 159
Cullen, Mark 132
curb cuts 6, 161, 225, 230
custom manufacturing 1, 8–9, 226

Data Processing Management Association 185
Davis, Lennard 3, 235
Deaf Gain 144, 154, 155 n.7
deaf people/deafness, NTID facilities. *See* National Technical Institute for the Deaf (NTID)
deaf people/deafness in British India 77–88
   colonial and missionary impact 78–81
   hearing devices 81–4
   Kar Pallavi Bhasha system of signs 78, 85–8
   misconceptions about the causes of disability 79, 80
   prevalence of 79–80
   schools for the deaf 80–1
   sign language 78, 84–7
DeafSpace 8, 98, 144, 154–5
deaf studies 143–4
Deaver, George 52
decentralization 120
dentaphones 90 n.50
DePoy, Emily 232–3
Desai, Rao Bahadur Gopali 85
design
   ideologies 103–6, 228–9
   and innovation 98–9, 131
   "model of disability" 5–6
design development 1–2, 105, 193
Designing for the Disabled (Goldsmith) 101–2, 105–6, 108, 109, 110
Design Meets Disability (Pullin) 213
Design Museum Boston (DMB) 209
design standards 96, 105, 108
diabetes 181
Dibner, Andrew 194, 195
diet issues 21, 181
Diffrient, Niels 186
digital technologies 7, 173–5, 209, 214, 215
disability
   beliefs attributed to 4, 95, 114–15, 160
   definitions 5, 134, 144, 229, 235
   as dismodernism 3
   forms of 4
   material history of 225–9
Disability Discrimination Act 2, 7–8
Disability History Museum 226
disability identity 1, 227
Disability & Industrial Society 226
disability insurance scheme 121
disability rights 96
Disability Rights and Deaf 98
Disability Rights movement 5, 173
#DisabilityStories 225, 226, 228
"disability things" 175
disabled people
   as agents in design 2, 4, 164–7, 229
   techno-ableism 6
   veterans 3, 52, 61–71, 95–9, 209–19
Distinctions: A Social Critique of the Judgement of Taste (Bourdieu) 131
dog-drawn carts 230, 239–40
Donnay, Albert H. 134
doors 95, 101, 102, 104, 105, 109, 118, 120, 124, 201
Downey, Robert, Jr. 214
Dreyfuss, Henry 3, 183–4, 186
Drinker, Elizabeth 25
Dupont, Richard 213
dwarfism 4

Eames, Charles and Ray 212
ear cornets 82
Earl, Ralph 27
Earth Day 132
ear trumpets 16, 78, 82–3, 89 n.32
Easterling, Keller 196
easy chairs 19, 20, 25, 34 n.60
easy-to-grip cutlery sets 98
electricity 83, 178
electrophones 16, 78, 83, 84, 90 n.50
Elementary Education (Blind and Deaf Children) Act 103
elevators 120, 161
Ellcessor, Elizabeth 174, 193–203
E-Nable 216, 217
Enabling Community Foundation 217–18
Enabling the Future (ETF) 210, 214
Enlightenment 4, 82, 120, 125
environmental philosophy 120
Environmental Protection Agency 132, 133
Environmental Working Group (EWG) 137

equitable use 8
ergonomic design 177–87
European Union (EU) 137
Everest, Herbert 4
Everest & Jennings Wheelchair 4, 229
EveryBody: An Artefact History of Disability 226
eyeglasses 235

Fallace, Michael 136
"Fall of the House of Usher, The" (Poe) 134
falls and fractures, prevention of 53, 54
Farm for Epileptics 115
fatigue 132, 180, 181
Finkelstein, Vic 95, 96, 97
First World War 3, 69, 103, 220 n.12, 221 n.32
Fiske, John 199
FitBit 209–10
flannel 23, 27, 28, 36 n.73
flexibility 1, 8
Follansbee, Moody 22, 24
food allergies 134
footwear 27–8
Foul and the Fragrant, The (Corbin) 132
fractures 53, 54
fragrance-free zones 135–6, 137
Franklin, Benjamin 21, 35 n.64, 56 n.13
Frisina, Robert 153
Fritsch, Kelly 6, 8
functionality 3, 15, 24, 25, 27, 71, 117, 168, 216–17, 219, 229

Garden Cities of Tomorrow 115
Garner, Eric 138
Gawley, Andrew 232–3, 240 n.30
General Act on Exceptional Medical Expenses 117
Gibson, Stephen 232–3
Gilbreth, Frank 3
Gilbreth, Lillian 3
Glabau, Danya 134
Goethals, George Washington 63, 68–9
Goldsmith, Selwyn 97, 101, 102–3, 105–10
Google 215, 217
Gordan, Henry 69
Goudsmit, Ellen 134
gout 15, 19–28
    causes and medical condition (in early America) 21–5
    disability aids and equipment 25–8
    social stigma associated with 24–5, 35 n.71
    treatment 23–4
Greene, Julie 63
Groase, John 27
Guffey, Elizabeth 1–9, 97, 98, 101–10, 159–68
gutta-percha 82, 89–90 n.33

Hamilton, Marilyn 4, 230
Hamraie, Aimi 6
hand-cranked wheelchairs 230, 239 n.27
Hanger Clinic 209
Haraway, Donna 211
hashtags 175, 225
headaches 132, 180
Health Canada 137
healthy environment, notions of 96
hearing aids 15, 20, 90 n.50, 148, 149, 197, 230, 239 n.19
hearing tubes 90 n.50
Heart Building Law 161, 167
heating, ventilation, and air conditioning (HVAC) 133
heating services 102
HEPA (high efficiency particulate air) filters 135
Hepplewhite, George 25
Herman Miller Equa chair 186
Het Dorp, Netherlands 97, 113–25
    commercial area 124
    eugenicist values 125
    mobility requirements 119–20
    neighborhood idea 120
    "normalcy" of residents, idea/policies/media depictions 122–5
    street design 120–2
Hill, David 47
history of design and disability
    Industrial Revolution 15–16
    preindustrial era 15
    twentieth-century 95–9
History of Disability, A (Stiker) 114–15
Hollerith, Richard 183
Holliday, Robert Cortes 49, 51
Hoshikawa, Yasuyuki 163
Howard, Ebenezer 115
Howes, Sandra 134
Hsu, Hsuan 132

Hugh Stubbins and Associates 145
Humanscale (Diffrient) 186
Hunter, George 19
hygienic sublime 134
Hymison, Melford 62, 70

IBM 178
idealism 101, 185
imperialism 2, 62, 66, 70
inclusive design 6, 7, 8, 9, 46, 96–8, 113, 115–18, 122, 125, 155 n.9, 213, 225–6, 228, 230
In Direction (Dupont) 213
indoor air quality (IAQ) 133
Indo-Pakistani Sign Language 87
Industrial Revolution 15–16, 131
infanticide 161
infrastructure 70–1, 105–6, 147–8, 153, 164, 175, 195, 196
integration and independence model 97, 105
Interdata CRT 183
International Style 131
Invacar 104, 110
invalid, definition 37 n.80
Invention of Comfort, The (Crowley) 34 n.59
iPad 7
Isei, Shugei 163, 166
Isthmian Canal Commission 61, 64, 66, 68

Jackson, Andrew 47
James Murray Company 83, 84
Japan Braille Library 163
Japan's disabled population 159–68
  Aoi Shiba no Kai (The Green Grass Club) activist group 160–1
  domestic legislation 161–2
  E&C Project, toys for disabled children 163–4
  ergonomic policy 182
  international legislation 161
  nonprofit organizations 163
  robot cafés for 173–4
  social stigma and invisibility 160–1
  Swany Bag, Miyoshi's assistive device 159–68
Japan Times, The 161, 162
Jennings, Harry 4
Johanna Foundation 113, 118
Johnson, Lyndon B. 37 n.80, 143, 145

Kar Pallavi Bhasha (indigenous sign language) 78, 84–8
Kaufmann-Buhler, Jennifer 174, 177–87
Kelley, Andrew K. 135, 136
Kennedy Center's Office of VSA and Accessibility 225
Kerkelijk Kultureel Centrum (Church and Cultural Centre) 114
keyboard 174, 179–82, 184, 185, 186
Kitchin, Rob 143
Klapwijk, Arie 113, 115, 118, 119, 124
Knoblauch, Joy 121, 225
Knoll Diffrient chair 186
Kodama Architects 136
Koonings Jaght 116
Kuhn, Adam 22, 23
Kyoyo-hin Foundation 163–4

Labor World 67
Lamb, Thomas 52
Lamb Lim-Rest 52, 53
Lancet, The 80, 104
language, as technology 91 n.60
Le Corbusier 3, 131
Liebermann, Wanda 97, 113–25
LifeAlert/LifeCall 174
Lifeline/Philips Lifeline 193–203
Life magazine 198
lighting 102, 148, 177, 179, 180
LimbForge 217
Limbitless Arm 214, 216
London smog tragedy, 1952 131, 133
Long, Richard 136
Los Angeles Herald 67
Lovell Demonstration Health House 131
Lovell Health House 139 n.5
Lukens, John 15, 19–28, 29 n.1, 29 n.9, 30 n.12
Lukens, Sarah 23
Lung Association of Canada 137
Lyon, David 201

Mace, Ronald 8, 97
Madison, James 56 n.13
Madonna 198–9
Madras Mail 87
Maginn, Francis 77
Makerbots 215
male Leg 27–8, 35 n.65
Manero, Albert 214

Manigault, Ann Ashby 23
Marks, Amasa Abraham 62
Markwood, Sandy 200
Mason, Charles 69
mass production 1, 2, 3, 8–9, 15, 133, 173, 209, 211, 215, 230
McDonald, Wilfred 62, 68–9
Measure of Man (Dreyfuss) 3, 186
medical models 4–6, 226, 227
Meijden, Henk van der 115–16
memory loss 132
Microsoft 214, 215
Mills, Mara 203
Miyoshi, Etsuo 159–68
mobility-impaired people 2, 5, 104, 159, 164–5
models of disability 4–6
   medical model 4–5, 226, 227
   moralistic model 4
   social model 5–6, 229
modernism
   definition 2–4
   postwar design efforts 95–9
Modulor, The (Le Corbusier) 3
monitoring 194, 195, 196, 200, 201–2, 209
monitors 174, 179, 180, 182, 184, 185, 186, 194, 195, 202
Morlan, Krysta 225
Morris, Matt 136
Morton, Agnes 47
Morton, William 53
Mufwene, Salikoko S. 86
Mullins, Aimee 218
multiple chemical sensitivity (MCS) 132–9
Murata, Minoru 161–2
muscular dystrophy 116
musculoskeletal problems 177, 180, 186
Museum of disABILITY 226
myoelectric limbs 209, 227

Nair, Aparna 16, 77–88
nasal congestion 132
National Advisory Group 145, 153, 154
National Association of Area Agencies on Aging 198
National Health Service (NHS) 103–4
National Safety Council 53, 54
National Technical Institute for the Deaf (NTID) 98, 143–55
   architectural planning and design 145–6
   creation of 143–5
   dormitory and dining commons 151–2
   government pushback on special services 152–3
   LBJ design 147–50
   NTID Act 143, 145
   special services 146–7
neurasthenia 133
Neutra, Richard 131, 139 n.5
Newspaper Publishers' Association 182
New York Herald 67
New York Times 51, 67, 185, 187
Niewenhuis, Marijn 138
Nike 226
Nineteenth-Century Disability: Cultures & Contexts 226
Nixon, Richard 153
Nobel, Wycliffe 109
No One's Perfect (Ototake) 162
normal/normality, concepts of 2, 3, 5, 53, 103, 104, 107, 122–5, 218, 228–9, 232
Norrgard, Lee 198
Nugent, Timothy 103, 105–7
Nussbaumer, Linda L. 133

obesity 181
objects of disability
   definition 228
   materiality of 225–9
Occupational Medicine 132
occupational therapy 7, 227, 234, 235, 240 n.39
office chairs, ergonomic 186
online exhibitions 175, 225–6
Ontario Assistive Devices Program 239 n.19
Open Het Dorp 113–25
oralism 16, 78, 81, 87, 88, 148, 149, 150
orthopedics 7, 51–2, 54, 104
orthotics 7
OSHA 187
osteoporosis 53, 54, 58 n.65
Ototake, Hirotada 160–2
Ott, Katherine 20, 29–30 n.9, 226–7, 233, 234, 236
Out from Under: Disability, History and Things to Remember 226
Out of Hand exhibition (Museum of Arts and Design) 213
Owen, Ivan 215

Panama Canal 61–71
Panara, Robert 154
Pantalony, David 226
parking spaces 97, 114
Parr, Debra 98
peg legs 68–71
Pemberton, Israel 22
Pennsylvania Gazette 22
perfumes 135–7
Perkhin, Mikhail 44
personal emergency response systems (PERS) 174, 193–203
  camoflage features 197
  components 195
  cultural circulation of 198–200
  design 194–7
  independence/security/surveillance enabled by 200–2
  ornamental design 196–7
petrochemicals 133, 138
phaeton carriage 15, 19, 20, 25, 27, 28, 29–30 n.9, 30 n.13
Phillips, John L. 68, 69
"Phoenix" model 216
phonoscopes 90 n.50
physiatry 7
Pitt, William 21, 34 n.58
Poe, Edgar Allen 134
polio 51, 97, 102, 116, 160–6
Porter, Eileen J. 197, 201
posture 34 n.59, 82, 181
Pring, Alex 214, 216
printing press 133
Proctor & Gamble (P&G) 137
progressive diseases 116
Project for Building Barrier-Free Cities 161
prosthetics
  Bespoke Bodies exhibition 209–10
  Bespoke Innovations 210–14
  crowdsourced 217, 218–19
  DMB exhibition 209, 210
  3D-printed limbs 209–19
  ETF models 210, 214–17
  Gawley's 232–3
  as metaphor 211
  split-hook prosthetic arms 209
prosthetics (used by the maimed in the Panama Canal project) 61–71
  A.A. Marks's 61, 62–5, 70
  Chandler's case 69–70
  Comba's case 66–8

Hymison's case 70
  McDonald's case 68–9
prototyping 3, 8, 118
Puar, Jasbir 62
Public Disability Act 117
Public Health Journal, The 109
Pullin, Graham 197, 213, 228

Queen Victoria 43, 47, 77
Quickie chair 4, 230

ramps 5, 6, 97, 101, 102, 106, 108, 136, 161
Randolph, Theron 134
Randolph, Thomas J. 56 n.13
"Raptor Reloaded" 216
rationality 3
Ratto, Matt 213, 219
Red Cross 52
Ree, Robert 213
rehabilitation 6, 7, 52–4, 67, 97, 103–4, 107, 109, 113, 115, 116–22, 125
resonant design 9
respiratory diseases 131–9
Rhodes, Richard 83
RIBA Publications 110
right to breathe 98, 132–8, 139 n.10
"Right to Breathe, A" (Niewenhuis) 138
Ripley's Believe It or Not! 232
robots 173–4, 214
Rochester Institute of Technology (RIT) 143–54, 155 n.13, 215
rocking chairs 230, 239 n.25
Roebuck & Company 48, 51
Rogers, Ernesto 96
Rosen, Russell 143
Rowlandson, Thomas 24–5, 27
Royal Commission on the Blind, Deaf and Dumb and Idiots and Imbeciles 77
Royal Institute of British Architects 102, 108
rubber 43, 52–3, 58 n.58, 62, 65, 68, 82, 83
Rush, Benjamin 25, 28, 29 n.6

Samsonite spinners 167–8
Sauter, Steven 180
Schull, John 215
Sears 48, 51
second-hand smoke 135
Second World War 3, 97, 101, 103–4, 110, 160, 212, 229
seizures 132

self-advocacy movements 81, 98, 186
self-governance 116, 120
self-help aids 7, 110
sensescape model 143
Serlin, David 210, 227
"Seven Principles of Universal Design" (Mace et al.) 8
Shakespeare, Tom 5
Shew, Ashley 6, 218
shoes 20, 27–8, 36 n.74, 36 n.78, 228
Siebers, Tobin 229
sign language 78, 81, 84–8, 150
Silk Quilt 35 n.68
skin allergies 137
slave caretakers 32–3 n.42
Smithsonian National Museum of American History 225, 226
smoking 122–3, 135, 136
social media 175, 225–6
social model of disability 5, 229
social responsibilities 2
software 179, 184, 186, 211, 215, 218, 236
specialized schools 77, 96
Staggs Aluminum Rawhide Artificial Limb Company 64, 70
Stamp Act 34 n.58
standardization 1–2, 3, 43, 52, 182, 186, 211, 220 n.12
Star, Susan Leigh 196
steam engine 133
steel 2, 3, 58 n.58, 68, 131, 166, 167, 230, 232, 233
Steelcase Sensor 186
STEM 215
Stiker, Henri-Jacques 114–15
Stokoe, William 155 n.7
Stoler, Ann Laura 62
Stolz electrophone 83, 84
stress disorders 180, 181
style 2, 3, 15, 27, 47, 49, 50, 51, 54, 210, 211
Sullivan, Louis 3
Summit, Scott 211, 212, 213
Sumner, Charles 47
support rails 102
surveillance 200–2
Swainson, Florence 81
Swann, Thomas 47

Taft, William Howard 67
Team 10 114, 117, 120

technoableism 6, 218
telegraph 90 n.33, 133
telethon 113, 114, 115, 116, 118, 122, 126 nn.11–12
"Tell-Tale Heart, The" (Poe) 134
Thingiverse 215, 216, 218
3D-printed prosthetic limbs 174, 209–19, 226
3D Systems 213, 214
Tiffany & Co. 43, 44, 46, 50
time-motion studies 3
toilet 19, 102, 106–10, 118, 161
tolerance for error 8
Tomes, Nancy 225
Towards a New Architecture (Le Corbusier) 131
Town and the Wheelchair, The (Murata) 161–2
Toynbee tympanums 82
transportation 78
Trauner, Ken 211
Trent, Robert F. 34 n.60
Trumbull, Joseph 25
trusses 82
Turner, David 82, 226
Twitter 225

United Kingdom
  air pollution impacts 131
  building code 101
  NHS design culture 103–4
  post-war welfare policies 103–4
  vs. US design standards 101–10
United Nations
  International Year of Disabled Persons, 1981 161
  United Nations Convention on the Rights of Persons with Disabilities 2, 7–8
United States of America
  accessible design 97
  building codes 105
  Clean Air initiatives 131–9
  Department of Health, Education, and Welfare (DHEW) 145, 152–3
  design for deaf education 143–55
  design standards 97
  disability rights movements 173
  ergonomic policy 182–7
  vs. UK design standards 101–10
  veterans' policies 104–5

universal design 6, 8, 144, 154, 183, 236
Universal Design movement 163
USA Today 198, 199
US Center for Disease Control 138
US National Archives 225
Utica crib 234

vaccination 78
Van As, Richard 215, 218
Van den Broek, Jo 114, 119, 120, 123, 127 n.26, 127 n.33
VDT (video/visual display terminal) 177, 179–85
Virdi, Jaipreet 175, 225–37
vision issues 181, 186
volatile organic compounds (VOC) 133, 134, 136

walkers 43, 159, 166, 167, 198
Walking Bag 98, 159–68
walking cane 43–54
    aluminum 53
    and crutches 49, 52–3
    design 49–50
    fashionable 43, 46–51
    functions 49
    handles 43, 44, 45, 47, 98
    history 43–51
    medical 43, 51–4
    as status symbol 43, 46–7
    stigma of 53–4
    violent use of 47
Walking-Stick Papers, The (Holliday) 49
Washington, George 56 n.13
Washington Post 64
Waterbike 225
Watson, Nick 229

wearable devices 174, 202
Wellington County Museum 230
Wesley, John 21, 31 n.23
wheelbarrow 235
wheelchair 4, 15, 19, 43, 53
    with activism stickers 226
    bath 230
    control consoles 118
    design history 101–10, 229–30
    foldable 229
    hand-cranked 230, 239 n.27
    Het Dorp's vision 118–24
    motorcycle-type 239 n.25
    NHS 104
    ramps 97
    user-designed 95–9, 230
Wheelchair History of Disability in Canada, A 226
Whitney, Kristoffer 98, 143–55
wicker chairs 230
Williamson, Bess 1–9, 135, 174, 209–19
Willis, Anne-Marie 96
Wilson, Harold 109
Wilson, Woodrow 69
Wolfson, Penny 230
Woods, Amelia 230, 231
word processors 179
World Congress of the Deaf 77

xenophobia 136

Yokota, Hiroshi 161

YouTube 214
Zenana Mission for the Deaf 77, 80, 81
Zola, Irving 5, 118, 122, 124, 126 n.17

www.ingramcontent.com/pod-product-compliance
Ingram Content Group UK Ltd.
Pitfield, Milton Keynes, MK11 3LW, UK
UKHW050223090425
457269UK00006B/292